A THIRD CONCEPT OF LIBERTY

A THIRD CONCEPT
OF LIBERTY

JUDGMENT AND FREEDOM IN
KANT AND ADAM SMITH

SAMUEL FLEISCHACKER

PRINCETON UNIVERSITY PRESS

PRINCETON, NEW JERSEY

Library of Congress Cataloging-in-Publication Data

Fleischacker, Samuel.

A third concept of liberty : judgment and freedom in Kant and Adam

Smith / Samuel Fleischacker.

p.   cm.

Includes bibliographical references and index.

ISBN 0-691-00265-7 (cloth : alk. paper). — ISBN 0-691-00446-3

(pbk. : alk. paper)

1. Kant, Immanuel, 1724–1804—Contributions in political science.

2. Smith, Adam, 1723–1790.   3. Liberty.   4. Judgment (Ethics)

I. Title.

JC181.K4F58   1999   323.44—dc21   98-30484

For Noa and Benjamin

WHO HAVE TAUGHT ME MOST

OF WHAT I KNOW ABOUT

"SMALL PLEASURES"

CONTENTS

PREFACE

IN THE FALL OF 1988 I taught a course on eighteenth-century moral sentiment theory that ended with a brief consideration of Adam Smith's *Theory of the Moral Sentiments.* I was struck by the way much of it seemed to look forward to Kant and, after teaching Kant's moral philosophy in the spring of 1989, pursued the possibility of a link between these two thinkers over the summer. To my delight, I discovered both that Kant had in fact read Smith and that this connection had never been made the subject of thorough scholarly study. I developed the connection in an article published by *Kant-Studien* in 1991. Even before the article was completed, however, I became interested in pursuing the connection between these two thinkers in the opposite direction: what might Kant have had to say about Smith's economic theories?

1989 was of course an auspicious year to take an interest in the philosophy of economics. As the summer moved into fall, I found myself, like many others, riveted less by scholarly work than by the almost daily political revolutions in Eastern Europe. But scholarly work on Adam Smith seemed about as timely as any such work could be. I agree with those who take the 1989 revolutions to sound the death knell not only of Soviet-style totalitarian politics but of Marxism as a plausible ideology. That need not mean, however, that Marxism's "antithesis," dogmatic libertarianism, has won the day. The events of 1989 make clear the need for an alternative to Marxism as a critique of the untrammeled free market. Very important and difficult issues remain about what the state can and should do to alleviate poverty, prevent oppression in the workplace, and guarantee everyone the education and information by which they can make judicious choices. And the debate over such issues needs to be informed, at least in part, by an adequate political philosophy. Contemporary advocates of the welfare state tend to share an unfortunate commitment to utilitarianism—an excessive emphasis on what people *want* and how to get it to them, as opposed to what they *do* and how they can carry out their projects with maximum freedom and hope of success. Libertarianism, on the other hand, while claiming to take up precisely the latter attitude, places too much emphasis on the sacredness of property, misconstruing freedom as a matter solely of having rights to act however one likes within one's "private" realm. There seems consequently to be a need for an approach to political economy that is neither Marxist, nor libertarian, nor excessively utilitarian, and a reconsideration of Adam Smith's philosophical foundations promises just such an approach. Smith is a highly nuanced and deeply humane philosopher, whose own view of capitalism was not nearly as rosy as that of his followers. He was not a systematic philosopher, however, so if his views are, as I believe, close to Kant's, then making use of Kant to reread him should clarify those views. And together the two promise a considerable infusion of strength and depth to the ideology of today's "left." Kant's moral philosophy, as John Rawls has shown, can be used to support a welfare state on other than utilitarian grounds. Rawls's own approach remains too oriented towards satisfying desires rather than enhancing action, however, and I arrive at a rather different picture by using Kant's aesthetics to supplement his moral philosophy.

Rawls is also far too vague a thinker to supply a healthy critical voice in real political debates. An interweaving of Kant and Smith offers a more concrete and accessible ideology as well as a richer vision of freedom. Since that interweaving proceeds in good part by way of the shared *aesthetic* views of the two figures, the vision we arrive at fits moreover into an old but relatively little discussed tradition of liberalism: the series of thinkers, from Friedrich Schiller and Wilhelm von Humboldt in the late eighteenth century to Hannah Arendt in our own day, who have been inspired by Kant's *Critique of Judgment*. Via Humboldt, that tradition also includes John Stuart Mill; via Schiller, it may include Charles Taylor; via Arendt, it can stretch to such liberal communitarians as Ronald Beiner or Michael Walzer. But these are not figures who all agree among themselves, even about the relationship between aesthetics and politics. I shall lean away from the view shared by Schiller and Taylor, for instance, by which artistic *creation* is a model of free action, the view generally labeled "expressive individualism." Artistic *appreciation* is a much better model, I believe, for both philosophical and political reasons. On the other hand, I shall also lean away from Arendt's emphasis on "spectatorship" in the *Critique of Judgment*: the account of judgment itself is much more valuable. These are important quibbles, affecting how we might so much as define the tradition of liberalism I want to bring out. But in the end they are still quibbles. What is of greater importance is that Smith, Kant, Schiller, Humboldt, and Mill share a core of views at all, and that that core is distinct from, and thus capable of criticizing and enriching, the more mainstream clusters of views that have defined "liberal" politics over the past two centuries.

The notion that political doctrines consist in clusters of views rather than single arguments or theories, and the notion that the history of such a cluster is crucial to defining what it amounts to, should themselves make clear that this book has been inspired in more than its title by Isaiah Berlin. Berlin died just as I was working on the final revisions. I never met him, never communicated with him, but he has been an inspirational figure for me from the beginning of my academic career. That intellectual history and philosophy might be intertwined; that they can be exciting, and beautifully written; that liberal politics and good academic work both do well to grow out of a commitment to pluralism; that, in the name of pluralism, it is worth attending to the insights of even such "fuzzy" thinkers as Herder—these are all propositions to which Berlin devoted his life, and of which, in the rarefied world of British and American philosophy at least, Berlin was one of the few respected defenders. Berlin is widely said to have reopened the entire field of political philosophy with his "Two Concepts of Liberty" in the late 1950s. He also, I think, helped open the way for such valuable history of political thought as the work of Quentin Skinner, John Pocock, Charles Taylor, and Alasdair MacIntyre. In any case, I have always felt that he made such work possible for me, that his writings literally kept doors open for me to do the kind of philosophy I find most worth doing. For that, along with, I would guess, many other people, I shall always be grateful.

On a more immediate level, I would like to thank a few foundations and a large number of individuals. Ann Wald, of Princeton University Press, first helped me see that this project might amount to a book and has provided encouragement and good advice throughout. The University Center for Human Values at Princeton provided me with the most delightful work environment I have ever inhabited, and the conversation that ensued when I presented an early draft of this book provided me with enough material for, literally, a year of revisions. To the participants in that conversation—George Kateb, Amy Gutmann, Hilary Bok, Elizabeth Kiss, Kent Greenawalt, Yael Tamir, Daniel A. Bell, Stephen Macedo, and Chris Bobonich—and especially to Hilary, who led off the discussion with a brilliant set of comments, I owe an irreplaceable debt. For similar reasons—for reading large parts of the manuscript and discussing them in detail with me—I also want to thank Daniel Statman, Alan White, Russ Muirhead, Georges Dreyfus, Elijah Millgram, John Cooper, Beatrice Longuenesse, Nicholas Phillipson, David Frum, Amy Reichert, two very helpful readers for Princeton University Press, and above all Charles Griswold and Jeff Weintraub. I am grateful to Williams College and the John M. Olin Foundation for support of a more concrete kind, making possible a year and a half of research time. The Institute for Advanced Studies in the Humanities at Edinburgh University, by way especially of its wonderfully welcoming director Peter Jones and the ever helpful Anthea Taylor, provided an elegant workspace for six months of that time. Peter also arranged a conference at which I could present some of this material, which I appreciated very much.

In addition to the critical assistance I have already mentioned, Amy

Reichert has given me love, support, and help well beyond what I deserved, especially during my crankiest moments of work on this project, and Noa and Benjamin, two relatively new explorers of what freedom might mean, provide daily delights to remind me that being a father is more important than being a philosopher. This book is for them.

Sam Fleischacker
Williamstown, 1997

ABBREVIATIONS

I use the following abbreviations for primary texts by Aristotle, Smith, and Kant. Unless otherwise noted, all translations are from the volumes given below.

ARISTOTLE

NE   *Nicomachean Ethics,* in *The Basic Works of Aristotle,* ed. Richard McKeon (New York: Random House, 1941).

P   *Politics,* in *The Basic Works of Aristotle.*

ADAM SMITH

Corr   *Correspondence of Adam Smith,* ed. E. C. Mossner and Ian Simpson Ross, 2d ed. (New York: Oxford University Press, 1987).

ED   "Early Draft" of the *Wealth of Nations,* included in the volume that contains *Lectures on Jurisprudence* (LJ).

HA   "History of Astronomy," in *Essays on Philosophical Subjects,* ed. W. P. D. Wightman, J. C. Bryce (Oxford: Oxford University Press, 1980); unpublished in the author's lifetime.

Letter   "Letter to the *Edinburgh Review,*" in *Essays on Philosophical Subjects*; published (anonymously) in 1756.

LJ   *Lectures on Jurisprudence,* ed. R. L. Meek, D. D. Raphael, and P. G. Stein (Oxford: Oxford University Press, 1978); unpublished in the author's lifetime.

TMS   *Theory of Moral Sentiments,* ed. D. D. Raphael and A. L. Macfie (Oxford: Oxford University Press, 1976). First published in 1759.

WN   *An Inquiry into the Nature and Causes of the Wealth of Nations,* ed. R. H. Campbell, A. S. Skinner, and W. B. Todd (Oxford: Oxford University Press, 1976); first published in 1776.

KANT

The German text in all cases is from what is known as the "Akademie" edition: *Kant's gesammelte Schriften,* Königlichen Preussischen Akademie der Wissenschaften (Berlin: Walter de Gruyter & Co., 1902–). Citations

from Kant will be given as follows: abbreviation, page number of the
Akademie edition/page number in the relevant translation.

A   *Anthropology from a Pragmatic Point of View*, trans. Mary J.
        Gregor (The Hague: Martinus Nijhoff, 1974); first published
        in 1798.

CF   *The Conflict of the Faculties*, trans. Mary J. Gregor (Lincoln:
        University of Nebraska Press, 1979); first published in 1798.

CJ   *Critique of Judgment*, trans. J. H. Bernard (New York: Hafner,
        1951); first published in 1790.

CPR   *Critique of Pure Reason*, trans. Norman Kemp Smith (New
        York: St. Martin's Press, 1929); first published in 1781, sec-
        ond edition in 1787. As is standard, "A" will designate the
        first edition, "B" the second.

CPrR   *Critique of Practical Reason*, trans. Lewis White Beck (Indi-
        anapolis: Bobbs-Merrill, 1956); first published in 1788.

E   "An Answer to the Question: What is Enlightenment?" in
        Kant's Political Writings, 2d ed., trans. H. B. Nisbet, ed.
        Hans Reiss (Cambridge: Cambridge University Press); first
        published in 1784.

FI   "First Introduction" to the *Critique of Judgment*, in *Critique of
        Judgment*, trans. W. S. Pluhar (Indianapolis: Hackett, 1987);
        unpublished in the author's lifetime.

G   *Groundwork of the Metaphysics of Morals*, trans. Lewis White
        Beck as *Foundations of the Metaphysics of Morals* (New York:
        Macmillan, 1959); first published in 1785.

IUH   "Idea for a Universal History With a Cosmopolitan Purpose," in
        Kant's Political Writings; first published in 1784.

MM   *Metaphysics of Morals*, trans. Mary J. Gregor (Cambridge: Cam-
        bridge University Press, 1991); first published in 1797.

PP   "Perpetual Peace: A Philosophical Sketch," in *Kant's Political
        Writings*; first published in 1795.

R   *Reflexionen*, translations my own; unpublished in the author's
        lifetime.

Rev   "Reviews of Herder's Ideas on the Philosophy of the History of
        Mankind," in *Kant's Political Writings*; first published in
        1784–1785.

TP   "On the Common Saying: 'This May be True in Theory, But it
        does not Apply in Practice,'" in *Kant's Political Writings*; first
        published in 1793.

A THIRD CONCEPT OF LIBERTY

Chapter 1

INTRODUCTION

"**A** LIBERAL,**"** pronounces one recent writer, "is a person who believes in liberty, as a nudist is a person who believes in nudity."[1] Most Americans are liberals in this sense, as are, at least nominally, most people in democracies throughout the modern world. It has been plausibly argued that liberalism in the sense of a concern for liberty is the *only* appropriate mode of politics in the modern age. What marks modernity, so goes the argument, is the loss of any substantial agreement about what constitutes the purpose of human life, and in that context it is essential that individuals have the liberty to explore that question, and pursue the answers they find, on their own. I think this is right, and am for that reason myself committed to liberalism as the right framework for modern politics. But the central term of liberalism—liberty—is an unclear and deeply contested one. This book is an attempt to lay out one tradition of what liberty means, and thereby to clarify—and ideally to enrich—liberalism.

The tradition I am referring to has received relatively little attention. It has been rendered virtually invisible by the much better known notions of freedom promoted by libertarianism, on the one hand, and the various liberationist movements that see freedom in some sort of collective identity, on the other. I take the title of my book from a famous essay diagnosing these two traditions by Isaiah Berlin, one of the most profound, sensitive, and honest contemporary thinkers about liberalism and modernity.[2] Berlin described two concepts of liberty: a negative one, by which I am free *from* constraint insofar as other people refrain from interfering with me, and a positive one, by which I am free *to* act insofar as I am included in the political units managing my environment. Both concepts have serious failings, as Berlin showed, and upholders of the one often accuse the other of not being a notion of liberty at all. Moreover, the debates here are not merely academic. Those who construe freedom as noninterference tend to promote hands-off government policies to a degree that can be breathtakingly callous to the poor, while those who construe freedom as political inclusion have repeatedly endorsed totalitarian attempts at utopia. To cut through some of these debates, both academic and political, I propose a third concept of liberty, a third way to divide up the history of freedom. I begin with a brief overview of the nature of this concept, and of its political implications.

Freedom from Tutelage

> Enlightenment is man's emergence from his self-incurred
> immaturity. Immaturity is the inability to use one's own
> understanding without the guidance of another. . . . I hear
> on all sides the cry: *Don't argue!* The officer says: Don't
> argue, get on parade! The tax-official: Don't argue, pay! The
> clergyman: Don't argue, believe! . . . All this means
> restrictions on freedom everywhere.
> *Kant, "What is Enlightenment?" (E 36–7/55)*

The third concept of liberty focuses on the important human skill known
as "judgment," and it construes freedom above all as that which enables
one to judge for oneself—unlike a child, who requires others to judge for
her, who requires tutelage. Kant, above all, explained what judgment
amounts to, and Kant also, in a classic formulation, construed the goal of
liberalism as enabling people to come out of tutelage. "Think for yourself!" is the motto of enlightenment, he maintained, and that entails both
that we are able to criticize the various authority figures around us
(politicians, church leaders, academics) and that we do not rely blindly
upon them when making our own decisions. The first of these conditions
for enlightenment is primarily a political one—the protection of free
speech—while the second is primarily something we all, as individuals,
must do for ourselves. Yet it may be possible for the institutions of society to foster a *culture* of enlightenment: an entire society of individuals
who encourage each other to think for themselves. This, implies Kant,
would be a truly liberal culture, and it constitutes the ultimate goal of
liberal politics.

What thinking for oneself has to do with judgment is a long story,
which I can only sketch in this chapter. Before we get to that sketch, let
us look a little at what it means *not* to think for oneself, and why it is so
important that one do. Kant characterizes the unenlightened state as
"tutelage," the condition in which we place children, along with adults
who cannot handle their own affairs. He rightly notes that the law can
encourage tutelage, both by suppressing such things as free speech and
by the paternalistic attitude by which a ruler or ruling party tries to take
charge of making the people happy:

> A government might be established on the principle of benevolence towards
> the people, like that of a father towards his children. Under such a *paternal
> government* . . . the subjects, as immature children who cannot distinguish
> what is truly useful or harmful to themselves, would be obliged to behave
> purely passively and to rely upon the judgement of the head of state as to how

they *ought* to be happy. . . . Such a government [would be] the greatest conceivable *despotism*. (TP 290–1/74)[3]

This charge has remarkable resonance even today. We are rightly proud, in the United States, of the protection we give to civil liberties—freedom of speech, freedom of religion, and the like—but we do not tend to worry as much about the subtle ways in which political as well as other institutions take a paternalistic attitude towards those they affect. Sometimes defenders of "laissez-faire" economics point out (justifiably) the stifling paternalism that comes with much of the welfare state, but they rarely worry in turn about the paternalism that comes with our prison system and the large number of people it monitors, and never about the paternalism of our corporations, by means of which the vast majority of our society works in demeaning, powerless positions.[4] Activists on the left, on the other hand, usually think there are more important things to worry about than paternalism. In a world that still contains great poverty, discrimination, and violence, being able to "think for oneself" is surely a luxury. Perhaps we should worry about it someday, in a social world of much reduced suffering, but at the moment even raising it as a problem is a distraction from the real evils that face us. Surely policies that alleviate or eliminate these greater evils, as long as they do not actually violate anyone's civil liberties, are justified whether they are paternalistic or not.

What is so bad about paternalism? Why should we worry if adults remain in tutelage—so long, at least, as the "tutor" cares sincerely about her charge's best interests? Tutelage is the relationship our parents have over us, which, when it works well, is something that provides us with comfort and support. We are certainly unfree when enchained, blocked in, tortured, or threatened with death, and hardly less so when lied to, slipped psychoactive drugs, hypnotized, etc., but how can the gentle protection of our parents be counted as a threat to freedom? Parents—at their best—impress their children with their superior wisdom, and use mild incentives to encourage certain kinds of conduct and discourage others. If some people are wiser than others even among adults—and surely some are—why should they not be given power to guide the rest of us to healthier, richer, more decent kinds of behavior? If there are more and less virtuous ways of living, why should society not set up incentives to guide us to the former rather than the latter? Most Western political philosophers (indeed, most political thinkers all over the world), from Plato, Aristotle, and Aquinas, to Francis Hutcheson and John Adams, have believed that that is exactly what politicians should do, and we hear echoes of such a view even today: in the "war on drugs," in campaigns against pornography or for "family values," and in many other political positions.

Nevertheless, I think Kant was right to insist that governments should release us from, not encourage us in, "tutelage," that paternalism in government is "the greatest conceivable despotism." An excess of "parental love" can severely threaten political freedom, can provide an all-too-easy disguise for unjustifiable force and manipulation. We also hear voices declaring this today, when conservatives cry out against "the nanny state," while people on the left wax indignant over governmental attempts to promote prayer in public schools, suppress artistic expression, or discourage homosexuality. But saying that we need to be released from parental relationships is much easier than explaining what is wrong with such relationships. After all, even many of those who say they believe in freedom insist also that the reason we need freedom is to find happiness, to pursue satisfying projects.[5] But then, if we can pursue more satisfying projects by way of a little well-meaning guidance, that should *enhance* the value of our freedom, not detract from it. If governments can help keep us from destructive drugs, or to leave the loneliness of single, urban life for (what we will find to be) the true happiness of family life and community, surely they ought to put their resources into such efforts. Is the case against such efforts solely that they may lead to abuses of power?

I would say not. To begin with, parents themselves, even or perhaps especially at their best, can be stifling. Their protective love keeps us from standing independently, from having confidence in our own decisions. The freedom that comes of *not* having such protection is exhilarating, although also frightening: unprotected, we may fall to destruction. Now if we still lived in a world confident that it knew its final end—confident that God had spoken to it, or that philosophers had worked out the true, or only rational, way to live—then we might want to accept the slight loss of courage, loss of strength, that reliance on one's parents brings, and thereby eliminate, or at least much reduce, our risk of falling. If we felt that people discovered true wisdom with age, that our parents, and elders in general, were connected to deep truths handed down from the past,[6] then we might be willing to live under tutelage forever, or at least until we each developed the age and wisdom to become elders ourselves, to have nothing but the Truth Itself as our parent. Such a hierarchical view of society, and access to truth, was common in the distant past of Western culture, and in both the distant and recent past of most other cultures in the world. But since the Enlightenment, we have not tended to believe this. We have tended to be unsure, instead, that anyone knows what the end for humanity is, even whether there is any such end at all. So we see all human beings as fallible and falling, picking their way as best they can in the directions that each, with very partial vision, selects for herself. On such a picture, we each need to pick ourselves up when, by our own lights, we fail, for ultimately each of us must determine our own standard for how to live a successful human life. But then there is no reason to expect that our parents will be wiser about such things than we are, and no reason, either, to consider the appearances of traditional authority—the parental glow by which customary ideas and practices come down from our past—to be more than an illusion, an image of confident directedness towards an end that, when examined, will turn out to be just as hesitant, as weakly based, as our own individual convictions about how to live. "Enlightenment" then means coming out from under the illusion of parental protection, and out from under the illusions, born of childhood attachments to our literal parents, that hallow and thus bind us to authority figures in church, state, and academy. What we must recognize is that the appearance of wisdom in others is an appearance *we* put upon those others. If they are truly wise, our own judgment will confirm theirs; if not, the appearance is a misleading transference of childhood affections. As Simon Schama and Robert Darnton have emphasized, it was precisely the shattering of such appearances that laid the ground for the French Revolution, and Gordon Wood has made much the same case for the origins of the American Revolution.[7] In Kant, the point unites his Critical philosophy with his politics. He declares "Think for yourself!" to be the Enlightenment cry in both politics and philosophy: the shattering of illusions of certainty is for him the key both to overcoming metaphysics and to living a truly human life. After we pass through the tribunal by which reason criticizes itself, we realize we are just as uncertain of what we need to do in life, and just as certain of it, as our parents. Anything—church dogmas, political mantras, philosophical proofs—that creates appearances to the contrary is an illusion. What we are uncertain of (e.g., the existence of God), *all* human beings should be uncertain of; what our parents rightly claim with confidence (e.g., the requirement that we act morally), we can likewise claim. Only if we act in the light of both of these truths can we be free of illusions, hence truly free. But to *learn* to walk the tightrope between certainty and uncertainty, we must each in fact begin to walk it, unprotected.

Now Kant also suggests, but does not precisely say, that the mode of thought appropriate to this tightrope is judgment, that we emerge from tutelage by using our own judgment.[8] "Let me judge for myself": this is the characteristic expression of someone emerging into full independence, full maturity. It is in this freedom of judgment, I shall argue, that a third concept of liberty can be found, a concept richer than the absence from constraint and manipulation that has obsessed upholders of negative liberty, and more sensible, as well as less dangerous, than the obsession with communal identification characteristic of believers in positive liberty. It is a notion we can find in Adam Smith, insofar as he supplements the "natural liberty" that he regards as essential to justice with a concern for "independence," in Kant, and, via Kant's *Critique of Judgment*, in Friedrich Schiller, Wilhelm von Humboldt, and J.S. Mill.[9] These five figures are rarely taken together—Schiller (usually), Kant (often), and Mill (sometimes) tend to be characterized as theorists of "positive liberty," while Smith and Humboldt are among the "negative" theorists' favorite spokespeople. That they had significant influence on one another itself suggests that Berlin may have cut up the history of freedom too broadly.

But in making this criticism, I mean also to be following Berlin's own understanding of moral argument. Like Berlin, I believe that to grasp the nature of a concept, one must grasp, among other things, the effect of that concept on the lives of those who have made use of it. Berlin is often taken to have moved away from philosophy to the history of ideas. I think this is a mistaken way of reading his work, and especially of the essays on liberty. I believe Berlin recognized, rightly, that good philosophical analysis of ideas—moral and political ideas, at least—is inextricable from the history of those ideas; history defines what, concretely, the ideas mean.[10] Accordingly, the historical investigations of this book are crucial to its philosophical claim: to the claim that there is a real third possibility in between the notions of negative and positive liberty, combining the most attractive features of both.

JUDGMENT

What is "judgment"? I will argue that judgment is a complex skill that draws on what we do in aesthetic interpretation, in sorting through empirical evidence, in making decisions in the common law, and in evaluating our ends for cogency and value. For the moment, however, let us rely on the most ordinary sense of "judgment," by which we say, "Use your own judgment," or "In my judgment [that shoe needs repair, you behaved rudely, America needs more public transportation, OXFAM is a good charity, etc.]." What exactly goes into such judgments is a complicated question, but the differences between "that shoe needs repair" and "you behaved rudely" alone indicate that a rather wide variety of factual information, normative standards, and feelings can inform judgment. "To judge" is paradigmatically to apply a general rule to a particular case, a universal to an instance of that universal. It can be contrasted, then, to "feeling" or "drifting" or mentally lazing around rather than thinking in any sense, to musing on generalities or particulars without drawing any conclusion about them, and, above all, to thinking in the sense of drawing general conclusions from other generalities—what we do in advanced mathematics or physics, what we call, standardly, "theorizing." It is opposed, that is, both to feelings that have no cognitive content and to the strict deduction of conclusions from premises. Since it is not merely a matter of subjective feelings, there can be expertise in it, but since it does not fall out neatly from any theory, real experience with the particulars to which it is applied is necessary to do it well. One becomes an expert judge of a thing by encountering it often and making judgments about it that other people witness and correct. At home most familiarly in the law, and in literary and other aesthetic criticism, judgment also plays a role in such academic disciplines as history and the historical sciences (all the social sciences, plus evolutionary biology, geology, and cosmology): anywhere that conclusions depend in significant part on grasping the features of complex and unreproducible particular cases.

I intend to use the word "judgment" in a way that coheres fairly readily with these common, everyday understandings of the term. But to hold on to a stricter definition until we have examined the various aspects of judgment more closely, let us stipulate the following: "judgment" will refer to the conclusion of a train of thought where the interpretation of particular cases is essential to that train of thought, and the practice under whose rules the conclusion is reached therefore allows for further reasonable disagreement over that conclusion.[11] Sometimes the verb "to judge" is used for any attempt to claim knowledge, even the drawing of mathematical conclusions. Perhaps this is reasonable, since every time we come to a conclusion we bring our general beliefs and modes of accepting evidence or proof together to yield a single truth claim. We conclude our thought at a particular instant, and upon a particular sentence or small set of sentences. When the sentence is a mathematical truth, however, following unequivocally from the premises given, or a purportedly universal scientific law, then the word "judgment" sounds out of place. In English, at least, "judge" is a word whose meaning is dominated by its legal heritage, and in law—as opposed to mathematics, physics, and the like—the conclusions to which one comes will always be open to further debate.

To grasp the nature of judgment, the reader must be aware of, and take as an example, what she herself does when making a judgment. To clarify the nature of judgment, therefore, I need among other things to awaken the reader's faculty of judgment into action. Take this as my excuse for rather painstakingly offering evidence for some of my conclusions.

Thus, to the claim that "judgment" in English is dominated by its legal heritage:

The OED gives sixteen definitions for the verb "to judge," of which ten refer to the mode of action of someone in charge of judicial proceedings, two use that mode of action as a metaphor for authoritative declarations in everyday life—"8. To declare or pronounce authoritatively . . . c 1400 *Rom. Rose* 6311 God iugged me for a theef trichour . . . 1617 MORYSON *Itin.* III.4 Hee was judged an unprofitable servant"—and the remaining four, which are all variations on "to form an opinion about" or to pronounce such an opinion, are given forty illustrations among which thirty-eight can be readily seen as using legal judgment as a model.[12] One judges of aesthetic or ethical merit,

> Tindale, *Matthew*: "Iudge not lest ye be iudged," Shakespeare, *Henry V*: "Who Prologue-like, your humble patience pray, Gently to heare, kindly to judge our Play," Walton, *Angler*: "I hope you will not judge my earnestness to be impatience," Pope, *Ess. Crit.*: "But most by Numbers judge a Poet's song"

or of some particular fact which one cannot know with certainty,

> 1679 Hobbes: "If he judg, he must judg either of that which is to come or of that which is past," 1774 Goldsmith: "If we were to judge of its size by the horns," 1871 Freeman "It was judged better to begin the attack at once"

which one will judge best if one has "discretion" or the appropriate experience,

> 1535 Coverdale: "I speake vnto them which haue discrecioun: iudge ye what I say," 1711 Shaftesbury: "To be able to judg of both, 'tis necessary to have a sense of each," 1850 Scoresby: "Some whalemen judge it does not attain its full size until twenty-five years"

and for which the final court of appeal is ultimately each individual listener or observer, not some set of theoretical experts or well-trained logicians,

> 1535 Coverdale: "I speake vnto them which haue discrecioun: iudge ye what I say," 1796 Eliza Hamilton *Lett. Hindoo Rajah*: "Judge how this shocked and offended me?"

So the model for judgment is the particular, always potentially controversial conclusion at which the authority in a courtroom arrives. But judgments in a courtroom are also decisions we all will have to live with. This places important limitations on the decisions to which a judge can come, makes irresponsible those who let highly theoretical issues, or pride in their own ingenuity, rule their interpretations. A scientist can postpone decision out of respect for the demands of theoretical accuracy. A literary critic adds color to her work by putting her ingenuity or biases on show. An historian can hold out for theoretical purity or put his ingenuity on show, tend towards scientist or critic, and the world is probably better for having both kinds of historian. A judge cannot do such things; a judge, no matter how much her thinking may resemble history or criticism, must answer for her conclusions to strangers who will suffer unnecessarily from unwise or unfair interpretation. Hence judgment in the courtroom represents a paradigm case of something which is both open or indefinite and needs to be responsible. Kant, as we shall see, regards an open, indefinite "play" of reflection to be essential to aesthetic judgment, while maintaining that scientific and moral judgment must end such play with a determinate conclusion. In legal judgment, there may be a lot of playroom within which to work, but ultimately the interpretation cannot be playful.

An example: in *Board of Education v Grumet*, Justice Souter argued that New York's law creating a public school district for children of the Satmar Hasidim was unconstitutional because it separated out one religious sect for special treatment. In order to do this, he had to read the clause in the First Amendment that prohibits establishing religion, and the history of precedent cases by which that clause has been interpreted, as essentially about not favoring any one religious sect over other such sects and not favoring religious groups in general over secular ones:

> The general principle that civil power must be exercised in a manner neutral to religion is one the Larkin court (*Larkin v. Grendel's Den*) recognized. . . . [T]he principle is well grounded in our case law, as we have frequently relied explicitly on the general availability of any benefit provided religious groups or individuals in turning aside Establishment Clause challenges. In *Walz v. Tax Commission of New York City* (1970), for example, the Court sustained a property tax exemption for religious properties in part because the State had "not singled out one particular church or religious group or even churches as such," but had exempted "a broad class of property owned by non-profit, quasi-public corporations."[13]

Justice Scalia countered with a different reading of the same cases, according to which the crucial issue in the First Amendment is not the favoring of religious *groups* but the granting of power to religious *institutions* (churches):

> Justice Souter believes that the present case "resembles" *Grendel's Den* because that case "teaches that a state may not delegate its civic authority to *a group chosen according to a religious criterion*." That misdescribes . . . what that case taught (which is that a state may not delegate its civil authority to a *church*). . . . The court had little difficulty finding the statute [in *Grendel's Den*] unconstitutional. "The Framers did not set up a system of government in which important, discretionary governmental powers would be delegated to or shared with religious institutions." . . . The uniqueness of the case stemmed from the grant of governmental power directly to a religious institution, and the Court's opinion focused on that fact, remarking that the transfer of authority was to

"churches" (10 times), the "governing body of churches" (twice), "religious institutions" (twice) and "religious bodies" (once). . . . Justice Souter's steam-rolling of the difference between civil authority held by a church and civil authority held by members of a church, is breathtaking.

He also proposed a different reading of the facts in the case at hand:

[W]hat this case involves . . . is a group chosen according to cultural characteristics. . . . On what basis does Justice Souter conclude that it is the theological distinctiveness rather than the cultural distinctiveness that was the basis for New York State's decision? The normal assumption would be that it was the latter, since it was not theology but dress, language, and cultural alienation that posed the educational problem for the children.

Now, both Souter's and Scalia's readings make sense, and could be considered equally good interpretations in a literature or history class. The principle of "neutral treatment," or equal treatment across sects and between religious and nonreligious groups, is a readily graspable general rule and seems a plausible candidate to fit much case law, including *Walz v Tax Commission*.[14] The principle of not transferring civil authority to churches, as opposed to groups of religious citizens, is an equally graspable general rule and seems a tighter reading both of what the Constitution probably means by "establishment" and of *Grendel's Den*.[15] On the other hand, Scalia's reading of the facts is strained: it is a theologically-grounded belief about the proper role of women, and not merely general cultural differences, that motivated the Satmars' request for a separate school district. The judges obviously pick different features out as salient in the precedents they are looking at and regard different kinds of problems for their own arguments as insignificant. As regards its precedents alone, is *Grumet* really more like a series demanding that benefits to religious groups be generally available or more like a series insisting that government not share power with religious authorities? It is probably somewhat like both series, and many of the precedents can probably themselves be read in both ways, depending on what features one emphasizes, what overall understanding one has of the political purposes and philosophical content of the Constitution, and what other concepts and distinctions one brings to bear. *Grumet* is thus a paradigm of a possible clash of interpretations—of the details, creation of patterns out of details, and overall views that go into such interpretations—and of the way that judgment concludes in spite of the reflective "play" that makes it look as if it can go on forever. In our system of law, we grant some recognition to the interpretation that is not accepted by recording it as a dissenting opinion and by allowing such dissents to be invoked as at least weak support for a view in subsequent decisions. In addition, as in most systems of law, the legitimate values in a minority opinion will usually find some expression in other laws, executive practices, or public discourse.[16] As long as both opinions are well reasoned, and the decisive opinion is then followed with suitable respect for the value claims dismissed, we can usually live with either opinion: that is ultimately our only protection against Supreme Court "misinterpretation." At the same time, the different ways of lumping cases together, and different lessons thereby learned, will shape profoundly different notions of, for instance, "church" in our society.

Edward Levi has shown that judicial decisions in the Anglo-American system are always a matter of aligning and realigning cases into patterns that can be used to make sense of a new case, and that different judges may form quite radically different patterns.[17] I suggest that this is what we do every day, upon reading the newspapers or hearing the local gossip from our friends, in judging a new event to be an instance of "terrorism" or "legitimate guerrilla warfare," of "love" or "mere infatuation," of "bureaucratic incompetence" or the "slow procedures required by justice." And as we assimilate new events to one or another of two opposed categories, we adjust our definitions of those categories accordingly.[18] Then, when we face significant changes in our own lives, we evaluate them using the categories as most recently readjusted. Kant says: "Judgment in general is the capacity to think the particular as contained under the general. If the general (the rule, the principle, the law) is given, then the judgment that subsumes the particular under it is *determining*. . . . If, however, only the particular is given, for which the general must be found, then the judgment is merely *reflective*."[19] So judgment is both the application of rules to particular cases and the interpretation of cases such that rules can be formed from their similarities.

Another example, a fictional one this time and from a nonlegal arena of practice. Suppose I work for a seller of furniture and art objects from various islands in Indonesia. She goes away on a two-month buying trip, leaving me with the following instructions: "Customers who make a down payment should be allowed to take items home to try out for a week, except for the chairs. Once people sit on the chairs they leave an indentation in the cushions." "Oh," I say, "Are any of the other items like that? Anything I should look out for outside of the chairs?" "Use your own judgment," she responds, "I can't tell you everything in advance." I am new to the store and at first I blindly follow the principle my boss laid out; I do not use my judgment at all. Then she sends back from Indonesia some wicker tables with cushioned surfaces, rather like the sacrosanct chairs. I wonder whether to treat these like chairs or not. I am tempted to "play it safe": not to allow them out of the store in case they might also be thereby dented, at least to my boss's keen eyes. But it occurs to me that there is a danger on this side too. Displeasing customers is no part of my job, and I will just as likely anger my boss by driving away a good sale as by making an item here or there less readily saleable. Eventually I decide that the less sturdy among the tables are unlikely to be used for sitting, hence may be taken home; the sturdier ones I judge are "chairs" for the purpose of the rule. Finally, my boss sends me a four-foot-high chest of drawers with a cushion across the top. It doesn't occur to me to treat *this* as a chair, until I see a customer in the store playfully holding his baby on top. My first impulse now is to apply the "chair" rule to the chest of drawers, but then I think, "How often and for how long is a baby going to sit on top of something that's four feet high? And of course no one else will sit on it." After the customer takes the baby off, moreover, I notice that it has made not nearly as deep an impression as the one I have gotten used to looking for in the Indonesian cushions. Now *my* "keen eyes" perceive how the rule I have been given applies to particulars; now I fully understand the reason for the rule and its limits; now I can truly "use my judgment." I have gotten to this point by disciplined practice, by repeated observation, but also by reflecting on the reason for the rule, connecting it to other general considerations (what kinds of objects people sit on, what safety precautions people take with babies) and to general norms derived from the interests I am supposed to be pursuing (protecting cushions, pleasing customers). I give this example as a case of how even a category like "chair," which seems to apply most straightforwardly to its instances, can in specific circumstances need to be broadened or narrowed, of how the use of even the most ordinary categories can require judgment. That we need to reinterpret instances is always a possibility in applying rules: this fact is one reason, I shall argue later, why Kant was right to see the way by which we come up with rules (reflective judgment) and the way by which we apply them (determining judgment) as different sides of the same operation.

I have given some rather special examples, to make vivid just how pervasive judging can be, and just what is involved in it, but of course I use my judgment most often neither to revise straightforward categories like "chair" nor to shape the most complicated issues raised by the separation between church and state. Instead, I am most commonly called on to judge when I apply or reflect on concepts like "love," "duty," "fairness," or "humanity"—concepts that are ordinary but whose ordinary boundaries are vague, concepts that are normative but whose normative bite is sufficiently innocuous that ordinary citizens can make up their minds about how to use them without legal help. Thus when I judge that Mr. and Mrs. McGillicuddy are unhappily married, I self-consciously employ *my* concepts of what counts as "a fight," of what counts as "dissatisfaction" or "repressed tension," of what furthers or counters "human dignity," and of how much indignity or dissatisfaction is compatible with "love," as against what I know to be the similar but in many detailed respects different conceptions of all these things that my neighbors, friends, and relatives hold. I do the same, of course, when I judge that *I* am happily or unhappily married, and I can only judge well about myself if I have had some practice in judging others. I contribute to my society's discourse about moral and political affairs, at times dissenting from its common views, by making my own judgments; those judgments in turn define a set of concepts that I use, at least ideally, in determining principles for, and judging, my own conduct. I build up, that is, an idiosyncratic vocabulary, an idiolect, of moral terms which together help reflect and shape my personal picture of what human nature is like and what ends it is most appropriately suited for. That I *have* a moral idiolect allows me to participate in shaping the judgments my society makes, although its judgments also influence my own concepts and views. In the end, however, I set my limits to those controversial moral and political terms my society cannot decide how to bound, and thereby build up my personal set of moral and political concepts. My moral idiolect, as displayed in and defined by the series of my moral judgments, thus constitutes *the most specific, most personal expression of my freedom*. My moral idiolect is the arena of my concrete freedom, set within the arena—linguistic communication—in which, more generally, human conceptions both shape experience and are shaped by it. So, at least, this book will argue.

POLITICAL IMPLICATIONS

Consider the following five mental skills, all of which are highly valued in our society, and each of which is considered by some people to constitute "intelligence" by itself:

1. calculative skill
2. "originality," or "creativity"
3. perceptiveness
4. argumentative skill, or "analytic rigor"
5. judgment

The names are undoubtedly somewhat inept, and the divisions are undoubtedly not as neat as this, but I think these categories are at least well entrenched, important, and importantly distinct. Originality (2) and analytic rigor (4) are often at odds with one another, as are calculative skill and perceptiveness, perceptiveness and originality, analytic rigor and judgment, etc. Yet all of these skills can rightly be called "intelligence," if "intelligence" is a word for mental skills that societies must value. All are needed for a society to run well: someone must be amassing observations, someone must be making good calculations, someone must be assessing arguments, and someone must be coming up with new ideas and conjectures. Different skills are needed in different social niches: a good logician makes a poor waiter, while an exciting artist is, often, a poor philosopher. This alone suggests that the project of some cognitive psychologists to identify *one* unified capacity as intelligence is misguided.

Indeed, the first four skills, at least, are measured by separate, incommensurable, canons of success. Excellence in calculation is measured by getting the right results a large percentage of the time, while the very notion of "right results" has no clear application in the realm of constructing good arguments and no application at all in the realm of creating original works of art. Philosophers and artists use the term "genius" in extremely different ways, enough so that a person often could not possibly fit the description under both usages. Similarly, while those who do empirical research in the physical or social sciences tend to agree on how to recognize an excellent work in their field, they may be quite incompetent at discerning such excellence in philosophy and art. We might compare the various intellectual fields and skills with games, each having methodologies and marks of success peculiar to itself.

As we shall see more fully in the rest of this book, it is left to judgment to move *among* all these various fields, skills, and canons for success. Judgment is what we have to use when making a decision under conditions of uncertainty—where this does not mean, as it does in mathematized "game theory," a decision in which the option with the best chance of success can be calculated as a matter of probability, but where the uncertainty concerns precisely, at least in significant part, what *canons of success* it is appropriate to use. I employ my judgment when I am not quite sure whether I ought to be doing what is legally right in a given situation, or where one option risks my happiness and another my spiritual integrity and it is not clear which ought to take priority, or where a single canon for success, whether aesthetic, moral, religious, or prudential, has a less than clear application. Kant rightly describes judgment as *bridging* different mental skills; it is what we use precisely when we want to bring to bear a theoretical principle on a body of observations or an aesthetic standard on a theory, or when we want to evaluate a given field's canons for success themselves. Is philosophy today pointless or boring, art lacking in intellectual depth, industrial technology ugly? To make such judgments is precisely to cross fields, to bring different canons together. But that suggests that judgment is essential to the construction of canons in the first place, to the process of second-order reflection by which we stand back from what a field does and try to decide where it succeeds and where it fails.

If this is so, then it begins to be clear why judgment, unlike calculation, originality, perceptiveness, etc., is the proper focus for a liberal approach to the intellectual virtues. For if the modern world is one in which various religious and ethical doctrines are reasonable but no single such doctrine can be proven more satisfactorily than another, then judgment is the skill we need in order to choose which of these doctrines we will follow—even if the doctrine we opt for itself gives pride of place to a different intellectual skill. We might say, a bit crudely, that Platonic religious doctrines see the highest human achievement ultimately in an exercise of logic, while Romantics emphasize creative expression above all, and thoroughgoing aesthetes, along with some Buddhists, seek a state of pure perception, stripped as much as possible of intellectual content. Perhaps only Aristotelian ethicists will say that judgment itself is essential to the highest human flourishing. But to *pick* any comprehensive doctrine about how to live, one must move among the different canons of achievement they value, and only judgment will allow one to do that. If absorbed already in the wonders of Platonic dialectic, the sensuous joys of a wine connoisseur will look simply trivial, and if already entranced by a movement along the sensuous surfaces of life, Platonic argument will appear just as obviously cold and lifeless. The twelve-hour-a-day computer programmer finds Dickens long-winded and religious ritual bizarre; the hard-boiled businesswoman finds the artist and mystic obviously irrational. To assess the canons of another way of proceeding, we must stand beyond our own, and it is only judgment that enables us to do that. So the liberal must make sure that people have well-developed capacities to judge whatever other intellectual skills they have, for judgment is essential to one's choice *of* way of life, even if one chooses a way of life that regards it as having, at best, only instrumental value.

We may make a similar point about the controversies we face over how "human nature" should be defined (not unrelated, of course, to controversies over how human life should be led). Considering human beings as, above all, *judging* creatures enables us to finesse a final answer to the question of who we "really" are, to leave metaphysical questions about the nature of the self up to each individual to decide for herself. In particular, emphasizing judgment enables us to avoid the question of whether our empirical desires or our rational will better defines our true nature. What one judges it best to do in a situation may well not be what one particularly *wants* to do. I may judge that I should see a doctor, despite my fear of medical professionals; I may judge that I should visit a sick aunt, despite my dislike of her or aversion to illness. Nor will my judgment ordinarily be equivalent to a deliverance of my "will" or reason, at least when the latter is construed in Kantian fashion. Will sets very general ends (a just world, my happiness, the flowering of human capacities) and reason provides very general principles ("treat all human beings as ends"). Judgment, by contrast, is always particular ("In my judgment, it would be best to visit Aunt Minnie"), although it may and usually will be informed by general ends and principles. Thus certain deliverances of the categorical imperative may well influence my judgment that I should visit Aunt Minnie, but that does not make my judgment identical with my reason. I can also judge, after all, precisely to *ignore* my overall ends and principles on occasion. It may well be rational always to use judgment when attempting to act on reason, but it is by no means so clearly judicious always to have reason—in its capacity of demanding general principles—determine my judgments. In the ordinary sense of "freedom," therefore, we may call someone free when using her own judgment about what to do, regardless of whether she directs her judgment towards what she "ought" to do or towards what would satisfy her desires. Yet it is to be presumed that anyone with a well-developed capacity for judgment will at least have spent some time reflecting on what she ought to do. So a freedom based on judgment allows us to finesse the question of whether freedom necessarily serves my "higher" purposes, while at the same time ensuring that a person driven by desire to the extent that she cannot even consider whether she has such purposes will not count as free.

The contrast with desire brings out, moreover, the fact that our judgment is something we need to cultivate, not something we simply have or fail to have, like a desire. The conditions that make for a well-developed capacity for judgment will take up a lot of this book, and they will turn out to require favorable material and social circumstances, as well as action on our own parts. To learn how to judge for ourselves, it will turn out, we need: enough food, clothing, shelter, and health care to be independent of pressing bodily needs; a wide base of knowledge; a deep understanding of interpretation; enough leisure to engage in reflection; and a social position in which we are held responsible for our own decisions. If judgment is central to liberty, then it will be in bad faith to say that individuals have the liberty to make their own decisions where these conditions are not in place.

At the same time the compelling intuition behind libertarianism can be put just as well by saying that government ought not to obstruct what I *judge* it best to do as by saying that government ought not to obstruct what I *desire* to do. That some outsider should override my judgment about a situation that, by being immersed in it, I know better than he or she does, is at least as impertinent as that someone should prevent me from fulfilling my desires. Hence the intuition about liberty generally associated with Adam Smith can be characterized as a basic right of people to come to and act on their own judgments.

But if we put the last two paragraphs together, we get a picture quite unlike the typical libertarian one. For if the making of judgments is essential to liberty, then a government concerned to protect the liberty of each of its citizens must *provide the conditions* for those citizens to develop their judgment, and not merely stand aside to let them act on untutored desires. A truly "libertarian" government, according to the third concept of liberty, will have to *both* make the conditions for judgment readily available *and* stand back from people's decisions once they have had the chance to use the conditions. The third concept of liberty thus weds a number of the demands for government action usually associated with the "positive liberty" tradition to the general presumption in favor of restraining government advocated by the "negative liberty" tradition.

I will return to such policy issues towards the end of this book. First I want to clarify more precisely what judgment is and why it matters to politics. In chapters 2 through 4 (Part I), I use Kant, Smith, and elements of Aristotle to develop an account of how judgment works. I proceed in chapters 5 through 8 to an examination of the politics by which, I believe, Smith sought to create a society that would encourage individuals to develop their faculties of judgment as fully as possible. Chapters 9 and 10 use the influence of Smith on Kant to reinterpret Kant's moral and political writings, and the book concludes with a return to contemporary political questions in chapter 11.

The position to which I ultimately come is one that plays down the importance of politics in our lives, that plays up instead the filtering of liberal, "enlightened" attitudes as much as possible into the course of everyday life. Far from urging the active citizenship that communitarians and civic republicans have recently been encouraging, or even the notion that we all need to cultivate the "public reason" that John Rawls has identified as essential to citizenship, I think political theorists need to help make politics less necessary, to promote institutions enabling individuals to lead rich, independent private lives. Insofar as political theorists have been concerned about pain and oppression, they have tended to consider violence, poverty, racial and sexual discrimination, and the like, and to seek, therefore, justifications for economic equality, for affirmative action, for political action that combats embedded sexism or racism, and for other ways in which the powers that be might directly alleviate suffering. What goes missing in all this is the way that the theorists' own activities, insofar as they succeed in influencing policy, further entrench a division of status in our society between "experts" and everyone else. The status of those who develop such good theories gets enhanced, and their abilities are brought into stark contrast with the foolishness of the masses who vote for less progressive policies. For the nonacademic masses, moreover, such enhancement of the status of academics exacerbates a fear they have in any case: that their understanding of moral questions is weak, that they have no real idea of how to lead a human life, whether their own or anyone else's. In America's high divorce rate, in the proliferation of fundamentalist religious groups and extremist political ones, in the large numbers of drug and alcohol addicts and the addiction of an overwhelming number of other Americans to television, and in what is sometimes decried as an increasing culture of consumerism, we see what has been called "a crisis of meaning," a culture of monotonous and empty lives, of barely suppressed despair about how to find a goal or set of activities that would make life worth living. These are the issues that left-wing academics impatiently brush aside as a distraction from real suffering.

I suggest, on the contrary, that until this problem is addressed there will be little movement on any other social problem. Not only are such crimes as theft, rape, and political violence often direct responses to a sense of ennui or lack of direction in one's ordinary life, but an electorate made up of people who have difficulty caring about their own lives is unlikely to find the generosity or energy to care much about other people's lives—to make the necessary financial sacrifices, for instance, to help the poor. When consumption is all that gives my life meaning, I will be very reluctant to give up any of my consumer goods to help others. But the skill that most enables people to find a purpose or direction to their lives, I shall argue, is judgment. So a politics that cultivates everyone's judgment should also, albeit indirectly, help people to the position from which they need no longer hold tight to their financial position in desperate self-protection. A side effect of no mean importance is that a citizenry capable of good judgment should be more capable, among other things, of good *political* judgment: should be less likely than our current population is to vote for career politicians who make empty and dishonest promises, or for demagogues who make foolish and dangerous ones.[20]

PART I

THE NATURE OF JUDGMENT

Chapter 2

AESTHETIC JUDGMENT

I BEGIN with a reading of Kant's *Critique of Judgment* (CJ), probably the richest account of aesthetic judgment ever written. Aesthetic
judgment may seem far removed from the moral and political issues
with which this book is concerned. But one of the main claims I want to
advance is precisely that knowing how to make judgments of beauty is
essential to making any judgment, that one condition for fostering moral
and political judgment across a citizenry is to ensure that people understand well what beauty is, and have broad access both to art and to natural beauty. In addition, the workings of aesthetic judgment richly illuminate the workings of judgment in general. So the time spent here on
Kant's aesthetic theory has a direct as well as an indirect payoff for the
moral and political case I want to build.[1]

Part I of this chapter offers an account of what Kant calls "the harmony of the faculties."[2] Parts II and III suggest some morally useful
implications of this account.

I

Kant famously refers the pleasure behind any judgment of beauty to what
he calls the "free play of the imagination and the understanding" (CJ
218/52). What exactly is this, and why is it pleasurable? The understanding is the faculty of rules or concepts; the imagination is that which
gathers, and places into space and time, the manifold of intuition. According to Kant, the state of mind that leads one to make judgments of
beauty is one in which these "cognitive powers . . . are . . . in free play,
because no definite concept limits them to a definite rule of cognition"
(217/52). This sentence is often read to elide the word "definite," thus:
"the cognitive powers . . . are . . . in free play, because no . . . concept
limits them."[3] If that is what Kant had said, he would have expressed the
common Romantic view that aesthetic appreciation is wholly an exercise
of the imagination. Aesthetic appreciation would then be something independent of knowledge, of the concepts, the classificatory structures, of
the understanding. But Kant does not say this; he says only that no *definite* or *determinate* concept limits the free play of the faculties.[4] And his
account of free play would make no sense if the understanding had no

role to play in it. The free play of the faculties is a play not *of* the imagination by itself but *between* the imagination and the understanding: "the
excitement of both faculties (imagination and understanding) to indeterminate but yet . . . harmonious activity . . . is the sensation . . . postu-
lated by the judgment of taste" (219/53–4).[5] This means that the understanding, the faculty of knowing, cannot be absent in judgments of
beauty. It must somehow interact with the imagination, albeit differently
from the way it does in knowing proper.[6] To think without a "definite"
or "determinate" concept might be best understood as to use concepts
without defining or determining precisely which concept one is using: to
allow a range or array of concepts to play with the contents of one's
imagination instead of fixing one of them determinately to that content.[7]

What might *that* mean? Well, suppose you are trying to show a friend
the beauty in a Jackson Pollock or Anselm Kiefer painting. The sensory
material is confusing but you feel it has some kind of order, and you
point out to your friend Pollock's ways of questioning the traditional
distinction between line and color, or Kiefer's ironic use of myth. These
concepts—these organizational tools—help give some coherence to the
sensory intuitions, and there is a pleasure in using them to bring erstwhile
confusion into focus. But your friend, if she is at all aesthetically sensitive,
will not long be satisfied by your remarks, and will complain that there is
much *more* in the paintings, that your conceptual tools are inadequate.
The randomness of Pollock's way of distributing paint, she might say,
defeats any thematic reading of his work, or the thickness of the painting's texture is too much left out by a bald contrast between line and
color. And there is a pleasure, too, in being able to knock down the
conceptual tools of aesthetic criticism, in showing how the sensory manifold overflows the concepts that are supposed to contain it. All the same,
having had one interpretation knocked down, you will come back with
others—well aware that, if the work is richly interesting, these tools will
also prove to be inadequate. *This* is the free play of the faculties, and your
friend will find the work beautiful not if one of the interpretations is
finally unanswerable but if she feels able to continue the play indefinitely.
I think we have here an accurate, and reasonably familiar, description of
aesthetic pleasure.[8] But if so, we should note that, just as the play may
not be ended by any definite concept, so it also cannot continue unless
some concept seems capable of organizing the imagination's material.
Aesthetic enjoyment is no more a matter of mindless absorption in a
work than of correctly finding the work's "message." If nothing else, the
imagination needs intellectual constructs to fight with, to find wanting; it
cannot play without some friction.

Now why, according to Kant, is all this pleasurable? Because pleasure is
the satisfaction of a need, and free play satisfies a cognitive need, a need

that any being whose knowledge depends on the organization of sensory material has to have (183–4/20). This need, quite simply, is for the world to be organiz*able*. To have knowledge, we must be able to make what Kant calls "determining judgments," judgments that apply concepts or rules to particular cases, that determine whether a particular thing is a house or flower or tree. But to make these judgments we need to *have* concepts or rules, and that means we must be able to unify our particular intuitions into concepts in the first place. We need to find general terms that fit the particular sense-data around us. To "fit" is not the same as "to be imposed on," however, so the process of coming up with general terms is both a matter of trying out a structure on the data and of deciding, sometimes, that that structure doesn't work and substituting another one for it. We realize that the world is organiz*able*, rather than something we merely impose organization upon, both when we succeed in getting a conceptual framework to apply to the world of our experience and when our experience bucks our frameworks, when we have to repair a framework or start again. Indeed the first part of the process depends upon the latter: it makes sense to think of some concepts as fitting experience only if it makes sense to think of others as failing to fit. Precisely when experience bucks our concepts do we have reason to regard the application of concepts as something we may succeed or fail in. Someone who understands thoroughly how interpretation works is someone who can say, "This interpretation (this set of concepts) doesn't fit the data—as opposed to that one." Concepts must satisfy two conflicting needs: they must protect us against the chaotic "manifold" of raw sensory intuitions, but they must also be responsible *to* the very chaos against which they protect us. It is this two-sided process of developing responsible conceptual frameworks that Kant calls "reflective judgment," and it is this process that constitutes the free play of the faculties.[9]

Thus our judgments of beauty are a precondition for our judgments of knowledge, and they are pleasurable *because* they show knowledge to be possible. A completely chaotic world would not allow for knowledge; the confusion we feel when we first approach a Pollock is disturbing because it threatens our entire capacity for making cognitive judgments. Once we begin to interpret the painting, we are relieved, and the relief of this cognitive need is the pleasure on the basis of which we call something beautiful. In addition, the demand on interpretation to be responsible, to "fit" the sensory data in some sense, keeps its pleasure energetic, mentally stimulating, while the potential endlessness of interpretation gives the pleasure an inexhaustible quality, a hint at eternity, traditionally associated with the experience of beauty. Kant repeatedly indicates that aesthetic pleasure is something that extends over time, that indeed can go on indefinitely. The play of the faculties is supposed to "quicken . . . both faculties . . . to indefinite but . . . harmonious activity."[10] The facts that we cannot endure an artificial nightingale's song for long (§42), and that one day in a Sumatran pepper garden would be enough (§22), let us know that these are not experiences of the beautiful. Something that inspires interpretation, by contrast, "quickens" our faculties for an indefinite period of time: "That with which the imagination can play in an unstudied and purposive manner is always new to us," Kant says, "and one does not get tired of looking at it. . . . We *linger* over the contemplation of the beautiful because this contemplation strengthens and reproduces itself."[11]

II

I have been suggesting that Kant sees judgment as a movement between two incommensurable ways of approaching phenomena that yet need one another. The play of the faculties is just that—a "play," an interaction that cannot be resolved and hence can go on indefinitely. By contrast, the standard reading of Kant's harmony of the faculties does without concepts, without the understanding. Paul Guyer presents this view: "The harmony of the faculties is . . . a state in which, somehow, a manifold of intuition is run through and held together as a unity by the imagination without the use of a concept" (85–6). The word "somehow" reveals Guyer's unease about exactly how a manifold might be unified without a concept. He is right to be uneasy, since such a unification is impossible. Nor did Kant think it possible. Guyer himself acknowledges that his reading is "far from self-evident" and only "suggested" by Kant's text (87).[12] A few words on Guyer's reading will help clarify the model of reflective judgment I prefer.

Guyer says that reflective judgment "leads to aesthetic response . . . by discovering that a given object fulfills the *general condition for the possibility of the application of concepts* without having any concept at all applied to it" (89). I quite agree that what we seek when we respond to an object aesthetically is "the general condition for the possibility of the application of concepts," but I think that condition consists in our recognizing many different concepts that might fit an object, not in our being able to grasp the object without applying any concept at all to it. That is, I believe that what makes it possible to apply concepts to an object, both on Kant's account and in fact, is that we have *already applied some concepts* to that object.

I put this point especially paradoxically because I think it is the appearance of paradox that makes Guyer and others shy away from such a claim, but the paradox disappears on fuller examination. Essentially, the point is just that we can never apply any one concept to an object without already having other concepts to serve as a background against which to apply it. There can be no "first" application of concepts, either in the sense that a child might be entirely innocent of concepts and then come to a first one, or in the sense that a sophisticated concept-user might mint a "first" concept for material which hitherto resisted all general categories. We are always already in the midst of concepts; it makes no more sense to be able to apply just one concept than it does to be able to pick out just one point in a perceptual field. Points in a perceptual field are defined by their relationship to other points in a coordinate system, and concepts are similarly defined by their relationship to one another in a conceptual field. To call an object a "dog" or a "coffee cup" is to say that it is *not* a lion or a beer mug. Concepts are functions of *determinate* unity: they unify intuitions not into a general mass but into discrete objects. Indeterminate unity might characterize the universe as a whole, but it cannot enable me to pick out a specific object among other objects. Concepts *consist in* what enables us to contrast one specific object with another—without which contrast, we could not pick out objects at all. Concepts are *specific* forms of similarity, *specific* ways of "seeing what is common."[13] Without their specificity, without the fact that they define a limited kind of similarity bordered by other limited kinds of similarity,[14] we could and would see everything as similar to everything else. That would mean that notions of similarity—on which all "notions," all concepts, in turn rely—would cease to do any work. We could, quite literally, no longer think.

Inter alia, we could not think reflectively. We could not make even reflective judgments about what Guyer and I both take to be the essential locus for Kantian judgments of beauty: a "given object" or "particular." Judging a particular object presupposes that we have distinguished it by means of *some* concepts from other objects. I reflect on *this* Pollock painting, not the whole room of paintings in which it hangs, much less on the whole museum, the whole city, or the whole universe.[15] Any suspension of conceptualization in reflective judgment will have to wait on the application of concepts that allows us to pick out the object of our reflections. Herein lies the philosophical advantage of reading Kant's reflective judgment in terms of an interplay between concepts and a given particular, rather than a play of intuitions that somehow does without concepts altogether. What we do in reflective judgment is reinterpret an object that we feel we have hitherto insufficiently or inaccurately conceptualized. We open up conceptual applications that we previously took to determine the object; we shift the object into a different set of intellectual boundaries. We may also, thereby, shift the boundaries of our intellectual sets, our concepts, themselves. In science, we engage in this reflective judgment only in exceptional cases: when developing a new theory, or radically reworking an old one. In aesthetic appreciation, we engage in it all the time. We revel in finding responsible interpretation among the uncertainties, the indeterminacies, that scientific theories must keep in the background. The fact that even our scientific concepts must be responsibly applied to particulars means that this aesthetic play satisfies a need, and since scientific judgments must be determining, science cannot engage in the free play to satisfy this need for itself. Similarly, moral decisions must be determining, and therefore cannot satisfy their own need for responsible concepts. "Responsibility," in the sense we use that term when we speak of "responsibility to evidence," is something we learn in the first instance and paradigmatically from aesthetic interpretation, not from scientific procedures or moral choices. In this way, aesthetic interpretation is essential, if essentially in the background, to all our other thinking.

But in this way, also, it is interwoven *with* our other thinking. Not only does reflective judgment consist in a play between concepts and intuitions: it participates in an interplay with determining judgment as well. (Here I go beyond what Kant himself says, although his use of the single term "judgment" to cover both activities may suggest such an interplay.) The determining judgments of science and morality play into the interpretations we come up with of, say, a Tolstoy novel, while our interpretations of the novel inform the way we then use some terms in science and morality. Concepts have a definite meaning insofar as we have a definite set or system of scientific and moral determining judgments, but such systems must be constantly scrutinized for responsibility to evidence, to the facts, and that means that our determining judgments, and the concepts they define, must always stand open to being reinterpreted, reshaped into a new system, by reflective judgment. The play in reflective judgment, and between reflective and determining judgment, is what keeps our concepts honest, our beliefs responsible to the world around us.

III

Aesthetic interpretation, on Kant's own account, is more directly related to moral thinking in another way: it teaches us how to share our views with and learn from others. CJ contains Kant's deepest thoughts on the nature of communication. The "universal communicability" of beauty appears both in his account of the harmony of the faculties (§§ 6–9) and in a separate section of CJ devoted specifically to it (§§ 18–22). The overlap suggests a striking insight: that the tension between a sharable (intersubjective) and a purely subjective state of mind closely parallels the tension between conceptualizability and the inapplicability of any specific concept. The reflective state of mind is sharable in that it plays with all sorts of concepts; it is subjective in that it eludes definition by any particular concept. Furthermore, *because* none of our concepts quite fits the object, we find ourselves wanting to hear from other people about what concepts they are inclined to apply in this instance. My moments of reflective judgment incline me to talk with people, to converse. There is a delicate line to be trodden here: what I do *not* need to hear from other people is that they too find the object worthy of interpretation, that they too find it beautiful. Kant insists that in matters of reflective judgment, the subject must "judge by himself, without needing to grope about empirically among the judgments of others, and acquaint himself as to their satisfaction or dissatisfaction with the . . . object" (CJ 282/123).[16] Yet the fact that I find an object resistant to determination by a concept, that I judge it to be beautiful, makes me interested in hearing about other people's attempts to conceptualize it. Its interpretability makes it good matter for discussion. Thus although the play of the faculties does not *depend* on talking to others, it does *lead* us to such talk.

This would explain why Kant returns again and again to conversation in CJ (§§ 6–9, 17–19, 21, 22, 40–42, 44), to what we *say* about the beautiful;[17] it would explain why he describes beauty as of particular interest in society; and it would explain, above all, why in § 9 Kant makes the apparently bizarre claim that the communicability of the judgment of beauty is the foundation of our pleasure in it rather than the other way around. I believe we need to understand the harmony of the faculties and the communicability of that harmony as one and the same thing,[18] as a state that both constitutes and grounds a feeling of pleasure.[19] That a subjective "harmony" or activity should be identical with a capacity for an intersubjective activity seems odd, of course, but we can begin to make sense of it by stressing that "communic*ability*" is not the same as "communic*ation*": communicability is a mere capacity, not an activity. The communicability of a state or activity is thus a mere potential of that state to contribute to some other activity or state. And there is no reason, in principle, why a subjective state or activity could not have a potential to contribute to an intersubjective state or activity. What it means to say that the universal communicability of the harmony of the faculties is identical with that harmony need thus mean nothing more shocking than that we can communicate about something if and only if our faculties are in harmony when we perceive and understand that thing.[20] At the same time, Kant does seem to want to use the pleasure in aesthetic response as a basis for conversation—actual conversation, not mere communicability (§§ 7–9, 21–2, 40–1). This derivation is never spelled out, however. All

Kant says is that the harmony of the faculties is communicable because it satisfies a universal need shared by all beings that "judge by means of understanding and the senses in combination" (CJ 219/54). The pleasure achieved by satisfying this need is therefore one we know we can in principle share with other beings like ourselves. It is also based on a relationship, between the understanding and the senses, that makes communication possible. But it does not arise from our interest in actual communication.

I offer the following to fill in the missing steps: We get pleasure from aesthetic response in part because it uncovers to us a subject matter that allows of significant discussion with others. The mental state we have in aesthetic response can be communicated, and "[t]hat the ability to communicate one's mental state . . . carries a pleasure with it, could easily be established (empirically and psychologically) from man's propensity to sociability" (CJ 218/53). Communication becomes worthwhile only when two factors coincide: when there is enough agreement on a subject matter to make sharing our thoughts with others possible, while at the same time there is enough disagreement about it to give us some interest in learning from or teaching others. The play of the faculties will necessarily exemplify this coincidence.[21]

Why? Well, we know from ordinary experience that claims to beauty are simultaneously universalizable and highly idiosyncratic, susceptible of endless discussion and resistant to being resolved by such discussion. Conversation about beauty is thereby a process *continuous with* the very free play of the faculties that constitutes aesthetic response. Communication requires us to use concepts, so the fact that we can communicate buttresses our sense that the perceptions we have are amenable to concepts—and the fact that they seem amenable to concepts buttresses our sense that they can be communicated. Communication about beauty, at the same time, has the peculiar feature that we can never *quite* justify any particular claim we make, and that peculiarity similarly buttresses and is buttressed by our sense that the imagination eludes complete capture by the understanding, "plays" with the understanding in such a way as to make clear that it performs an independent role in the acquisition of knowledge. Thus our conversations about beauty serve as evidence for our belief that a given object has set our intuitions and our concepts into potentially indefinite play, while our sense that such an interpretive movement has begun encourages us to enter into conversation about the object inspiring such thoughts.

Kant can locate a yet deeper identity between these two activities. Understanding is for him a universal human faculty, governed by a transcendental unity of apperception that does not allow us to distinguish between one human being and another, while imagination responds to the history of empirical data peculiar to each human being.[22] So not only does the play between the idiosyncratic and the universal, in conversations about beauty, parallel the play between a single subject's imagination and understanding, not only does it flow continuously out of that play, but the two are, in kind if not in degree, *indistinguishable*. The play of the faculties is a play between *my* imagination and *some* understanding, the latter "belonging" empirically either to me or to any other human being. The understanding is universal, the play is communicable, and the difference between "universal" and "communicable" comes out in the hesitancy—the stops, starts, and repeats—that mark both my private reflections and my reflective conversations with others.[23]

On this reading, a profound theory of the origins of conversation and of the nature of sociability is at work here. Kant's own explicit attention to these subjects in CJ adds textual support to the philosophical reasons for adopting such a reading. The most individualistic of thinkers, Kant reserves judgment, among our mental faculties, for conversation with others. As Kant characterizes them, reason, understanding, and imagination are lonely and silent processes, shared with others and informed by others only via their coming together in judgment. We might say that reason and understanding are too sure of themselves, too definitive, to provide anything worth discussing, while imagination is too inchoate, too *in*definite to make conversation possible. What we have already placed into a rational theory or category of a theory is beyond interesting discussion; what we have merely sensed, with all the peculiarities of our individual capacities for sensation, is not yet expressible in linguistic terms. Only judgment is simultaneously formed enough to be discussible and indeterminate enough to be worth discussing. There is a hint here of what Wittgenstein eventually made explicit: that judgment provides the foundation of language, of what human beings have to share.[24] In any case, judgment provides the foundation of the kind of conversation relevant to morality: conversation about particulars that must be placed in some evaluative category but are, often, too distinctive to fit easily into any single such category. A feeling for the nuances of aesthetic interpretation will thus be essential to the nuances that morality requires. What else moral judgment needs is the subject of our next chapter.

Chapter 3

MORAL JUDGMENT

MUCH OF OUR DISCUSSION of aesthetic judgment can be carried over to moral judgment. In particular, the greatest mistake made by accounts of moral judgment is to identify it with a sort of perception, to overlook the role that rule-following plays in its development and use. In this chapter, I pursue various forms of this problem in some detail, then elaborate two other related features of moral judgment: the way it binds us to a society and a culture, and the way it depends on a kind of discipline, on a process by which we learn to take responsibility for our judgments.

The great difference between aesthetic and moral judgment is that the latter requires choice. At the end of the day one needs to act and therefore, among other things, to make a determining judgment, to put an end to one's reflections. But if the argument of the previous chapter is correct, every determining judgment presupposes a process of reflective judgment. In the case of moral, as opposed to merely cognitive, judgments, moreover, we must make conscious use of reflective judgment. To learn to choose with judgment—to choose "judiciously"—we need to become self-conscious about the importance of reflection to our choices. It may be acceptable, it may indeed be entirely reasonable, for us to take most of the concepts we use for granted in our cognitive judgments. But insofar as our judgments are moral ones, we must become self-conscious about our concepts: we are responsible not only for the acts we decide on but for the kind of thinking that goes into those decisions. This responsibility makes moral judgment dependent on our learning to interpret moral terms in a richly reflective way, makes moral judgment more answerable to social norms than is either cognitive or aesthetic judgment, and distinguishes it, deeply, from perception.

I

A favorite way of characterizing Aristotle, and of commending his approach to ethics, identifies what he calls "practical wisdom" (*phronesis*) with "moral perception." Thus John McDowell in a famous article calls virtue "a sort of perceptual capacity."[1] What we need above all in order to act well, he argues, is to see the particular circumstances of our world aright. He takes himself to be following Iris Murdoch in this, and he has in turn been followed over the past fifteen years or so by a number of other moral theorists. Nancy Sherman tells us that the emotions enable us to "see" human distress and injury,[2] and Martha Nussbaum calls practical wisdom "like perceiving in the sense that it is non-inferential, non-deductive."[3]

I am sympathetic to the aims of this body of moral theory—to its realism, its preference for the contexts of ordinary moral life over the outlandish counterfactuals of earlier theorists, its fondness for bringing moral philosophy together with literature, and above all its emphasis on properly grasping moral particulars as opposed to properly formulating moral rules. Abstract principles of morality are not sufficient for making real moral decisions, nor are intentions to follow such principles sufficient to make one's decisions virtuous. But the friends of "moral perception" have not adequately addressed the worry that turning simply from rules to perceptions may block the room we need to *correct* our moral judgments, or be open to such correction from others. If perception is "non-inferential, non-deductive," then it need not be responsive to objections based on inferences or deductions. In its ordinary as well as its technical, epistemological uses, perception does in fact tend to be independent of inferences and deductions, directed towards particular objects as opposed to universals, rules, or theories. Descartes notoriously supposed we could clearly and distinctly "perceive" general truths; we sometimes say that we "see" how or why a theory is correct; and some people even claim to perceive the point or the emptiness of all existence. But if these are not aberrant uses, saying one stands for moral perception will not be saying much. Perception cannot stand for everything and still mark off a distinctive way of knowing. Insofar as it is a distinctive mode of knowing, however, a mode directed to particulars as opposed to universals, some other faculty of knowledge must do the work of correcting it when attention to the particular alone is misleading.

And, for moral purposes, attention to the particular alone can be very misleading. Many people in modern societies give charity or support causes exclusively on the basis of pictures they see or stories they read about particular sufferers.[4] When a bomb goes off in Tel Aviv, newspaper readers become pro-Israel; when reports of Palestinian sufferings appear a few days later, they switch sides. One day Haiti seems an outrage, the next day Bosnia, then Rwanda, then something else. The rule is "He who cries loudest is most worthy of concern." This turns every issue into a matter for anger and breast-beating rather than a disengaged search for solutions, and it blocks the thought "This pain is merited" or its opposite. Perhaps no human pain is merited, but even then we want to distinguish at least between the *degree* of wrong in pain suffered by an innocent victim and pain inflicted upon that victim's abuser.

Indeed if we do not make room for such distinctions as a matter of appropriate moral concern, simulacra of them will crop up as a matter of natural inclinations. Bigotry, erotic attraction or rivalry, clan loyalty, and other arbitrary sources of bias will lead us to care greatly about the pain of some individuals and not at all about others. In Jerusalem a few years ago, a woman who described herself as an Orthodox Jew threw her body on an Arab teenager to save him from a lynch mob that had just seen him stab and wound a young Jew. A few days later, all the participants in the event except the Arab were gathered together on TV for a bizarre, Oprah-like conversation. The woman who had thrown herself on the stabber repeated several times, in a low voice, that without respect for the due process of law a civilization cannot survive. To which the mother of the stabbing victim cried, "You don't understand the feelings of a mother!" Here concern for abstract principles led fairly obviously to better action than immersion in the particular would have done. In the conditions of war that have structured Jewish/Arab relations in the Middle East throughout this century, it is to be expected that Jews and Arabs will commonly see each other there as "enemies" first and foremost. Moreover, the few seconds of the first woman's acquaintance with this particular Arab consisted almost entirely of seeing him in the process of fleeing the scene where he had just tried to kill one of her fellow Jews. So it is highly unlikely that she was immune to the clan loyalty, the collective fear, and the sense of righteousness making the other Jews so angry, that she saw this particular Arab as anything other than the dangerous, wrongful agent he seemed to them.[5] But an abstract ideal of justice enabled her to overcome her particularized reactions—and for that ideal she was willing to risk her life. Sometimes, especially when we face a stranger or an enemy, we can recognize other people's humanity only via the filter of very general principles and procedures, ones which do implicitly express our shared humanity, as Kant insisted, but only by *distancing* us from the particular circumstances in which we find ourselves and the emotions those circumstances evoke.

So however much we may want to avoid the mechanical, emotionless models of morality associated with the worst of Kantianism, we err if we just dismiss that tradition's emphasis on the importance of rules. In particular, we need to make sure that a stress on moral perception does not bring along the position of incorrigibility that, in standard cases, goes with cognitive perception. We should not want people to be so focused on the way they "see" or "feel" a situation that they are unwilling to step back and analyze their perceptions from a cooler, more distant perspective. Sometimes moral theorists stress perception precisely because it brings our emotions, our "embodied" characteristics and not merely our minds, into the middle of moral thinking. But such embodiment can easily bring with it a complacent or stubborn satisfaction with one's own reactions, a refusal to humble oneself to outside voices.

It happens that McDowell and Murdoch, especially, argue for their brand of moral particularism precisely on the ground that it can humble us. By thinking of ourselves as trying to perceive correctly in particular situations rather than deriving the proper decision from antecedently given principles, they say we will attend more carefully to what is out there, restrain ourselves from rushing into situations with the arrogance of an answer already known—restrain the all-too-ready human inclination to impose ourselves on the world rather than responding to and living within it. McDowell praises Murdoch for her Platonic conception of Good because it encourages humility.[6] Making perception fundamental to moral thought turns out, however, to reintroduce a kind of arrogance.

The point is made most easily by way of Murdoch. Murdoch tells us repeatedly that the purpose of moral philosophy is to thrust down our arrogance[7] and concludes *The Sovereignty of Good* by calling "humility" the best synonym we have for goodness.[8] Yet in what she calls "the ideal situation," the agent combines submissiveness with a cocksure certainty of having found a truth to which to submit:

> One is often compelled almost automatically by what one can see. . . . [I]f we consider what the work of attention is like, how continuously it goes on, and how imperceptibly it builds up structures of value round about us, we shall not be surprised that at crucial moments of choice most of the business of choosing is already over. . . . If I attend properly I will have no choices and this is the ultimate condition to be aimed at. . . . The ideal situation . . . is . . . to be represented as a kind of "necessity." This is something of which saints speak and which any artist will readily understand. The idea of a patient, loving regard, directed upon a person, a thing, a situation, presents the will not as unimpeded movement but as something very much more like "obedience." (pp. 37, 40)

Murdoch presents this sense of compulsion as an unqualifiedly good thing, seeming not to notice how dangerous it can be. Suppose, like Yigal Amir, I direct such a loving regard to the land of Israel, and attend so deeply to the tragic situation Prime Minister Rabin is inflicting on Jewish settlement in that land, that I am "compelled almost automatically" to kill him. . . . Surely it is precisely when I "attend" so deeply as to suppose I have no choices left that I should worry about whether I am attending *properly*. It is at least as likely, when I have this fixed regard, that I have been allowing moral conventions around me, elements of my culture or subculture, to so dominate my way of perceiving that I can now see only one course of action as proper. I "obey," indeed, but therein lies the *danger* of such an uncritical, such a passive relationship to moral reality. A moral realist like Murdoch should be the last person to give up on moral criticism. But only bringing the cultural structuring of my perception explicitly to the surface, only *rejecting* the apparent necessity of my perceptions, can keep moral criticism richly alive.

McDowell takes pains to insulate his position against this objection. He explicitly denies that moral perception is immune to correction:

> It is not to be supposed that the appreciation of the particular instance . . . is a straightforward or easy attainment on the part of those who have it; that either, on casual contemplation of an instance, one sees it in the right light, or else one does not, and is then unreachable by argument. . . . 'Don't you see?' can often be supplemented with words aimed at persuasion. A skilfully presented characterization of an instance will sometimes bring someone to see it as one wants; or one can adduce general considerations, for instance about the point of the concept a particular application of which is in dispute. . . . [A]ny such arguments will fall short of rationally necessitating acceptance of their conclusion in the way a proof does. But [they remain] . . . appeals to reason. (p. 342)

Presumably, what McDowell has in mind is the sort of performance that Wilfred Sellars recommends when we want someone to see a green tie as blue instead.[9] Sellars, telling a story about John, a shop assistant at a time when electric lighting was first introduced, has a member of John's community (re)educate him in the reporting of color perceptions by taking the tie out of the electrically lit shop into daylight—which counts, as John already knows, as a "standard condition" for the viewing of ties. In moral thinking, the analogue would presumably be to place a given case in a different context—to get Yigal Amir to see killing the prime minister in the light, say, of the sacredness of human life. But there is a serious disanalogy between moral and ordinary cognitive perception. Sellars's recommended exercise requires some prior agreement as to what counts as standard conditions in which to see the situation. In the moral case there may well be no equivalent to this agreement. We all pretty much agree that bright daylight is a good context in which to view ties, but precisely what tends to be at stake in morals is what should count as a good context for viewing particular situations. Yigal Amir can reasonably refuse to accept our interpretation of why, and when, human life is sacred. What McDowell calls "a skilfully presented characterisation of an instance," moreover, directs us to the wrong *kind* of moral correction for a case like this. We want Amir to shift his attention precisely *away* from the particulars of Jewish law and history with which he is obsessed, towards a universal principle by which he might consider his entire constellation of particular reactions to be misguided. Presenting other instances is likely to shift Amir's reaction to this particular case only if the presentation itself expresses the very emotional configuration we want to change.[10] And that would defeat the purpose of our correction. The proper "words aimed at persuasion," in this case, seem very much to be words aimed at getting the agent to *stop* perceiving—at least until he can perceive in an entirely different way.

Unlike some of his interpreters, Aristotle takes pains to avoid identifying phronesis with perception, although he certainly compares them. Consider four passages bearing on the relationship between the two:

> a) Practical wisdom is . . . concerned with the ultimate particular, which is the object not of scientific knowledge but of perception—not the perception of qualities peculiar to one sense but a perception akin to that by which we perceive that the particular figure before us is a triangle. . . . But this is rather perception than practical wisdom, though it is another kind of perception than that of the qualities peculiar to each sense. (NE 1142a23–31)

Here Aristotle brings practical wisdom together with perception but also distinguishes them. The perception practical wisdom resembles is not that "of qualities peculiar to one sense" but a kind of "seeing as" by which we interpret a variety of sensory perceptions as fitting into one category or another, and even this interpretive, conceptually infused perception is in the end "rather perception than practical wisdom." To describe practical wisdom as concerned with the same *object* as perception, moreover, is not to identify it with perception. The passage hints that there are various ways of being concerned with this kind of object (the "ultimate particular"), of which perception is but one. 1143a26–8 confirms such a reading: "When we speak of judgment [*gnomen*][11] and understanding and practical reason we credit the same people with possessing judgment and . . . with having practical wisdom and understanding. For *all* these faculties deal with ultimates, i.e. with particulars" (my emphasis).

> b) Nor is practical wisdom concerned with universals only—it must also recognize the particulars. (1141b15; cf. 1147a1–5, b1–5)

Phronesis is not concerned with universals only, but, if this needs to be said, not with particulars only either. The line follows a discussion of how the *phronimos* (practically wise person), unlike the theoretician or (implicitly) the craftsman, aims in deliberation "at the best for man of things attainable by action," so the universals relevant to phronesis are presumably components of this "best for man." 1147a–b makes explicit that there are "universals" in virtuous action, on the order of the medical claim "dry food is good for every man"—defeasible, empirical generalizations about the purposes we seek. Universals of this sort, unlike the starting points of logic or metaphysics, will always require interpretation in particular cases and will always be open to revision in the light of that interpretation. But at the same time they provide guides to the significance, the explanation, the very categorization, of every particular we perceive. Practical wisdom, unlike theory, needs to be concerned above all with particulars because practice is a matter of bringing about one particular rather than another, a matter, therefore, oriented towards the features that distinguish one particular from another.[12] This does not mean practice can do without general rules, however, even for the purposes of grasping precisely those distinguishing features. Distinctions show up only against a general background. Phronesis is therefore unintelligible if it is not a grasp of general similarities exactly as much as it is a grasp of distinctive particulars.

We find a concern with generalities, in any case, throughout the passage surrounding our quotation. "Nor is practical wisdom concerned with universals only" is a phrase marking Aristotle's transition from a discussion of universals to the famous illustration of the importance of particulars by way of the doctor who knows that "chicken is wholesome" versus the one who knows merely that "light meat is wholesome." This illustration in turn gives way to the following summation: "Now practical wisdom is concerned with action; therefore one should have both forms of it, or the latter in preference to the former" (1141b21–3). Perhaps it is better for action, if one has to choose, to know only particular facts than only theory, but the best is to have "both forms" of phronesis. The "theory" of what's good for human beings belongs to any full achievement of practical wisdom.

> c) Hence [understanding] is about the same objects as practical wisdom; but understanding and practical wisdom are not the same. For practical wisdom issues commands, since its end is what ought to be done or not to be done; but understanding only discerns [*kritikê*]. (1143a7–10)[13]

To command an act, and to act on a command, are in part to *limit* one's discernment, to limit one's survey of the features of a situation, emotional responses to what they mean, and the like. Action requires eventually deciding that one overall view will do, that one can stop looking for others. Subsumption under a single view like this is ordinarily, and perhaps necessarily, a debatable and less than adequate interpretation of a situation. But what is the alternative? Scanning details and sifting through universals until every possible interpretation of the situation has been laid out, along with its respective level of plausibility? Laying out the possibilities for interpretation may at this asymptotic point coincide with simply grasping every particular, with not bringing the particulars under any interpretation at all. We not only have too little time for such an endeavor before each of our decisions, but the full picture could in any case yield no directive for action. Action depends in the end on a willingness to follow our passions beyond the limits of their perceptiveness; hence the need, as Aristotle stresses so often, to habituate them so that they normally direct us in healthy ways. Thus practical wisdom differs from understanding not merely in that it *adds* action to discernment[14] but in that it knows how to *stop* discernment at some point so that we can act. To command is to call for obedience regardless of understanding, and at some point, practical wisdom must command.

> d) But to say to what point and how much someone is blameworthy [for diverging from the correct] is not easy to determine by a principle: nor in fact is this the case with any other perceptible item. For things of this sort are among the concrete particulars, and the discrimination [*krisis*] lies in perception. (1109b20–25)[15]

Note that this passage does not actually mention practical wisdom. Nussbaum emphasizes the ineptness of translating the final phrase as "the *decision* rests with perception," but goes on to use the passage as support for her identification of perception with practical wisdom.[16] But her philological point cuts against her conclusion. For if Aristotle is concerned here with discrimination rather than decision, then the distinction we have just drawn *between* discrimination and phronesis should come into play. Perception is a good faculty for discriminating—for picking out the particular differences among concrete particulars, perhaps also for assessing those differences, giving them greater or lesser importance, etc.—but so analyzing a situation is not yet phronesis, and cannot become so until the particulars and their differences are brought under some general rule, or set of rules, for action.

I think "judgment," rather than "perception," is the faculty that best grasps moral particulars. I mean thereby to include what Kant, under the name "reflective judgment," regards as the faculty that best appreciates aesthetic particulars: interpretation, a negotiation between rules and the particular situations to which they are supposed to relate. "Moral judgment" then adds to reflective judgment the activity of *choosing*, by which we take the chance of acting on our (necessarily incomplete) interpretations of a situation. A consideration of rules and the act of choice bring us much closer to what morality demands of us than appreciation of the particular alone. At times, indeed, the Aristotelian "perception" theorists themselves agree with this. After devoting most of her attention to perception alone, to immersion in the particular, Nussbaum concludes that good Aristotelian deliberation actually consists in "a flexible movement back and forth between particular and general" (p. 316):

> [T]he particular case would be surd and unintelligible without the guiding and sorting power of the universal. (We do not even love particular individuals in the Aristotelian way without loving, centrally, repeatable commitments and values which their lives exemplify). Nor does particular judgment have the kind of rootedness and focus required for goodness of character without a core of commitment to a general conception—albeit one that is continually evolving, ready for surprise, and not rigid. There is in effect a two-way illumination between particular and universal. (p. 306)

The unnerving endlessness of moving between universals and particulars, of a process of interpretation akin to aesthetic reflection, makes a more apt match than perception does for the uncertainty that permeates moral thinking at its best. Consider how interpretation, in the aesthetic context, supervenes on simple perception. If I see only the scene represented, in a realistic painting, or globs of color on a canvas, in an abstract one, I do not yet see the painting as a work of art. If I hear music as I hear all other sounds, I cannot yet hear it *as* music. Even Duchamp's "found objects" count as art at all, if they do, because their placement in a museum calls for a process of interpretation—in part, of the very nature of art itself. If I have not yet noticed the difference between the urinals in the men's room and the urinal in the gallery, I have not yet noticed the latter as so much as a *candidate* for being an art object. It is part of what we mean by aesthetic interpretation that this is so, that we grasp something as art only once we understand it as having features that supervene on all its perceptual qualities. It defeats the purposes of aesthetic interpretation to perceive art objects in the matter-of-course, semiconscious way we do the stuff of our ordinary cognitive negotiation with the world. Even if I do casually note, "There's a sculpture in my way," as I walk across a lawn, by acknowledging it as a sculpture I allow for the possibility of a more conscious reflection on it at some other time. Similarly, even when I casually note some generous or cruel act in the course of, say, assessing the agent as a potential business partner, by acknowledging the moral qualities of the act, I allow for the possibility that I might think more critically about those qualities at another time. It defeats the purposes of moral interpretation to allow for any more matter-of-course acceptance of what I "see" morally. Insofar as "perception" designates a straightforward, direct contact between ourselves and the objects we encounter, we have reason to prefer "interpretation" to describe both our aesthetic and our moral relationships with the world: precisely in order to *rule out* such immediacy.

Of course, interpreting moral acts is sometimes easier and sometimes more difficult. Sometimes it is so easy that we may overlook the need for interpretation altogether. No reflection seems necessary to praise Gandhi or to know that we should not be cruel to children; to praise Lyndon

Johnson (if we should) or to urge vegetarianism (if we should) requires a lot more work. But similarly we are much quicker to say something about Brecht or Rembrandt than about Beckett or Pollock. Yet Brecht and Rembrandt, and likewise the character of Gandhi and the nature of cruelty to children, are also susceptible of a wide variety of interpretations. Any connoisseur of Rembrandt knows that it is not in fact easy to figure out what is going on in his self-portraits, why he chooses just this background, why he shades in just that way. Similarly, we can complicate the story we tell about Gandhi (what about his weird relationship to his wife? his remarks on the Holocaust?) or even about cruelty to children (is corporal punishment always cruel?). The point is that, even in the apparently easy cases, openness to widely differing construals of the particular is a defining mark of the aesthetic and the ethical grasp of reality, and in this, aesthetic and ethical knowledge differ from the perceptions on which they depend.

It should now be clear that reflective judgment can handle many of the intuitions behind the fondness for moral perception very nicely. Quite obviously, to regard interpretation as central to moral thinking is an approach as friendly to the moral importance of literature and concrete examples as anything Nussbaum and others get from their emphasis on perception. Furthermore, there is every reason to suppose that interpretation will be as seriously skewed as perception is by a lack of appropriate emotional dispositions. Not merely a general love for beauty, but a fine sensitivity to details of shading and texture and an ability to be shocked, delighted, moved, etc., by painterly expression are necessary for good aesthetic interpretation, and we need demand nothing less for good interpretation in the moral sphere. So the role for desire and care, for the cultivation of proper emotions, that perception theorists have reintroduced into moral philosophy remains just as necessary if we shift the description of their central concern from "perception" to "interpretation." Finally, to emphasize the movement between rules and their cases is not to adopt a blueprint picture of the application of rules.[17] Interpretation is neither primarily perceptual nor primarily conceptual. It is as much the one as the other and the precise balance required in each particular case can be grasped only by further interpretation.[18] Insofar as interpretation is central to practical wisdom, therefore, a nuanced and flexible use of rules will be essential to such wisdom.

II

Kant, of course, is identified above all with rule-based conceptions of morality. But Kant's account tends to get distorted by an overly rigid and simplistic caricature of what moral rules amount to. Adam Smith, with

whose work Kant was greatly impressed,[19] provides us with an account of
moral rules that is sensitive to our individual experience, as well as to
social and cultural influences—an account, moreover, that brings in the
kind of balance between particularizing and generalizing tendencies that
we have seen to be central to Kant's notion of reflective judgment. I
propose to enrich Kant's moral theory by way of both Smith and the
Critique of Judgment. Bringing rule-following into judgment, I argued in
the previous chapter, allows Kant's suggestive but obscure aesthetic theory to be read as a plausible, empirically recognizable account of what we
actually do in appreciating beauty. Bringing judgment into rule-following
similarly allows Kant's inspiring vision of freedom to be realized within
the contours of ordinary moral experience.

Smith vigorously criticizes reliance upon "casuistic rules" in the pursuit
of friendship, gratitude, and other virtues whose nature requires particularized sentiments (TMS VI.ii.1.22). In TMS VII.iv he inveighs against
books of casuistry for seeking precise rules where no precision is to be
found and thereby tempting us "to chicane with our consciences." His
argument here is with a long tradition of Christian moralists. Fear of
having done wrong "is a load upon every mind," he says, "and is accom-
panied with anxiety and terror in all those who are not hardened by long
habits of iniquity" (VII.iv.17). We have a deep psychological need for
someone who can alleviate this anxiety, so a class of people promising
such relief has an assured socioeconomic niche. Clerics fill this niche,
both in their capacity as confessors and in the collections of "cases of
conscience" they publish as books of casuistry. The latter, says Smith,
attempt, "to no purpose, to direct by precise rules what it belongs to
feeling and sentiment only to judge of." The result of such false precision
is that those who want to can find "innumerable evasive refinements" by
which to get out of their duties.[20] Who consults a book of casuistry? Not
someone who is ready to do what he ought to do: "One, who is really
anxious to do his duty, must be very weak, if he can imagine that he has
much occasion" for such books.

But Smith does not leave rule-following out of morality. It is casuistry,
not rules, to which he objects. Rules, and the faculty of reason with
which they are associated, can be crucial to morality. Smith vehemently
denies Hume's claim that it is "not contrary to reason to prefer the destruction of the whole world to the scratching of my finger." It *is* contrary to reason, insists Smith, and indeed reason is *all* that it is contrary
to. If a man "was to lose his little finger to-morrow, he would not sleep
to-night; but, provided he never saw them, he will snore with the most
profound security over the ruin of a hundred millions of his brethren"
(TMS III.3.4). Our sentiments are ultimately too limited to extend much

beyond ourselves, and only reason can correct for this parochialism: "It is reason, principle, conscience, . . . who . . . calls us, with a voice capable of astonishing the most presumptuous of our passions, that we are but one of the multitude, in no respect better than any other in it" (III.3.5).[21] And reason comes up with rules by which we treat anonymous others fairly. Each of us must rely on his or her *own* rules, however, not on rules culled from books or confessors.

What are my "own" rules? How, and why, do I establish rules for my decisions? Smith explains:

> [G]eneral rules of morality are . . . ultimately founded upon experience of what, in particular instances, our moral faculties, our natural sense of merit and propriety, approve, or disapprove of. . . . To the man who first saw an inhuman murder, committed from avarice, envy, or unjust resentment, and upon one too that loved and trusted the murderer, who beheld the last agonies of the dying person, who heard him, with his expiring breath, complain more of the perfidy and ingratitude of his false friend, than of the violence which had been done to him, there could be no occasion, in order to conceive how horrible such an action was, that he should reflect, that one of the most sacred rules of conduct was what prohibited the taking away the life of an innocent person, that this was a plain violation of that rule, and consequently a very blamable action. His detestation of this crime . . . would arise instantaneously and ante-cedent to his having formed to himself any such general rule. The general rule, on the contrary, which he might afterwards form, would be founded upon the detestation which he felt necessarily arise in his own breast, at the thought of this, and every other particular action of the same kind. (TMS III.4.8)

At first glance, it looks as though the general rule arises directly from my own experience, and a very immediate experience at that. I stand over the dying innocent, his decency made evident to me in his words as his blood oozes away onto the sidewalk, and "instantaneously" a condemna-tory judgment wells up in me at the act that has brought him to this state. I am using highly theatrical language to describe the incident—but so does Smith. A plethora of Handelian "Perfido!"s and "Ingrato!"s are evoked when we read about "the dying person . . . with his expiring breath, complain more of the perfidy and ingratitude of his false friend," etc. So to begin with, we need not assume that the quiet intellectual of the Scottish middle classes who wrote TMS actually witnessed a horrible murder before he recognized the sacredness of innocent life. He saw such things in the theater, as several of his other examples make clear.[22]

So this is not my "own" experience? Not if that means I have to have actually stopped on the road to catch the last exhortations of a murdered innocent. But that is too limited a conception of "my own" experience. I may have seen murders in the theater or read newspaper accounts of

dying Bosnians or Tutsis. The detail of lived experience is clearly important to Smith, else he would hardly present his cases in such elaborate
narratives, but what is most important is that at some point I *make the
relevant judgments independently.* It is "my" experience in the sense that
I visualize it and form the judgment against it, even if that visualization
and that judgment are informed by what others have said, and how
others react. And it is my visualization of the situation, and my appropriation of the gut-based reaction against it into the moral code guiding
my own life, that allow me to dissent from or modify what others say, to
find their rules and reactions too cruel or too forgiving. As we shall see,
a moral judgment for Smith is a balance between partial and impartial
feelings, and between feelings (all necessarily partial) and the cool im-
partiality of thought. By tracing our moral judgments to our own individual experience, Smith lets us know that this balance of feelings, and
between feelings and thought, must be reestablished in the heart of every
individual.

Now the distance of Smith's example from immediate experience
comes out not only in his use of theatrical language. For one thing, I
know, as I watch, *why* the act was committed. Furthermore, if immediate
experience were all I had to go on, how could I recognize that the murder victim is innocent? Nor could a sentiment within the breast alone
show me how to recognize avarice or envy, perfidy or ingratitude. But
the horror I feel has a lot to do with these modes of classification. The
murder would not be so horrible had the victim not been innocent, or
not been a friend of the perpetrator, or had the perpetrator been motivated by more honorable passions. (Imagine the situation instead if the
victim were a husband killed by his physically abused wife, expiring on
the words, "But I only meant to discipline her . . .") To know where
wrong lies in this situation is in part to know a *history*; it by no means
resembles the immediate compassion that Rousseau imagines a horse
might feel.[23] To know what "innocence" means, I must know what
"guilt" means, and that is hardly possible without a prior understanding
of law and justice. To recognize the evil of betrayal, I must understand
the importance of trust, which is something I normally learn from a combination of my own experience with the teachings of my parents and
peers. To respond to the added horror of the murderer's being a friend, I
must know about friendship, the shared experiences that make a friend
seem especially close, and the role friendship, as opposed to mere commercial or casual acquaintance, plays in society. I must have heard rules,
from my parents or peers, about how important it is to care for my
friends, to appreciate their generosity and show generosity in turn, etc.,
and I need to have learned, from my own experience, why these rules
carry weight, what precious experiences they protect. As Smith says, I do

not need to invoke the sacredness of a rule *to preserve innocent life* in order to condemn this act of betrayal, but I do have to invoke *other* rules, other principles and patterns, in order to understand so much as the situation itself.

So I come to the rule that prohibits the taking of innocent life in part by bringing other rules to bear on what I see and feel. But even then— am I really coming to this rule for the first time here? It is hard to believe I could have reached the stage of maturity at which I can understand the patterns that make up friendship and show the evil in ingratitude without being already at least aware of a rule against the taking of innocent life. Surely Smith's point is not that I now first become aware of such a rule, or first invent it for myself, but that I first truly take it *upon* myself as my *own* rule. Up until now, I have heard about the evil of murder and could parrot the rule against it.[24] I could also parrot the claim that the rule is supposed to be sacred. But now I judge that rule to be sacred on the basis of my own experience (mediated perhaps by the stage or newspaper) and integrate that judgment into how I approach the world from now on. Without such experience, Smith says, the rule would fail to be a moral guide.

A reflected-upon experience is therefore in principle the basis of all moral rules, although we may "parrot" the rule without having gone through the process of reflection. We establish a general rule for ourselves when we see an act that greatly shocks (or delights) us and we would like, in general, to avoid it (or seek occasions for performing it). It is my passion—my anger, in Smith's case, at the murder—that motivates my judgment. A rule does not *intervene*; it is, rather, *produced* by the passion: "His detestation of this crime . . . would arise instantaneously and antecedent to his having formed to himself any such general rule. . . . The general rule, on the contrary, . . . would be founded upon the detestation which he felt." If I needed rules about the preciousness of innocent human life to condemn a murder, I either would never get to the point of condemning murders at all (would never see what innocence means, or that human lives are precious) or would do so merely automatically, borrowing other people's terms and passion, never myself seeing the point of those terms—never myself *judging*.

At the same time, we actually come up with the rule only when we find ourselves in a "cool hour," in which we can survey the action and our reaction impartially and assure ourselves that any general resolution we have come to is appropriate. Smith describes the general rules to which each agent holds himself as "those measures of conduct which, *in all his cool hours*, he [has] resolved never to infringe" (III.4.12). They are "fixed in our mind" by "reflection," after which they fill us with "awe and respect," inspire "reverence," and "check the impetuosity of [our] passion." Occasioned *by* passions like the "detestation of [a] crime," they yet serve to check passion, and acquire their proper shape after reflection in a cool hour. This is closely connected with the purpose of the rules: they are supposed to "correct the too partial view which self-love might otherwise suggest, of what was proper to be done" when we are overcome by such sentiments as resentment. Smith sees self-deceit as a constant danger to moral action, but normally allows the sentiment-driven "impartial spectator" to correct for it. What is distinctive about resentment is that it is characteristically a *moral* sentiment, the sort of sentiment the impartial spectator normally can rely on. It is indeed, for Smith, the emotional foundation of justice. The impartial spectator alone is therefore of no use in correcting for it:

> The man of furious resentment, if he was to listen to the dictates of that passion, would perhaps regard the death of his enemy, as but a small compensation for the wrong, he imagines, he has received; which, however, may be no more than a very slight provocation. . . . [T]he fury of his own temper may be such, that had this been the first time in which he considered such an action, he would undoubtedly have determined it to be quite just and proper, and *what every impartial spectator would approve of.* (III.4.12, my emphasis)

The impartial spectator, reacting to the immediate situation alone, does not know how to draw the distinction between revenge and justice. Only a rule, based on past experience, can enable it to draw that distinction: "But his observations upon the conduct of others, have taught him how horrible all such sanguinary revenges appear. Unless his education has been very singular, he has laid it down to himself as an inviolable rule, to abstain from them upon all occasions. This rule preserves its authority with him, and renders him incapable of being guilty of such violence" (ibid.). In a cool hour I realize I have my best or only chance to make provision, in advance, against the habits of anger that might betray me into evil. My having resolved never to take a sanguinary revenge is all that prevents me from doing so when, later, I am filled with "furious resentment." I need to distance myself from myself, abstract myself from my immediate desires and situation, in order to force myself to do what as a spectator I would insist on others doing if they were in my place. The balance between "agent-feelings" and "spectator-feelings" here, and between passion and "cool" thought, nicely anticipates the balance between imagination and understanding in Kant's reflective judgment.

In addition, the *function* of Smith's moral rules closely anticipates the function Kant attributes to moral rules. For Smith, I both develop the rule by myself and use it to correct for my own temptation to violate it. Without correction by rules, even the moral sentiments in me may serve selfish anger rather than true righteousness. I say to myself, about partic-

ularly awful actions, "I will never do that," and about particularly wonderful ones, "I would like to do that," and when the circumstances next
arise on which "doing that" is a real option for me, the memory of this
general declaration helps me keep in line with my own commitments.
The function of rules is to remind me that I need to do what I expect
others to do, to remind me that I am just like everyone else, to humble
me and break through my self-centeredness. Exactly this is the function
of the categorical imperative. I apply it to prevent myself from wriggling
out of the similarities between the behavior I condemn in others and the
behavior I would like to indulge in my own case. In Kant's examples an
agent always debates with *himself* about his *own* conduct. Never does
Kant take as the paradigm moral question "what should all people do?"
or "what should so-and-so over there do?" The question is always, "what
should *I* do?" Or, more strictly: "how can I *convince* myself of what I
ought to do?" I am not really in doubt as to the nature of the appropriate
moral laws. I simply use a variety of stratagems to deceive myself into
thinking that somehow the "ought" doesn't really apply to my own case:
"When we observe ourselves in any transgression of a duty, we find that
we do not actually will that our maxim should become a universal
law . . . ; rather, the contrary of this maxim should remain as a law generally, and we only take the liberty of making an exception to it for ourselves . . . and for this one occasion" (G 424/42).

Barbara Herman notes that

> Kant's analysis of his own examples in the *Groundwork* (G 424) suggests that
> the need for judgment characteristically arises when an agent . . . [already]
> realizes that what he would do violates a known moral precept. The issue that
> brings the agent to the CI is his feeling that the need or interest involved may
> justify making an exception to the moral rule in his case. The agent who pro-
> poses a deceitful promise to extricate himself from financial difficulties knows,
> *without appeal to the CI*, that what he proposes *may* be impermissible. He
> knows in advance that deceit is the sort of thing marked for moral review.[25]

This suggests that the categorical imperative is not so much a moral rule
itself as a principle that I ought not to exempt myself from *whatever the
moral rules happen to be*. By making the categorical imperative demand
universality, Kant seems to be trying less to found a morality that will
embrace or transcend all empirical differences between people than to
cast a moral net wide enough to entangle the empirical self in strictures it
would rather apply only to others. The CI reminds me that the moral
rules I normally accept, as shown by my willingness to apply them to
others, also and necessarily apply to myself.[26]

Of course, Kant grounds his rules differently from Smith. Smith says that
regard for rules "is what is properly called a sense of duty" (TMS III.5.1),

and insists that it ought to be "the ruling and the governing" principle of our conduct (TMS III.6.1). Kant agrees with these claims[27] and shares Smith's notion that the everyday self is hidden and unreliable. Even when it seems that nothing except duty could have moved us to an action, he says, "We cannot by any means conclude with certainty that a secret impulse of self-love, falsely appearing as the idea of duty, was not actually the true determining cause of the will. For we like to flatter ourselves with a pretended nobler motive, while in fact even the strictest examination can never lead us entirely behind the secret incentives" (G 407/23).

But for Kant hypocrisy and self-deceit are more than mere empirical facts, features of the natural history of mankind. Having accepted Hume's epistemological critique of the self, Kant can claim that the empirical self is *necessarily* elusive: "Consciousness of self according to the determinations of our state is merely empirical, and always changing. No fixed and abiding self can present itself in this flux of inner appearances."[28] In response to Hume, he uses precisely this point to argue that knowledge requires the a priori assumption of a unified cognizing self and its epistemic rules. In response to Smith, similarly, he argues that morality requires the a priori assumption of a unified moral self and its moral rules. This self is necessarily elusive, since it stands outside the empirical phenomena that it synthesizes; it therefore also stands beyond each of the particular circumstances that it observes and reacts to, and beyond the sentiments, moral or otherwise, comprising those reactions. Hence it must ultimately give reason priority over sentiment. As purely empirical beings, we can always use one of our sentiments against the others, trump any one sentiment-based way of construing a situation with a construal based on different sentiments. Only reason, not the sentiments, can transcend the emotions that engulf us in every particular situation, and only reason, therefore, can set us free from those emotions. Reason is truly freeing, in that sense, freeing from the limitations of our own empirical selves. It allows us the "cooler," more reflective self to which, even as empirical beings, we aspire. In the process that enables us to come up with general rules and apply them to ourselves, we discover how we can be free. It is essential to this view that the internal judge of our passions not be merely an empirical product, and that the ultimate justification for its judgments not lie in experience. The categorical imperative thus has a grip on us very different from that of Smith's internal spectator.

But if the reading I have been pursuing is correct, then the CI, regardless of the source of its grip on us, serves much the same goal as Smith's spectator: it keeps up faithful to our own commitments, to the rules we lay down to ourselves as a result of our moral experience. It follows that the specific rules to which it keeps us faithful may, in principle, reflect the differences in our courses of moral experience as much as Smith's spectator does (Smith explicitly makes room for a significant degree of cultural pluralism on moral matters in TMS V.2). Specific moral rules need not be "universal" across all agents; only the principle that each submit himself to his own rules must be universal. The CI commands the latter, and since it stands beyond experience altogether, it must stand beyond all differences in experience. But the specific rules it underwrites need not be similarly oblivious to the empirical. Like the principle of causality, the CI must entirely transcend experience, but specific moral rules, like specific causal rules, must on the contrary *reflect* experience. We may thus see our way to a flexible version of Kantian morality, sensitive to the social and cultural surroundings of each individual agent.

III

Sensitivity to social and cultural surroundings is important because moral judgment, for each of us, plays a major role in defining our social bonds. We saw in the previous chapter how aesthetic judgment can open the way for communication, can interweave our thinking with that of others around us. Moral judgment is yet more essentially a socially oriented faculty. A society takes great interest in the moral judgments individuals make, since the actions they lead to can affect many others around the individual. Individuals, in turn, if only because they are similarly affected by the actions of others, likewise each take an interest in the moral judgments abroad in their society. If a person persists in a set of judgments radically out of synch with those of her society, she may well find she needs to leave—or convert, emigrate, etc. Or she may become a recluse, or hide her judgments, or suffer penalties ranging from ostracism to imprisonment to death.

This rarely happens, since it is the nature of judgment to bring each individual's thoughts into discourse with the thoughts of others. Individual judgments are, ultimately, constitutive of social norms, but social norms are also an indispensable source for individual judgments. Indeed, the process of moral judgment is the means by which individuals most deeply build the views of their society into themselves. Paradoxically, it is precisely by doing this that they can also most fully express their individuality.

This insight is the central achievement of Smith's TMS. On Smith's general view of moral development, we are awakened to reflecting on our own conduct only by the approval and criticism of others:

Were it possible that a human creature could grow up to manhood in some solitary place, without any communication with his own species, he could no more think of his own character, . . . of the beauty or deformity of his own mind, than of the beauty or deformity of his own face. . . . [T]hese are objects which he cannot easily see, which naturally he does not look at, and with regard to which he is provided with no mirror which can present them to his view. Bring him into society, and he is immediately provided with the mirror which he wanted before. It is placed in the countenance and behaviour of those he lives with, which always mark when they enter into, and when they disapprove of his sentiments. (TMS III.1.3)

We then internalize these external responses:

[O]ur first moral criticisms are exercised upon the manner and conduct of other people; . . . But we soon learn, that other people are equally frank with regard to our own. We become anxious to know how far we deserve their censure or applause, and whether to them we must necessarily appear those agreeable or disagreeable creatures which they represent us. We begin, upon this account, to examine our own passions and conduct, and to consider how these must appear to them, by considering how they would appear to us if in their situation. We suppose ourselves the spectators of our own behavior, and endeavour to imagine what effect it would, in this light, produce upon us. This is the only looking-glass by which we can, in some measure, . . . scrutinize the propriety of our own conduct. If in this view it pleases us, we are tolerably satisfied. (III.1.5)

Finally, at least in the ideal case, this "impartial spectator" within ourselves replaces external response as our primary criterion for whether we are behaving well or badly:

The man of real constancy and firmness, the wise and just man who has been thoroughly bred in the great school of self-command, . . . never dare[s] to suffer the man within the breast to be absent one moment from his attention. With the eyes of this great inmate he has always been accustomed to regard whatever relates to himself. . . . He does not merely affect the sentiments of the impartial spectator. He really adopts them. He almost identifies himself with, he almost becomes himself that impartial spectator, and scarce even feels but as that great arbiter of his conduct directs him to feel. (III.3.25)

Here moral behavior is dependent on social sanctions, not in the cynical or deterministic sense that we are incapable of acting well except as a sort of performance to win approval, but in a heuristic sense: in the sense that we learn to turn inwards only from society. Moreover, for Smith virtue consists, at least in good part, in what conduces to harmony between individual and society. Hence social approval is implicitly a means of rational persuasion, not just a mode of behavioral conditioning—it is an appropriate if not fully accurate indicator that we are in fact achieving virtue. Thus praise teaches us how we can seek, not praise itself, but praise worthiness: "to be that thing, which, though it should be praised by nobody, is, however, the natural and proper object of praise. . . . [S]o far is the love of praise-worthiness from being derived altogether from that of praise, that the love of praise seems, . . . in a great measure, to be derived from that of praise-worthiness" (III.2.1,3). If one succeeds in internalizing the ideal, internal spectator against which to judge one's own actions, one can judge oneself more or less freely, and contribute more or less freely to the social standards of judgment around one.[29] Individually free action and the social construction of the self are compatible, for Smith, even dependent on one another.

Insofar as we come to moral rules individually, now, and use them above all for compelling our individual selves into conformity with our own beliefs, the mirroring relationship between society and the individual is reversed. Each of us comes to moral rules—to the commitment we have *to* moral rules—by and for ourselves, but all of us engage in coming to such rules, we do so for the sake of other people as well as for our own sake, and as we do so, we come, and bring each other, into society. Smith continues the passage on rules I quoted earlier by noting that we talk, share our impressions with others, as we come to our rules, that we gather evidence supplementing our own experience and giving us reason to think that our judgment is appropriately impartial:

> Some . . . actions shock all our natural sentiments. We hear every body about us express the like detestation against them. This still further confirms, and even exasperates our natural sense of their deformity. It satisfies us that we view them in the proper light, when we see other people view them in the same light. We resolve never to be guilty of the like, nor ever, upon any account, to render ourselves in this manner the objects of universal disapprobation. We thus naturally lay down to ourselves a general rule, that all such actions are to be avoided. (III.4.7)

We talk about each other's sexual peccadilloes, professional rivalries, the astounding things others are said to have said, and the ways in which we wish we were, or are glad we are not, like them. This is gossip, often condemned because it can sully innocent reputations. But without it, says Smith, we would neither have reputations to sully nor terms with which to praise and condemn so much as our own acts.

Tolstoy, whose delight in small details and in the workings of society is strongly reminiscent of Smith, illustrates the process wonderfully:

> "If you follow me, I shall call the servants and the children! I'll let everybody know you are a scoundrel! I am going away to-day, and you may live here with your mistress!"
>
> She went out, slamming the door.

> Oblonsky sighed, wiped his face, and with soft steps left the room. "Matthew says 'things will shape themselves,'—but how? I don't even see a possibility. . . . Oh dear, the horror of it! And her shouting—it was so vulgar," he thought, recalling her screams and the words *scoundrel* and *mistress*. "And the maids may have heard it! It is dreadfully banal, dreadfully!"[30]

Note how deeply social- and self-judgment are here woven together. Oblonsky has presumably in the past "laid down a rule to himself" that he would never want to be guilty of an act that allowed him to be called a "scoundrel" or described as having a "mistress." He has heard "every body express detestation" of such people. Here suddenly he hears the ugly words justifiably thrown at him, and the experience puts his behavior in a light different from the one in which, presumably, he carried it out. But at the same time he seems concerned mostly over the "vulgarity" of his wife's outburst, and whether "the maids may have heard it." Tolstoy both shows us that our judgments of good and bad are informed by the language of judgment that surrounds us and quietly warns us that the result of this process may be mere fear of disgrace, not an impulse to true moral change. Tolstoy is himself known as both an exquisite portraitist of social habits and an eccentric individualist Christian who had no tolerance for commitments not rooted in "the heart." Of course, these two Tolstoys are in part chronologically divided, with the later Tolstoy condemning the author of the great novels as immoral, but even in the novels his most heroic characters reject the moral babble of their class and upbringing in favor of silent internal transformations. In the novels, however, moral transformation is inseparable from commenting on, and coming into harmony with, one's society. We can see this in Levin's meditations after Kitty has rejected him, early in *Anna Karenina*:

> "Yes, she was bound to choose him. It had to be so, and I have no cause to complain of anyone or anything. It was my own fault. What right had I to imagine that she would wish to unite her life with mine? Who and what am I? A man of no account, wanted by no one and of no use to anyone." And he remembered his brother Nicholas, and kept his mind gladly on that memory. "Is he right that everything on earth is evil and horrid? And have we judged brother Nicholas fairly? Of course, from Prokofy's point of view, who saw him in a ragged coat and tipsy, he is a despicable fellow; but I know him from another side. I know his soul, and know that we resemble one another." (p. 77)

Relief from self-judgment comes "gladly" in the form of reflection on his prodigal brother, Nicholas. That our judgments of others are in part the result of our reluctance to view our own conduct steadily and honestly, Tolstoy here good-humoredly notes, but the good humor signals not cynicism but an accepting recognition of the fact that by considering the case of others we can also *return* to self-knowledge, as Levin does here ("we resemble one another"). As to the content of his judgment on Nicholas: we have Levin directly adopting society's general point of view, by which Nicholas "is a despicable fellow," but then sensibly locating this external view in the external impressions likely to have evoked it and adding, not that his brother is the opposite of despicable, but that he has "another side." That his judgment of Nicholas stands in such a finely ambivalent relationship to the judgment of others comes out clearly in the rest of the passage:

> On the long way to his brother's he recalled all the events he knew of Nicholas's life. He recalled how despite the ridicule of his fellow-students his brother had lived like a monk while at the University and for a year after, strictly observing all the religious rites, attending service, fasting, avoiding all pleasures and especially women; and then how he suddenly broke loose, became intimate with the vilest people and gave himself up to unbridled debauchery. He remembered how his brother had brought a boy from the country to educate, and in a fit of anger had so beaten the lad that proceedings were commenced against him for causing bodily harm. . . . Then he remembered the night which Nicholas had spent in the police cells for disorderly conduct, and the disgraceful proceedings he had instigated against his brother Sergius Ivanich, whom he accused of not having paid out to him his share of his mother's fortune: and lastly, the time when his brother took an official appointment in one of the Western Provinces and was there arrested for assaulting an Elder. . . . It was all very disgusting, but to Levin it did not seem nearly so disgusting as it must have seemed to those who did not know Nicholas, nor his whole story, nor his heart. (p. 77)

It *was* all very disgusting, thinks Levin, but simultaneously that it seems less so to him. He divides himself in reflection between one who accepts a socially endorsed judgment that imposes itself upon him, and one who is tempted to modify that judgment in accordance with his experience. He never abandons the judgment of society even if he mitigates it: the very process *of* mitigating the judgment seems to entail understanding why it is justifiable. We, the readers, are subtly alerted, in the last line, to an irony in Tolstoy's attitude towards this social judgment—we are led to feel that the polite people who judge Nicholas to be disgusting without knowing him might themselves be disgustingly narrow-minded. Nicholas *in fact*, if this description is at all accurate, is a mixture of generosity and cruelty, high spirits, avarice, and courage. He is also one who rebels against "society" by means of the rites and practices of a different society, a religious subgroup of the world that ridicules him, and then rebels again by means of the typical behavior ("debauchery," gambling, drunkenness) of yet another social group, rebellious students. Both in his behavior and in the judgments Levin, and we, are asked to make on his behavior, there is constant play between a position inside and a position outside social groups. Levin will eventually find a balance between these positions; this balance, this reflective equilibrium, is mature judgment. We should not quickly dismiss people as disgraceful or disgusting, but when we know Nicholas's "whole story" we will still criticize much of what he has done. And Levin will truly be able to make this judgment himself only once he reconciles himself to the fact that he is constituted as a person in good part by the various social groups in which he participates and social judgments to which he responds.

One final implication of all this is that even as he reflects on and shapes his own character, Levin is always also a literary critic, an interpreter, of his own and others' moral judgments. So is Tolstoy himself. He seems throughout to imagine a community in which everyone is herself a mininovelist, reciting stories about the loves and scandals of one member of the community to the others and thereby implicitly or explicitly conveying a moral judgment.[31] Debate over the interpretation of such anecdotes then continues the process of morality as literature/literary criticism, and Tolstoy is both a critic *of* such proceedings and delightfully in love with the details of how they go on. He is also in love with his own role, by the very production of this immensely popular serialized novel, in shaping the way discussions of character go on in the community of his readers. Insofar as he did shape those discussions, it was surely by infusing an element of irony toward gossip—his true heroes (Levin, Pierre, Prince Andrei) are all individualists, dissidents even, resisting the everyday flow of society— so there is level upon level of irony in this most self-reflective novelist/ moral judge, writing about a fictional community made up of novelists/ moral judges, and mocking their fictions/judgments for the benefit of a real community of novelist/judges, who take this ironic mockery into the midst of their own moral productions. But for all Tolstoy's *distance* from the social process that goes into moral judgments, nowhere does he encourage us to stand *outside* society and its talk. Levin, Prince Andrei, Pierre dissent from much of what their society has to say, criticize some of it, and have powerful individual experiences that make the whole world of party chatter and tea conversation look foolish, but they always return from these experiences to society—to an estate, a marriage, the court, the Freemasons. They never adopt the life of a hermit or Romantic adventurer. For Tolstoy, as for his characters, moral independence is won by wrestling with society's judgments but not by abandoning them. And we wrestle with those judgments by making judgments ourselves. Judgment is indeed, for Tolstoy as for a long tradition that includes Smith and Kant but stretches back well before them, the characteristic expression of the *sensus communis*—"common sense" in the meaning that phrase has when it denotes the sense each person has in common with other members of his or her society. Judgment, the common sense, makes social interaction possible, gives rise to sociability. And social interaction, for Smith and Tolstoy at least, is essential to judgment.

Some version of this point may even be acceptable to Kant. Presumably we must construct our general moral rules out of particular cases, even if those rules themselves must be brought into accordance with the categorical imperative (CI) in order to be autonomous. Everyday moral generalizations, like scientific ones, are constructed out of a process of reflection between received particulars and the understanding's effort to classify those particulars. As in aesthetic interpretation, the effort is ongoing and never completely satisfactory. But we will have no moral concepts to regulate by reason at all, as, analogously, we would have no scientific concepts, unless we interpret some sort of perceptual given, unless we treat the diverse instances on which our parents and teachers offer us paradigms for what "ought to be" as an appropriate beginning point for moral thought. Herein lies a way in which morality may depend on community. Insofar as our parents and teachers belong to a relatively coherent community, their paradigms of what "ought to be" will more or less cohere, and to the extent that they do cohere, the starting point for our detailed moral views will be relative to some community or set of communities. Barbara Herman suggests that agents pick up morally relevant features of the world by individual observation but are influenced by a culture in what they take these features to mean.[32] I would say something rather stronger—that particulars do not so much as appear "morally relevant" until they are mediated by a culture[33]—but in any case we agree that the specific rules submitted to the CI are in the first instance drawn from a community.[34] The CI serves as a *regulative ideal* for moral theory, a *meta*-norm for the moral rules we use everyday. It works through, and shapes, our different communal paradigms for how to live. When pressed for a justification of some specific norm, we try to fit the norm in question into some larger view of what all human beings seek, or should seek—some interpretation, in Herman's words, of persons as ends-in-themselves.[35] The role of reason is thus to regulate the process of moral interpretation and, consequently, of socialization, above all ensuring that we apply whatever rules we come up with to ourselves. But an ineliminable connection remains between our rules and the rules of our society—between our *selves*, indeed, and our relationship to a society.

IV

My society must *inform* my judgments, but should not, and usually does not, *control* them. Ultimately, I alone am responsible for my own judgments. As we have seen, for Smith it is indeed the function of society to bring me to face this responsibility: "We become anxious to know how far we deserve their censure or applause, and whether to them we must necessarily appear those agreeable or disagreeable creatures which they represent us. . . . This is the only looking-glass by which we can, in some measure, . . . scrutinize the propriety of our own conduct" (III.1.5). But to scrutinize our conduct in this way is to become self-conscious about taking responsibility for it, to take the crucial step towards acting on judgment rather than merely having it. This is the hardest step in developing true moral judgment.

So far I have downplayed this feature of judgment, treating judgment on the whole as if it were *merely* interpretation, as if it were just like what we do in aesthetic reflection. But interpreting a situation well is neither a necessary nor a sufficient condition for acting properly in response to that situation. There are many perceptive and sympathetic people who cannot make up their minds to act. And there are unperceptive, unemotional people who carry out generous or just actions with dispatch. Hamlet famously exemplifies how excellent perceptions and decent emotions can be detached from a strong will.[36] For Hamlet, too much moral reflection seems to blur the focus, to incapacitate or at least detract from his ability to will. Reflection and strong will do not always conflict in this way, but a person good at discerning moral details may well find it difficult to make a decision. He may be paralyzed by the many options that seem open to him or, when his action would affect several people, by the conflicting hurt feelings he can foresee.

Taking action, however, and consciously accepting responsibility for that action, is essential to moral judgment. In morality, we must make the move from reflective to determining judgment; we must treat the particulars before us, ultimately, as one kind of thing rather than another. To dispense with determining judgments is to dispense with the simplifying directives that allow us to act, to be so afraid of simplification that we cease to act at all. Of course, we need not give up on moral interpretation once we do act, and sometimes can even use action to further the process of interpretation. Lawrence Blum has us imagine Tim, who, having jumped into a taxi that left a black woman and child standing to pick him up, begins to realize in the car that he has been complicit with racism.[37] Suppose now that Tim, after reflecting on what to do about this complicity, judges his situation as calling for "outspokenness," and begins to harangue the driver on the evils of discriminating against black customers. It may well turn out that the driver's response is so frightening, so dull-witted, or, on the contrary, so reasonable, that Tim decides it is not worth his while to continue, or that he was presumptuous ever to begin. He reinterprets the situation as one in which "discretion is the better part of valor," or in which correcting the driver is too vast a project to undertake in the time he will be in the cab, or in which his own elitist prejudices against taxi drivers led him to misunderstand what was going on. Here his act of speaking out helps him achieve a richer interpretation of the situation. Sometimes such experimental action is impossible. Tentative explorations of the situation, however desirable, have no place where one's decision can have momentous consequences. A president who declares war on a country can hardly plead, later on, that he hoped to learn from the decision. Most of the time, however, the situations in which we act call for a fluid movement between reflection and action, such that we learn more about our lovers, neighbors, employers, and indeed ourselves, by here yelling, there "making nice," being aloof at one moment and sensitive at another, one time hauling a landlord into court and another time trying to settle matters by tact, while using the results of all these actions as the basis for future interpretations. We learn from the effects of our own actions; often this is the most effective way for us to learn.

But to take the actions from which we learn, we need to accept risks that aesthetic reflection does not require. In Aristotelian terms, it is the realization that phronesis must "command," not merely discern, that moves us from reflection to action. Only one who makes that move truly emerges from tutelage into freedom, truly becomes able to "judge for herself."

I have said that this is the hardest step in developing moral judgment. Part of what makes it so difficult is that are chronically unwilling to face our own failings. Here Smith's psychological insight is just superb:

When we are about to act, the eagerness of passion will seldom allow us to consider what we are doing, with the candour of an indifferent person. The violent emotions which at that time agitate us, discolour our view of things; even when we are endeavouring to place ourselves in the situation of another, and to regard the objects that interest us in the light in which they will appear to him, the fury of our own passions constantly calls us back to our own place, where every thing appears magnified and misrepresented by self-love. . . . When the action is over, . . . and the passions which prompted it have subsided, we can enter more coolly into the sentiments of the indifferent spectator. . . . It is seldom, however, that they are quite candid even in this case. . . . It is so disagreeable to think ill of ourselves, that we often purposely turn away our view from those circumstances which might render [our] judgment unfavourable. He is a bold surgeon, they say, whose hand does not tremble when he performs an operation upon his own person; and he is often equally bold who does not hesitate to pull off the mysterious veil of self-delusion, which covers from his view the deformities of his own conduct. Rather than see our own behaviour under so disagreeable an aspect, we too often, foolishly and weakly, endeavour to exasperate anew those unjust passions which had formerly misled us; we endeavour by artifice to awaken our old hatreds, and irritate afresh our almost forgotten resentments: we even exert ourselves for this miserable purpose, and thus persevere in injustice, merely because we once were unjust, and because we are ashamed and afraid to see that we were so. (TMS III.4.3–4)

The difficulty we have in judging our selves is precisely the problem in moral practice that Smith's internal spectator and Kan'ts categorical imperative are designed to solve. But these are theoretical devices meant to help us overcome the problem once we already see the moral importance, and difficulty, of judging ourselves. How do we come to see this in the first place? In practice we usually need to be *forced* to judge ourselves, to be placed in situations in which we cannot but see that, and how, we constitute the originating source for both good and bad actions.

I suggest that we need two opposing kinds of experience to learn responsibility for our actions. Most important is the opportunity to exercise choice in a responsible position: a position where the decisions we make count for something. One learns responsibility by having to exercise it. The fact that so many people today spend their lives in positions where nothing they do matters very much, and where, insofar as it does matter, they are not allowed to make decisions for themselves, is the main reason for our widespread inability to accept responsibility. But, on the other hand, one gains a rich understanding of what it is to make responsible choices by spending first some significant period of time *explicitly deprived* of such responsibility: being ruled over, rather than ruling oneself. The two-sidedness of Kantian judgment, the play between passive and active faculties, again comes out here, but the essential insight is Aristotle's. To learn to rule oneself, one must know how to obey, and the people most suited for freedom are, as Aristotle says, "able to rule and to obey in turn" (P 1288a12–15). Let me elaborate each side of this Aristotelian dichotomy a little.

"Able to obey":

The virtue of a good man [is] that which rules, and the virtue of the citizen include[s] ruling and obeying. . . . [T]he ruler must learn by obeying, as he would learn the duties of a general of cavalry by being under the orders of a general of cavalry. . . . It has been well said that "he who has never learned to obey cannot be a good commander." The two are not the same, but the good citizen ought to be capable of both; he should know how to govern like a freeman, and how to obey like a freeman—these are the virtues of a citizen. . . . Practical wisdom only is characteristic of the ruler: it would seem that all other virtues must equally belong to ruler and subject. The virtue of the subject is certainly not wisdom, but only true opinion. (P 1277a27–1277b29)

We learn the virtues of the good man, that which rules, by obeying: "he who has never learned to obey cannot be a good commander." The good man has practical wisdom, which on Aristotle's terms is to have self-rule, but this self-rule requires a training period of being ruled by others. Even the general acquires his excellence only if he is first a foot soldier. But the general/foot-soldier relationship parallels, according to Aristotle, the relationship between "good man" and "good citizen"— which in turn seems to parallel the relationship Aristotle elsewhere delineates between virtue, dependent on *phronesis,* and mere continence (NE VII.9). So to have virtue at all, I need to know first how to obey. What can I learn by obeying? I suggest all of the following:

1. I make mistakes, and learn from them. I can make mistakes and learn from them also as an officer, but then the consequences will be large. Hence I will have to be more careful and can take fewer risks. Hence, also, I will feel an intense need to *cover* mistakes or doggedly pursue the wrong road, once taken, because admitting a mistake may undermine my authority, and because once an order is followed, it is logistically too difficult to reverse course. As infantryman—and as apprentice, as child, as "good citizen" in relation to the "good man"—I can be more flexible, experimenting, trying out all sorts of different little moves, and turning both failures and successes into lessons for future wisdom.

2. I get the details of battle into my pleasures and pains. Pleasure and pain are teaching devices, as Aristotle notes repeatedly.[38] When I make a wrong move, and get wounded, or waste a day, or am humiliated in front of others, I know, deeply, not to make that move again. The laziness that tempted me to take a bad shortcut, say, will in future be neutralized by a memory that evokes the same higher-order desire to avoid pain. When I perform successfully, the flush of self-satisfaction will engrain the relevant detail of practice into my memory with similar vividness. Of course, I can again do this kind of learning from practice as an officer as well, but as an officer I must worry both about handling subordinates and about handling terrain and technology. To learn just the latter—the *stuff* of the commands I must give to my subordinates—it is better that I let the details of terrain and technology sink into me independently of any pleasure or pain I get from successfully or unsuccessfully commanding human beings. The parallel for the relationship between virtue and continence is that virtue commands, lays a rule down for, passions, but it is those passions that actually modulate my movement around plant and animal, river and stone, artifacts and human beings. If I cannot build the

triumph of obdurately ignoring a fear, or the humiliation of succumbing to it, deeply into my immediate feelings and reactions, no amount of higher-level reflection on the appropriate things to fear and not to fear will make me courageous.

3. Finally, I learn what it is like to act without making my own decisions. I learn what it is to act blindly, and without ultimate responsibility. Having once thought, "I don't really need to worry; it's all the general's fault," invaluably adds to the power of thinking, "I'm all alone now; it's entirely my responsibility" should I become a general. At the same time, of course, as long as I remain a subordinate I will be blamed for my failings and foolishness whether I want to be or not. And when I am dressed down by a person to whom I am subordinate, I cannot use the casuistry I might employ when alone to wriggle my self out of the chain of causality that makes things come to pass. In this way I am forced to face ways in which I bring about events that I may long have claimed, wrongly, are "really not my fault." Sometimes I am blamed (or praised) wrongly, of course, but that too can be a valuable way of learning when people should be praised or blamed. Eventually, if I give orders myself, I will know how my subordinates will act. I will know from my own past experience when their blindness is dangerous and when it is helpful, as well as when they are using casuistry and when they are pointing rightly to a reason why they should not be blamed. In just these ways does virtue learn from continence. Only continence has a sufficiently intimate acquaintance with the temptations to incontinence to know where and how guards against such temptations must be constructed. At the same time, continence wears the half-resentful face of the obedient child, which follows rules but does not see those rules as its own; virtue can learn its proper role from that weakness, can see in continence what it needs to transcend. When, and if, I develop wise judgment, I will take care to design, communicate, and administer orders from one part of myself to another so as to exploit the advantages and avoid the perils of obedience.

The "rule/ruled" relationship between virtue and continence has several stages. We get our first training in virtue when we emerge from blind government by passion—the state of an animal or young child—to incontinence, where we are aware that there is a way of controlling our actions at which we are currently failing. Continence is then the silent, habit-induced transformation of this struggle to the point at which what one feels to be the right passions dominate most of the time. This struggle displays to us all the details of how passions can lead us to fail: the consequences of yielding to bad temptations, the factors that weaken our resistance or increase our liability to being misled—all the *fault lines* between a concern for our well-being and the feelings by which well-being is supposed to be played out. The struggle, I say, "displays" all this to us, but we are not conscious of it. We do not take up a fully conscious approach to our own behavior until we adopt the rule-governed striving for consistency and reason that characterizes virtue. Virtue may be more consistent, and also more flexible, in its handling of the passions than the repressive state of continence (it is a seasoned officer, rather than a drill sergeant), but it can learn about the fault lines it must handle only *from* continence: the content of the rules it forms must be drawn from a less articulate, more body- and world-connected self. It is precisely those points at which my continence has failed in the past that virtue will make the greatest efforts to correct. The failure of animal passions makes way for incontinence, the failures of incontinence for continence, and the failures of continence for virtue.

We might say: the "general" of practical wisdom in us learns from the "foot soldier" of continence. And what does this general learn? It learns to make explicit what continence knows only implicitly: "Practical wisdom only is characteristic of the ruler; it would seem that all other virtues must equally belong to ruler and subject. The virtue of the subject is certainly not wisdom but only true opinion." Practical wisdom is something reasoned and aware here, something that grasps truth rather than mere opinion, something articulate. It is founded on a discipline, a regimen of bodily pains and pleasures, but it is as much the *consciousness* or *understanding* of that discipline as the discipline itself.

On this view, discipline, living under the rule of others, is not merely a way of restraining the potentially dangerous wills of the immature: it is an intrinsic feature of becoming free. Discipline is always a restraint only if freedom is always the fulfillment of desire (and for those who do think this, from Rousseau to our own day, discipline is a regrettable necessity even in bringing up children). We need to spend a period of our lives in which we choose among options but play no role in determining the options available to us. We thus learn (a) the nature of error, (b) what range of options we would like to have, and (c) how to accept life within a limited subset of that range. Otherwise we will always live in the fantasy of having unlimited options, like the spoiled child who gets things too easily; we will direct our power of choice beyond the reality available to it, rather than using it, as we should, to craft realistic options for ourselves. Furthermore, only once we have made mistakes and learned from them, faced pain and endured it, absorbed experience and acquired a respect for its details, can our self-rule be trusted—by ourselves or by others. Only then do we know how to correct for bad judgment, rather than floundering around and only accidentally finding solutions when we do find them at all. Only then, therefore, can we truly "judge for ourselves," rather than following the lead of others. We need "tutelage" before and in order to reach the stage of freedom; we need an education in the components of what it takes to judge for oneself. The phronimos thus embraces his own prior period of tutelage, and willingly undergoes similar periods should he need to learn how to make judgments in new areas of life.

And "able to rule":

But the phronimos demands also to leave the period of tutelage once he feels he has absorbed its lessons. Indeed, one cannot really become a phronimos at all unless one leaves the period of tutelage. Here Kant and Aristotle are united. To learn deeply what goes into making decisions, we must *make* them, take responsibility for their consequences, and be held responsible by others for those consequences. We understand what taking responsibility means only after we start actually taking such responsibility. Only then can we fully recognize that we are ourselves each a source of consequences, an active force, not merely a passive object blown this way and that by natural or social forces. This is part of what has led many political theorists to hold up participatory democracy as an ideal: ultimately, only holding a position of power enables one fully to understand the seriousness, the dread even, of making decisions that significantly affect the lives of other people. In fact, we make decisions that impact importantly on others, at least on those close to us, every day. But it is when one occupies a position in which this impact is made explicit, and in which it falls on people one would otherwise avoid affecting, that the full implications of making decisions tends to sink in.

It is not just the power to affect others, however, that a period of participating in "rule" teaches. One can also learn one's power to affect oneself. Following other people's orders, useful as that may be in some ways, all too easily encourages the impression that things just "happen" to me, that other people, along with things outside of me in general, affect me without my having any power over how I am affected. Explicitly being given responsibility for decisions makes it impossible for me to ignore my control over my own actions, and from there I can begin to see that I also have control over my *reactions.* Until I take responsibility for my reactions, moreover, I cannot change my character. Only once I realize that nobody else can instill in me how I regard the world—how, or whether, I can see myself as fitting into it—do I realize what it means to take control of myself.

Indeed, until I take responsibility for my reactions, there is an important sense in which I cannot see myself as existing. What marks individual human beings as distinct entities is their faculty for pleasure and pain, the constellation of emotional reactions by which they, each for themselves, receive the world. No one else can feel my pleasures and pains for me, and once I recognize that fact I may begin to see the sense in which I am radically alone, in which I exist as an individual. The experience of pleasure and pain serves as a paradigm for subjectivity. As we shall see in the next chapter, Kant says that the governing principle of our faculty for pleasure and pain is precisely judgment. If he is right in this, it follows that judgment gives us the power by which we can define who, subjectively, we are.

Before we get to this, a political point: I do not want to claim that either military training or political participation is essential for the development of virtue. Military training serves as an important metaphor for Aristotle, and it has served us well here, I think, in explaining some features of his account of self-rule. In the past, political theorists have taken the further step of insisting that *literal* military service and participation in government is essential to citizenship. I think there is something to this (especially if one construes "participation" strictly: to involve not merely democratic elections but, say, the assigning of some political positions by lot), but to develop full judgment all we need is some experience that will similarly inculcate the two-sided virtues of self-rule. Many kinds of experience can teach us the ability to "obey": a loving but fairly strict childhood might be one, or the attempt to master a difficult craft, or the experience of seeking and trying to keep a first job. Similarly, the experience of participating in "rule" can be had outside the realms of either military or political leadership. Working as an independent master of a craft, managing a household independently, or even working for others—provided that one is given a significant amount of independence—can all teach the virtues of responsibility. Natural forces, or anonymous social forces, may thus accomplish what Aristotle's general does for the foot soldier, may indeed accomplish it better. I shall argue in a later chapter that Adam Smith considers precisely the "discipline" of market forces to substitute in the modern day for the moral education that war once provided.

First, however, we need to complete our investigation into the nature of judgment. In the next chapter we consider how, in its moral as well as its aesthetic form, it defines our subjective freedom.

Chapter 4

JUDGMENT AND FREEDOM

FAMOUSLY, for Kant reason defines our freedom. Reason takes us beyond the empirical world and thereby frees us from its constraints. But this leaves obscure the ordinary sense of "freedom," the sense in which it is something we may have or not have as natural beings in a natural world. How does our nonempirical faculty of reason come to get a grip on the details of our experience? How do we figure out which of the many specific moral interpretations we encounter—specific claims about our duties or purposes—actually makes best moral sense of the world? The previous chapter has indicated that judgment carries out this process, thereby constituting the essential intermediary by which we each, individually, find our moral way. But if so, then our judgment would seem to define our freedom at least as much as our reason does. How the freedom of judgment goes together with the freedom of reason is the subject of this chapter.

Part I of the chapter concerns Kant's notion of "purposiveness without purpose," showing how it may inform our attempts to change our characters or redirect our lives. Parts II and III take up Kant's suggestion that judgment is a means of transition from one mode of thought to another, a "mediating link" among our scientific, our moral, and our aesthetic selves. Part IV moves from there to a set of reflections, inspired by Kant but not necessarily things he would have said himself, on how judgment and subjective freedom are bound together.

I

We may begin a movement from reason to judgment by considering how judgment teaches us about our purposes. In order to make a reasonable decision about any action, we must see it as achieving some purpose. Kant's rule for determining the moral acceptability of actions is of course a formal one, one that abstracts from our immediate ends, but that does not mean that we are supposed to make decisions without considering ends at all. Indeed, figuring out what our ends ought to be is a central moral task.

Now, according to Kant, we learn what defines "purpose" in general not from judgment but from reason: this is a crucial feature of the reconception of reason which Susan Neiman has rightly described as the heart of Kant's entire Critical enterprise. Reason is the faculty *that sets ends,* for Kant[1]—which is to say that it is essentially "practical." This implies that we could make at least dim sense of what it might be to have a purpose even if there were no natural world at all. A fortiori, our capacity to reason allows us to transcend any empirically given purpose we may seem to have.

But reason in relationship to nature has a problem: *every* state of affairs can be construed as contributing to its ends, while no state of affairs can fully realize those ends. Natural objects, in their spatio-temporal finitude, can never embody the ideals of a faculty that demands absolute perfection. As regards morality, Kant talks about the impossibility both of knowing whether any of one's acts are truly good (G 407/22–3) and of achieving the rational intentions for which we continually strive (CPrR 32–3, 84–5/32–3, 86–8). Reason sets goals for itself that finite creatures who merely *partake* of reason can never fully achieve. In the first *Critique,* reason transcends the very categories of the understanding. It thereby provides a standpoint from which we can see how our thought gets directed towards objects, but also eludes the limitations by which it might itself be able to take an intelligible object. No object of reason can be unified and individuated from other objects, as the spatiotemporal objects of the understanding can be. It goes with these views that nothing in the nature of reason itself can tell us which particular natural conditions—which states of ourselves or of the world—are particularly well suited to reason's needs in the realm of morality. What enables us to bring nature and morality together is judgment, the faculty concerned precisely with the fittedness and unfittedness of natural objects to transcendental conditions. So, to work in the natural world, reason needs judgment, although it needs judgment precisely as a faculty it can distinguish from itself and govern, not as a part of itself.

What this means becomes clearer if we look at the relationship between reason and judgment from a strictly moral point of view. In both the Third Antinomy of the first *Critique* and the Typic of the second, Kant uses divine creation as his model for moral action: we must see ourselves, for the purposes of action, as if we create both our ends and their fulfillment ex nihilo. This model captures what I called earlier the "dim sense" of what a purpose might be even in the absence of any natural world and captures the demand of reason that any natural condition may require alteration for moral purposes, but it is also, obviously, not an intelligible model for what action *within* natural conditions should look like. In fact, whenever I act I must take for granted that some conditions of my environment will not be alterable by me and that what I can achieve will be significantly determined by those conditions as well as by my rational decisions.

Herein lies the role for judgment. Judgment is a faculty whose job it is to note the similarities between one set of conditions and others, to come up with general principles likely to suit the particular conditions given, and to work out, in accordance with those principles, how and to what end those conditions may be altered. Judgment can get a foothold on particulars because it always works out from its foothold on other particulars. We can decide to show a specific kind of courage in specific circumstances that seem to call for courage, but only by holding fixed, at least for the moment, what we have so far held to constitute the kind of circumstances calling for courage. We could alternatively revise the concept at any given moment. But we cannot simultaneously revise it and appeal to it for justification, and we can only revise it bit by bit, here in accordance with one general consideration, there in accordance with another new particular. Judgment works *within systems,* and cannot get outside those systems to see them as a whole.

This is the feature of judgment that makes it unsatisfactory to reason as the final arbiter of what counts as "a purpose." Reason demands that we never pass over the question, "what purpose(s) do the systems within which we work themselves serve?", the possibility that the interconnected concepts we have gotten used to employing are globally irresponsible or corrupt. Thus reason needs judgment to apply itself to the natural world, but judgment also needs reason to provide it with an ideal of infinite revisability that governs, but can never be part of, its own workings. To perform their complementary roles, the two must be conceived as distinct. Kant seems increasingly to realize this as he separates judgment off from reason in the later development of his Critical system.[2]

Indeed, perhaps because he was afraid that we would miss the need for judgment to be governed by reason, that we would mix up the freedom within empirical constraints that belongs to judgment with the necessarily nonempirical freedom of reason, Kant insists in CJ that judgment is, and must be, altogether independent of morality. Still, he winds up giving judgment a more significant moral role than he may intend when he says that it aims at "purposiveness without purpose."[3] He admits, in fact, that judgment thereby "makes possible the transition" between concepts of nature and concepts of freedom (CJ 176, 196/12, 33). Sometimes he translates this as meaning that judgment enables us to see how it is possible that moral "purposes [can] be effected" in nature (176/12). The aesthetic judgment, the subjective feeling that there is "purposiveness" in a natural object, prepares the understanding to apply the notion of a purpose in moral judgment. This does not mean that reflective judgment teaches us the purpose of life. But it does seem to teach us *how to look* for such a purpose, or at least how to recognize it should we find it.

A first interpretation of the mysterious phrase, "purposiveness without purpose," might tie it, as Kant himself does, to what is sought by the free play of the faculties. At one point Kant defines a purpose as "the object of a concept" (220/55), but elsewhere he recognizes that a purpose may itself be a concept, insofar as it is held in the mind of a creator prior to creating the object in question (180/17). Insofar as purposes are themselves concepts, "purposiveness without purpose" is very close to "conceptualizable without concepts." But if we make use of the interactive model proposed in chapter 2 for understanding the latter, we can readily translate "purposiveness without purpose" as "purposiveness without any *definite* purpose." An object is purposive without purpose, then, if it seems more or less to satisfy an indefinite range of purposes without being exactly tailor-made for any of them. The moral and cognitive value of grasping such a property is fairly clear: by separating objects from any single purpose they might seem to serve, we simultaneously broaden our notion of what ends are available to us and remind ourselves that purposes, like concepts, must *fit* the objects to which they are applied, that "purposiveness" presupposes the possibility of a gap between the purpose assigned to an object and the aptness of the object for the purpose assigned. The experience of beauty once again comes to teach us the notion of "fittedness to."

What purposes might be "fitted to," however, what imposes responsibility upon them, remains unclear. I think we can make some progress on this by considering Kant's tendency to juxtapose the purposiveness of judgment with its "systematicity." Systematicity, in CJ, is the primary means by which we establish unity in the world of our experience, the primary governing principle of science. One function of reflective judgment is "to establish the unity of all empirical principles under higher ones, and hence to establish the possibility of their systematic subordination" (180/16). The ultimate principle of nature's unity is "unknown to us" (ibid.), and of course the full system of nature, if there is one, is something we should not expect to complete, but the fact that we can meet with system*aticity*—here a particular that fits neatly under a given general term, there a general concept that seems nicely to account for a set of particulars—allows us to hope that all of nature can be unified, to hold out the systematic subordination of all particulars in one whole as at least a possibility. Here systematicity has priority over actual system, although we maintain, at least in principle, the ideal of an actual system.[4]

Now if systematicity and purposiveness can be treated similarly, then we can see each particular purpose as necessarily belonging to a hierarchical network of purposes even though no complete such network is actually available to us. It belongs to the nature of purposes that we can attribute a purpose to a thing only if we can explain what purpose that purpose itself serves. Thus I adequately give the purpose of my going on a walk as "to get a cup of coffee" only if you already know, or I can also give, the purpose of my getting a cup of coffee—and if necessary, I must be able to give the purpose of *that* purpose and so on ad infinitum (I need the coffee to work harder, I need to work harder to advance my career, I need to advance my career to buy a bigger house, etc.). Thus, also, in older, teleological versions of science, one explained the purpose of the human finger by reference to the human arm, and the purpose of the human arm by reference to the human body, and the purpose of the human body by reference to the role of human beings in a wider, God-designed universe. If purposes come in hierarchies, it is natural to suppose that all the separate hierarchies must themselves be adjudicated by reference to higher-order hierarchies, such that ultimately there will be only one system, giving all entities their place in the universe, and one purpose at the zenith of that system.

Today we tend to reject any such view. We tend now to understand different sciences, and the differences among scientific, aesthetic, and ethical approaches to the world, as dependent on systems of explanation that need not be mutually translatable: such that both the highest-order concepts in each system and the canons of explanation for each system may not be adequately commensurated by any single standard. This leaves us with purposes and explanations still coming in hierarchies and still plausibly linked to one another, but with different fragments of hierarchies, more or less linked by different sets of judgments, rather than any single clearly best hierarchy. We judge new explanations in physics according to canons specific to physics, or at most according to general scientific canons, and we make decisions about whether to regard scientific information as relevant to our moral and aesthetic decisions based on canons specific to moral and aesthetic reasoning. If there is anything right about cultural relativism, moreover, members of different cultures may judge according to differing canons of scientific, moral, and aesthetic evidence. In any case, modern pluralism makes judgment prior to hierarchy and system.

Pluralism does not, however, get rid of the fact that judgments always depend upon and create hierarchical systems of evaluation. We may not be able to derive our judgments from any single systematic order, but each judgment must still fit into *some* system. As Wittgenstein says: "We . . . are taught *judgments* and their connexion with other judgments. *A totality* of judgments is made plausible to us. . . . My judgments themselves characterize the way I judge, characterize the nature of judgment."[5] This allows for the following explanation of what Kant means by purposiveness without purpose: (1) a thing is *purposive,* we may say, if a judgment that it has purpose fits into some totality of judgments, some system for making sense of the world, while at the same time (2) it lacks *purpose* as long as we do not endorse that system of judging itself. A natural object may suggest "purposiveness without purpose" to us, therefore, as long as we retain the notion that *some* comprehensive explanatory and teleological system might fit the natural world and that among such systems there are reasonable ones in which this particular object would have a place. This is then the model for objective purposiveness that aesthetic response provides: a beautiful object suggests to us what it would be for a thing to have an objective purpose *if* any teleological view of nature were to be (objectively) true.

There seems to be some handwaving here, however. The beautiful object is supposed to be "purposive" to *us*, to serve a need of *our* faculties. But how can the object be purposive for us, satisfy our needs, without the purposiveness of the object collapsing again into something purely subjective? To preserve the sense that the object, and thus the universe, might have an objective purpose, we need to suppose that the hierarchical systems of purposes we are considering do not have their root in us, that they make room for us, too, to have an objective purpose in the system of nature. But can we regard ourselves as objectively being given a purpose without violating the autonomy both of beauty and of morality?[6]

Let us explore the possibility that the experience of beauty reveals something about what I might *consider* objectively to be my purpose. It does not *give* me an objective purpose, or let me assume objective purposes for things in the world—that would be teleological judgment. But it tells me something about *what it would be like* for me to have an objective purpose, how I could fit into some overall purposive scheme. When I experience beauty, I feel I have a place in the world. It is as if the world were made for me, or at least with me in mind. This is a feeling beyond all specific purposes either I or any thing in the world might have. I do not know *what* purpose the things in the world, or I, might have, only that *if* they all have a purpose, those purposes will fit together and mine will have a place among them. For a scheme giving me such a place to be true, every particular thing must in fact have a specific purpose, but the conceit in imagining the scheme without committing ourselves to its truth value is that we presume I would be able to work out the specific purposes only after reaching the point at which the whole scheme was before me. Each specific candidate for the purpose of the object I judge is suspended, from the perspective of beauty, in recognition of the fact that any system of purposes I currently accept stands open to revision unless and until someone can determine the highest-order purpose of human being and universe. Purposiveness without purpose is then the feeling that *if* we knew that highest-order purpose, this particular object before us would be given a purpose by it, and the system giving it purpose would also give a point to our lives. We feel as if the object were purposive from God's perspective and as if, therefore, we could see our own purpose from that perspective.

This would explain a feature of the third *Critique* to which Anthony Savile draws attention: "Kant wants to talk about the supersensible substrate of humanity at least as centrally as that of objects of our aesthetic attention themselves, because what it is that gives rise to the purposive way in which things impinge on us is ultimately something unfathomable at the bottom of our own nature as well as what lies at the bottom of the nature of things to which we attend. Reference to only one of the noumenally involved parties would be radically deficient."[7] Kant talks of judgment as pointing to the "supersensible substrate" of both the universe and our subjective selves, to what underlies both our freedom and the world to which that freedom relates. He does not say that there *is* any such substrate, but that the feeling that there *might* be is necessary to human freedom. This is what makes the experience of beauty so important to us. The feeling is comforting, bringing us into harmony with the world, but it is also freeing: it can help us shake off some of the ends we have been blindly pursuing. The priority of systematicity over system allows for no end of scientific criticism. Any piece of empirical system we construct is always open to the possibility that another, more comprehensive attempt at system will show that our piece is radically incorrect, that we need to redo or reinterpret our canons of explanation. Similarly, the priority of purposiveness to purpose allows for no end of moral criticism. Any hierarchy of purposes we set for ourselves stands open to the possibility that it may have to be shaken up, in light of its failure to fit some evidence about what pleases or displeases us, or about how our moral duties can best be realized in the empirical world, or of its comprehensive inferiority to another, neater attempt to systematize our purposes.

So the feeling that my "supersensible substrate" is unified with a similar substrate of the world obligates me never to rest satisfied with a single, fixed view of how I should act. At the same time, it allows my empirical, emotive self some possibility of reconciliation with the demands of reason. This comes out in several ways. In the first place, the sense that the world is purposive holds out a promise for the possibility of reconciling my scientific and my moral views of the world. This explains Kant's insistence on the priority of the beauty of nature over the beauty of art, and belief that only an interest in the beauty of nature, not an interest in the beauty of art, is "always a mark of a good soul" (CJ 298/141).[8] The discursive account I have given of what Kant means by the harmony of the faculties may seem to overlook this priority of the beauty of nature. I described reflective judgment as quintessentially a conversational experience. Yet, while we enjoy talking in museums, we would usually rather be silent before mountain landscapes. All the same, I think there is a kind of conversation even in the appreciation of natural beauty. We may not talk to someone else at the top of the Grand St. Bernard Pass, and we are certainly not likely to talk about the landscape itself, but the beauty of a natural scene can well encourage us to think discursively about *other* subjects. Walking alone along a mountaintop or through a beautiful forest, our minds come alive with insights and internal discussions. I suspect this is something Kant himself felt much of the time and is here justifying as philosophically important. The happiness I feel in the presence of natural beauty *encourages me to feel my scientific and moral researches are worthwhile,* and that is not just a psychological fact but something the pleasure in natural beauty implicitly teaches.[9] It gives us a hint that the world is well-ordered, that rational investigation can succeed, and that science and moral purposes are reconcilable. This is the ultimate *hopeful* experience, the closest we can get in experience to an answer to Kant's third question for philosophy: "what may we hope?"

In the second place, the pleasure in experiencing beauty gives me a sign as to how I might solve an important worry in moral practice. Reason demands that I bring my feelings in line with my duties, but most of the feelings motivating me to acts that accord with duty—the self-love out of which I preserve myself, the sexual desire out of which I marry and procreate, the impulse to revenge out of which I act justly—may equally well motivate *violations* of my duties, such that I may have to ignore or suppress those same feelings. Desires and their satisfactions are normally *amoral*, and I can therefore worry whether an entirely good "me" living in an entirely good world would be happy. Now the experience of beauty—and especially of natural beauty—is a satisfaction that in itself never conflicts with my duties. The experience of beauty enhances rather than takes away from my cognitive skills and moral judgment; it is never used up, never subject to the need for new sources of excitement; and it demands the possession of no object (CJ 204–5/38–9). Hence, even if I were perfectly good and living in a perfectly good world, I could experience the pleasures of beauty endlessly. This is the deepest harmony of the faculties: not only a harmony of my cognitive faculties but a harmony that brings together my moral, cognitive, and affective faculties. Experiencing this harmony, I know that striving for moral perfection need not entail either getting rid of all my desires, as reason sometimes threatens, or knowing how to satisfy all of them, as sensibility sometimes demands. Instead, there are pleasures whose satisfaction is compatible with both duty and cognition. The experience of beauty thus shows me how I might overcome the very temptation to evil. It gives me a picture of how a good world might *feel.*

In practice, one thing this means is that I can use my judgment to refine and alter my own purposes. Knowing that I will never lose all possibility of happiness, that the pleasure of enjoying beauty will be there regardless of the other pleasures I may have to give up, I can work on weaning myself from bad habits, from addictions to pleasures that harm me or my relationships with others. I can, moreover, use the process of interpretation beauty inspires to change myself—and, thereby, to *enjoy* changing myself. If I see myself as part of a beautiful whole, I can adjust my feelings about the rest of that whole as well as adjusting it to me. I am myself, after all, something purposive without any definite purpose. I can therefore take any of my specific ends, assess its connection both with the system of purposes I currently uphold and with the empirical world in which it is supposed to be realized, and transform it into a new specific end if, in either direction, it does not fit. I need not identify myself with my specific ends; as purposive without purpose, I understand myself to be able to transcend any of them.

This is to say that Kant's purposiveness without purpose allows me deliberation over ends. Philosophers have often denied that this is possible. I deliberate, they say, over the *means* to my ends but never over the ends themselves. Of course, I may deliberate over whether my "end" of becoming a professor, say, is conducive to my happiness or not, but then it would seem becoming a professor is really not my end at all, only a means to my real end: happiness. And how could I deliberate over whether I want to be happy or not? What further criterion for the adequacy of my purposes would even make sense of such a question? My ultimate ends, like happiness itself, would seem to be "set" for me, not something I can even make sense of deliberating over. But to give purposiveness priority over purposes, as Kant does, is to deny that I must start from some overall end from which I then derive my more specific purposes. Instead, I can reflect on each of my ends in the light of its fittedness to my system of ends, as I currently construe that system. This, it seems to me, suits the normal shape of deliberation very well. At each moment we find ourselves faced, not with an overarching purpose from which to derive our particular goals, but with a set of already given particular ends whose relationship to one another we need to assess.

But since my ends are so essentially particular, judgment, not reason, is the appropriate faculty for assessing them. With judgment we always find ourselves *in medias res*. It is the nature of any single judgment to be interlocked with other judgments. It is the nature of interlocking judgments to form hierarchical systems, moreover, in which some judgments, judged more important or better evidenced, are used for judging others (Wittgenstein: "My judgments themselves characterize the way I judge"). And it is the nature of hierarchical systems to recede to a point—a final cause, if normative, or a foundation, if descriptive. All the same, we neither know nor need to know the contours of the whole system we have embarked upon when we make an initial single judgment nor whether, indeed, a system in which it fits is complete at all. Our judgment must connect to other judgments to be intelligible, so once we climb onto the one judgment there must be others to move to from it. In that sense, each judgment belongs to a system. But we may clamber around a system for some time, exploring here one connection, there another, only to find in the end that, like some massive construction project abandoned halfway through for lack of funds, it stands pointlessly in the middle of nowhere, lacking both a ground floor and a roof.

In seeking a purpose for life, people frequently go through precisely such a "clambering" process. Rather than being persuaded of the foundational principles of, say, Marxism or fundamentalist Christianity, many people find themselves drawn to particular stances or practices that they see a Marxist or fundamentalist they know maintaining. They then explore the system more fully, trying out here an extension of its judgments to sexuality, there an extension to engagement with community. Eventually they are either more or less drawn into the whole system that the judgments form, or they find themselves more or less disillusioned with it. While sometimes they get disillusioned because of a particular aspect of the system, often they were drawn originally to it precisely by its claim to comprehensive explanatory power and get disillusioned when they find its grounding weak or overall vision unappealing. This is not to say that no Grand Platonic System of judgments exists, only that we cannot presume in advance, by the mere act of grabbing one judgment, that in fact there is such a whole. Here is systematicity without system, purposiveness without purpose. The interlocking of judgments precedes the holistic systems that their interlocking seems to promise; the responsibility of judgments, downwards to evidence and upwards to canons of argument, is something we build systems out of, not something derived from the foundational principles, or ultimate telos, of an already given Absolute System. So if judgment does not exactly provide us with a comprehensive conception of how to live, it at least points the way to how we might search for such a conception. It thereby teaches us how to seek the purpose of our own lives—and how, with that search at least vaguely in view, to shape our particular moral ends.

II

That "purposiveness without purpose" helps us develop specific concepts of our moral ends is but one example of how judgment translates very general moral ideas into terms suitable for our specific, daily practices.

Reflective aesthetic judgment, for Kant, forges the link between nature and our concepts of nature; reflective and morally determining judgment together, I want to say, forge the link between nature and freedom.

This is not far from Kant's own view. Between the perspectives of theoretical reason, by which we see human beings as fully determined in their choices, and practical reason, by which we see them as free, there seems to be no common measure, no commensuration. But there *must* be some way of bringing them together, for it is an empirical being, the human me or you, who is supposed to have freedom: "Even if an immeasurable gulf is fixed between the sensible realm of the concept of nature and the supersensible realm of the concept of freedom, so that no transition is possible from the first to the second (by means of the theoretical reason) . . . , yet the second is *meant* to have an influence upon the first" (CJ 175–6/12). Kant says that judgment "makes possible the transition" between the concept of nature and the concept of freedom. We have seen that purposiveness provides one way to understand this transition. Here are some others:

1. Judgment provides what Kant calls the "law of the specification of nature" (CJ 186/22) to science and can similarly make possible articulation in the realm of freedom. The very way in which it leads us to particular empirical laws serves as a model for the specification of freedom, for regarding one particular empirical thing or event as morally relevant, another as not. On the one hand, this means that we can begin a transition down from the concept of "freedom" to the details of everyday life, where freedom must be exercised. We can begin to speak not merely of being free, but of freely displaying "courage," or freely overcoming "racism," of using one's freedom to "preserve one's talents," or to "help the poor." On the other hand, it means that we can begin to move up from particular cases towards moral ideals. Does a jeweler's barring young black men from her store reveal racism or merely a statistically based notion of who is likely to endanger her security? Is the danger of working in a Rwandan hospital so great that seeking such an opportunity would be foolhardy, or so outweighed by the possible good I can do that proper courage demands that I do so? Does a slight here, an injury there, morally require remedy? If so, what remedy and by whom? Only a network of judgments, not freedom or the practical reason it represents, can begin to answer these questions. Judgment *articulates* freedom, allowing us to talk of specific moral cases and virtues, which in turn are linked together systematically but not derivable from the overarching pure idea of freedom alone.

2. A similar point we might make is that a free reason requires free concepts. Reason organizes concepts into potential totalities called "ideas," according to the first *Critique,* and if practical reason wants to establish a

totality of concepts under the auspices of the overarching idea of freedom, it surely requires that we come to those concepts themselves freely. "Free," for Kant, always means grounded, as opposed to merely caused. So a "free concept" is one that is properly grounded rather than just a product of my environment's impact on me. One of the facts about me that can be either caused or a result of my choices is what empirical concepts I have and use. I can, for instance, merely absorb a concept of "witches" from my social milieu and allow it to infest my thought, or I can choose to regard that concept as empty, to ignore it, to apply it only to fictional entities, etc. I can accept an ongoing application in my milieu of the concept "symptom of late capitalism" to explain every social ill, or modify or reject those applications. If I do take control over what concepts I accept, if I keep my concepts responsible to the particulars they unify, I must recognize that they may at any point require revision. Conversely, if I do keep my concepts open to revision, I have some ground for assuming that they are responsible to their particulars whenever I do *not* find a need to revise them. Insofar as the transcendental idea of freedom demands that the concepts it unifies be themselves free, therefore, it demands precisely that they be revisable and responsible, that they be respons*ive* to good grounds. But that is the job of reflective judgment. So transcendental freedom demands that I submit my everyday moral concepts to a constant scrutiny by judgment.

The relationship between transcendental and empirical freedom is thus represented by the relationship discussed earlier in this chapter between reason and judgment. Our judgments—concrete, indexed to specific situations and dependent on specific moral concepts—form a network by which we make all our everyday choices. Practical reason's role is to provide a regulative ideal for this network, insisting that we transform particular decisions into rules for general types of action, that we aim to make the rules themselves at least compatible with and preferably constitutive of a single order under which we could will all rational beings to live, and, above all, that we hold ourselves up to our own rules when deciding how to act. These demands do not immediately produce any concrete directives; rather, they are "meta-rules" for a system of directives against which our actual set of directives will always fall short and will therefore always be capable of approximating more closely. Our judgments need to be thus grounded in reason to make sure that we act responsibly on them, but our reason needs judgments as well if it is to act, as it must, in concrete situations. The cultivation of judgment thus becomes a duty, a part of reason's demands on itself, a mandate of the categorical imperative.

3. A third possibility, more far-fetched in terms of Kant's own thought but not implausible in its own right, is that the experiences we normally

associate with beauty—in particular, the telling and interpretation of stories—are essential to the freedom of morality. This is a way of taking seriously Kant's claim that aesthetic judgment makes moral concepts possible. What would it mean in practice? Perhaps, as Kant himself says at times, that we learn morality most powerfully from examples in history and literature; perhaps also that the freedom to spin imaginary tales prepares us for the kind of imagining of alternate possibilities that is essential to practical reasoning. Someone very literal-minded is likely to suppose she has fewer alternatives than she in fact does, to blunder into tactlessness or dogmatism or a thoughtless conformity to bad social practices simply because she is not imaginative enough to find other ways of doing things. The sort of aesthetic reflection I am urging is notoriously not a sufficient condition for being a good person, but it may be a necessary one.[10]

4. Perhaps the deepest way that judgment can commensurate the seemingly incommensurable transcendental and empirical freedoms is simply by *being the faculty of commensuration*. A faculty that brings particulars and generalities together is a model for how the apparently incommensurable can be brought together at all. What it is to view a particular from the perspective of a concept and try to figure out whether it ought to be brought under the latter or not, or to view a concept from the perspective of a particular and try to figure out whether its use should be altered or not, is precisely what it is to try to reconcile two notions which appear at first to have no common measure.

Let me try to clarify this by means of what seems like a different kind of commensuration. Most often, the issue of commensurability arises today across cultures or languages. Can we, for instance, find a common measure that adequately grasps the meaning of both "duty" and "dharma"?[11] Well, suppose for the sake of argument that every term or more extended description in English, Sanskrit, and every other known language badly fails to capture the connotations of either one or the other of the words. Something like this tends to be the grounds for saying that the terms are incommensurable. But if you are an earnest anthropologist, or international lawyer, or person interested in bringing English and Indic peoples together, you are unlikely to let the matter go at that. What would you do? Well, what you would probably do is investigate more closely how the term foreign to you actually works in context. You might study literature or legal cases in which appeals to "dharma" are made. Then you could ask which of the actions characterized by "dharma" fit under the way you understand "duty." You could try to bring the objects that fit under "dharma," that is, one by one under "duty" as well. Some may fit fairly easily; some will fit only if you revise "duty" a bit; and some will just not fit at all—but there may be room for regarding them as inauthentic or inessential examples of "dharma," or for recommending, to the members of the culture with whom you are conversing, that they revise "dharma" *such that* these objects become inauthentic or inessential examples of it. In any case, you will have to reinterpret either "duty" or "dharma" or both if you want to reconcile them. At the end, if you succeed, the concepts will no longer be incommensurable, but that will be *because* you have used reflective judgment to change their usage, and perhaps the entire context in which they are used.[12] There is no guarantee that you will succeed: reflective judgment is unconstrained, impossible to pin down in advance, by natural concepts or the moral law. If you do not succeed, you may say that you have encountered incommensurability in principle rather than merely in practice, but you will not be able to prove that that is what happened rather than that you failed to use judgment long or well enough. If you do succeed, it will be clear that judgment allowed you to build a bridge that was not there in the beginning. And if you do build such a bridge, the changes in each of the two cultural contexts will not have been imposed from some position outside but will have been found from within by, will feel "their own" to, the people whose cultures are so altered.

Now apply this to the transcendental and empirical notions of "freedom." Empirically I am free when I can satisfy my desires, while transcendentally I am free precisely when I can stand *beyond* my desires. Philosophers have spilled much ink trying to show either that the latter must be possible or that the former is the only intelligible notion of freedom. On my view, freedom requires *both* the possibility of satisfying my desires *and* the possibility of standing beyond them.[13] These two conditions are indeed severely in tension with one another, but judgment reduces that tension. The more we judge particular desires and their satisfaction as free or unfree from the transcendental perspective of reason, and the more we judge particular reasons for action as allowing or not allowing for human satisfaction from the empirical perspective of desire, the more we can alter our conceptions of both the desires we want to have and the reasons on which we think we should act, to the point at which we can generally identify our desires and grounds as in accordance with both transcendental and empirical freedom. And if the analogy with the cultural case holds, both our desires and our reason will regard a reconciliation brought about by judgment as something they come to of their "own" accord, something that expresses them adequately and to which they come freely.

III

Kant's own way of describing judgment as a faculty of commensuration is to call it a "mediating link" among the cognitive faculties. He calls judgment a "mediating link" several times in CJ, but what it mediates differs from occasion to occasion. It is the mediating link between understanding and reason (CJ 168, 177/4, 13), but it is also the mediating link between understanding and imagination (52–4 and throughout most of the "Analytic of the Beautiful"), between imagination and reason (in the "Analytic of the Sublime"), and, finally, between nature and freedom (168, 177, 179, 195–7/4, 13, 15, 32–4). That judgment mediates between each pair of our faculties makes clear that it is a way of moving among faculties in general, not the province of any single one of them. I think Kant wants it to represent the subjective form of *all* thinking, although he cannot find a good way of fitting this point into his architectonic. We might do so for him by defining "nature" as understanding applied to imagination under the guidance of theoretical reason and "freedom" or "morality" as understanding applied to imagination under the guidance of practical reason. Then judgment moves among all three faculties in two different ways, producing two kinds of concepts directed at two kinds of objects.

I draw from this an extremely important and surprising conclusion, probably rather more surprising than Kant himself intended: that hermeneutics, the unfixed mode of interpretation to which we are inspired by the experience of beauty, is the ultimate precondition for both adequate moral thought and morally useful scientific thought, the ultimate point of unity or at least transition between the two, and the fullest and truest expression of how, overall, we come to a subjective view of the world. As subjective selves, we find our freedom more precisely in our use of judgment than in our use of reason. Kant never explicitly says anything like this—that would threaten his insistence that only reason can be a free cause—but there are three indications that the notion of judgment as a kind of freedom may lie somewhere in the background of CJ:

1. Famously, he uses the phrase "free play" to describe the harmony of the faculties. This is not simply a loose use of words. Kant repeatedly contrasts the freedom of the imagination in the harmony of the faculties with the "limitations," "compulsion," or "constraint" that rules, laws, or concepts would otherwise place upon it:

> There is presupposed no concept of any purpose which the manifold of the given object is to serve [in a pure judgment of taste]. . . . By such a concept the freedom of the imagination which disports itself in the contemplation of the figure would be only *limited*. (229–30/66, my emphasis)

> If . . . the imagination is *compelled* to proceed according to a definite law, its product in respect of form is determined by concepts as to what it ought to be.

But then . . . the satisfaction is not that in the beautiful, but in the good . . . and the judgment is not a judgment of taste. Hence [the judgment of taste] is a conformity to law without a law. (241/78, my emphasis)

[N]ature . . . that is subjected to no *constraint* of artificial rules, can supply constant food for taste. Even the song of birds, which we can bring under no musical rule, seems to have more freedom, and therefore more for taste, than a song of a human being which is produced in accordance with all the rules of music. (243/80, my emphasis)

The imagery of freedom is pervasive and deep here, but I think it makes Kant nervous. He quite sidesteps the question, at any rate, of how this freedom is supposed to relate to the freedom of morality. For the freedom of taste or judgment is explicitly a freedom from moral concepts as well as natural ones: "[T]aste in the beautiful . . . is the only free satisfaction. An object of inclination and one that is proposed to our desire by a law of reason leave us no freedom in forming for ourselves anywhere an object of pleasure" (210/44). Readers of the *Groundwork* and second *Critique* would be pardoned for supposing that "ourselves," in this passage, properly refers to our reason, and that nothing proposed by a law of reason could leave those selves in any way unfree. Instead Kant almost acknowledges another notion of "freedom" here, one that comes closer than his austere freedom of reason does to what we ordinarily mean by the freedom to do something or experience something "for ourselves." But he does not quite acknowledge this. Judgment for him is free, inter alia, *of freedom,* since it is "free" of the moral law. Still, that is to say that Kant keeps himself from the position I am urging only by insisting on a single, rigid use of the term "freedom." I suggest that exactly his point can be put alternatively by talking of two meanings for "freedom," an objective and a subjective one, with judgment providing a subjective freedom to mirror the objective freedom of reason.

2. Kant describes the principle of judgment as a principle of "heautonomy." This seems virtually a conscious dodge away from the unnerving connotations of the plain term "autonomy," and indeed Kant twice defends his usage against such an objection:

the judgment has therefore also in itself a principle *a priori* of the possibility of nature, but only in a subjective aspect, by which it prescribes not to nature (autonomy), but to itself (heautonomy). (CJ 185–6/22)

But that the *imaginative power* should be *free* and yet *of itself conformed to law,* i.e. bringing autonomy with it, is a contradiction. The understanding alone gives the law. . . . Hence [judgment] is a conformity to law without a law. (241/78)

The philosopher doth protest too much. A law which one gives oneself is precisely what Kant elsewhere means by "autonomy," and judgment certainly gives itself its own law. That there is no realm of application for this law outside of judgment itself merely brings us back to the fact that we have a different *kind* of autonomy here—a subjective rather than objective kind.

3. Kant describes CJ as "the critique of the judging subject" (194/31), as something that has no objective realm, no object at all other than its own principle (176/12). Judgment is also the faculty that somehow represents or embodies the feeling of pleasure and pain, which at one point Kant describes as another name for "the subject and . . . its feeling of life" (204/38). In the same passage, Kant says that in judgment we compare a given representation to our "whole faculty of representations, of which the mind is conscious in the feeling of its state." And he repeats, later, the claim that when the faculties are in harmony, "our *whole faculty* of representative power gains" (231/67).

I suggest that judgment represents or even is identical with the subject. *As* Sam Fleischacker, as opposed to reason encased in one of many human bodies, I *am* the set of my judgments, together with the experiences and capacities they express. The specific person who has been reading Kant, and indeed the specific Immanuel Kant who has been writing all these critiques, are first and foremost *judging subjects:* that is why CJ is "the propaedeutic of all philosophy" (194/31). I probably identify more closely with my feeling of pleasure and pain than with my cognition or desire, and I certainly identify above all with my "feeling of life" and "whole faculty of representation." So to say that I am free when I judge is not merely a metaphor. My judgments best represent the specific me—hence they are the best expression of my specific freedom. Perhaps I have another freedom as well, which regulates and revises the freedom of my judgment, but that freedom, the freedom of reason, represents a transcendental or noumenal me. And for a transcendental me to be meaningfully a form of "me" at all, it must be connected to, or even expressed by, the specific me who makes judgments.

IV

So according to CJ we are, as specific individuals, first and foremost judges, which is to say that something paradigmatically represented by literary interpretation is the quality in ourselves with which we most identify. Both our moral concepts and our empirical concepts are dependent on this quality, so the freedom to develop and use it is essential to any other freedom we might possess. Let me expound this view a little now in my own voice.

The most striking way I can put the claim is to say that our specific selves are literary interpreters; more dully but more accurately, we might say that the individuality characteristic of literary interpretation is one version of the movement between conceptualization and experience with which we identify our empirical selves. This seems too abstract, too intellectual a notion of freedom only if one misunderstands what is involved in judgment. It is not, after all, just the abstract "having" of concepts, but an active *application* or *use* of concepts, such that involvement in the empirical world is an inextricable part of it. Our judgments are not our experience, but they track it. My judgments follow my experience wherever it goes: each instant of my life presents new particulars to be placed under some rule and new occasions to maintain or revise rules, to apply them in expected and unexpected ways. Judgment changes with experience, unlike both reason, which is supposed to transcend all experience, and our sensations, which do not maintain enough of an identity over time that change can meaningfully be ascribed to them. Judgment is something abstract or intellectual only in that it insists on a certain capacity for *reflection* on, conscious appropriation of, experience, which is surely in line with what we consider to be a truly human—free—relationship to experience. If we humans are between beasts and gods, creatures that maintain some integrity over time but do not transcend time, who have a more connected sense of self than a snail or a goat but no eternal and completely unified essence, then judgment expresses us perfectly.

We say: "Use your own judgment," but never, "Use your own senses," "Use your own understanding," or "Use your own reason." Perhaps the latter might be an instruction not to get help from another student on a math assignment, but the "own" still sounds odd. What is my "own" reason, as opposed to Jimmy's reason, or Jane's? "Use your own senses," on the other hand, sounds otiose—whose senses *could* I use, other than my own? There's nothing I "own" about my understanding and reason, and no choice about using my own sensibility, but my judgment seems both intimately related to my character, and something I can control.

As I compare a set of particulars, perhaps this similarity among them or perhaps that one occurs to me as more relevant to their explanation or classification. No concept can *compel* me to apply it to a given particular, and certainly no concept alone can do so. I may decide this thing is granite or I may decide it is a slightly different material or a subspecies of granite.[14] Considerations playing into such a decision include the marks of the particular, but also how I use the term "granite" in various scientific, or pragmatic, or aesthetic contexts. I may change the concept slightly to accommodate or rule out this particular. Some concepts, and some contexts, give me more playroom than others for such modifications. Scientific contexts and terms make fairly strict demands, while aesthetic contexts make weak ones. But none of the decisions I make about following or altering a concept are arbitrary. There are always better and worse judgments, and on granite, for instance, only a well-trained geologist will normally make a good judgment in favor of altering the concept. Experience imposes responsibility on my judgments.

A speaker advocating greater democracy in Asia is asked whether Singaporeans are culturally unsuited for democracy, whether an Asian temperament or tradition makes people prefer to submit to authority. In response he does not invoke arguments against all generalizations, or all generalizations about culture, but cites the fact that Singapore, until the early 1960s, was in fact a thriving, lively scene of democratic debate. *This* is responsibility in argument: picking precisely the evidence that best meets a specific question. Fitting one judgment in with a network of others means learning the subtle norms of each language-game of argumentation and the subtle differences among them. Stupidity, in the ordinary sense which I think Kant captures well when he calls it "deficiency in judgment" (CPR B 173n), comes out when a person is not sensitive to these details of evidence and argument. Someone who responded to the question about Asian temperaments by baldly parroting leftist shibboleths against "stereotyping" would strike others as stupid, would be embarrassing to sympathizers and opponents alike by his or her tin ear for what counts as an appropriate defense for a position. What makes many multiculturalists and deconstructionists today seem so outstandingly stupid is that they have lost all sensitivity to the difference between a good and a bad defense for a position. They seem unable to defend themselves coherently, appealing to empirical instances here or there without considering whether the instance is a representative or even a relevant one, or proclaiming against "Western rationality" without so much as recognizing the difficulties in an attack on reason.

And Sherlock Holmes seems the exact opposite of stupid precisely because of his lively and subtle appreciation for just what evidence fits what position, just what detail, just how interpreted, can serve as evidence for the case he wants to make ("the dog that failed to bark in the night"). A philosopher would have to use different kinds of argument, relying on general considerations rather than details; an art critic would interpret details differently and for different purposes; a physicist needs concrete data like the detective and art critic but can never rely on any single instance, and indeed must read idiosyncrasies out of all the details he uses. Someone who does not understand the differences among these fields, and applies kinds of evidence appropriate to one in another, seems slow, flat-footed, unable to find her way around—literally "stupid." And she seems culpably so, since we consider good judgment something of which every human being is capable, something "we regard as the least to be expected from anyone claiming the name of man" (CJ 293/135).

Revising accepted concepts and canons of explanation is, however, also a part of freedom, a part of what we daily, as subjective, specific selves, mean by "freedom." I am free when I judge in that I ultimately make up my own mind, and I am also free in that the judgments I form and conversations which inform my judgments are open-ended: I can interpret the particular case or formulate the general rule somewhat differently from you. For me "innocence" may properly extend only to members of a particular human group, or as far as animals or even plants, or "revenge" may denote some but not other kinds of retaliation. It is of the nature of language to allow such shifting and idiosyncratic interpretations, of the nature of conversation to allow, indeed to presuppose, dissent.

I express my freedom by extending a concept to a new or slightly different instance from the ones I've been taught. I have more license to do this in some areas than in others. That concepts are revisable does not mean they are revisable always or in all contexts (the mistake of deconstruction). It simply means that they are always *potentially* revisable, and each may actually be so in some context. Reflective judgment takes place at the margins of determining judgment, necessarily *not* all the time.

The most difficult exercise of judgment, and one its aesthetic paradigm is not well-suited to convey, is the application of it to our own psychological and moral failings. We may hone our interpretive skills to a fine art, astutely picking up on the subtlest of details in the behavior of people around us, in our environment, and in our history. In this, however, we remain always a spectator, never having to take responsibility for our actions. To accept our actions *as* ours, and condemn them, change them, or repent for them when necessary, we must immerse ourselves in action and, consciously taking responsibility for our acts, turn the all-too-blind eye of self-criticism on what Adam Smith calls "the mysterious veil of self-delusion, which covers from [our] view the deformities of [our] own conduct" (TMS III.4.4). Yet turning this eye of criticism on ourselves and using it to change what we do, turning from set habits to self-revision, is itself an act of reflective judgment, itself an act that requires self-interpretation.

Judgment mediates, not only between reason and understanding, or understanding and sensibility, but among all the various skills and interests that compose our subjective selves. As Aristotelian phronesis, it can be thought of as a craftlike skill that extends itself from sphere to sphere of our activities until eventually, at least in the ideal case, it takes over our entire lives. I hone skills in assessing details and responding to them appropriately in repairing cars, say, or practicing pediatric medicine, or working for political candidates. But then I can turn what I have learned about assessing detail from cars and medicine to politics, or vice versa. By analogy, at first, I see the lack of investment in a nation's infrastructure as like an abandonment of regular tune-ups or checkups. Then I have to watch out, if I want truly to develop judgment in the new sphere, for *disanalogies* that make auto repair or medicine a bad model for politics. Finally, the skills transfer: I work my way into the new sphere and no longer need analogies. Clearly the transfer can fail to go through. We need to attend carefully to the similarities and differences among spheres, to give the same judicious attention to the process of transferring itself as we do, or hope to do, to the spheres transferred among. A doctor who takes his superb knowledge of medical facts as an excuse for never learning the details of law, or who adopts the same paternalistic attitude toward national ills as he did, with more justification, to the problems of his patients, a businessman thinking the canons or rituals of politics are the same as the canons and rituals of business, will remain with a craftlike simulacrum of judgment, a judgment limited to one realm of human activity.

By contrast, the phronimos extends judgment beyond all particular realms, beyond all limited aims. The highest use of judgment, but also the most difficult, is to train my craftlike abilities on myself, to distance myself enough from myself that I can suspend and reflect on my own ends and habits, and that I can alter those aspects of myself with the freedom by which, in aesthetic play, I abandon one interpretation in favor of another. I ask myself whether medicine, or political activity, is really what I ought to be doing, although until now I have always identified myself above all *as* a doctor or a politician. I take a hard look at my attitude towards my wife or parents, towards certain colleagues or holders of certain views, towards psychotherapy or a religion I have been practicing, and try to see from a distance whether I am responding as I should to the facts around me or to changes I have accepted to my evaluative beliefs. The consequences of such reflection are wide open: I might re-embrace everything I have already been doing, or alter my views mildly, but I might also decide to divorce, to change my sexual or social or eating habits, to enter or leave therapy, to convert from one religion to another, or to become an atheist. If I change beliefs, as in the last example, I will use judgment as just one of the intellectual faculties that plays a role in all reasoning. But if I have to change my habits, what I do and what I enjoy, judgment will come to the fore. The use of judgment has its own pleasure to it, which can be worked into the habits by which I attend to the details of any activity. I will need that pleasure if I have to give up deeply entrenched other pleasures. By holding fast to the pleasure in reflection, in the free play of my faculties, I may wean myself from other pleasures. By way of self-interpretation, I can figure out how to change myself, and why, and the pleasures of interpretation itself help provide a way station, a transition point, in which I can immerse myself while undergoing the changes that produce the new set of desires I think I should have.[15]

But if judgment provides a way station or transition point, how can it also constitute my "true" self? I suggested earlier that our capacity for judgment might "represent or even be identical with" our (authentic) selves, but in fact the greatest advantage of relying on judgment rather than either desire or reason to define ourselves is that we need no notion of essential or authentic selves. So my own use of such language is a sort of Wittgensteinian ladder, to be kicked away once ascended. *If* one wants to locate an essential human self, the self that judges is as good a candidate as any, fitting in well with the canons by which such claims are normally evaluated. But better yet to do without any such claims. I may judge that I am reducible to the biological facts about myself, or that I am a transcendental will—in either case, that I am *not*, most fundamentally, a being who judges. But then I will still have *judged* myself to be the one or the other, which means that I must consider my capacity for judgment crucial to me at least insofar it leads me to self-knowledge. Someone who treats my capacity for judgment as what is all-important about me will therefore deserve my appreciation, since he or she protects my ability to figure out who I am. Someone who treats my capacity for judgment as if it were my "true nature" will also come closer to my own view of myself than someone who focuses on the view of myself I reject: on my capacity for transcendental reason, if I regard myself as fundamentally an animal, or on my biological embodiment, if I regard myself as fundamentally a rational process. A focus on my capacity for judgment, rather than on what I might judge, will always do this, will always approach who I am more the way I do myself, than will a focus based on a theory of human nature that I judge to be wrong. As a political strategy, therefore, protecting and fostering people's capacity for judgment has the advantage of being able to finesse comprehensive theories of human nature. As long as people disagree vehemently on the latter, freedom will be best preserved as freedom of judgment.

Relatedly, by protecting judgment we protect the individuality of human beings. This comes out clearly in the aesthetic paradigm on which judgment is modeled. Because I experience beauty independently of other people—alone, or in disagreement with others—I become aware that individual experience matters, that I as an individual may have as much to contribute as anyone else to how the world should be interpreted, even if some of those "anyones" are better at scientific or mathematical theories than I am. Difference over beauty, that is, gives a hint as to legitimate difference over morality, and as to how those differences can be responsible. The latter comes out especially after I first learn to appreciate an initially unappealing source of beauty, and discover that another can guide me in so changing or deepening my aesthetic appreciation.[16] So one learns authority as well as legitimate disagreement from the experience of beauty. One also learns proper individuality: just as ultimately *I* must experience the harmony of my own faculties to judge something as beautiful, so, I recognize, I must ultimately appropriate the judgments that constitute my own standards of morality. Judgment, as opposed to reason, understanding, and perhaps even sensibility, *consists* in irreducible part in something specific to the individual's own specific faculties. None of this is true of practical reason: recognizing the principles of morality is a matter of bringing one's specific self to what *anyone* can regard as moral. The principles of reason are necessarily colorless. If there is any specific or individual color to moral action, it must come from judgment rather than reason.

It is but a small step from here to the conclusion that judgment, in its aesthetic as well as its moral roles, grounds the individual's right to liberty. If the development of judgment crucially requires individual experience, it becomes clear why legal attempts—necessarily general, necessarily theoretical—to institute morality will necessarily run roughshod over people's concrete experience of their moral freedom, why such attempts will necessarily miss the point, *even if in truth there is ultimately only one right moral code,* of living out the moral life for oneself. It becomes clear, that is, how a Kantian account of moral experience leads to the politics of Adam Smith: ordinary individuals must develop and live out their own faculties of judgment as much as possible by themselves.

But it should also be clear that this type of politics is not identical with what today gets called "libertarianism." Clearly, letting people alone to use their judgment and live with the consequences is essential to the self-rule in which moral judgment ultimately consists. At the same time, other features of judgment that we have discussed, in this and previous chapters, suggest that "laissez-faire" is not the whole story. Developing the capacity for judgment requires that we learn the workings of interpretation, that we have a community of people around us whose opinion we care about, and that we have a stretch of experience in which we are forced to take responsibility for our acts. Since judgment depends on socially structured conditions in this way, one who cares about it will also have to be concerned to bring about the kind of society that will foster it. This takes us to the difficult question of what kind of political arrangements favor judgment. There is a delicate line to be trodden here, between structuring society so little that it fails to provide the conditions for judgment and structuring it so much that it paternalistically squelches judgment itself. The line is, however, one that any thoughtful liberalism must tread. We will be concerned with it for the rest of this book.

PART II

THE POLITICS OF JUDGMENT

Chapter 5

PROPER PLEASURES

ONE WAY of drawing political implications from the theory of judgment we have developed is to use it to enrich standard conceptions of "pleasure." Modern utilitarians, who include most contemporary political scientists and almost all contemporary economists, vaunt their "value-free" definition of pleasure—whatever satisfies people's "expressed preferences," regardless of what those preferences might be—over earlier utilitarian views that distinguished between better and worse kinds of pleasure. I shall argue in this chapter that the earlier views were in fact superior, and that we can offer stronger support for those views than their original defenders did by building into pleasure a role for phronesis or judgment. There *are* better and worse pleasures, and the difference between them has significant political consequences, but we can see the difference only by looking first away from pleasure altogether—to the kinds of activities on which our pleasures ensue.

I begin, in sections 1–5, by exploring a notion of "small tasks," activities that require the solution of a small problem and can be completed in a relatively brief time. These are activities that yield pleasure by exercising and developing our judgment, and their characteristic pleasures are therefore, I believe, very valuable. In section 6, I contrast this emphasis on small tasks and their pleasures with a more standard view of life that I think is flawed. The next four sections (7–10) consider what happens when success in small tasks must get deferred, and the extent to which approval by other people can substitute for such success. I close (sections 11 and 12) by arguing that what today often gets called "malaise" has much to do with an absence of small tasks from our lives, and offering some suggestions for what we might do about that.

1. For moral excellence is concerned with pleasures and pains. . . . Hence we ought to have been brought up . . . both to delight in and to be pained by the things that we ought; . . . For an activity is intensified by its proper pleasure, since each class of things is better judged of and brought to precision by those who engage in the activity with pleasure. (Aristotle, NE 1104b7–13, 1174a29–32)

The rules for practicing virtue . . . aim at a frame of mind that is both *valiant* and *cheerful* in fulfilling its duties. . . . [W]hat is not done with pleasure but with compulsory service has no inner worth for one who attends to his duty in this way and such service is not loved by him; instead, he shirks as much as possible occasions for practicing virtue. (Kant, MM 484/273)

Aristotle tells us that it is "by the rudders of pleasure and pain" that we can steer our young towards the acquisition of virtue (1172a19–21); Kant, while of course uncomfortable with talk of "rudders" and "steering" to describe moral education, agrees that virtue should ultimately be something one enjoys. I begin here with something less than "virtue" as my concern. I begin with "excellence" or "skill" in the broad sense that covers artistic, intellectual, social, and professional abilities as well as strictly "moral" ones (the sense Aristotelian philosophers sometimes like to limit to "craft"). It is my contention that only with skills or abilities in this broader sense can we develop mental powers with a regular, reliable connection to the shaping of events in the world, can we possibly acquire—or discover in ourselves—a power of will, and corresponding notion of "excellence," in the specifically moral sense. A philosophy of pleasure is thus important, at least for political purposes, even for a Kantian. But the Kantian insists, here with the enthusiastic agreement of the Aristotelian but contrary to popular opinion, that pleasure is not one kind of thing, and that some kinds of pleasure, not merely some kinds of pleasurable activities, are as worthless and destructive as other kinds of pleasure are good.

Aristotle defines "proper pleasures" as those that "complete" the activities on which they supervene (NE X.4, 5). Presupposed, in this definition, is a view that life *has* more than one activity, that it consists of a series of discrete, small movements that can be completed, rather than a continuous striving for some single end or condition. This localized, broken-up conception of our lives strikes me as both deeply out of synch with modern views and deeply right. We spend much of our lives setting ourselves small tasks, and we live, much of the time, for the pleasures of completing these tasks successfully. In each of these tasks, we want a problem to solve, on which we can exercise our judgment. Hence I will call activities that involve these tasks "phronetic" ones. And I shall call the pleasure of mastering a moderately difficult task a "proper pleasure": a pleasure proper to a specific kind of activity, in the sense both that it comes with the successful carrying out of that activity and that it enhances our ability to carry out the activity successfully in the future. Aristotle himself uses the phrase more broadly, for pleasures that complete any kind of activity, not just ones involving judgment—but for reasons that will come out below, I will treat the pleasures "proper" to biological functions rather differently.[1]

2. A farmer gets up in the morning prepared, not "to farm," but to milk the cows, collect eggs, and spend the rest of the day weeding potatoes;

tomorrow, "farming" will take different small, specific forms. An auto mechanic congratulates himself today on having determined that the electrical problem in the Toyota was due to the alternator rather than the battery; tomorrow he will devote his expertise to why the fifth gear seems to be unavailable in a Subaru. His supplier handles people and economic abstractions more than mechanical troubles, but here too there are tasks to perform that require skill, at which he can fail, and that yield pleasure when he succeeds. He must figure out how to apologize to an irate customer without accepting responsibility for a late shipment, or decide whether it is cost effective to use a small but reliable trucker rather than switch to a larger firm despite its occasional failures. What makes these tasks interesting is that they demand good judgment. If the problems they set can be solved merely "mechanically," with a calculator or a rule book, if they require only untrained or minimally trained perception (getting a peg in a hole), then completion of the task brings no pleasure. And if there is too small a problem, or too great a problem, or if we hardly ever see completion or get confirmation of success, or if the marks of success are suspect, we fall into despair. Note that one test of the adequacy of the problem, and its associated task, is that we *fail* sometimes. If success is too constant, we suspect, rightly or wrongly, that we're being set up, that we are not getting true marks or the problem is too easy.

A fortiori, of course, if there are no problems, the task will be merely boring. If the problems are always the same, moreover, if essentially there is only one problem so that once you learn how to solve it future problems require no new judgment, if, that is, there is no *tyche,* no luck, in the task, then it will also quickly become boring, give no pleasure. Finally, the farmer will feel retrospectively as if milking his cow was a waste of time if the milk spills or is stolen, or if people everywhere stop eating dairy products, and the mechanic will feel similarly if the Mercedes' owner junks his car the day after it is repaired. We like to think that our small tasks fit into one another, that they form a network, and fit into the wider network of our society's activities, indeed of all human ones.

Now I said we set *ourselves* constant small tasks, but of course in the examples I have given tasks are very much set *for* the worker. Not all tasks set for workers have this pleasantly phronetic character, moreover; people whose professional life does not allow them such tasks must seek them elsewhere. The assembly-line worker or receptionist whose tasks are extremely repetitive, who has no problems to solve or only very simple ones, looks for phronetic tasks to carry out in the church choir, at the bridge or golf club, in organizing demonstrations for the local trade union or Save-the-Animals fund, in pick-up basketball games, bowling leagues, stamp collections, or a series of seductions and affairs. The completion of a small phronetic task brings a small pleasure, and a pleasure for which one respects oneself; one who must go without any such tasks quickly loses much delight in life and all sense of self-worth.

This has important consequences for political economy. For example: much that is understood today as a search for "community" is more a search for an arena in which one can use, and be honored for using, phronesis; conversely, any community that does not allow each of its members to exercise phronesis is a stifling of personality, rather than something that can enhance one's sense, and achievement, of one's own individuality. For example, again: what goes under the heading of "alienation," for Marxists, and "malaise," for cultural conservatives, is I think very much a matter of people not having enough small phronetic activities to carry out in their lives, or not receiving the rewards of such activities often or directly enough. Marx may have overemphasized the importance of having such activities specifically in one's work life, and the utilitarians never did better than Mill's limp argument for "higher pleasures" to explain why someone can have most of her desires met while feeling overall despair. The claim I want to make is that no one is happy without the opportunity to use judgment, or at least, no one is happy in a way that allows them freedom, allows them what Mill rightly identified, without properly explaining, as a *human* happiness. If this is right, it becomes incumbent on the state to do what it can to compensate for an absence of phronetic activities, to provide opportunities for such activities to those whose work lives do not do so.

3. I decide my house needs cleaning and that the best way to do that is to pick books and children's toys off the floor, do the dishes and clean the counters, and make the beds. On completing these tasks, I feel a palpable sense of relief, of pleasure in having solved a problem successfully. OR: I find the house still looks like a mess, I have no time to do any more cleaning, and I realize that the real problem lies in a pervasive dustiness, so my time would have been better spent on vacuuming alone. I feel frustrated and depressed. OR: It becomes clear to me as I go on that I am quite right that the completion of these tasks *would* solve my problem, but the amount of junk on the floor is so enormous, and my time is so limited, that it also becomes clear to me that I will not in fact reach completion. Again, I feel frustrated, and wonder whether it was worth starting at all. OR: I complete my tasks successfully, am about to breathe my sigh of satisfaction, when my children come tearing in and quickly turn the place back to a disaster area. This time my frustration may turn outwards more than inwards, but again I am likely to wonder whether it was worth my while to bother with cleanup at all.

Some features of this example:

(a) My pleasure in succeeding, if I succeed, is likely to encourage me both to take on housecleaning again and to pursue that end in the same or a very similar way. The pleasure here is thus part of what psychologists call a "feedback mechanism": the pleasure at the end feeds back into the habits of my behavior as a means encouraging me to act in a similar way again; which action, if I once more succeed, results once more in pleasure as an end; that pleasure then becomes a means once more to further action of the same kind. As long as I keep getting rewarded by success, the motivation to behave similarly in future should become greater and greater, such that the pleasure does not merely maintain the habit but strengthen it. The frustrating pain I talked about in each of three ways I might fail will similarly feed back into a motivation *not* to behave similarly in the future, and indeed a series of successes can be badly stymied by one or two striking failures.

   (b) The feedback mechanism can equally well be regarded as a cognitive tool. The pleasures and pains I feel on succeeding and failing in my tasks *teach* me something. It is not merely natural to abandon the putting away of toys if one's children continually defeat every attempt one makes in this direction: taking the task as unachievable is a *rational* response to such failure. Of course, one could learn something more subtle—clean up when the children are in bed, perhaps—and the natural reaction does not always track the most intelligent reaction. The natural reaction to striking failure may well be to give up on a task altogether; a more intelligent one is to do the task differently. But pleasures and pains do generally track something we ought to take note of in our proceedings, some feature of the world with which we are successfully or unsuccessfully negotiating. So this particular kind of pleasure and pain is a cognitive one, something from which we can learn. That is not as true of the "brute" pleasures that come with the satisfaction of bodily needs: the pleasures of ingestion, excretion, rest, and copulation. Not that one cannot learn from the latter as well. Pleasure can indicate that a food is healthy for us, the pain of nausea often indicates that a food is unhealthy, pain in excretion can signal illness, ecstasy or boredom in copulation can signal the appropriateness or inappropriateness of a love partner. But these are blunt and broad mechanisms, perhaps for good biological reasons, and are notoriously unreliable indicators in particular cases. They are also, perhaps again for biological reasons, pleasures and pains that sweep over us mostly without our conscious control. We cannot easily *choose* to enjoy a particular meal or act of copulation by attending to its objectively advantageous features. *Only* attention to such objectively advantageous features, by contrast, can give us pleasure in housecleaning—the task itself hardly conduces to bodily delight. Hence the pleasure achieved or missed is more likely to index some real success or failure than a pleasure tripped off by a biological mechanism. Biological pleasures can be so sweeping, moreover, that they leave little room for thought at all. They overcome us *at the expense of thinking,* and this is indeed part of the relief they bring: satisfying bodily needs, we are relieved from the strain and responsibility of thought.

Finally, there is a category of pleasures that distract us from thinking without satisfying any bodily need, that work directly on brain centers for the activation of positive sensations, or the dulling of negative ones, without going via the completion of either a task-based or a biologically necessary process. Such are the pleasures of alcohol, of narcotics, and, probably, of much TV watching and "light" reading. The mind is directly stimulated to pleasure, or directly dulled to pain, or distracted from all thoughts, including the worrying ones about whether one's tasks are completed and bodily health in order. Very ill and very unsuccessful people notoriously devote much of their lives to pleasures like these, a fact which I take as empirical evidence both that the pleasures in question require little effort, and that they are satisfying precisely because they allow one to set aside one's objective situation.

For convenience, let us label the three pleasures here considered "task completions," "biological pleasures," and "distracting pleasures." I will have more to say in a bit about the consequence of substituting the second, and especially the third, for those of the first.

(c) If I learn from these pleasures and pains, and what I am learning is some set of empirical facts, then I need to have not one or two but many, many of the relevant experiences to learn my subject properly. How, for instance, to determine whether my children's messing up what I have done is a one-time contingency to be generally disregarded or a regular feature of the world I must in future take into account? No other way than by seeing what happens across a *number* of occasions, perhaps with slight alterations here and there, sometimes with precautions of one kind or another to keep the damage under control. Over such a series of occasions, I will learn both whether I need to be concerned about this contingency and how to deal with it. For this reason, the pleasures and pains of housecleaning are appreciated best only when one actually performs many, many small acts of housecleaning, not when one cleans house just once in a long while or hears about it from others.

(d) Note that in the last of the scenarios for how I might fail, I do for a moment achieve the pleasure of success. Then my children come and ruin my work. What this means is not just that a moment of pain follows upon a prior moment of pleasure. Rather, the prior pleasure itself is "reread," in retrospect, as unmerited. Just as a love note turns sour as soon as it is revealed to be a practical joke, so the latter-day failure of my task transforms the pleasure it gave, in memory, into pain. Indeed, like the false love note, a ruined task may bring more pain than a mere failure to complete the task would have brought. Regret at being foolish enough to have thought one had succeeded gets added to the disappointment that comes of failure. The mechanic whose customer junks his Mercedes the day after the repair may wish he hadn't bothered at all—if he sets aside, at least, the monetary reward he gained by his work.

4. Aristotle understands pleasure and pain to be the primary forces in shaping character (NE VII.11, X.9), distinguishes between the biological pleasures that human beings share with other animals and the pleasures proper to particular skill-requiring activities (III.10, VII.12, X.4–5), distinguishes, again, all the latter pleasures as differing in kind according to the activities to which they pertain (X.5), and says that these latter "complete" their respective activities "as an end that supervenes as the bloom of youth does on those in the flower of their age" (1174b33). An activity is "intensified by its proper pleasure" and hindered by a foreign one: "people who are fond of playing the flute are incapable of attending to arguments if they overhear some one playing the flute . . . so the pleasure connected with flute-playing destroys the activity concerned with argument" (1175b2–6). Phronesis generates its own pleasure, moreover, in addition to those generated by the activities requiring phronesis: "the pleasures arising from thinking and learning . . . make us think and learn all the more" (1153a22–4).

Phronesis is also destroyed by excessive indulgence in the purely biological, the animal pleasures (1153a30–33). Hence the importance of moderation. Relying on a strained etymology that modern linguists consider inaccurate, Aristotle says, "This is why we call temperance [*sophrosyne*] by this name; we imply that it preserves one's practical wisdom [*sodsousa ten phronesin*]" (1140b11–13).[2] We preserve our humanity by moderating our animality.

Etymology or no etymology, the point is, I think, quite right. If I fail, over and over, in my phronetic activities, I may increasingly substitute for them alcohol, or sex, or food, or the dull, cowlike reception of the passing scene that makes television diverting. As I do so, a new feedback mechanism comes into play. By immersing myself in pleasures that divert from phronesis, I implicitly tell myself and my neighbors that I am no good at human activities, that I cannot act, only take in stimulation. The more I do this, the more I in fact do lose the skills, habits, and social support that enable me to take on human activities and complete them, to set myself moderately difficult tasks and carry them out. Animal pleasures destroy the human ones. They teach me no facts or specific skills, in part because they require none to be enjoyed, and they destroy the pleasures of phronesis by overwhelming them, by distracting me from something that requires so much more effort. The more I indulge in these animal pleasures, therefore, the more I have no other sources of pleasure, until I really become the choiceless animal I have been advertising myself to be.

5. Since I learn what I can do by setting myself, and succeeding or failing at, many small tasks, what I learn comes from a *habit* of having and expecting certain pleasures, and from pains that squelch contrary habits. What I learn phronetically, unlike what I learn from "intuition" or "argument," can be truly grasped only after my body has actually experienced, and reacted to, a series of particular instances. Contrast how I grasp even an empirical argument. You present me with data, with the results of a series of tests, conducted indeed over time but not necessarily a time *I* experienced by running the tests, and I can "immediately," "in a flash," draw the conclusion. You may need time to show me the appropriate conclusion, but I then grasp it, as it were, "in no time." I can*not* do this with regard to my own habits; I must develop them first. So my use of phronesis, unlike my use of empirical induction, depends constitutively on my actually undergoing the experiences from which it abstracts. Habits of pleasure take the place of test results in such learning, and habits of pleasure cannot, even in principle, be presented in a graph or summary on a piece of paper. I develop my skills at, say, fixing cars only by fixing so many that my body revolts before my head does at, say, the thought of using the wrong tool for a transmission adjustment. Or I spend enough time in politics to feel its incompatibility with my temperament and ideals viscerally. The mode of cognition appropriate to grasping a pattern of particulars with which we must interact is a bodily habit rather than just an exercise of *theoria*.

That we develop habits in this way has the consequence that, once entrenched in a pattern of tasks, we find it difficult to switch to a very different pattern. Adam Smith notes that the differences in human beings are mostly a product of the division of labor rather than the basis of that division, but he insists nevertheless that once each person has gone through the process of differentiation, going back and starting again is rarely an option. He recognizes, ahead of his time and of simplistic biological determinists today, that acculturation is no less difficult to break or reverse for not being "built in" to the body or, indeed, for being a mere influence on behavior rather than a strictly "determining" force. (The baby, but not the adult, can learn any human language.) Phronesis, in the strict Aristotelian sense in which it extends across the human character, keeps us always open to the possibility of change: keeping one's pleasures moderate is a dictate of phronesis precisely because it makes change easier. But even a habit guided by phronesis, as opposed to a twitch or obsessive symptom, can only be unworked the same way it has been worked in, by the slow undoing of our experience and expectation of small pleasures and pains. So to fail in one's main sphere of phronetic activity, even if it is something one wishes one had never undertaken, entails an enormous crisis in what to do with one's life. A career criminal can hardly be expected *simply* to adopt the habits of a gardener or accountant.

6. [S]ince without activity pleasure does not arise, and every activity is completed by the attendant pleasure . . . , pleasures seem, too, to differ in kind. For things different in kind are, we think, completed by different things . . . ; and, similarly, we think that activities differing in kind are completed by things differing in kind. (NE X.5)

One answer to why it is so difficult to find "the purpose of life" may be that life actually has innumerable small purposes, incommensurable with one another because indexed to our innumerable, separate tasks. To sum all of these ends together by means of the pleasure their achievement brings is to substitute a feature of a thing for the thing itself. Pleasure provides a comfortable ethical focus for the arithmetically inclined, since it holds out the possibility that there is something, ethically, we can add up, but that is precisely what makes it such an *in*appropriate measure for what it is being abstracted from. For the pleasure of achieving a task, at least, consists in the achievement of *that* particular task and not in the thin abstraction all task-completions may have in common. (That is what makes it a *proper* pleasure.) By contrast, biological pleasures may be, and distracting ones usually are, fairly interchangeable. Making pleasure central to ethics requires that one blur the distinction between proper pleasures and interchangeable ones; this is the great mistake of Bentham and contemporary preference utilitarians. Focusing on our pleasures as if they were interchangeable "raw feels," rather than respecting the way in which some of them are a mere sign and crown of the successful task-completion at which we are really aiming, constitutes a way of demoting the importance of phronesis in our lives, of trying to substitute an empirical theory instead. Luck, and the irreducible uniqueness of particulars, might thereby be conquered, but so would the reason we want to conquer luck and mystery in the first place: to achieve our ends, which are particular.

We can bring the essential fragility of these ends out more sharply by attending to the temporal dimension of small tasks. I have, say, two hours to clean my house, and I succeed or fail if I achieve my task *in that time*. I may overlook this, thinking, "Well, if I don't clean up now, I can always do it later." And of course this is often true. I'm not a complete failure if I pick up the toys but leave the dust—I simply have more to do when I get home that evening, or later in the week, or maybe the next week. Housecleaning is a task particularly conducive to such thoughts because it always needs to be done again, and only occasionally needs to be done with any urgency. But sometimes it *is* urgent (I have guests coming over), and often I have a chance to do it now and no chance to do it later. Then, even if the strictness of "two hours" is illusory, it is a greater illusion to imagine there is no time frame at all. We should note, finally, that housecleaning is a task with an *a*typical time frame. Many tasks are not accomplished at all unless they are accomplished within a set amount of time. Housecleaning illustrates how elastic that amount of time can be, but also how strictly, despite the elasticity, we remain within temporal bounds.

The philosophical importance of all this is that the small tasks we are considering are deeply *unlike* those generally picked out as capable of making life "meaningful" or not. Faith in Christ, contemplation or meditation, maintenance of one's integrity, even contributing to societal well-being have in principle either no time frame at all, or an infinite time frame. Faith, meditation, contemplation, etc., are literally "eternal" goods—they take one out of time—while Kantian, Marxist, and utilitarian goals lay claim to all time, but to no part of it more than to any other. This makes such goals a bit suspect as truly human ones. Only God could fully achieve the first few; only the entire human species, at best, can achieve the others. An individual human being must have goals she can achieve or fail to achieve within limited periods of time—at most in a single lifetime, but because life is so precarious, better within a few hours, or a day, a few days, at most a year, so that she can take pleasure in her achievements as she goes along, not just before she dies, much less have to face failure then and have no time at all left in which to correct herself.[3]

"Purity of heart is to will one thing," says Kierkegaard. Perhaps, but how then does one live from day to day? (A question he was acutely aware of himself: see the remarkable, frustrating meditation on an outing to Deer Park in the *Concluding Unscientific Postscript*.) If my life were shorter, I could will one thing all right. But I have to get through many days until I can really act on my willing, if I will one thing, and little of what I do on those days is needed for the one thing. If my life consists in a quest for the Holy Grail, how do I make each day that I am *not* on the quest matter? And what do I do if I find it? If all I have to do in life is achieve faith in Jesus as the Christ, what do I do after I succeed? The Christian responds, annoyed, that faith is not a one-time event but an ongoing, lifelong struggle, but even then, what does that amount to in terms of everyday tasks? One traditional response to that question is precisely that faith redeems one from the drudgery of the everyday, that small temporal tasks fade to insignificance once a life becomes consecrated to eternity. It is this view, which has parallels in other religions and even in many secular movements, that I want to combat.

If my overall goal is to attain nirvana, or faith in Christ, or the revolution of the proletariat (so far as this depends on me), I still need to get dressed, eat, and do something with my day, to keep from being bored until my next worship service or rally. I will still learn, if I fail at every ordinary profession I try, or fail repeatedly in my attempts to fill such humdrum needs as finding a comfortable pair of shoes, avoiding hunger or stomach upsets, maintaining friendly relations with the people around me, and attracting a romantic partner, that I am incapable of knowing how to act properly in the world. Among other things, this should, and often will, shake my confidence in the very overarching, supposedly redemptive act of faith that is supposed to free me from these petty failings. If my judgment is so poor in everything else, why should I trust it when it comes to religious or political matters? If my actual, particular will is so ineffective, why should I believe that I can make use of a transcendental, general will, by which I might plunk for faith or political utopia? Success in small tasks gives me psychic energy and direction, so I need a constant supply of that success if I am to aim at anything larger.

Now I might be able to suspend all daily activity if I knew that I would die, or see redemption, very soon. It was wise of the Albigensians to baptize people only just before they died. One gets one's ordinary tasks completely out of the way, *then* plunks for "willing one thing." Paul preached redemption in the immediate future, and the excitement of preaching it and holding communities together in the interim (itself a set of small tasks) probably sustained him through his short and extraordinary life. One can imagine also that, for a few days, a new follower of Jim Jones, David Koresh, or any of the other contemporary millenialists, might be able to forego all professional activity, all ordinary entertainment, all sex, perhaps even all food, in the thrill of expecting an immediate, unprecedentedly radical change in her life and the world around her. After that initial ecstasy, however, the extraordinary regimen of the cult must simply take over from her prior ordinary regimen, sustaining the thrill with periodic emotional reinforcements while providing at the same time a social world and set of tasks to substitute for the lost temporal world she thinks she has abandoned but still needs.

Aside from joining such a cult, you can blind yourself to the regimen required by daily life by being so immersed in satisfying bodily needs and desires that you have no time to adopt small ends of your own. This can be accomplished in two ways, a very painful and a very pleasant one. You can be forced to work, by a master or by desperate poverty, for many hours in some hard, exhausting activity—mining, chopping trees, carrying goods or people around all day—so that you need every ounce of energy to keep your body going while you work, and then you eat, drink, excrete, and drop off to sleep. Or you can smother your senses in food, drink, light entertainment, and sex, dull them with alcohol or directly satisfy them with heroin, and thus never face the challenge of how one finds small and worthwhile activities in which to succeed. Traditional religions, and Marxist movements before the revolutions at which they aimed, thrived on the first way, on the fact that so many lives were overwhelmed by pain. Exhausted people with no "life of their own," no small temporal tasks other than those forced on them by biological need, fell into their beds with hope for some kind of ultimate salvation as their only comfort. If one works hard and then dies young, it is almost as though the salvation offered is something in the immediate term: before one has time to worry about the delay, it will be time to gain or lose one's lifetime goal. Cults and political ideologies in the contemporary world thrive on the second way, on the fact that people now desperately want to be overwhelmed by pleasure. A world that despairs of any task's being worthwhile is one in which a steady stream of unearned pleasure seems most appealing. In both cases the individual fades from existence as an independent entity, becomes hardly discernible from someone comatose or severely retarded, someone who needs to be fully cared for by others. If I never have the opportunity, or never take the opportunity, to set myself tasks, I don't know whether I can achieve *anything*, including faith in Christ, or proletarian consciousness, or a contribution to a more decent world. I can be a subject only of a paternalistic regime, and I can worship a God only blindly, not with my rational faculties intact. I cannot emerge from tutelage, in the political, spiritual, or any other realm.

All this is not meant entirely to delegitimize religions and secular movements with singular, overarching visions of the human end. But such a religion or movement can respect individuality only if it combines its goal with daily activities—as both Christian churches and Marxist political parties have tended in fact to do. You go out to work again as usual, but you say a blessing this time before you take up the spade, reminding yourself that your efforts serve a higher goal. Or you make sure to discuss the class struggle, and the emptiness of liberal "rights" theories, with your fellow workers. Perhaps you tithe your earnings and give that to the church or the Movement. You have sex after reminding yourself that procreation helps spread your guru's word, or increase your class's power. Your church or union forms choirs, reading groups, even a theater, in which everyone can excel at some particular skill while believing that this will keep alive the revolutionary spirit, or serve the greater glory of God.

A faith can also be translated directly into a set of tasks of its own. If sexual temptation gets designated as a sin, one can turn every day into a struggle against the Devil, or Evil Inclination, with small battles to be constantly lost or won. Add anger and pride as sinful modes of thinking, and there are battles everywhere. "Today the Evil One appeared to me as a river," a believer declares, having that morning gotten frustrated when he couldn't find a boat or bridge. But he squelched his anger without venting it on anyone, so he adds triumphantly, "I thwarted him!" Another time Evil might appear as a political movement, or a potential friend, whose tendency to encourage my pride I only belatedly discover. The work of *uncovering* appearances of evil, let alone of defeating them, becomes a task that requires ingenuity. So phronesis and its associated small, temporal pleasures return to the heart of the faith, no matter how much that faith may proclaim that it lifts one out of the moment and into eternity. What kept most Christians christian over the centuries was not residency in some eternal now, but the ongoing process of defeating God's enemies, both inside and outside themselves.

The problem with all this today is that struggling against lust, anger, and pride becomes much less interesting when, at most, one sees the impulse to that struggle as a product of the superego rather than of God. I suppose one could take every day as a fight of ego to wend its way through the foolishness of id and superego—and some convinced Freudians, or people whose therapists are convinced Freudians, do see the world that way—but the knowledge that only one's own health demands such a struggle, that only one's own choice makes health, mental or otherwise, so important, that it will all be over when one dies, and that one can spend the intervening years distracted by work or sensory pleasures instead, makes the struggle seem, to most people, petty and uninteresting. Unless a modern faith can convince its adherents of the same Good/Evil battle in the desires that used to make sense in a psychologically more innocent world, it must find new daily tasks if it wants to survive. This is not easily done. Reform Jews and liberal Christians have tried to substitute social causes for the personal projects that occupied earlier believers, but improving society has but a limited appeal if we believe that each individual, once society is adequately improved, will have nothing much to live for. Perhaps the modern equivalent of the old daily struggle against the devil is the 12-step program, where alcoholics and addicts of various kinds manage to turn every social occasion, sometimes every meal, into a world of temptations to be resisted, and share the stratagems they devise for these battles with a group of like-minded believers. But a world in which only the unhealthy can take their small successes seriously is a world in which small people—individuals—no longer have a healthy place.

7. The pleasure attendant on completing a phronetic task does not always come immediately. A mechanic may solve a problem with a carburetor but have to leave before it becomes clear that his solution has

worked. A financial expert may propose a cost-cutting measure whose success will appear only after a year or more has gone by. Where there is such a long lag time between completion of a task and evidence of its success, the approval of peers and supervisors commonly stands in, temporarily, for objective confirmation. But such approval may also be delayed, and where it is, the agent whose reward is thus denied tends to become depressed, to lose confidence and interest in his or her work. The feedback mechanism works here exactly as though the task had been unsuccessfully completed. The agent learns the *wrong* message, even if she had reason to believe she was acting competently. "Gratification deferred is gratification denied," a wit once quipped, and the quip contains a good deal of truth. If we go too long without the pleasure of savoring our phronetic successes, our ability to judge will deteriorate. We will lose confidence in it and, therefore, the will to use it.

On the other hand, of course, neither gratification nor justice can but be deferred in many cases, and it is a significant part of human maturity to come to terms with that fact. We cannot always see our successes as soon as they happen, nor can we expect other people to appreciate our abilities always and immediately. Certain professions, especially, require a good deal of patience in awaiting success. Financial consultants, politicians, artists, and intellectuals—in these and a number of other professions, successful people are precisely those who have a knack for seeing long-term trends that others do *not* see, for anticipating an economic or political condition, a mode of aesthetic appreciation or a method of investigation, the reality or acceptability of which is a long time coming. We all know the stories of the scientist or artist who struggles for years to get her ideas known, and then finally becomes a huge success. Here the small phronetic successes that had to be amassed over the years went, for the most part, without the pleasure that should have attended them. That we should especially admire someone who manages such a life is only appropriate, both because without people of such patience great novelty could never come about and because their lives are undoubtedly very difficult—they are long deprived of a crucial element, perhaps the crucial element, of happiness. The ability to defer the pleasures of phronetic tasks is important to society, but it is important the way extraordinary strength and courage are: as something we all would like some members of our society to have but cannot demand of anyone. In fact it is something we should rather *not* see too much of. A few of those whose artistic or scientific or financial success is long deferred will turn out to have been geniuses in the making. Most, however, will turn out to be just the failures everyone took them for. The feedback mechanism we described earlier would not work at all, there would be no reason to attribute cognitive value to the proper pleasures and pains of phronetic tasks, unless in general we can read off the evidence of our successes and failures fairly readily, and correctly infer from them whether we should or should not continue to pursue the paths we have been taking. Thus the regularly disappointed scientist or artist may, should, and often does change careers. Adopting a stoic attitude towards one's failures, even towards the deferral of evidence of one's success, may on occasion be a virtue that makes for a great scientist or artist, but more often it is a barrier to recognizing the changes one should make in one's life. Indeed, many who are halted by this barrier and then succeed against the odds do so at the cost of acquiring an arrogance and paranoia that makes them quite impossible as human beings. Even at its best, then, too much stoicism about proper pleasures can be a virtue of mixed value to society.

Stoicism is important to this discussion because the stoic philosophy, more than any other, plays down the importance of proper pleasures. Stoics recommend performing one's tasks without expecting a proper "completion" for them, whether in terms of objective success or societal approval. The task alone is in one's own hands, runs the familiar line from the likes of Epictetus, so one should be satisfied with doing that well, regardless of whether it is crowned with success or approval. Success and failure depend on luck, which is out of one's hands, hence not to be expected or regretted. But most of us do not feel this way. Most of us share Aristotle's view on this crucial difference between Aristotle and the Stoics: luck in fact irremediably makes up part of what counts as "happiness," and failing to have the luck, in particular, of seeing our best efforts crowned with the end at which they aim is something we cannot afford to ignore. To ignore it means not to learn from it. To take pleasure in one's "best efforts" regardless of repeated failure in achieving their aims is just to aim badly, not to put forward one's best efforts at all. Repeated failure is a sign that one should alter one's aim, or give up a kind of task altogether.

8. We get pleasure not only from achieving *some* end but from achieving the particular end we foresaw when we undertook the task: it is part of phronesis to know what it is aiming at. While I can take a sort of bemused pleasure in helping humanity, or myself, quite accidentally, it is a tribute to my *lack* of ability, *lack* of skill in knowing what means bring about what ends, that my writing what I take to be a serious philosophical treatise, say, should wind up providing great hilarity to connoisseurs of academic parody, or my attempt to fix a car should provide a comfortable feeling of superiority to everyone with the chance to observe my ineptitude.

But it is also part of phronesis, indeed what distinguishes phronesis from mere *techne,* that I learn about and work on my overall character in

all my small activities, rather than simply complete those activities themselves, and it is part of improving character to learn what talents one
lacks, and how to fit oneself into a world of luck, a world that limits the
effectiveness of one's choices. It is thus part of phronesis to take unexpected results in any one activity as a guide to what to expect, from that
activity and others, in the future. I therefore can in fact take a certain
pleasure in my own failures, especially my failures to attain the exact end
I have set for myself, despite their simultaneous tendency to induce frustration. There is a certain pleasure in realizing that I am good at academic parody, or not good at repairing cars. Learning from one's mistakes, including one's mistaken expectations, is a large part of learning
from experience in general. There is a certain pleasure to be gained precisely from wryly putting the pain of embarrassment or frustration to
good use, and a pleasure in having the maturity to take precisely that
kind of pleasure in one's pains—especially since the more one can do it,
the more one achieves the virtue of patience and overcomes the vice of
anger. So phronesis enjoys succeeding in its small tasks, but it can also
enjoy learning from failure.

   The stoic goes from here to the claim that one need never take pain in
the results of one's actions. As long as the intentions are right, the results
will always either pleasurably satisfy those intentions or disappoint the
intentions only to provide the pleasure of learning from failure. But, as an
exceptionless rule, this is a serious mistake. I may set out to write a paper
today, fall into conversation with someone instead, then have that conversation broken off by a need to take care of some errands, and then fail
to accomplish any of my errands. After all that, I am likely just to be
annoyed, not to be capable of taking up failure into the pleasure of learning about myself and the world any further. When unsuccessful tasks
form a long chain, I will find the always mixed and dubious pleasure in
learning from failure weakening and weakening until it peters out altogether. And this is a *justifiable* reaction, since repeated failure indicates
that I lack the skills to find my way around, even if a single failure here or
there can enrich those skills. Eventually I must stop just cultivating my
phronesis and use it: success at some finite point is precisely the aim of
phronesis. There is no elegant criterion for determining where that point
lies, simply the empirical facts of human time—the time span over which
individual human beings grow up, act fruitfully, age, and die. In my
large-scale projects, I can probably afford to fail for about ten to fifteen
years after reaching maturity, or, if I am very patient or distracted, perhaps until the age of fifty. In small scale projects, I can afford to fail for
only a few weeks, or days, before self-doubt and despair justifiably take
over. I am a noble stoic if I take disappointments in work, love, and play

as simply "learning experiences" for a year or so; I am a fool if I so take them for a lifetime.

9. When it is necessary to defer the pleasure of one's phronetic tasks, one way to do so is to take on other such tasks, in which one has a better chance of succeeding. I have to wait a long time before I know if my article has been accepted, my grant application has come through, my book has been well received, etc. So I go regularly to the gym and play basketball. The pleasures I would like to get from the problem-solving I do in my writing I get instead from—I transfer to—the problem-solving I do on the court. Of course there is no direct connection between the two, and no necessity that the pleasures of the second should make up, even in the short term, for being deprived of the pleasures of the first. But perhaps, for contingent, psychological reasons, the substitution more or less works. Most people have some such means of substitution, and that is how they get through the failure, or deferral of success, of tasks in what we might call their primary phronetic arena. One comes back from an unsatisfactory job to cook happily; another substitutes professional or charitable work for a frustrating domestic arena; a third identifies himself increasingly with his musical skills, to distract from or compensate for what he regards as an unsuccessful marriage or job or political life. These substitutions often do not quite work, but they do well enough to ease the pain of failing where one most wanted to succeed. (The best stoic advice may well be to cultivate such an alternative arena when one fails in one's primary tasks, rather than to ignore the failures altogether.) Ideally, one has a primary arena of small phronetic tasks and an array of secondary ones on which to fall back here and there. Then trouble starts only when one fails, for a significant period of time, in the office *and* at the kitchen counter *and* on the basketball court *and* in the church choir or bridge club. Failure in all one's phronetic tasks, either where they are located in just one arena or across a series of alternative arenas, can bring on suicidal depression.

It can also lead to addiction, the characteristic American way of running away from one's individuality. I decide to seek satisfaction by exercising when my day at the office goes badly. And if the weather is bad and the gym is closed, I decide to transfer my desire for a small success, again, to a game with my children or a piece of much-needed travel planning. The more of these transfers I can achieve, the more I can pride myself on internal strength, patience, self-command. But what if the office goes badly *and* the gym is closed *and* my children crankily reject my game *and* the call I make to my travel agency never gets through? Then I sink into a chair to read a silly book or watch television, or in some other way distract myself from myself for a little while. Everyone has a day like this here and there. When they start to add up, however, one thing they start to add up to is overall failure at the office and in my family and in my leisure activities, and therefore, perhaps, to an overall turning to distractions of myself from myself—more and more TV, alcohol, even long hours simply spent asleep. The accumulation of these failures, and certainly of these distractions, is not only a clinical criterion of depression, but the beginning of *evidence* that I do not know how to "get on in the world," to "find my way about." If I fail in each phronetic activity, then I may well lack phronesis altogether, and if I lack phronesis altogether, I lack the psychological wherewithal by which to connect any dreams, desires, or willed ends I may have to the empirical world in which they can be realized. Unless I desire or will purely to be a fantasist—I suspect no one in fact does the first[4] and no one rightly, on Kant's account at least, does the second—I might as well then globally give up not only on the hope that I might *achieve* what I will but on willing itself.[5] I might as well see myself as a passive part of the world, something to which things happen rather than something with its own power to make things happen, and to start watching myself undergo fate, watching even the irritating features of my personality simply play themselves out, rather than trying to change either my self or the things it bumps along through. The dullness of alcohol, of endless channel-surfing, perhaps best of all of prolonged sleep, comes to seem appropriate to what I am; I seem to be, properly, more a "what," a dull thing, than a person at all anymore.

10. One solution to the deferral of completion in small tasks is to substitute social approval for the objective measures of success. Then the rewards of phronesis become bound to the presence of a "supportive community," surrounding each individual with emotional warmth. To value this emotional support by itself is to put the cart before the horse, to misunderstand the characteristic way in which communal ties reinforce phronetic success—by *supervening* on such success rather than by *constituting* it (much like proper pleasures themselves). But there are good reasons why social approval can stand in provisionally for the criterion of success in a small task, and those reasons provide whatever grounds there are for supposing that communism or communitarianism can alleviate the moral ills that come of liberal, individualist society. Having a community is indeed necessary, for most of us, if we want to maintain our confidence in our own capacities for judgment, and insofar as communities do this, insofar as they reinforce the phronetic activities of individuals, they are indeed empirical aids to freedom. Insofar as they merely provide direct emotional bonds, however—a sense of "belonging" and unconditional

love—they tend to be stifling and dangerously parochial. This is a point difficult and important enough to deserve some elaboration.

Adam Smith, who had the deepest respect for the importance of community to our individual senses of self-worth, also wrote: "In proportion to the degree of self-command which is necessary in order to conquer our natural sensibility, the pleasure and pride of the conquest are so much the greater; and this pleasure and pride are so great that no man can be altogether unhappy who completely enjoys them. . . . [T]his complete enjoyment of his own self-applause, though it may not altogether extinguish, must certainly very much alleviate his own sufferings" (TMS III.3.26–7). This strikes me as exactly right. But if so, then it is a mistake, commonly made, to assume that the pleasures of success in a task are identical with the pleasures of being acclaimed by others *for* such success. The lonely life need not be a miserable one, as long as it requires a high degree of self-command. The humble life chosen by an Albert Schweitzer or forced on an Indian peasant is one whose hardships do not lie in a lack of things to accomplish; it is filled, on the contrary, with opportunities for well-deserved "self-applause." The mountaineer struggles mightily but achieves constant small successes; the soldier and the itinerant worker have lives packed with tasks to accomplish, and tasks, indeed, of unquestionable importance: failure, in many cases, literally means death. These people may face wounds, illness, disfigurements, and great bodily pain; they may face humiliation and loneliness; but they do not face the dull emptiness that comes of having nothing phronetic to do, nothing with any interesting choices to which one might bend an intelligently sifted experience. These people *must* use their judgment and they know, without being told by others, when they succeed and when they fail. Hence one pleasure they do have is that of self-applause, and if they remain psychically strong and confident, it is in good part because "this pleasure and pride are so great that no man can be altogether unhappy who . . . enjoys them."

So one *can* live on the pleasure of self-applause alone. But if this pleasure is not to be deluded, one will do well to lead a life of truly harsh struggle. Otherwise the self-applause will tend to drown out the self-censure with which, to be properly earned, it must be mixed. In a life of struggle, real external pains will regularly prompt, and can in any case replace, the pains of self-censure. To some extent, this balance can be achieved also where there is clear material evidence for success in a task, evidence that the agent performing the task can recognize by him or herself. We need, not only to succeed, but to *know* we have succeeded. That's fine for the car mechanic or the housecleaner. At the end the car either works or it doesn't, the house is either clean or it isn't. Perhaps at some early stage one needs training, socialization, to learn how to *recognize* what counts as a car's working or a house's being clean, but after that point recognizing one's own success is not something that itself requires much judgment, thus not something for which one needs the help of other people. Quite without social approval, even without social contact, a mechanic or gardener or housecleaner can carry phronetic tasks to successful completion and receive the small, proper pleasures that constitute the reward of such completion. But that is not so for all trades or skills. Most of us need the applause of others to supplement our self-approbation and self-censure: "We must endeavour to view [our character and conduct] with the eyes of other people, or as other people are likely to view them. When seen in this light, if they appear to us as we wish we are happy and contented. But it greatly confirms this happiness and contentment when we find that other people, viewing them with those very eyes with which we, in imagination only, were endeavouring to view them, see them precisely in the same light in which we ourselves had seen them" (TMS III.2.3). For the pleasures of approbation, and for keeping the pleasure of our self-approbation honest rather than deluded—these are the reasons, above all, for which we need a community.

With this we come, finally, to an intersection with Hannah Arendt's famous account of judgment.[6] Arendt views judgment as a paradigm of human action because it is a type of *performance*, something done at least implicitly before spectators. What kind of action can be worthwhile in and of itself? It is depressing and ultimately self-defeating to think of all action as instrumental, everything we do as serving some end that in turn serves some other end, that in turn . . . and so on in an infinite chain. It is hardly less depressing, hardly less undermining of meaningful action, to suppose that all we do serves our biological needs alone. Arendt responds to these lines of reasoning by envisioning our striving as ultimately a performance that can be worth watching for its own sake. What kind of action can be *intrinsically* worthwhile? That done on a stage, which people watch purely for the excellence it displays.

But this has the unsavory implication that some of us, indeed most of us, will have to be spectators so that others can play out their lovely performances. Arendt's view is thus at least implicitly elitist. That, however, is not its only problem. It also, in the end, does not solve the problem it sets out to solve. For performances are themselves, normally, things we enjoy for instrumental reasons, because they entertain us or teach us something or "elevate" us morally, and if we refuse this line of thinking by holding beauty to be a good in and of itself, we threaten to make beauty less worthwhile than at first it seemed. The slogan "art for art's sake" notoriously produced something less than art at all. In addition, there is something uncomfortably trivializing about construing judgment as "an act," in the theatrical sense, about a notion of action that blurs the distinction between virtue and hypocrisy, that dissolves our selves entirely into our social appearances.

To get a finer sense of the relationship between judgment and social approval, we can return to Smith:[7]

> The all-wise Author of Nature has . . . taught man to respect the sentiments and judgments of his brethren; to be more or less pleased when they approve of his conduct, and to be more or less hurt when they disapprove of it. He has made man, if I may say so, the immediate judge of mankind. . . .
>
> But though man has . . . been rendered the immediate judge of mankind . . . an appeal lies from his sentence to a much higher tribunal, to the tribunal of their own consciences . . . , to that of the man within the breast, the great judge and arbiter of their conduct. . . . The jurisdiction of the man within, is founded altogether in the desire of praise-worthiness, and in the aversion to blame-worthiness, in the desire of possessing those qualities, and performing those actions, which we love and admire in other people. (TMS III.2.31–2)

Ultimately we seek, says Smith, not praise but praiseworthiness—"to be that thing, which, though it should be praised by nobody, is, however, the natural and proper object of praise." (III.2.1) In some cases, at least, "so far is the love of praise-worthiness from being derived altogether from that of praise; that the love of praise seems, . . . in a great measure, to be derived from that of praise-worthiness" (III.2.3). Smith here distinguishes himself from the blind emotional determinism of Hume—the pleasure in praiseworthiness and displeasure in blameworthiness arises from whether, in truth, we deserve praise or not, rather than from any mere behaviorally programmed response to external stimuli—and, as Nicholas Phillipson has pointed out, from Mandeville's identification of virtue with hypocrisy.[8] The standard for virtue is ultimately something individuals can assess, just as they assess ordinary factual claims, independently of other people's opinions;[9] virtue itself, correlatively, is not mere performance. So Smith places a severe obstacle in the way of any Arendtian reduction of phronetic activity to something aimed at the applause of spectators, something essentially "other-directed."

This is only one side of the picture, however, and not the one Smith characteristically emphasizes. We can in principle satisfy the desire to be praiseworthy without external approval and disapproval; we can therefore in principle live by "self-approbation" and disapprobation alone. In fact, however, on many if not most occasions, we need external reinforcement for our own opinion as to whether we have hit the right mark or not. Other people's "approbation necessarily confirms our own self-approbation. Their praise necessarily strengthens our own sense of our own praise-worthiness." This is especially true where we have some reason to doubt our own judgment, where it is hard to tell with any exactness whether we have successfully achieved our end or not: "The agreement or disagreement both of the sentiments and judgments of other people with our own, is, in all cases . . . of more or less importance to us, exactly in proportion as we ourselves are more or less uncertain about the propriety of our own sentiments, about the accuracy of our own judgments" (III.2.16). Smith illustrates this both with the uneasiness a person of nice sentiment might feel "lest he should have yielded too much even to what might be called an honourable passion; to . . . just indignation, perhaps," and by the uncertainty a would-be artist feels at his first, inexperienced efforts: "The beauty of poetry is a matter of such nicety, that a young beginner can scarce ever be certain that he has attained it. Nothing delights him so much, therefore, as the favourable judgments of his friends and of the public; and nothing mortifies him so severely as the contrary" (III.2.19). By contrast, mathematicians and natural scientists can achieve by themselves "the most perfect assurance, both of the truth and of the importance of their discoveries," and therefore tend to be "very indifferent about the reception which they may meet with from the public" (III.2.20). The latter are not, therefore, while poets and people of nice sentiment are, inclined "to form themselves into factions and cabals, either for the support of their own reputation, or for the depression of that of their rivals" (III.2.22). Only people who are uncertain whether they have succeeded or not—which is all of us, in our moral activities, and most but importantly *not* all of us in our professional ones—must worry about the judgments of "the man within" being overwhelmed and "confounded by the vehemence and clamour of the man without" (III.2.32).

I think this delineates, with nice care, the role social approval plays in granting us completion for a phronetic activity. The car mechanic can be satisfied with the quiet pleasures of knowing he is doing a good job, although a nice word from the boss or a customer now and then will not come amiss. The same goes for the scientist, for the farmer, and perhaps for innumerable craftspeople, at least once they have learned the standards of excellence in their particular field. But many people, especially in the service economy that increasingly dominates the West, measure their success in their small tasks entirely by whether their bosses or colleagues give them a compliment, a raise, or some other token of approval. I don't know whether I have given a good presentation, as an academic to a class or a business person to a meeting, or whether I am doing an appropriately friendly or efficient job as a salesclerk, unless I hear from the people I work with to that effect. Of course, there are some external signs of success in these arenas—it may clearly be due to my efforts that certain customers keep coming back—and I don't need to receive approval in so many words: an offer of a job from another company can be rather more satisfying than any compliment. The point is that without *some* sign of social approval, my self-approbation will not do the job of keeping up my self-respect. Success in these arenas is so nebulous, so difficult to judge with nicety; self-deceit is so easy where vagueness prevails; and self-deceit is such a danger, so severely obstructive of my ability to change my character; that without the reinforcement of approbation from others, my own silent praise for my own efforts falters, fades, and eventually may turn right around into bitter self-hatred or insecurity. I cannot get the proper pleasure of succeeding in these small tasks without approval from others, and over time I will start experiencing the pain proper to failure instead—even *if,* were judicious and disinterested spectators to be consulted, my work would be adjudged a success. Hence the cloying dependency on their bosses so many people who work in business feel, for their psychological health as well as for material support; hence the dissatisfaction work in a large, anonymous business often gives people, even when it has reasonable hours and affords a decent living; hence the tendency of many people today to turn from phronetic to animal pleasures, to drown the sorrows of feeling like a failure, in alcohol, television, or casual sex. An excellent example of the importance I am attributing to social approval is the main complaint of the air traffic controllers who struck in 1981: that the nature of their work was such that their work elicited a response only when they failed—when a plane crashed or almost crashed—and that this made the painstaking efforts required of them particularly grueling. And an excellent example of the widespread failure to understand the place of phronetic pleasures in our lives is the way most people dismissed the traffic controllers' complaint as petty.

Those who do recognize the need for social approval often respond to the problem of its absence by proposing a restructuring of the workplace such that bosses are encouraged, or required, to say nice things to their workers. This is not only a policy likely to be cumbersome, at least in businesses where there are large numbers of people under each supervisor, but it misses Smith's point that people seek not praise alone but praise*worthiness,* and that praise itself is valuable only as a marker for praiseworthiness. Artificially jacked up social reinforcement is counterproductive, at least if the motivation for so spreading "good will" becomes, as it inevitably will become, widely known.[10] Better responses to lack of regular approval in the workplace are (1) to restructure the nature of workers' daily activities so that they always have some phronetic tasks in which they can measure their own success, or (2) to provide opportunities for community, centered around some phronetic activity or activities, *outside* the workplace, such that one who occupies an uninteresting job can use her judgment to achieve ends, and be rewarded with approval for achieving those ends, in a musical or athletic or political arena.

Arendt is thus partly right. Phronesis, and the activities it guides, is first of all and most of the time a performance. It is just not *essentially* a performance. We judge with and towards others, in an arena surrounded by spectators, but only in an attempt to grasp a criterion that lies beyond our own individual judgments. That leaves us with a number of arenas, perhaps secondary ones, in which we do not need social approval at all, and more importantly means that the approval we do need must track some higher, less subjective standard of worth. Judgment is social but its success or failure is not *constituted* by society's judgments. To compensate for the lack of phronesis and its proper rewards in modern society what we need is, not "consciousness-raising," not a program of empty pats on the back by bosses to their secretaries, but more *arenas of phronetic activity*, more realms in which people can work on tasks that have small successes and failures, and in which they can be recognized, by others around them, for the achievements they make in these arenas. Not empty honors, but the chance to win real ones, can alone compensate for a sense that one's life means nothing to the world. Hence the solution to the alienation, the anomie, so many people experience can be neither cheap nor theatrical, as a proliferation of meaningless honors would be. Instead it requires the real costs in efficiency that come of recongregating labors rather than only subdividing them; giving low-level workers and officials more responsibility than, at least at the beginning, one has any reason to think they can competently handle; and giving power to unreliable people rather than reliable machines. If we refuse to do these things in our political, social, and economic arenas, then we may indeed build technology that gives us smoother, healthier, and more bodily pleasurable lives, but the people living those lives will more and more resemble dumb animals rather than human beings.

11. The idea that phronetic activities take place in a number of arenas has important implications. Far too many political philosophers and political economists identify just one arena as the appropriate, the best, or even the only realm in which phronesis can be developed. The so-called civic humanists, from Machiavelli through James Harrington to the latter's English and American followers, identified military prowess, or at least military training and the readiness to defend oneself with one's own arms, as this realm.[11] From Aristotle they learned that the nature of man is to rule and to direct one's particular end towards a more universal "common good," and that both ends are achieved by phronetic activity in the defense of one's community. "To rule" can also mean to shape or administer laws, of course, and another tradition that grew out of Aristotle and Machiavelli calls for citizens to participate in politics: this comprises the participatory democrats from Rousseau and Jefferson to

Hannah Arendt and Benjamin Barber. The debates of a governing assembly here take the place of armies as the proper venue for developing and displaying phronesis. And yet a third tradition influenced by both Aristotle and Machiavelli is the Marxist one, according to which labor, and only labor, is the proper realm for phronetic activity.[12] Man is a *homo faber*, says this tradition, so choosing phronetically means exercising phronesis in one's worklife above all. Judgment in one's leisure time and dullness in the office is a mere dispersal of oneself, a disintegration of one's personality.

In contrast with all these monists, who not accidentally tend to favor revolutionary reworkings of society to bring about the centrality of the sphere they favor, there stands in great relief the sensible pluralism of Adam Smith. Yes, military participation can help one develop phronesis, he says; yes, the workings of politics can also be a realm for such exercise of the ability to choose (TMS VI.ii.13, WN V.i.f.60); and yes, again, the increasing dullness of worklife in advanced societies can severely retard or corrupt human personality. But *all* these realms, not any one of them, allow for the use and display of judgment, and one's failure in or absence from one can be compensated for somewhere else. The nature of man is not to defend oneself phronetically, nor to debate politics phronetically, nor to labor phronetically, but simply to engage in phronetic activity, and only in *that* sense is it to rule—to rule, that is, over oneself. The spheres of war, politics, and labor can all serve the individual's need to develop phronesis, but the point is that *they* ultimately serve each of *us*, not that our individual development matters only if it serves one of them. Philosophically more astute than the other traditions we have mentioned and closer to Aristotle,[13] this view also allows for a more flexible, more gradual, and more commonsensical approach to politics. Thus Smith's suggestions that society compensate for the dullness induced by very specialized work with militia training and public education (V.i.f). Thus his indication (V.i.g) also that small churches and similarly small-scale communal organizations may provide arenas of social approval, against the background of which phronetic activity can be performed and judged, for the masses in commercial cities.[14] These are not mere Band-aids on a huge social wound, not mere homeopathic remedies, as Marx bitterly called them,[15] but intelligent hints, still useful today, as to how we might move towards a world in which all have meaningful lives without violently overthrowing the societies we already have, or abandoning the liberties and material growth that have come with capitalism. The gradualism of Smith is a reflection of his own phronesis, but also of his placement of phronesis alone, and not of any more specific activity, at the heart of his account of human nature. If human beings are essentially "phronetic," but not phronetic in any particular way, then their freedom consists in any activity that enhances or preserves phronesis. A state that enables us to gain judgment, and live it out according to our own judgment of how it should be used, will be a state that guarantees liberty. No further intrusion into the details of our lives, and no more radical change of human nature, is necessary.

12. Men lose their high aspirations as they lose their intellectual tastes, because they have not time or opportunity for indulging them; and they addict themselves to inferior pleasures, not because they deliberately prefer them, but because they are either the only ones to which they have access or the only ones which they are any longer capable of enjoying. (Mill, *Utilitarianism*, ch. II, ¶ 7)

Another political implication. A minimal condition for participation in a sphere of phronetic activity, especially if one's work life lacks any interesting tasks, is that one have the *time* to discover, and develop the skills for, such a sphere. It follows that from the importance of judgment and its proper pleasures we can resuscitate the old liberal idea that government needs to ensure adequate *leisure* for its citizenry. Once a prominent part of reform movements everywhere, that idea has all but disappeared in recent years,[16] partly, I think, because of philosophical weaknesses in the standard arguments for it. John Stuart Mill distinguished between higher and lower pleasures, using the distinction to urge public financing for education, voyages of exploration, and scholarly research; his follower, Alfred Marshall, developed the argument for giving working people more leisure. "It is better to be a human being dissatisfied than a pig satisfied; better to be Socrates dissatisfied than a fool satisfied," said Mill, and "if the fool, or the pig, are of a different opinion, it is because they only know their side of the question. The other party to the comparison knows both sides."[17] The pleasures of our "higher faculties" are simply better in kind than those we share with "the lower animals," and the proof of this is that the former are preferred by "the only competent judges" to render such a verdict: those educated well enough to know what the pleasures of the higher faculties are. It follows that there can be commodities of which the average consumer is not "a competent judge," "of the worth of which the demand of the market is by no means a test." These will tend to be things that, instead of "ministering to inclinations [or] serving the daily uses of life," improve the character of human beings, make us "wiser and better"—among other things, presumably, in the pleasures we choose to enjoy.[18] From this it follows neatly, as Mill argues, that a host of goods must be chosen for the public by the judgment of an educated political elite, rather than by consumer demand. Marshall shows how leisure for the working classes will be one of these goods: "[I]t is only through freedom to use leisure as they will, that people can learn to use leisure well: and no class of manual workers, who are devoid of leisure, can have much self-respect and become full citizens. Some time free from the fatigue of work that tires without educating, is a necessary condition of a high standard of life."[19]

Laudable as both Mill's and Marshall's policy recommendations are, they as well as their philosophical justification have been vigorously attacked by thinkers on the left as well as the right. To the former, Mill's distinction of higher from lower pleasures is elitist nonsense that entrenches upper-class entertainments at the cost both of popular culture and of moneys that could go to more important projects (housing, job training, public health). To the latter, Mill's distinction encourages violations of people's liberty to do with their labor, and their incomes, whatever they please. For both, it represents unjustifiable paternalism.

Now, working from expressed preferences has been a methodological dogma among both left- and right-wing economists since the 1940s,[20] and if we begin with expressed preferences alone, Mill's argument is weak indeed. There is little empirical evidence that people, once exposed to his "higher pleasures," will express preferences for them. That he and his friends preferred scholarship over entertainment, or leisure over work, is evidence for nothing but their own tastes. Many people who have encountered Beethoven and Shakespeare continue to prefer Elton John and Danielle Steel. And people widely accept contracts giving them higher pay rather than more leisure, widely seem to prefer more material comforts over the time to develop new, active pleasures.

But Mill's argument can be reconstructed as a case for the priority of choice, and specifically phronetic choice, over pleasure of any kind.[21] The higher pleasures are higher, on this reading, because to enjoy them we need to reflect on their objects, and they thereby encourage us in the use of the faculties by which we make choices. Not only does this fit the language by which Mill repeatedly identifies the higher pleasures with "activity," with what we choose once we "exercise [the mind's] faculties,"[22] but it makes better sense than his own presentation does of how a philosopher who was concerned to draw human ends from what we actually choose, rather than to impose on us a theory of what we should choose, could suddenly claim that only some objects of choice are truly human. In general, Mill's *Utilitarianism* is a tract deflating the pretensions of those who insist that people have ends "higher" than the ends they set themselves, so a controversial theory of true human nature is the last thing one expects in the middle of it. But if the point of chapter II really depends on a theory of desire-*formation* rather than of the proper *ends* for desires, such that our desires are truly our own only if they have been sifted through the power of choice, then one and the same concern to validate people's actual choices runs through the work.

So it is backwards to say we should choose phronetic activities because they yield higher pleasures. Rather, we should choose higher pleasures because only they can preserve our phronesis, hence our power of choice itself. A recognizably liberal argument now emerges for favoring "active" preferences, and the leisure to develop active preferences, over passive ones, an argument that flows directly from the liberal's emphasis on freedom rather than making a competing, paternalistic appeal to our "true" or "higher" nature. More active preferences use and therefore develop our capacity for choice itself—for intelligent, which is to say phronetic, choice. So the political powers that be must guarantee us substantial opportunities to satisfy these preferences because otherwise we will lose our freedom. The rights of employers to set whatever terms they will on employment, of advertisers to say what they like about their products, of businesspeople in general to go about their business on the assumption that the people they affect freely choose their part in each interaction, are all justifiable only if the individuals on the other end can exercise phronesis, and become more and more tenuous the more a citizenry is made up of people whose means of satisfaction are so passive that one can literally say, "They don't know what they want." And people with two or three weeks of leisure a year are unlikely to develop the interests or skills with which to exercise phronesis in any of their choices—including the very choice by which they trade off their leisure for more material goods.[23]

"The study of pleasure and pain belongs to the province of the political philosopher" (NE 1152b1). We tend today to ignore this advice in political philosophy, believing either, with most utilitarians, that all pleasures are alike and study is required only to work out how best to distribute them, or, with most Kantians, that pleasure and pain are irrelevant to the properly philosophical issues of rights and justice. I think Aristotle was right, and that a distinction among kinds of pleasure can greatly enrich our understanding of many political issues. This is illustrated by, although not limited to, the argument for leisure I have just sketched.

At the same time, I think Kantians are right to be wary of letting moral questions ride on such empirical determinations. In Aristotle's own hands, the insistence on the political importance of pleasure is a bit disturbing, going all too neatly together with his notion of politics as providing the "rudders" by which an enlightened elite guides a less capable populace to virtue. Yet it is Aristotle, too, who substitutes *phronesis*, a skill open more or less to any human being, for Plato's *sophia*, something achievable by philosophers only, as the central intellectual excellence required by human activity. And *phronesis*, unlike *sophia*, excels by grasping particulars first and foremost, ethical theories only secondarily. But that means that the moral pleasures to which Aristotle refers us are in principle open to everyone and linked to our many particular activities and ends, not merely to the overall Good contemplated in the philosophical life. Aristotle's ethics, that is, are open to egalitarian uses, to incorporation in the multifold activities of nonphilosophers, and to being uncoupled from any overall philosophical theory about what human beings, or nature in general, should aim at. In the next three chapters we turn to Adam Smith's *Wealth of Nations*, the political work that I think most successfully lays out an egalitarian, and nonteleological, version of Aristotle.

Chapter 6

THE *WEALTH OF NATIONS* (I): JUDGMENT

BETTER THAN anyone else, I believe, Adam Smith has described the politics that the freedom of judgment requires. Both the regulations he thinks government should avoid and the institutions he thinks it should foster would spread phronesis as widely as possible across a population. Once people have judgment they should be free to act on it, for Smith, but he is not laissez-faire about the institutions enabling them to develop judgment in the first place.

The claim that Smith urges a politics that would foster judgment is a contentious one, running against most readings of the *Wealth of Nations* (WN). According to the usual interpretations of Smith, at least of Adam Smith the political economist, the main reason governments should leave people alone in economic matters is that this serves efficiency, that the total production of a nation's economy will be greatest when directed by private interest alone. Moral reasons for such policy are supposed to be secondary, and insofar as there are any, the received interpretation would have them be (a) that economic growth is essential to the most basic of human needs, above all the provision of adequate food, and (b) that everyone then can fulfill her absolute right to pursue her desires as she likes, as long as she does not harm others. I believe this entire interpretation is misleading, the last claim especially so. That Smith believed governments should generally leave people to act on their own interests is clear, but it is not at all clear that he saw such noninterference either in purely utilitarian terms or as the fulfillment of some individual right to satisfy one's selfish desires. If character depends centrally on a virtue—phronesis—that each individual must ultimately develop for herself, then governmental noninterference with human actions can itself be a way to help people develop their characters. That Smith had such Aristotelian hopes for his politics of restraining politics is the burden of my interpretation of him. In this chapter I try to demonstrate his closeness to Aristotle; in the following two, how he turned Aristotle to nonteleological and egalitarian uses. These claims require a considerable amount of indirect reading, but so do any claims about Smith's normative views. Smith rarely lays out the philosophical foundations of his ethics, and in WN never so much as explicitly declares his ideals, whether political or moral. His skills lie less in rigorous philosophical argument than in astute observation of society, and the provision of clear, well-informed explanations of what he sees. He is a phenomenologist of the human mind and social world. But his *Wealth of Nations* was admired in its time—by Kant, by Condorcet and the Abbé Sieyès, by Tom Paine, by Jefferson and Madison, as well as by such very different figures as William Pitt and Henry Dundas[1]—in large part because his phenomenology seemed to convey an inspiring moral vision. And the book has had a similar effect ever since. It continues to be WN, after all, not the writings of Malthus, Ricardo, or any other economist, that is most often used to make the normative case for laissez-faire economics. People of very different political persuasions find themselves admiring WN when they read it. It is unlikely, I think, that the crude utilitarianism or libertarianism normally foisted upon Smith can explain this. (The same people often do *not* admire Milton Friedman or George Stigler.) Teasing out the moral vision of WN is thus a project worthy of some effort.

I

There *were* people in Smith's day who believed governments should give free rein to self-interest—either because self-interest is inevitably the primary, even the sole, motivating force in human beings, or because laissez-faire policies, while poor for shaping character, are good for economic growth. Thomas Hobbes, Pierre Bayle, and Bernard Mandeville were the prime authorities for the first view; David Hume and Francis Hutcheson for the second.[2] Hutcheson seems to have combined with the second something like the libertarian view that people have a right not to have virtue instilled in them: "Such as judge truly [about the Deity, religion, and virtue], act virtuously: and as for weak men, who form false opinions, it may do good to instruct and convince them of the truth, if we can; but to compel them to profess contrary to their opinions . . . must always be unjust."[3] Hume was a close friend of Smith's and the philosopher Smith most admired; Hutcheson was Smith's teacher and predecessor in the chair of Moral Philosophy at Glasgow. If Smith has a different justification from theirs for liberalism in politics, it should come out in twists he places on their ideas.

I locate four such twists:

1. Smith has a notion that there is a distinctive kind of thinking peculiarly appropriate for making moral decisions, by which he fends off both Hume's noncognitive view of morality and the common view, held by Hutcheson among others, by which thought is relevant to morality but the thinking needed is the kind of calculation also used in science and mathematics. The standard Smith sets for the proper direction of our passions is an internal balance among the passions themselves, rather than

an external object, like utility, at which we might aim. It follows that a certain kind of self-understanding, rather than a calculation of external objects, will be the mental skill most important to morality. That skill is a highly particularist one, informed by sympathy, and trained by experience. Often, but not always, he calls it "judgment."

2. Smith is more of an individualist than either Hume or Hutcheson, concerned with the development of individual human beings for their own sake, rather than for the sake of some larger social system to which they might belong.

3. Relatedly, Smith differs from Hutcheson by giving concern for oneself a legitimate place in morality. Hutcheson defines virtue such that it is equivalent to benevolence. Smith sees virtue as directed towards a balance within ourselves that consists in a moderate degree of concern for ourselves as well as a moderate degree of benevolence: excessive benevolence can *detract* from virtue, for him.

4. Finally, Smith considers honor, the approval of others, a proper incentive to and reward for the pursuit of virtue, rather than a mere distraction from that pursuit. Hutcheson, like most other eighteenth-century moral theorists, had recognized that people are often virtuous primarily because they want to be honored, but regarded this motivation as conducive more to hypocrisy than to true ethical achievement.

In each of these ways, Smith is considerably more Aristotelian than either Hutcheson or Hume. His Aristotelian bent is actually not hard to see. In TMS, Aristotle is the only moral philosopher coming in for no criticism, and the long chapter in which Smith officially seems to be declaring his sympathies for Stoicism turns out rather to urge an Aristotelian moderation, in relation to one's passions, over Stoic attempts to eliminate or ignore them. Unlike Hume and Hutcheson, moreover, Smith identifies the sentiments relevant to moral theory as those we have as socialized adults, rather than ones with which we happen to be born. Only the adult, for him as for Aristotle, has enough prior emotional training to grasp what ethical issues are all about.

Now Hutcheson himself is already quite Aristotelian. He quotes Aristotle favorably on a number of occasions,[4] stresses, like Aristotle, the need for education and good habits for the proper development of moral feelings,[5] discusses virtues as discrete qualities of character,[6] sees human beings as essentially social creatures, derives his ethical theory from an account of human nature, and treats ethics as leading immediately to an account of politics. With the exception of the last, these are features uncharacteristic of eighteenth-century moral thought. Attacks on Aristotle had in fact been a hallmark of the new "moral science" ever since Hobbes's groundbreaking work of the mid-seventeenth century. "The fame . . . of Aristotle is utterly decayed," says Hume, in one of his few references to that figure.[7] Pufendorf took the "cleans[ing] of natural law from its grounding in the Aristotelian and Thomistic concept of nature" to be one of his main purposes in political philosophy.[8] Perhaps because Hutcheson, like Smith after him, returns with a vengeance to the notion that our nature is essentially social, he elevates Aristotle well above his usual standing in the intellectual circles of the time. So if Smith is yet more Aristotelian than Hutcheson, it is not a mark of his intellectual faddishness. Rather, his ties to that ancient source of ethical theory must run deep.

I take the connection to Aristotle as a general framework within which to set the more specific point of this chapter. Of the four "twists" on Hume and Hutcheson that I listed above, I shall be concerned at the moment only with the first. Smith has an unusual and important, if never fully worked out, conception of what it is to think about moral and political questions. That conception brings him much closer to Aristotle's notion of phronesis, and belief that phronesis differs essentially from the skills necessary for good philosophical or scientific thinking, than practically anyone else was to come in the eighteenth century.[9] And insofar as he uses that conception, under the name of "judgment," as a central term in WN, his notion of why governments should leave markets alone has to be thoroughly reinterpreted. We will see why as we work the conception out in more detail.

II

Hume had argued that reason is "inactive" and amoral. For him, it plays a purely instrumental role in ethics, helping us determine how to satisfy our passions, which can be virtuous as well as vicious. Smith vehemently denies this, while trying at the same time to avoid slipping into the rational intuitionism Hume had been criticizing in Samuel Clarke and William Wollaston. Reason belongs essentially to morality, for Smith, but its role is not to make contact with ideal standards of right and wrong. Rather, it comes up with general rules reminding us that we are "but one of the multitude, in no respect better than any other in it" (III.3.5). Exactly how reason performs this equalizing function is not clear, but the passage comes in the context of Smith's reaction to Hume's " 'Tis not contrary to reason to prefer the destruction of the world to the scratching of my finger," and it is clear that he rejects Hume's picture of an entirely amoral rationality, and an entirely arational morality.

Equally, however, he rejects a picture of reason, to be found in a wide variety of eighteenth-century writers, as calculating pleasures and pains in order to figure out right actions. As we shall see below, Smith deemphasizes the importance of consequences in evaluating right action, but in any case he has an aversion to overly calculative conceptions of how moral reasoning works. Hutcheson, Wollaston, Beccaria, Jefferson, Condorcet, and of course Bentham all tried hard to come up with exact calculi of pleasures and pains as a guide for moral decisions.[10] Wollaston is typical: "[T]he man who enjoys three degrees of such pleasure as will bring upon him nine degrees of pain, when three degrees of pain are set off to balance and sink the three of pleasure, can have remaining to him only six degrees of pain: and into these therefore is his pleasure finally resolved. And so the three degrees of pain, which any one endures to obtain nine of pleasure, end in six of the latter."[11] Never does Smith indulge in this eighteenth century intellectual sport, nor does he ever characterize pleasures and pains in a way that would lend them to quantification. The "father of political economy" uses numbers in WN only for prices, lengths of time, and amounts of material goods, famously avowing that he has "no great faith in political arithmetick" (IV.v.b.30). Instead of "political arithmetick," his own method is a sort of "political history," drawing together real events and hypothetical psychology into a plausible narrative about how human beings produce and exchange. Knud Haakonssen has pointed out that Smith regards "contextual knowledge," the proper grasp of unrepeatable particulars, as central to the workings of human practice,[12] and he makes use of such knowledge himself in the construction of his jurisprudence and political economy. WN displays a very Aristotelian attention to the particular, a respect for the way in which knowledge of particulars differs in kind from knowledge of universals. The work is known for its abundant detail, both in the sense that Smith scatters delightful tidbits all over the place—"The first person that wore stockings in England is said to have been Queen Elizabeth. She received them as a present from the Spanish Ambassador" (I.xi.o.11)—and that he proceeds through careful examination of specific historical cases (the corn laws, the navigation laws, the history of the price of silver, the American crisis).[13] The people one meets in WN are always particular individuals, they want somewhat different things in life, and they live in situations that differ widely in detail.

This fits well with the particularism Smith attributes to sympathy, the engine of his moral system: sympathy is always the result of my imagining myself in some particular person's position, in some particular set of circumstances. As the person with whom I am to sympathize moves further from my direct experience—from my family, neighborhood, country—as the person dissolves more and more into a vague representative of "humanity at large," my sympathy grows weaker and weaker. Hence the need for general rules of justice to supplement sympathy in political morality. Hence, also, the difficulty of abstracting useful general rules other than these principles of justice to guide moral behavior. What sympathy tells me an impartial spectator should do in any given set of circumstances is quite strictly limited to those, and very similar, circumstances. A politics that attempts to figure out what it is right to do across all human situations, what would make people happy in general, is therefore doomed to failure. Smith considers it the greatest hubris to try to decide how people should live on the basis of an abstracted view, without knowing their particular situations from the inside: "The statesman, who should attempt to direct private people in what manner they ought to employ their capital, would . . . assume an authority which could safely be trusted, not only to no single person, but to no council or senate whatever, and which would nowhere be so dangerous as in the hands of a man who had folly and presumption enough to fancy himself fit to exercise it" (IV.ii.10). Accordingly, Smith's politics are minimalist, and his policy proposals are always directed to specific contexts.

Now this emphasis on a judicious grasping of the particular simply is *phronesis*, and in the philosophy of the social sciences, Smith's approach to the subject represents perfectly what a turn to *phronesis* over *theoria* has come to mean, what is urged by those who argue that human beings cannot be fitted to the numerical calculi of the physical sciences.[14] In that sense, Smith can be said either to look forward to Kant, whose distinction between *reinen* and *praktischen Vernunft* has helped ground the narrative approach to the social sciences, or back to Aristotle, whose account of *phronesis* was designed above all to refute an assimilation of moral to scientific knowledge in Plato. The calculating conception of reason, the notion that "reason" is just one kind of thing that applies indifferently to any subject matter, comes out nicely in Jefferson's "Head and Heart" letter to Maria Cosway. As Garry Wills nicely puts the point of that letter, the Head is supposed "to limit itself to matters of technique, of perfecting the means toward higher ends," while the province of duty and virtue belongs to the Heart.[15] Morality is entirely a matter of feeling; science is entirely a matter of amoral calculi. For Smith, by contrast, the Head has a substantial role in ethics, but a *different* one from its role in science. There is a moral "Head," which means both that reason can be moral and that morality is not grounded in sentiment alone. But to give reason a moral role while identifying that role with proper self-understanding and the construction of narratives—this is to have quite an unusual account of reason, in the eighteenth century.

Smith's view of intellectual skills in general resembles Aristotle's. Like Aristotle, Smith takes cognitive activities to require development and to affect our actions only in conjunction with other, more passion-based habits. The notion that human qualities are developed above all by habit runs through both TMS and WN, and in WN intellectual qualities especially get treated more as shaped by, than shapers of, bodily activities. WN is overwhelmingly concerned to root *what* people think in the distinctive activities contributing to *how* they think, in what we might want to call "habits of mind":

> [T]hough the interest of the labourer is strictly connected with that of the society, he is incapable either of comprehending that interest, or of understanding its connection with his own. His condition leaves him no time to receive the necessary information, and his education and habits are commonly such as to render him unfit to judge even though he was fully informed. (I.xi.p.9)

> It seldom happens . . . that a great proprietor is a great improver. . . . To improve land with profit, like all other commercial projects, requires an exact attention to small savings and small gains, of which a man born to a great fortune, even though naturally frugal, is very seldom capable. The situation of such a person naturally disposes him to attend rather to ornament. . . . The elegance of his dress, of his equipage, of his house, and houshold furniture, are objects which from his infancy he has been accustomed to have some anxiety about. The turn of mind which this habit naturally forms, follows him when he comes to think of the improvement of land. He embellishes perhaps four or five hundred acres in the neighbourhood of his house, at ten times the expence which the land is worth after all his improvements. (III.ii.7)

> A young man who goes abroad at seventeen or eighteen . . . commonly returns home more conceited, more unprincipled, more dissipated, and more incapable of any serious application either to study or to business, then he could well have become in so short a time, had he lived at home. By travelling so very young, by spending in the most frivolous dissipation the most precious years of his life . . . , every useful habit, which the earlier parts of his education might have had some tendency to form in him, instead of being rivetted and confirmed, is almost necessarily either weakened or effaced. (V.i.f.36)

That the way we think is shaped by what we do is a point commonly thought to have been made by Aristotle and then rediscovered, after long neglect, by Marx. But while seventeenth- and eighteenth-century epistemologists do indeed overlook this fact, do indeed treat cognitive abilities as independent of habit, Smith does not.

III

The term "judgment" was not much attended to by Smith's predecessors, but when they did use it, they tended to give it a sense by which it corresponds closely to Aristotle's *phronesis* and Kant's *Urteilskraft*. Locke defined judgment as "The Faculty, which God has given Man to supply the want of clear and certain Knowledge in Cases where that cannot be had,"[16] distinguished it from both perception and "demonstration" (logical proof), tied it to our ability to discern differences and similarities among ideas, and understood it to be commonly, if inaccurately, associated with "wit" (IV.xiv.3, II.xi.1–2). He at one point brings judgment close to reason (IV.xvii.2), but distinguishes them in that reason achieves knowledge—correct and certain grasp of the connections between ideas—while judgment puts ideas together when their agreement or disagreement is, "as the word imports, taken to be so before it certainly appears" (IV.xiv.4). The notions that judgment is informed by perception and reason but identical with neither, that it bears some relation to the "common sense" that makes "wit" possible, and that it consists in the assimilating and discernment of ideas that Kant was to call "reflection" are all present here. Above all, judgment is for Locke, as for Aristotle, the appropriate faculty for coming to conclusions under uncertainty, the appropriate faculty for grasping unrepeatable particulars. This means, again as for Aristotle, that it is central to moral thinking. In several famous passages of another work, Locke designates judgment as the appropriate faculty for what he seems to have considered our most important, and most individual, moral decision:

> Here . . . the common question will be made, *who shall be judge,* whether the prince or legislative act contrary to their trust? . . . To this I reply, *The people shall be judge*; for who shall be *judge* whether his trustee or deputy acts well, and according to the trust reposed in him, but he who deputes him? . . . But farther, this question, *(Who shall be judge?)* cannot mean, that there is no judge at all: for where there is no judicature on earth, to decide controversies among men, *God* in heaven is *judge.* He alone, it is true, is judge of the right. But *every man* is *judge* for himself, as in all other cases, so in this, whether another man hath put himself into a state of war with him, and whether he should appeal to the Supreme Judge, as Jephtha did.[17]

When we move from Locke to Smith's contemporaries, we find Hume calling the notion that judgment merely discerns differences and similarities among ideas, while reason articulates arguments, to be an "establish'd maxim," although he himself regards the distinction as a false one.[18] Hume is uncharacteristically vague about where to place judgment, treating it now as a process by which we draw inferences from our perceptions, now as a perception itself, at other points as the affirmation of a fact, however arrived at.[19] And he does not think judgment has much to do with morality: "Morality is more properly felt than judg'd of."[20] One constant between his views and Locke's, which Thomas Reid, Smith's successor at Glasgow, likewise maintained even in criticizing Hume, is the assumption that judgment is the final act in the mind's assessing of a proposition for truth or falsehood, and that as such it may be *informed* by perception or reason but is not identical with either. Reid puts this last point explicitly: "I take it for granted, that there can be no . . . judgment of things, abstract and general, without some degree of reason."[21] And at the same time: "A man who has totally lost the sense of seeing, may retain very distinct notions of the various colours, but he cannot judge of colours, because he has lost the sense by which alone he could judge."[22] That there is something conducive to uncertainty about the *objects* of judgment is lost here (one could presumably judge, for Hume and Reid, of a perception directly in front of one, or of a mathematical proposition for which one has seen the proof), yet there remains something open to risk about the *act* of judgment. Reid, moreover, tries to elucidate judgment by way of the reasoning appropriate to "the office of a judge" (§ 936), in which a decision must be reached in spite of uncertainty, and while he does not emphasize that aspect of the matter, his discussion is informed by the fact that judges must reach finality in cases where final truth is available only to God. Judgment thus remains, even for Hume and Reid, something that each individual must complete for herself, in spite of the infirmities her faculties may have and the limitations on the knowledge available to her. So it remains a risky enterprise, an activity by which one ventures convictions and assessments despite all that one does not know.

In this context, it is surely no accident that Hutcheson identifies "natural liberty" with an individual's right to "exert his powers, according to his own *judgment*,"[23] adding that those "who judge well about their own innocent interests will use their liberty virtuously" while "such as have less wisdom," as are "imprudent" (note the Aristotelian echoes!), should still, generally, be left alone to live with the consequences of their bad judgments. This right is immediately followed, moreover, by a right "to judge according to the evidence that appears to [the individual]" of God, religion, and virtue. The connotations of "judgment" that we have seen in Locke, Hume, and Reid clarify Hutcheson's point: we decide on the fundamental questions of how to lead our lives and what to believe as if we were sitting in a courtroom, having to come to some final conclusion even where there is insufficient knowledge to reach certainty, having to assess the relevant evidence for our conclusion by an indeterminate movement among all our faculties, among all the ways we know of evaluating evidence—perception, reason, and any other mode of knowing.

Hutcheson is not merely *a* teacher and professional predecessor of Smith's. When Smith took over the chair of Moral Philosophy, he followed almost exactly the same course of topics in his lectures as Hutcheson had, moving, like Hutcheson, from the grounding and nature of everyday moral conduct to the principles of property, contract, marriage, family, and finally political economy. He also relied on many of the same author-ities and took over specific doctrines ranging from the primacy of the moral sense to the rootedness of commerce in conversation.[24] When Smith takes over Hutcheson's "natural liberty" as the prime moral con-straint on politics, therefore, we should expect to find "judgment" play-ing at least as central a role in that liberty as it does for Hutcheson. There is indeed reason to see Smith's use of "judgment" as invested yet more heavily with the connotation that one has it when one acts like a court-room judge, in assessing one's inclinations with the degree of informa-tion, distance, and wisdom that a member of the judiciary is supposed to have. For Smith transformed Hutcheson's moral sense theory with the notion of an "impartial spectator," and the function of that spectator is above all to set up a courtroom inside ourselves.

In Hutcheson's theory, the proper motivation for virtuous action is the moral sense or benevolence, but the proper end or object of that benevo-lence is "the greatest happiness of the greatest number."[25] Hutcheson thereby posits a basic desire for virtue while making room for the obvious fact that even when we have this desire we often go wrong. To ensure that our moral sense leads us in the right direction, we need to correct it by the power of reason, which Hutcheson understands to entail calculat-ing what, in each situation, would best conduce to overall happiness. Smith corrects the moral sense he posits rather differently.[26] We learn over time, he says, to have just that amount of sympathy in each situation that an "impartial spectator" would have. Actions that meet with the approval of this imagined spectator have "propriety," a "proportion or dispropor-tion, which the affection [acted upon] seems to bear to the cause or object which excite[d] it" (TMS II.i.intro.2), regardless of the conse-quences that may ensue from those actions. To judge in advance whether a proposed action has propriety, we think back over past situations, con-sidering how people we respect have reacted to similar cases, rather than projecting the presumed effects of our action into the future. Smith ac-knowledges that the anticipated overall "utility" of our acts normally has some impact on what we consider right, but he treats this as a secondary matter, indeed a distortion ("irregularity") of the moral sentiments, rather than a proper part of their use (II.iii).[27] Consequences should come into morality, but indirectly, as one among the factors that, over time, shape the way people in fact react to types of situations, and therefore something that eventually shapes our internal norms for such reactions.

This substitution of an internal standard for Hutcheson's external one, as the device correcting our moral sentiments, has immense implications for the teleological structure of Smith's moral philosophy and politics. I will come to these in the next chapter. At the moment, I want to focus on the fact that Smith, again and again, describes the activity of the impartial spectator as "judgment," and indeed uses "impartial judge" or "equitable judge" as a synonym for the phrase "impartial spectator" itself.[28] In an important passage, he makes the courtroom metaphor explicit. Hearkening back to Locke—the echoes are remarkably strong—and rejecting Hume's replacement of moral judgment with moral feeling, he extends the arena in which the individual should play "judge" over himself from the decision about whether to rebel or not to the whole course of moral life:

> The all-wise Author of Nature has . . . taught man to respect the sentiments and judgments of his brethren; to be more or less pleased when they approve of his conduct, and to be more or less hurt when they disapprove of it. He has made man, if I may say so, the immediate judge of mankind, and has . . . created him after his own image, and appointed him his viceregent upon earth. . . . But though man has, in this manner, been rendered the immediate judge of mankind, he has been rendered so only in the first instance; and an appeal lies from his sentence to a much higher tribunal, to the tribunal of their own consciences, to that of the supposed impartial and well-informed spectator, to that of the man within the breast, the great judge and arbiter of their conduct. (TMS III.2.31–2)

As in Locke, we each judge for ourselves and hope thereby to approximate God's judgment on us. And what we do when we judge is modeled explicitly on the process of law. If rejected by the "tribunal" of society, Smith says, we divide ourselves internally into a judge and defendant and carry out an inspection of our conduct in the higher court of our consciences. To do this, we make use of general rules for conduct that our "reason" comes up with (III.3.4 and III.4), interpret our situation to figure out how those rules should properly apply, and come up with a verdict that we command ourselves to live with on pain of self-hatred or self-contempt if we do not. The centrality of judgment to this account could hardly be greater.

Consider, in this light, the many uses of "judgment" to characterize proper thinking about one's situation in the *Wealth of Nations*. The words "judge" and "judgment" appear in WN, outside of discussions about courts and justice, around forty times by my count,[29] and most often in contexts like the following:

> When the landlord, annuitant, or monied man, has a greater revenue than what he *judges* sufficient to maintain his own family, he employs either the whole or a part of the surplus in maintaining one or more menial servants. (WN I.viii.19, my emphasis)

But the man who ploughs the ground with a team of horses or oxen, works with instruments of which the health, strength, and temper are very different upon different occasions. The condition of the materials which he works upon too is as variable as that of the instruments which he works with, and both require to be managed with much *judgment* and discretion. The common ploughman, though generally regarded as the pattern of stupidity and ignorance, is seldom defective in this *judgment* and discretion. (I.x.c.24)

It is the interest of the people that their daily, weekly, and monthly consumption, should be proportioned as exactly as possible to the supply of the season. . . . By supplying them, as nearly as he can *judge,* in this proportion, [the corn dealer] is likely to sell all his corn for the highest price and with the greatest profit; and his knowledge of the state of the crop, and of his daily, weekly, and monthly sales, enable him to *judge,* with more or less accuracy, how far they really are supplied in this manner. (IV.v.b.3. See also IV.v.b.25)

There are no publick institutions for the education of women, and there is accordingly nothing useless, absurd, or fantastical in the common course of their education. They are taught what their parents or guardians *judge* it necessary or useful for them to learn. (V.i.f.47)

Three such occurrences are situated in statements of what is usually taken to be Smith's central doctrine, indeed in some of the most widely quoted passages of the whole book:

The patrimony of a poor man lies in the strength and dexterity of his hands; and to hinder him from employing this strength and dexterity in what manner he thinks proper without injury to his neighbor, is a plain violation of this most sacred property. . . . To *judge* whether he is fit to be employed, may surely be trusted to the discretion of the employers whose interest it so much concerns. (I.x.c.12, my emphasis)

What is the species of domestick industry which his capital can employ, and of which the produce is likely to be of the greatest value, every individual, it is evident, can, in his local situation, *judge* much better than any statesman or lawgiver can do for him. (IV.ii.10)

But the law ought always to trust people with the care of their own interest, as in their local situations they must generally be able to *judge* better of it than the legislator can do. (IV.v.b.16)

In every one of the cases I have cited, "judging" is something (1) done by a single individual, (2) in and with reference to his or her local situation, (3) where the information needed cannot be given with scientific or logical certainty, (4) that depends instead on experience of the local situation that no one will have who has not herself lived through its details, for which reason (5) Smith contends interference with the decision by outsiders to the situation, including government officials, would be foolish and presumptuous. I submit that the consistency of this context of use is no accident, that Smith carefully selects "judgment" when he wants a cognitive term to carry the implication that the people in a situation should be able to decide for themselves how best to act. Smith is not, in general, a casual or loose writer. Indeed he carries precision to a point at which it can seem frustratingly plodding. When he once uses a term in a certain context, he almost always uses the same word in similar contexts.[30] Much of the book looks like it was written on a word processor, with certain phrases programmed into the function keys, or block-copied from place to place, so that every similar idea is given exactly the same wording.[31] While inelegant, this precision is perhaps Smith's most philosophical characteristic, ensuring that his abstract modes of classification are carried along consistently, so that one can see at a glance how one point or piece of evidence fits together with the others.

The vocabulary Smith develops for designating cognitive abilities is precise in just this sense, and it includes a variety of other terms besides "judgment." To "ascertain," for instance, usually means to find something out that can be known with exactitude, while "rated," "valued," and "considered" are terms for stipulations of fact or value, especially when such stipulations are somehow suspect.[32] The words "calculate" or "compute" appear in most of Smith's attributions of mathematical knowledge to people,[33] while empirical knowledge either is "observed,"[34] "appears evidently [from experience]," or "is found by experience." When he himself is unsure of something, or wishes to make an assumption that he knows may not be strictly accurate, he "supposes" or "apprehends" it.[35] When others *should* be unsure of what they think, but are not, we see the words "presume," "fancy," "imagine," and "represent."[36]

So Smith has a wide vocabulary of terms for cognitive activities, all of which he uses with consistency and precision. We may therefore presume that his use of "judgment" is meant to pick out a specific one among these activities, and that he is well aware of how it may differ from the others. Two features of his use of the term, in that light, deserve comment. First, Smith frequently talks of what is or can be "valued," "considered" or "known," but almost never uses "judge" in the passive voice.[37] This may indicate that he regards judgment, not as a simple "reception" of knowledge, a taking in of what is "out there," by any knower at any time, but as an *activity,* which must be undertaken by particular agents at particular times and in particular circumstances. Unless someone has personally engaged in the activity of judgment, there may be no judgment at all to be had.

Second, Smith virtually always uses "judgment" as a favorable term. Mercantilists may "presume" or "suppose" all sorts of false beliefs, metals and people can be "rated" or "considered" above or below their real value, but she who judges for herself in her own local situation rarely if ever needs to fear that she is thinking improperly about her decisions. In the passages I have quoted, Smith treats judgment as something almost sacrosanct, something that even uneducated people can do well and should be allowed to do by themselves. This is not because he thinks we can in principle never be wrong in our judgments, that there is nothing to go wrong about or there is some guarantee that we will always judge aright. On two occasions he portrays "the judges who were to determine" a particular preference or decision as, respectively, childish and confused (III.iv.10, IV.i.10), and on several occasions he implies or says that "prejudice" can "direct our judgment."[38] Rather, what Smith recognizes is that there is no higher authority over an individual judging for herself in her local situation who is likely to be able to judge any better.[39] In the examples with which I began, the corn merchant judges as well as anybody can how the overall demand for corn is likely to fluctuate; the ploughman judges how to use his animals as well as such things can be judged; and parents, whose judgment determines the education of their daughters, do a better job with them than school officials, necessarily less well acquainted with the peculiarities of each individual child, do with their sons. Judgments can be informed, and pervasively corrupted, by general doctrines—"National prejudice and animosity, prompted always by the private interest of particular traders, are the principles which generally direct our judgment upon all questions concerning [the so-called balance of trade]" (IV.iii.a.2)—but on the whole our faculty for judgment works better than our faculty for grasping general principles, and no particular judgment, responsible as each judgment must be to the details of the situation it judges, is likely to be bettered by someone who possesses simply a more adequate *general* view. I shall return to this point when discussing some of Smith's purposes in writing WN.

IV

On several occasions, Smith links "judgment" with "dexterity" (intro.3, I.i.3, V.i.e.30), his favorite word for "skill." Such dexterity, which consists above all in an attention to detail, is one of the main products of the division of labor:

> the division of labour, by reducing every man's business to some one simple operation, and by making this operation the sole employment of his life, necessarily increases very much the dexterity of the workman. (I.i.6)

> Men are much more likely to discover easier and readier methods of attaining any object, when the whole attention of their minds is directed towards that

single object, than when it is dissipated among a great variety of things. But in consequence of the division of labour, the whole of every man's attention comes naturally to be directed towards some one very simple object. (I.i.8)

Smith's account of the division of labor is importantly the reverse of Plato's[40] in that (1) the division is the *origin* of differences in talent, not the consequence of such differences, and (2) (relatedly) the division is not a fixed element of nature but a process that continues indefinitely, expanding through greater and greater sectors of the economy and sub-dividing professions into smaller and smaller parts.[41] What is natural is thus not, as in Plato, a given set of crafts and craftspeople but the human tendency to discover the different elements of an activity, to focus intently on those differentiated elements, and to develop "dexterity" by so focusing. At the same time, Smith tries hard to build a capacity for generalization into the very workings of this dexterity. The second passage I quote above goes on to suggest that the intense focusing brought about by the division of labor leads our thoughts to take flight towards inventing new ways of performing our tasks, while in another passage Smith argues that the kind of business to which merchants, at least, devote their attention enhances their "acuteness of understanding" (I.xi.p.10). At these points the division of labor seems to combine perception and intellectual activity in just the way that I have suggested judgment does. It becomes not a mode of immersion in particulars alone but something that simultaneously yields particularized attention and a broad enough grasp of what the particulars have in common that one can project them into as yet unperceived contexts and invent new ways of bringing them into existence.[42]

This linking of judgment to dexterity, and notion of an "acuteness of understanding" arising from immersion in detail, strongly recalls Aristotle's descriptions of *techne* (craft) and *deinotes* (cleverness or know-how)—faculties that he suggests might be, respectively, a model and a necessary condition for phronesis.[43] Just as these faculties are concerned with perception, the proper grasping of particulars, so must phronesis be. Judgment requires "care" and "attention" (WN I.x.b.38, III.ii.7, III.iv.3, V.i.e.30), and better yet "exact" and "vigilant" attention (III.ii.7, V.i.e.30), for Smith. Similarly, Aristotle compares phronesis to a perception by which one is alert to and worried about details. Concerning a creditor who has no knowledge of any "particular portion" of capital stock, Smith says, "He has no inspection of it. He can have no care about it" (V.iii.56; see also IV.v.b.25). Inspection and care are linked here just as perception and the sentiments moving one to act are in Aristotle's theory of motion: I perceive details *insofar as* I am worried about achieving a certain end to which they are relevant. For both Aristotle and

THE *WEALTH OF NATIONS* (I)   135

Smith, my perception is a biological function, the workings of which are inseparable from its ability to guide me around the world, so the particulars I perceive must be similarly inseparable from the emotions I have about those particulars. One thing that follows from this—a point of great importance to which we shall return—is that "self-interest" functions above all to guide us toward certain *cognitive* abilities, for Smith. Smith yokes judgment, both directly and indirectly, to "prudence" on several occasions (II.ii.64, II.ii.77, IV.ii.11–12), and in the eighteenth century "prudence" is the badly attenuated descendant of, and common if misleading translation for, Aristotle's "practical wisdom."[44] The importance of prudence to Smith's account of human nature has been widely recognized but equally widely misunderstood. As we shall see shortly, Smith's point is not so much that prudence is directed to the care of one's own interests but that it is *judiciously* so directed. To be prudent is to have judgment; it is also to be self-concerned. But the former, rather than the latter, is what primarily interests Smith.

At the same time, the notion that all ordinary economic agents need for good judgment is "care" and "inspection" suggests strongly that this "judgment" is not yet "phronesis" in the rich sense that Aristotle makes central to ethical thinking. Perhaps it is not much more than *deinotes*. But Aristotle allows for several levels of "phronesis," and for the possibility that higher levels build upon the structures put in place by lower ones. This comes out most clearly in his remark on the relationship between phronesis and "political wisdom": "Of the wisdom concerned with the city, the practical wisdom which plays a controlling part is legislative wisdom, while that which is related to this as particulars to their universal is known by the general name 'political wisdom'" (NE 1141b24–27). Here political phronesis can float free of the general principles that are properly its "controlling part," when it is exercised by agents other than legislators.[45] Political skill *resembles* "legislative wisdom," but it should recognize that it ought to be controlled *by* legislative wisdom. I suggest that the "judgment" of Smith's ordinary economic agent resembles this lower kind of phronesis. It may be perfectly adequate for finding one's way around ordinary economic affairs, but ideally it needs to be controlled by a higher conception of one's ends as a human being. Like deinotes and techne, it depends on detailed information while incorporating the grasp of some general principles about how to get around the world. It thus resembles phronesis in structure if not in overall aim. But if so, the dependence of this lower, economic judgment on participating in the situations about which one judges may carry over to the higher, moral form. And for Smith, this clearly does carry over: legislators are no more justified in presuming to know our proper interests than in presuming to know how we should satisfy those interests. Smith, here unlike Aristotle, considers moral knowledge, knowledge of the properly "controlling" principles, as widely spread around as economic knowledge. Legislators who judge situations of which they are not a part thus display an impertinence that is as much moral as it is economic.

V

Two broader points. First, consider Smith's overall style and method in WN. We might treat Smith as a sort of commonsense philosopher. He takes what seems "natural" to us, in the sense of "ordinary" or "obvious," as having at least a prima facie claim to truth, although it can also on occasion be corrected by an understanding that has put these natural intuitions into some sort of comprehensive, systematic order. That is, our common sense is normally correct, at least about social phenomena, but where it is systematically misguided, the cure is more common sense. Now, "common sense" is standardly understood to be synonymous with "judgment," so insofar as Smith vindicates common sense about economics, we may say that his overall intent is to delineate a system of people following out their own economic judgments and to correct that system, where necessary, with better judgment.

This fits well with how Smith treats what he opposes, what he calls the "prejudices," "delusions," "absurdities," or "follies" that get in the way of sound economic policy.[46] Absurdities and follies are not just falsehoods but falsehoods so glaring that once pointed out, no reasonable person can go on believing them. Delusions are diseased perceptions, fancies, or fantasies that ought simply to vanish once one's senses are cured. And prejudices are unconscious commitments that block or preempt judgment. All of these are the sort of problems that characteristically plague common sense, not the sort of cognitive error characteristic of theoretical understanding—a failure to follow rigorous argumentation or to be aware of crucial empirical information. (If you are at the point where you can appreciate arguments and evidence, you are beyond the point at which you can be fooled by cognitive illusions.) Now, the way one would expect to dispose of obstacles to common sense is simply to point them out, and to clarify the context that produced them. But we must *judge* the accuracy and adequacy of a clarification. So to remove obstacles to good judgment, we must remind the very judgment that is being misled of facts and arguments it already knows, or that lie readily within its grasp. Prejudices, follies, etc., are not sophisticated mistakes. One *dispels* them, like perceptual illusions; one cannot, strictly speaking, refute them. One appeals to judgment to cure itself.

As it happens, Smith characterizes his writing precisely as an effort to clarify economic issues, and thereby to dispel prejudices: "I shall endeavor to explain, as fully and distinctly as I can, [these] three subjects in the three following chapters, for which I must very earnestly entreat . . . the patience . . . of the reader: . . . in order to examine a detail which may perhaps in some places appear unnecessarily tedious; . . . I am always willing to run some hazard of being tedious in order to be sure that I am perspicuous" (I.iv.18; cf. II.ii.66). Perspicuity is Smith's great aim and achievement. WN has been said not to contain a single original idea,[47] but it has rarely been accused of obscurity in style or argumentation. WN's lucidity is indeed what most drew readers to it. "What an excellent work!" wrote Gibbon, ". . . an extensive science in a single book, and the most profound ideas expressed in the most perspicuous language."[48] Smith has a gift for words, for vivid and pertinent examples, and for organizing his arguments in clear sequences that he follows rigorously. He believes, moreover, that the British have had the wool pulled over their eyes by clever but misleading merchants, and considers it his responsibility to provide a clear and comprehensive picture of economic workings that can combat this mercantilist nonsense. At one point, although here in a context where he is coming to the defense of merchants, he compares his job to that of dispelling "the popular terrors and suspicions of witchcraft" (IV.v.b.26). Laws abolishing the prosecution of witchcraft seem at the same time "effectually to have put an end to those fears and suspicions," and Smith thinks that if he can persuade lawgivers to pass similar laws encouraging sound economic policy,[49] he can also help the populace lose their false beliefs about the importance of hard currency or the need to restrict trade. So to describe Smith as writing a book combating a set of bad judgments with clarifications that allow us to make more, better judgments is very close to his own way of presenting his method and main themes.

The second broader point is that we can understand Smith's emphasis on letting people pursue their own interests as in large part a way of activating good judgment:

The law which prohibited the manufacturer from exercising the trade of a shopkeeper, endeavoured to force [the] division in the employment of stock to go on faster than it might otherwise have done. . . . It is the interest of every society, that things of this kind should never either be forced or obstructed. The man who employs either his labour or his stock in a greater variety of ways than his situation renders necessary, can never hurt his neighbour by underselling him. He may hurt himself, and he generally does so. . . . But the law ought always to trust people with the care of their own interest, as in their local situations they must generally be able to judge better of it than the legislator can do. (IV.v.b.16)

[I]f a merchant . . . buys up corn . . . in order to sell it again soon after in the same market, it must be because he judges that . . . the price . . . must soon rise. If he judges wrong in this, . . . he not only loses the whole profit of the stock which he employs in this manner, but a part of the stock itself. . . . If he judges right, instead of hurting the great body of the people, he renders them a most important service. By making them feel the inconveniencies of a dearth somewhat earlier than they otherwise might do, he prevents their feeling them afterwards so severely as they certainly would do, if the cheapness of price encouraged them to consume faster than suited the real scarcity of the season. When the scarcity is real, the best thing that can be done for the people is to divide the inconveniencies of it as equally as possible through all the different months, and weeks, and days of the year. The interest of the corn dealer makes him study to do this as exactly as he can; and as no other person can have either the same interest, or the same knowledge, or the same abilities to do it so exactly as he, this most important operation of commerce ought to be trusted entirely to him. (IV.v.b.25)

In these passages and many others,[50] Smith's concern is not to advocate acting on self-interest over acting on some other motivation but to ensure that, *where self-interest will be the motive in any case,* the self whose interest motivates whatever action takes place is the one located closest to the scene of the action, the one most likely to be informed by judgment. The choice, in the above cases, is between the self-interest of a private person and the self-interest of legislators or those who influence legislators. If legislators restrict the corn trade, or ordinary people's choice of occupations, the corn dealers and the ordinary people will obey the law out of private, self-interested fear rather than pursuing their private, self-interested desire for material well-being, while the legislators will gratify the self-interested desires for material well-being of some group of their constituents who benefit from the restrictions. What concerns Smith is how to get interest to motivate good rather than bad judgment. But if so, "judgment" is exactly as important a theme in WN as self-interest has been taken to be. Interest is but the engine that can call judgment into action, the source of energy that when properly harnessed can transform a nation from a static, inefficient set of paternalistic rulers and dependent subjects into a society of independent judges, each determining what actions to take in his or her own situation.

The focus on "self-interest" in nineteenth- and twentieth-century readings of WN is in any case misplaced. Everything Smith says about the importance of self-interest is humdrum, for his time. He keeps far away from Mandeville's cynical reduction of human nature to self-interest, is a greater believer in the possibility of concern for others than Hume, allows more room for sincere religious faith than Voltaire, and differs barely at all from the gentle Hutcheson on the role of interest in economics. It is highly implausible to suppose that he took his remark about appealing to the self-love of butchers and bakers to be anything other than a platitude, that he expected his contribution to our understanding of human nature to rest in the least on this position. Even among "left-wing" radicals in the eighteenth century, according to Bernard Bailyn, "If there was one absolute certainty, one unqualified fact, it was that in his deepest nature man was 'restless and selfish,' ruled 'not by principle, but by passion,' [and] driven by an uncontrollable lust for domination."[51] That human beings are creatures of selfish lusts was such a platitude in Smith's time that one would be hard-pressed to find anyone who disagreed with it. What Smith took to be unusual in his own views, and rightly so, was the claim that people, even the most ordinary of people, can usually judge best what is *in* their own interests, that they can pursue those interests without being guided by others. It is the egalitarianism of his view of human judgment, and not any claim about the nature of human motivation, that sets him apart from other thinkers of the time and that provides the essential premise for his arguments against government interference. Smith's controversial claim is about cognition: that all human beings, civilized and uncivilized, educated and uneducated, are capable of *judging well* about their own interests and situations, and in particular are generally better at so judging than any administrator or legislator trying to plan society from above. Only because this is true does an unregulated market distribute labor and goods efficiently. Whatever our interests, when we make and act on judgments about our own local situations, we do rather better than anyone who tries to figure out what is in everyone's interest from beyond all local situations. Napoleon's minister of finance, the Comte de Mollien, claimed above all to have learned from Smith "the multitude of points at which public finance touches every family, and raises judges of it in every household."[52] That people "in every household" can judge financial matters perfectly well, and that they should be left alone to do so, was central to Smith's egalitarian conception of judgment—and his egalitarian vision of a world in which governments would supply only the institutions we need to develop our capacity for judgment. In this, I shall argue, he wrested a modern, liberal vision of politics from Aristotle's ethics.

Chapter 7

THE *WEALTH OF NATIONS* (II):
VIRTUE AND INDEPENDENCE

I F JUDGMENT OR PHRONESIS is an intellectual skill usually associated with Aristotle, "virtue" or "excellence" is the central term in the approach to ethics it is supposed to define. Among other things, "virtue ethics" connotes a notion of the good life in which the vagueness and difficulty of ethical choices, and the role of luck, are given realistic acknowledgment, in which human beings are understood to aim at a bundle of different achievements rather than a single, overriding one, and in which good character is taken as something one develops rather than is born with, and education, correspondingly, is taken extremely seriously. All of these features recommend virtue ethics over its Kantian and utilitarian competitors. Only the extreme conservatism of Aristotle and his followers makes readers since the Enlightenment reluctant to endorse it. How Smith dissents from Aristotle is then what marks him as a modern figure. Were he to follow Aristotle down the line, rooting ethics in a teleological conception of nature and praising hierarchical structures for governing polities, he could offer nothing to the ethics of a modern scientific world or the politics of a liberal democratic one. As it happens, he differs from Aristotle in two crucial respects. The first is that he submerges, if not quite eliminates, the teleology that characterizes Aristotelian ethics. The second is that he refuses to grant any natural superiority to one human being over another. I shall say more about the ways in which Smith resembles Aristotle in the beginning of this chapter, then move to their differences over teleology. In the next chapter, the last on the *Wealth of Nations,* I discuss Smith's egalitarianism and what I take to be his concrete political vision.

I

I noted in the beginning of the previous chapter four ways in which Smith is closer to Aristotle than to his contemporaries Hutcheson and Hume. The three I did not discuss in detail all concern Smith's individualism. His treatment of honor as having an intrinsic rather than a merely instrumental value, and the moral place he gives to self-love, are closely bound up with his strong orientation, shared with Aristotle, towards seeing the point of ethics more in the perfection of individuals than in the good of society. Let me elaborate these points a little.

For Smith, approbation by others, and even more so self-approbation, is a suitable reward for virtuous action, and as such a rightful part of virtue itself. He is here much more Aristotelian than either Hutcheson or Hume. The delight in being approved of by others and in being able to approve of ourselves are immediate natural passions for Hutcheson, but not in themselves morally valuable.[1] Hutcheson denies Aristotle's claim that we "relish honor *as* it is a testimony to our virtue,"[2] and treats the pleasures of approbation as instruments to the development of virtue rather than themselves a part of virtue. Virtue itself he takes to be our positive feelings for others, not any selfish feeling.

Smith regards this as too ascetic a picture of virtue, an excessive avoidance of self-love in construing the highest human character. Smith and Hutcheson agree that there are realms of human life—economic exchange, in particular—in which self-love will inevitably be our dominant motivating passion. But while Hutcheson takes self-love to be at best morally neutral, even in such realms, Smith sees self-love within proper limits as intrinsic *to* virtue. We have a *duty* to take care of ourselves, he says.[3] The impartial spectator inside us approves of individuals taking care of themselves, and condemns those who commit suicide or put up with gross humiliation.

But to allow self-love a place in virtue, Smith must have an altogether different definition of "virtue" from Hutcheson's. And indeed "virtue" is not benevolence but human excellence for Smith, precisely as it is for Aristotle, consisting in a moderate degree of, and a balance between, self-regarding as well as other-regarding feelings:

> [T]o feel much for others and little for ourselves, . . . to restrain our selfish, and to indulge our benevolent affections, constitutes the perfection of human nature; and can alone produce among mankind that harmony of sentiments and passions in which consists their whole grace and propriety. As to love our neighbour as we love ourselves is the great law of Christianity, so it is the great precept of nature to love ourselves only as we love our neighbour, or what comes to the same thing, as our neighbour is capable of loving us. (I.i.5.5)

The *criterion* for virtue on Smith's model is what an impartial spectator would admire in a human being. The *essence* of virtue is therefore whatever is impartially admir*able* in human beings. This is far from the synonymy between "virtue" and "benevolence" in Hutcheson. And while Hume would agree with Smith's conclusion on the question of whether the pleasure taken in approbation is virtuous, he would do so for quite different reasons. Virtue is a social construct for Hume, projected upon

some passions and characters rather than others insofar as they conduce
to the utility of society as a whole. Precisely the instrumental value that
Hutcheson noted in the pleasures of approbation suffices to make them
virtuous for Hume. They are good tools for making sociable people out
of us, and we therefore rightly denote them as virtuous.

Smith shares neither Hume's noncognitivist metaethic nor his dissolution of the self into a social artifact. Indeed, Smith's view of approbation
brings out his unusual, subtle conception of the relationship between self
and society. Contrast his belief that honor is an honorable pleasure, for
instance, with Mandeville's attitude toward the opinion of other people,
or Rousseau's view of "amour propre."[4] For Smith, honor is the appropriate marker for virtuous achievement—what Aristotle would have
called the "proper pleasure" that "completes" virtue—not the neutral
source of pleasure that it is for Hutcheson, and certainly not the distraction *from* virtue, the source of hypocrisy and loss of integrity, that it is for
Mandeville and Rousseau. Smith considers self-approbation as higher
than the approval of others, but he also regards the latter as a necessary
step on the way to the former. Mandeville and Rousseau, the former
mockingly and the latter despairingly, take the search for others' approval
to show how the self betrays its own standards in favor of what society
expects of it. Smith, here like Hutcheson, regards this notion of a pure,
presocial self with "its own" standards as a myth, regards the self as dependent, for its understanding of itself, on its transactions with society—
although not, as Hume held, *reducible* to those transactions—and therefore as needing, rather than being threatened by, the social influences
upon it.

But unlike Hutcheson, Smith does not take the social embeddedness
of the self to imply that the good of the self *is* the good of its society.
Hutcheson sees individual human beings as essentially part of a larger
system. Benevolence extends in principle to every other human being,
thereby connecting us to all of them: "[I]f we enlarge our views with
truth and justice, and observe the structure of the human soul, . . . we
must find a sacred tie of nature binding us even to foreigners, and a sense
of that justice, mercy and good-will which is due to all."[5] As much as we
can, we should stretch our goodwill, first beyond ourselves to our families, then beyond our families to our particular society, then to all humanity. The system to which we belong, we should realize, takes absolute
precedence over our private desires. Indeed, humanity as a whole has
rights over each of us, which explains what is wrong with suicide:
"[M]ankind, as a system, seems to have rights upon each individual, to
demand of him such conduct as is necessary for the general good. . . . As
each individual is part of this system, . . . as every one may be of some
service to others in society, . . . each one is obliged to continue in life as

long as he can be serviceable, were it only by an example of patience and resignation to the will of God."[6] These rights also include a demand that we procreate (from which Hutcheson derives prohibitions against homosexuality and abortion), that nothing "useful to men" be vainly destroyed, that useful inventions be made public, and that everybody do some useful work.[7]

Smith has no truck with such dissolution of individuals into larger systems. His well-known admonition against utopian politicians can be taken equally well against Hutcheson here: "He does not consider that the pieces upon [a] chess-board have no other principle of motion besides that which the hand impresses upon them; but that, in the great chess-board of human society, every single piece has a principle of motion of its own (TMS VI.ii.2.17)." More directly, he says, in the course of an attack on Hume's utilitarian account of justice: "[O]ur regard for the individual [does not] arise from our regard for the multitude: but . . . our regard for the multitude is compounded and made up of the particular regards which we feel for the different individuals of which it is composed" (TMS II.ii.3.10).[8] Smith's reliance on propriety rather than utility as the touchstone of good action allows for the evaluation of each action and each person on its own, independently of their contribution to larger purposes. If "the perfection of human nature" is a "harmony of sentiments and passions" (TMS I.i.5.5), then the perfection of human nature is an *individual* achievement. Smith never talks of people as being "serviceable," in TMS or WN, never holds that humanity has rights over human beings, or that anyone has a duty to procreate, to have a useful profession, to make inventions public, or even to refrain from suicide.[9] Much as for Kant, individual human beings are ends in themselves for Smith, not means to the well-being of others. Smith and Kant dissent sharply from the utilitarianism that dominated eighteenth-century ethical theory. The goal of ethics, for them as for Aristotle, is the self-perfection of individuals.

This reading runs contrary to that of an important recent article by Charles Griswold and Douglas Den Uyl. They maintain that "the final object of Smith's [moral] theory is not the self-perfection of the individual (as in Aristotle) but rather social cooperation."[10] I disagree. Smith's virtues are, as they say, "oriented towards" our fitting into society, and justice especially is essential to the survival of "the whole edifice [of society]" (TMS II.ii.3.4). When we bring the commitment to individualism we surveyed in the previous paragraph together with these points, however, they entail merely that society be an essential *framework* for our individual lives, not their end, and that justice be a condition on which that framework depends. What something is "oriented towards" need not be its true end, as Smith famously stresses throughout TMS and WN.

Society shapes us so that we are capable of virtue, Smith argues in Books I to III of TMS, but in Book III it becomes clear that this, far from making us tools for society's ends, makes society a means to the ends of each of us.

II

But it is not so clear what ends each of us is supposed to have. When we ask, "What end does the life of practical virtue serve?" we discover a crucial difference between Smith and Aristotle. Smith's constant emphasis on unintended consequences suggests an unusual suspiciousness towards accepted notions of ends. TMS argues that we take pleasure in things as beautiful not when they are actually useful, as Hume had supposed, but when they *seem as if they might be useful,* and moves from this to the famous "invisible hand" passage declaring economic activity to be spurred on by the poor's inaccurate supposition that wealth is useful. This belief in the elusiveness of human ends shows up only more strongly in WN. Smith had begun his lectures on political economy with a series of reflections on the nature of demand, of what people want, but he cut these out of the book that became the *Wealth of Nations.* Moreover, WN contains none of TMS's invocations of the beneficent designs of Providence. The later revisions of TMS tend likewise to play down the notion of God, and make God's existence, where they do touch on it, more something we posit than something we know to be true.[11] Thus both scientific and religious accounts of human ends fade from Smith's work as it proceeds. I suggest that this is deeply tied to the doctrine of "unintended consequences," the "invisible hand" teleology that is his best-known and most original view. People tend to aim at one thing but achieve something quite different. This is especially true for any practice that endures over a significant span of time. Smith's emphasis on the particularism of human knowledge resurfaces here. We grasp our immediate circumstances very well, but we grasp *only* such immediate circumstances well. Attempts to predict how people will act over a large set of different circumstances (extended either temporally, into the distant future, or horizontally, across a large swathe of society at a single time) are hubristic. They overlook the crucial place in human history of both happenstance and freedom, the fact that "every single piece [on the human chessboard] has a principle of motion of its own." What happens in history is very largely unpredictable, and that means that the detailed structure of human ends is also unpredictable. We may know in general what conduces to pleasure, and we certainly know some specific conditions that conduce to pain, but what specific pleasures and pains will constitute overall happiness for a specific person at a specific historical moment, let alone what constitutes happiness for humanity at large, depends so fundamentally on minute and unpredictable circumstances that a philosopher who tried to delineate that goal precisely would be guilty of unpardonable "folly and presumption."

I think there is good evidence in Smith's writing that he found the question "What is the end for man?" endlessly vexing if not unsolvable, and attempted to come up with a politics that would finesse that question. In addition to fitting with his notion of "unintended consequences," an agnosticism about teleological matters helps explain the absence of any talk in WN about ideological commitments, civic virtue, or any other source of human motivation. There is nothing in the book, on the other hand, to suggest that people want material goods for their own sake, out of uncontrollable avarice. So instead of attributing such a view to him, we may regard his economic writings as *abstracting* from the higher purposes in human life, taking those purposes out of the realm of legitimate policy concerns. Note, here, a subtle difference from Hume. For Hume, our passions set our purposes independently of our reason; reason "is and ought only to be the slave of the passions."[12] One can go from here to saying that our ends are strictly nonrational, without reason of any kind, and sometimes Hume seems to lean towards this view,[13] or one can say that whatever directs our passions explains our ends, and go from there, as Hume more generally tends to do, to a naturalistic account of human ends drawn from human biology. Neither of these options is open to Smith. Smith thinks that the passions are cognitively directed, even suggesting that reason has a motivating power of its own,[14] so it is intelligible for him, as it is not for Hume, that our passions might be comprehensively misdirected, that we could discover an objective purpose for our lives by reason and have to correct our passions in accordance with it. On the other hand, his suspicions of unsocialized human sentiments, of approaches to ethics that begin from our animal nature alone, prevent him, as well, from identifying what we *should* seek with what we simply *happen*, biologically, to seek.[15]

Consequently, Smith never defines "happiness" as the satisfaction of the desires we happen to have. In TMS Smith leaves the definition of happiness elusive, and usually employs it more as a normative term than a descriptive one. He tells us, for instance, that happiness is the only purpose for which it makes sense to suppose that God brought us into existence, and that by pursuing the happiness of humanity we "co-operate with the Deity." But he adds no clue as to what this happiness consists in. Again, when he tells us that happiness above all requires "tranquillity," or that it is best pursued by exercising our moral faculties (III.5.7, III.3.30), the first is at best a necessary condition for satisfaction, while the second is more a stipulation of happiness as the satisfaction we *ought* to aim at than a description of it as something we *do* aim at. Smith goes on to say, moreover, that tranquillity is achievable in almost any "permanent situation" of human life, and that what most detracts from happiness is exaggerating the difference between one such situation and another (III.3.30). This does not help anyone calculate the effects of her actions: if tranquillity can be achieved in any permanent situation, and tranquillity is the chief component of happiness, then putting people into a state of permanent "external" misery (jail, divorce, public disgrace, etc.) need not detract from their chances at happiness.[16] The point of the passage is to guide ourselves *away* from illusions of greed or ambition that will make us *un*happy, not to tell us what, positively, we should aim at in order to be happy.

In general Smith does little more than gesture toward a conception of happiness. We get a bit of content into the notion when he says that the "chief part of human happiness arises from the consciousness of being beloved" (I.ii.5.1; cf. also I.iii.2.12, III.5.8), but this is qualified by the claim that the warm attention received by the rich is counted part of happiness only by way of delusion (I.iii.2.2, IV.1.10). Similarly, he says that happiness can be obtained with but minimal material goods (IV.i.10), yet also that it requires being "in health, [and] . . . out of debt" (I.iii.1.7).

All this is remarkably vague and evasive, especially by contrast with the richly detailed accounts of other subjects in TMS. It is also vague and evasive by contrast with the detailed accounts of what goes into happiness to be found elsewhere in eighteenth-century writings. Wollaston and Bentham carefully analyze degrees and types of pleasure. Voltaire and Samuel Johnson write whole novels about happiness. Hutcheson spends two long chapters of his *System of Moral Philosophy* on the various types of pleasure—their duration, degrees of intensity, etc.—that go to make up happiness.[17] Smith, here less like Aristotle than his master, has no comparable discussion. Instead, he gives us tidbits, delineating mostly failings that take away from happiness, sometimes features that make up part, but not the whole, of happiness.

When we now turn to WN and read that "[n]o society can . . . be flourishing and happy, of which the far greater part of the members are poor and miserable" (I.viii.36), we should hesitate more than a little before reading utilitarian content into this claim. The sentence before it tells us that "what improves the circumstances of the greater part of society can never be regarded as an inconveniency to the whole," and it is clear that "improves the circumstances" is to be equated with lifting people out of "poverty and misery." It seems equally clear that lifting people out of misery is a good thing, a criterion, indeed, of any society's success. But the cautious wording, the double negatives in two successive sentences, and the term "flourishing" with which he pairs "happy," allow Smith to avoid committing himself to happiness as the be-all and end-all of human life. *Not* being *un*happy is clearly *one* of our ends; *being* happy, in the sense in which that means having "improved circumstances," is not clearly our total or final end.

As I have indicated earlier, Smith's view of how we should evaluate our acts renders a doctrine about the nature of happiness unnecessary. Substituting "propriety" for Hutcheson's "greatest happiness," as a corrective for our sentiments, allows him to turn moral decision-making into something fairly independent of the consequences at which our actions aim. It follows that he no longer needs any substantial view about the telos of human life, any conception of the human telos articulated enough to serve as a guide for action. We may therefore do best to avoid such a conception in reading him.

On one occasion, however, Smith does seem to lay out a final goal for moral development. We have already seen the passage in question: "[H]ence it is, that to feel much for others and little for ourselves, that to restrain our selfish, and to indulge our benevolent affections, constitutes the perfection of human nature; and can alone produce among mankind that harmony of sentiments and passions in which consists their whole grace and propriety" (TMS I.i.5.5). Propriety, say some commentators, is the goal of the virtuous life for Smith.[18] But recall Smith's refutation of Hume's aesthetics: it is our grasp not of a thing's *actual* usefulness, he says, but of its *suitedness to be useful,* that leads us to consider it beautiful. Its fittedness to a purpose takes priority over any actual contribution it might make to human purposes. This "utilitarianism without utility," this conduciveness to ends over actual ends—a clear ancestor of Kant's "purposiveness without purpose"—provides the best light in which to understand Smith's notion of propriety. Propriety is more a fittedness to ends than an end itself. We need a balance of affections so that we can feel our own pleasures and pains less strongly, and others' pleasure and pains more strongly. On Smith's account of moral judgment, this provides us with a criterion by which to approve and disapprove of our own and others' actions correctly, and puts us in a good position for coming to terms with our lives in healthy "tranquillity." But propriety is then a condition suitable for judging or coming to terms with *other things*—situations, passions, acts, lucky or unlucky circumstances, etc.—not something that it makes sense to identify with our ultimate purpose itself. Propriety is not identical with happiness and is important only in connection with what else we do with our lives. It makes best sense, that is, as a condition of being *ready* for human action, of being "all dressed up with nowhere to go," rather than an endpoint of our actions themselves. Where should we go, once we're "dressed up"? Here Smith's response would surely be to deflect us toward the particular ends that we set ourselves daily, rather than to worry about any overall, abstract end beyond these particulars.

Let me add now that insofar as Smith is agnostic about our overall ends, I think he is right.[19] It is perhaps the defining feature of the modern world, I believe, that we can no longer confidently claim knowledge about our telos. In what does our highest fulfillment lie? What is "the end" for human being? For Aristotle there was a universal and absolute answer to that question: to achieve the life of contemplation, or, failing that, of active participation in a polis. For Plato, there seems to have been a more obscure but equally singular and absolute one. Christianity, like other religions, has had its own definite answers to the question, differing slightly from sect to sect and time to time but bearing at least a strong family resemblance to one another. By the time Smith wrote—a time, politically, when Europe had finally recovered from the terrible wars of religion and moved towards toleration for religious differences, and a time, scientifically, when the notion that there are ends or purposes in nature was widely derided—it was much harder to say what all human beings do, or should, aim at. John Rawls has identified his liberalism as "political" rather than "comprehensive" because it attempts to come up with solutions to questions about how people ought to live together while abstracting from the problem, by his lights philosophically unsolvable, of what a comprehensive conception of the good life should look like. His liberalism tries thereby to enable society among people whose comprehensive conceptions differ widely. For the priority Kant gives to the right over the good, Rawls takes him as an important ancestor to this view. I believe that there are more Enlightenment figures who approach Rawls's (in my opinion eminently sensible) political liberalism than Rawls himself acknowledges, and that Smith, along with Kant, is among the closest.[20]

Neither Kant nor Smith are exactly "political liberals" in Rawls's sense, of course. Like Kant, Smith shares the "comprehensive view" of the Enlightenment to the extent that he regards "enthusiasm and superstition" as "poison" to the mind (WN V.i.g.14), looks forward to a day on which religion would be "pure and rational . . . , free from every mixture of absurdity, imposture, or fanaticism" (V.i.g.8), and believes that virtue and happiness are best pursued by way of a rational understanding of human nature. But he does not condemn religious belief, as his heroes Hume and Voltaire do, he does not think that intellectuals can work out a conception of virtue and happiness that would improve on what ordinary people already pursue, and his political economy is dominated by an insistence that governments should refrain from imposing conceptions of how to live on people. In these ways he is far removed from the comprehensive liberalism of most of his contemporaries.

III

One who rules out directing politics towards a comprehensive conception of the good life cannot quite be an Aristotelian. Some would say, indeed, that Smith cannot be considered an Aristotelian at all if he removes Aristotle's teleology.[21] I propose two responses to this claim. In the first place, much in Aristotle is more or less independent of his teleological views. Smith's focus on individual self-realization, combined with a view of individuals as inextricably interwoven with society, his focus on moderation, his emphasis on moral sentiments and habits combined with a controlling place for moral reason, and his particularist and nonscientific conception of that moral reason are all deeply indebted to Aristotle. Some influential recent readings of Aristotle have taken these features, especially the particularist and nonscientific conception of moral reason, to rule out any strongly teleological bent in Aristotle's own ethical theory. Sarah Broadie and John McDowell have argued, not implausibly, that if the particularism of phronesis is taken seriously, we could not possibly derive the way to act in any given set of circumstances from a "blueprint" or "Grand End" picture of human living.[22] So the picture of human flourishing or well-being with which the *Nicomachean Ethics* opens and closes must be either relevant to politics alone (Broadie) or only a general indication of how our more particular ends might hang together (McDowell). Without going as far as these readers, who have been criticized for their extreme particularism by other Aristotelians,[23] I think we can safely say that an Aristotle stripped of his overall telos is not an Aristotle stripped of his ethical views altogether.

In the second place, as a philosophical matter, it is not impossible to justify a set of character traits as virtues without relying on an overall picture of human ends. What makes trait x a virtue and trait y not? Some say the answer to such a question must be a substantial picture of the human telos such that x conduces to the achievement of that telos while y does not. Then the fact that Aristotle's specific virtues (temperance, courage, magnificence, etc.) were conducive to excellent life in a Greek polis would justify them if and only if the ultimate human end is to participate in a polis, and we can justify a contemporary set of such virtues if and only if we can show how they might be similarly necessary to an ultimate human end. But why should the virtues not be justified, equally well, by way of a necessary *constraint* on human ends? For Smith, propriety, and the self-command that allows one to achieve propriety, is certainly a constraint on the happiness we seek. But propriety, and the honor it brings with it, while also a part of happiness, are not the whole of it: Smith's repeated refusal of the Stoic identification of happiness with virtue makes that clear (TMS III.3.11–4, VII.ii.1.39–47). So if the virtues he adduces are conditions for propriety, they are conditions for a constraint upon happiness, not for its full achievement. But that provides a reasonable justification for them, and it points the way to how liberals in general can justify virtues. Those traits of character that conduce to human choice, and to the minimal ethical demands made by a world in which each enables the others to have choice, are legitimate descendants of Aristotelian virtue.[24] We can expect them of everyone, even take political measures to try to instill them, while leaving vast areas of life for each person to explore by him or herself.

So to say that Smith leaves open the detailed structure of human ends is not to say that anything goes, that his ethics allow human beings to aim at anything whatever. Propriety sets conditions on human ends. The first, and most rigid, of these is that our pursuits must meet the demands of justice. We may not pursue any end that requires the death, or despoiling, or defamation of innocents. Since this is a requirement without which society, and therefore the free pursuit of individual ends within society, would be impossible, government must protect it absolutely: hence the primacy of justice for Smith, and the core of truth in the libertarian reading of his work. But another condition on our ends that propriety requires, even if it should not be enforced by law, is that they be compatible with a decent balance of self-regarding and other-regarding sentiments. Both completely selfish ends and completely self-sacrificing ends are repugnant. And a third constraint propriety places on our ends, if only so that we can live up to the other two, is that they be compatible with the epistemic balance between reason and sentiment that we need in order to achieve the perspective of the impartial spectator. This latter balance constitutes what I have called "judgment," what Smith variously calls "judgment," properly calibrated "sympathy," or, at times, "wisdom."

If we have no clear ends, if the ultimate goal or "final cause" of human life is unknown, then virtue must consist in a fittedness for pursuing whatever ends there might happen to be rather than for pursuing any particular end. That fittedness consists in the ability to *choose judiciously,* the skill for deliberating well over both ends and means. Aristotle portrays the admirable human being with such specific traits and activities as temperance, courage, generosity, good humor, and friendship. By contrast, Smith is reticent about the specific qualities—the typical acts and emotional constellation—of a virtuous person: he concerns himself mostly with the bare *capacity* for pursuing specific traits, interests, and activities. Smith's notion of the virtues is a sketch or outline of Aristotle's, a rough drawing of the human character that leaves plenty for each of us to fill in by ourselves. It comprises simply the emotional configuration and intellectual skills needed to acquire and preserve phronesis—to preserve, therefore, our freedom of choice or independence.

IV

"Independence" is a term of great importance for Smith. It was a term of great importance throughout eighteenth-century Scotland, in part because Scotland lost its political independence in 1707, and spent much of the next seventy-five years or so wrestling with whether this was a good thing or not. And Smith's polemic on behalf of commerce returns frequently to the increase it allows in every individual's "independency."

Indeed it could be said that an interest in "independency" served as Smith's initial impetus to study political economy at all. The point at which he first discussed economic matters, according to both surviving sets of lecture notes from his jurisprudential courses, came in connection with the subject of "police." By "police" he means "policy, politicks, or the regulation of a government in generall" (LJ 331), which are supposed to aim primarily at three things: the cleanliness of a country, the security of its inhabitants against crime, and "the cheapness of goods of all sorts" (331, 333). The first, he says, is not theoretically interesting enough for a course on jurisprudence, so he moves immediately on to the second. And this second object of police, security against crime, takes him immediately to the subject of economics. For it is Smith's opinion that the greatest preventative of crime is not tough laws and energetic law-enforcement, nor yet good moral education in homes and schools, but economic independence for the poor:

> Upon the whole it is the custom of having many retainers and dependents which is the great source of all the disorders and confusion in some cities; and we may also affirm that it is not so much the regulations of the police which preserves the security of a nation as the custom of having in it as few servants and dependents as possible. Nothing tends so much to corrupt and enervate and debase the mind as dependency, and nothing gives such noble and generous notions of probity as freedom and independency. Commerce is one great preventive of [having many servants and dependents]. The manufactures give the poorer sort better wages than any master can afford; besides, it gives the rich an opportunity of spending their fortunes with fewer servants. . . . Hence it is that the common people of England who are altogether free and indepen-

dent are the honestest of their rank any where to be met with. (LJ 333; cf. 486–7)

So even before Smith gets to "the cheapness of goods of all sorts," he has found a reason to recommend commercial society. Throughout his work, moreover, this will remain one of the main advantages he adduces for commerce. WN I.viii presents the "independent workman" as a moral as well as economic ideal, attacking those "masters of all sorts" who prefer dependency in their workers and pretend to the public that a dependent labor force is in the nation's interest (I.viii.45–51). WN II.iii argues strongly for the superiority of manufacturing work over service. WN III.iv repeats, in great detail, the claim that commerce increases people's security and takes them out of a state of dependency, calling this "by far the most important of [its] effects" (III.iv.4). And WN III.i sings the praise of the agricultural life because of "the independency which it really affords," noting that in the American colonies agriculture allows practically everyone to become "a master, and independent of all the world" (III.i.3, 5).

What is "independence"? It is clearly not the same thing as "liberty." Scotland after 1707, and the American colonies before 1776, had *liberty* throughout the eighteenth century. Rights were generally protected; there was a free press; there was a fairly free market. What the colonies declared in 1776, and Scotland lost in 1707, was something else.[25] It is not entirely clear what that something else is. To "depend" is to "hang from," to follow from, to be entailed by. Perhaps, even where one's actual moment of choice is uncoerced, one does not want the options among which one chooses to follow from someone else's choices. For the colonies, this meant they wanted a governing body of their own that would not have to answer to King or Parliament. For Smith, the paradigm of "dependency" is the relationship of a feudal lord to his tenant farmers: "Those who were not bondmen were tenants at will, and though the rent which they paid was often nominally little more than a quit-rent, it really amounted to the whole produce of the land. Their lord could at all times command their labour in peace, and their service in war. Though they lived at a distance from his house, they were equally dependant upon him as his retainers who lived in it" (II.iii.9). Here one person's control over another's basic needs severely limits the latter's options. Control over basic material conditions for one's life seems to be necessary for independence.

But Smith also links independence to a certain kind of *mental* state: "Nothing tends so much to corrupt and enervate and debase *the mind* as dependency, and nothing gives such noble and generous *notions of probity* as freedom and independency." If we bring this together with the description of "self-command" in TMS, it appears that independence is an ability to stand apart from both the material pressures and the moral attitudes of others: to shape one's own individual life despite the fact that one's very ability to think has itself been shaped by immersion in society. At the heart of TMS, Smith makes clear that virtue aims ultimately at an internal transformation of one's self, even though it is brought into being by the quest for other people's approval. At least in the ideal case, the "impartial spectator" within our selves comes to *replace* external response as our primary criterion for whether we are behaving well or not:

> [A] wise man feels little pleasure from praise where he knows there is no praise-worthiness, [and] he often feels the highest in doing what he knows to be praise-worthy, though he knows equally well that no praise is ever to be bestowed upon it. . . . His self-approbation . . . stands in need of no confirmation from the approbation of other men. . . . This self-approbation, if not the only, is at least the principal object, about which he can or ought to be anxious. The love of it, is the love of virtue. (TMS III.2.7–8)

Not only does virtue consist in living up to our own standards, moreover, but we are enabled to develop such standards, and the correlative skills of self-judgment, only if we can achieve an ability to distance ourselves from all our immediate desires, including our desire for approval. Smith calls this ability "self-command," and devotes a long section of the last edition to it (TMS III.3.22–45). So virtue incorporates two levels of paradox, a definitional as well as a pragmatic one: (1) while brought into existence by the need we have to win others' approval, it consists in what allows for *self*-approval, and (2) it does not fully develop until we can *distance* ourselves from the need that brings it into existence in the first place.

Now one of the great virtues of the market, for Smith, is that it helps us achieve self-command. Sometimes Smith uses "the ordinary commerce of the world" or "the bustle and business of the world" to describe means by which we learn to discipline our passions (TMS III.3.7, III.3.25). Of course, they are not the only means, and it is somewhat unclear whether we should even take "commerce" and "business" literally in these descriptions.[26] More explicitly, Smith maintains that for people who neither have nor aspire to great wealth, "the road to virtue and the road to fortune . . . are very nearly the same" (TMS I.iii.3.5). The discipline of the marketplace, besides promoting efficiency, leads to "prudent, just, firm, and temperate conduct." Only the very wealthy are likely to be morally corrupted by the desire to improve their status, and that is precisely because they are exempt from the discipline of the market (TMS I.iii.3.6, 8).

And it is the importance of this discipline, not an exaltation of selfishness, that Smith primarily teaches in the famous passage about appealing to the self-love of butchers and bakers:

[T]o gain the favour of [the one] whose service it requires . . . , [a] puppy fawns upon its dam. . . . Man sometimes uses the same arts with his brethren, and when he has not other means of engaging them to act according to his inclinations, endeavours by every servile and fawning attention to obtain their good will. . . . But man has almost constant occasion for the help of his brethren, and it is in vain for him to expect it from their benevolence only. He will be more likely to prevail if he can interest their self-love in his favour. . . . Whoever offers to another a bargain of any kind, proposes to do this. . . . It is not from the benevolence of the butcher, the brewer, or the baker, that we expect our dinner, but from their regard to their own interest. We address ourselves, not to their humanity but to their self-love, and never talk to them of our own necessities but of their advantages. Nobody but a beggar chuses to depend chiefly upon the benevolence of his fellow-citizens. (WN I.ii.2)

But *of course* we address the butcher and the baker in terms of what they can get from us! Who would ever think otherwise? If Smith's point were that people are always motivated by self-interest he should have used a less obvious example—shown us, perhaps, like Mandeville, that charitable actions are really motivated by self-interest[27] or, like Gary Becker, that parents are so motivated in relation to their children. No self-respecting person, in ordinary circumstances, would dream of going into a butcher shop and begging for a cut of sirloin. Nor does Smith deny that in extraordinary circumstances people do beg: "Nobody *but* a beggar chuses to depend chiefly upon . . . benevolence," but a beggar does so choose. Hence the passage cannot possibly make the point that people are motivated exclusively by self-interest. If Smith wanted to advance this Mandevillian thesis, which he is elsewhere at pains to dismiss (TMS VII.ii), he would not have appealed to the paradigm cases in which we already expect self-interest to be at work.

Instead, he uses the ordinariness, the obviousness of the appeal to self-interest in interaction with butchers and bakers as background, as evidence, for another point. What other point? Smith's concerns throughout the paragraph center around what makes human beings different from other animals, and that is not our self-interest but our ability to be aware of *sharing* interests: to know how to persuade another.[28] Unlike the puppy or the beggar, the butcher's customer can speak to someone else's needs rather than bleating self-pityingly about her own. We come away from the passage with an appealing picture of relationships that do not require benevolence—of the reliable, independent relationships most of us have with our butchers and bakers, as opposed to the cloying, humiliating, and always uncertain life of a beggar. It is the contrast of my life as a butcher's *customer* with the life of the beggar, and not the life or self-love of the butcher himself, that stands at center stage. The main character, the character with whom we are supposed to identify, is the one who merely *appeals* to self-love: the one who is "more likely to prevail if . . . ," who "offers . . . a bargain," etc. It is not clear that this character is self-interested at all. He may be making dinner for a friend, for his parents, for a church or a charity . . . That is not the point: the point is to bring out his *strategy* as regards the butcher, his awareness that he can get the butcher to give him meat by offering him something in return. Whether or not this character is himself self-interested, he is able to perceive, and address himself to, *other people's interests*. Instead of giving us an almost Ayn Randian paean to self-love, we may now see this famous passage as focusing on our capacity to be *other*-directed.

That that is Smith's concern, that he is interested in our capacity for being aware of other people's needs and feelings, makes much more sense in terms of his moral theory than any normative endorsement of self-love. TMS emphasizes how perceiving other people's feelings, and building into ourselves their perspectives on our own feelings, is essential to proper moral judgment. Neither benevolence based on an immediate feeling of compassion towards others, nor prudence based on the feeling of self-love, nor justice based on the desire for revenge can count as virtue. Rather, these feelings must be refracted through the eyes of the impartial spectator, such that we feel them only to the degree, and in the circumstances, truly appropriate to each of them. For Smith, I come to an appropriate level of both self-love and benevolence by trying to have those feelings only to a degree I can express without embarrassment in front of other people: "The person principally concerned . . . longs for that relief which nothing can afford him but the entire concord of the affections of the spectators with his own. . . . But he can only hope to obtain this by lowering his passion to that pitch, in which the spectators are capable of going along with him. He must flatten . . . the sharpness of its natural tone, in order to reduce it to harmony and concord with the emotions of those who are about him" (TMS I.i.4.7). Initially, I respond to what actual other people let me get away with. As I get older, I build a model of the normal "impartial spectator" into myself out of these actual reactions (TMS, Book III, passim). I then moderate the expression of my emotions according to that internal standard, allowing my drive to fit into society to guide me toward a balance among self-directed and other-directed feelings. Finally, in order so much as to approximate this ideal balance, I need a certain distance from *both* types of feeling. Only self-command, the power to control my feelings, enables me to achieve this distance, and it is thus the precondition for all virtue whatever.[29]

Now plug all this in to the "butcher and baker" passage. I may not love my butcher and baker, I may indeed have no feelings for them at all, but to get what I want from them, I must at least moderate my self-

centeredness down to the point at which I can present to them a plausible understanding of their needs and a willingness to help fulfill those
needs. If Smith's paradoxical way of getting at the self only through the
other is at work here, it is reasonable to assume both that the butcher
and baker are more likely to be open to a true understanding of my
concerns if I thus moderate my self-love ("lower" my passion, "flatten its
tone"), and that *I* can achieve a more appropriate, better balanced sense
of my own worth and just deserts by forcing myself to lessen my demands
in the presence of others. Yes, I appeal to the butcher's self-love, but that
is likely to *lessen* his own concern for himself and his needs, to open him
more to understanding me. The market, that is, provides a condition
both for true benevolence and for the development of self-command. We
should not lay too much stress on the first of these achievements.[30] I do
not become friends with my shopkeepers merely by having commercial
relationships with them, nor does Smith think I do: "[Man] stands at all
times in need of the co-operation and assistance of great multitudes,
while his whole life is scarce sufficient to gain the friendship of a few
persons." Smith strongly implies that the market provides training in self-
command, on the other hand, by his contrast between human beings and
animals and repeated suggestion that participation in the market grants a
dignity of some kind. Exchange is a means to self-command, the ordinary
means for those lucky enough to live in a state not constantly at war, and
humble enough to have no political position. Commerce thus promotes
virtue, enables us to achieve the mental conditions for independence.[31]

V

"Independence," and "virtue," mean something different to historians of
political thought than they do to philosophers. John Pocock's work has
shown powerfully how a tradition beginning more or less with Machiavelli, and finding its way into English thought by way of James Harrington, developed an ideal by which republics should be governed by
men who live in agrarian conditions and participate in a militia that serves
as the nation's sole defense force.[32] Only thus can people become truly
equal and independent; only thus can they achieve "civic virtue"; only
thus can they realize their Aristotelian nature of "self-rule." The nearest
acquaintance of Smith to inherit this tradition was Adam Ferguson, who
drew from it a pessimistic view of modern society according to which
commercialism, and the division of labor giving rise to it, tears us apart
internally—"dismember[s] the human character"—in particular by pro-
fessionalizing politics and the military.[33]

Smith, of course, very much endorses the division of labor, and generally welcomes the coming of the commercial world. Some of Ferguson's concerns—in particular, the notion that workshops tend to become "engine[s], the parts of which are men"[34]—come up in Book V of WN, but that is late in the game and Smith has relatively little to offer in resolving them. Furthermore, he both endorses the professional army and wants governments to avoid favoring agriculture over industry. So is he not rather an *opponent* than a friend of "independence"?

One answer to this is to insist on the philosopher's notion of independence, holding Aristotelian approaches to ethics quite apart from whatever Machiavelli and company may have made out of Aristotle's politics. I shall want to have some recourse to this possibility, but I suggest in addition something else: Smith may say so little directly about the sorts of things that worry Harringtonians because he takes his whole work to be an indirect answer to those concerns. Michael Ignatieff has written interestingly on how Smith responded, as early as 1756, to Rousseau's version of the civic republican tradition, noting that Smith believed the egalitarian citizen-republic would necessarily be an *impoverished* state— that, in particular, the poorest citizens in such a state would be much worse off than they are under (inegalitarian) commercial conditions.[35] This is correct, and it is also part of what Smith has to say to Ferguson, but Ignatieff overlooks the extent to which Smith's response to civic republicanism is couched in Rousseau's own terms. Rousseau had complained that while "ancient treatises of politics continually made mention of morals and virtue; ours speak of nothing but commerce and money."[36] Ignatieff says that this description fits WN well. But if I am right about the importance of the market to self-command, then for Smith commerce *is* a matter of "morals and virtue."[37] Similarly, while Rousseau, like Ferguson, winds up admiring the precivilized "savage" as a model of human independence, Smith insists that it is the mark of the civilized person, not the savage one, to be independent—"more or less" independent, at least, but Smith sees independence as necessarily a matter of degree, not something that either exists fully or fails to exist at all. It is characteristic of commercial society to foster a greater degree of independence for all, first, as a byproduct of the *abandonment* of the constant need for military readiness that Ferguson finds so wholesome. With the absence of constant war comes security in property, and a lessening of the need for armed protection from powerful lords: "[C]ommerce and manufactures gradually introduced order and good government, and with them, the liberty and security of individuals, among the inhabitants of the country, who had before lived almost in a continual state of war with their neighbours, and of servile dependency upon their superiors. This, though it has been the least observed, is by far the most important of all their effects" (WN III.iv.4).

Second, the increased standard of living that commerce grants the poor enables them to have more independence than they had in agrarian societies. The gross inequality of agrarian societies makes the poor in such societies extremely dependent on the rich:

> In [the] age of shepherds if one man possessed 500 oxen, and another had none at all, . . . they who had no flocks or herds must have depended on those who had them. . . . They therefore who had appropriated a number of flocks and herd, necessarily came to have great influence over the rest. . . . It is to be observed that this inequality of fortune in a nation of shepherds occasioned greater influence than in any period after that. Even at present a man may spend a great estate and yet acquire no dependents. Arts and manufactures are increased by it, but it may make very few persons dependent. (LJ B 20–1)[38]

It is in the nature of economic relationships under commerce, not those in precommercial societies, to encourage the independence of each party to the relationship. In a commercial society, each person not only has more material means but depends rather less for his means on any single other person or small group of persons:

> In a country where there is no foreign commerce, nor any of the finer manufactures, a man of ten thousand a year cannot well employ his revenue in any other way than in maintaining, perhaps, a thousand families, who are all of them necessarily at his command. In the present state of Europe, a man of ten thousand a year can spend his whole revenue, and he generally does so, without directly maintaining twenty people, or being able to command more than ten footmen not worth the commanding. Indirectly, perhaps, he maintains as great or even a greater number of people than he could have done by the antient method of expence. For though the quantity of precious productions for which he exchanges his whole revenue be very small, the number of workmen employed in collecting and preparing it, must necessarily have been very great. . . . He generally contributes, however, but a very small proportion to that of each, . . . to many not . . . even a ten thousandth part of their whole annual maintenance. Though he contributes, therefore, to the maintenance of them all, they are all more or less independent of him. (WN III.iv.11)

Finally, as we have seen above, the market itself, by requiring us to appeal to other people's self-love rather than to their benevolence, provides a direct schooling in independence, while at the same time bringing out, if only indirectly, our relationships to others in our community. By means of the ordinary life of buying and selling, and (especially) of seeking and keeping a job, people acquire both self-command and an understanding of the way their own interests are enmeshed with those of others.

To revert now to the recourse of separating political from ethical independence: we should remember that Smith belongs more in a philosophical tradition than a political one, more in the line of Plato, Aristotle, Locke, and Hume than of Machiavelli and Harrington. The history of moral philosophy he traces in Book VII of TMS covers Plato, Aristotle, Zeno, Epictetus, Epicurus, Hobbes, Hutcheson, Mandeville, and Cudworth, with casual notes here and there to Cicero (described, correctly, as borrowing other people's ideas rather than inventing his own), Clarke, and Shaftesbury. This is a canon of *philosophers*, in the twentieth-century as well as the eighteenth-century sense of the term, not something one would expect from someone interested in the moral and political thought of polemicists and pamphleteers. That Addison and Steele, much less Machiavelli and Harrington, make no appearance, that Cicero plays such a minor role, all suggest that Smith regarded his own ethical work as belonging to the tradition of thinking that meditates on life in unpolemical and transhistorical ways. And it goes with that tradition, especially with the Stoic section of it that Smith particularly admired, to focus on how individuals should live out their own lives—on the relationship between individuals, not whole societies, and the human good. One effect, and symptom, of this orientation is that Smith developed his notion of independence as a largely *internal* quality, one that consists in self-command allied to a strong conscience, rather than in anything as external as participating in political or military "rule." In terms of judgment, we might say that Smith understands the republicans' concern for people to participate in the military and in government as a way for them to acquire the discipline necessary for good judgment, hence for true choice or "self-rule," and responds to this concern by saying that the relevant discipline may be equally well provided by the marketplace. So the material conditions for independence on which the Harringtonians insisted— landownership, the possession of arms, participatory citizenship—have at best secondary importance for Smith. He accepts the Harringtonian tradition's goals without its obsessions, seeing independence to be just as attainable in modern, commercial society as among the armed citizen-farmers of the civic republican imagination.[39]

It follows, moreover, from Smith's agnosticism about human ends that participating in a good society need not be the highest human achievement. He does not consider the political life to be the crown of the moral one: running a polis is a job like any other, for him. The identification of virtue with a willingness to die for one's society, implicit in Machiavelli, would be ridiculous or repugnant to Smith, and equally so the notion that only participation in government allows for virtue. Smith cannot accept Aristotle's "man is a political animal" as a statement about our ultimate ends any more than he can accept any other piece of Aristotle's teleology. He certainly does accept the notion that we are social beings, but that does not make our social nature one of our ultimate ends. Living in society may be a great good for human beings, but we cannot say whether it is our highest good or only an instrument for achieving that good.

It is this subtle difference from Aristotle that enables Smith to be such a truly *modern* figure, someone who can speak, from within a perspective that understands and respects virtue, to our own social and economic world. By turning virtue inward, by making the material conditions for virtue merely secondary to rather than constitutive of it, he was paradoxically more able to find a place for it in society than those who saw it as something essentially social; he was able to free himself from the nostalgia for precommercial society haunting civic republicanism. Self-command has material conditions, but they can be found in many different practices, including those as ubiquitous as the social interactions by which children learn to moderate their anger (Smith calls this "the great school of self-command" at TMS III.3.22). If such humble pie is capable of underwriting independence, then anyone can attain it, and neither war, nor citizenship, nor the agrarian life is necessary to it. Thus when Smith comes explicitly to consider the material conditions that allow each of us to attain the courage and intelligence without which we will be "mutilated and deformed in . . . essential part[s]" of our character (WN V.i.f.60–1), he proposes a variety of institutions, including but clearly not limited to public schools and a citizen militia, as helpful contributions to that end, without betraying the slightest worry that the problem might require a radical transformation of society. The smallness of these proposals—which Marx mistook for a vast underestimation of the problem—reflects Smith's sense that commercial society is not intrinsically hostile to independence, that no revolution is needed to achieve that virtue,[40] and that the spread of independence across a people, being something that in any case no political invention could either fully bring about or fully prevent, can and should proceed gradually, in accordance with a pace of change that people can incorporate easily into their everyday patterns of judgment.

Chapter 8

THE *WEALTH OF NATIONS* (III):

HELPING THE POOR

I

AN ADDITIONAL FEATURE of Smith's thought that separates him from Aristotle is his egalitarianism.[1] In both TMS and WN, he treats each human being as equally the locus of moral concern. We cannot attribute to Smith either Aristotle's elitism or the utilitarian belief that the good of some individuals can be added up and weighed against that of others. The good of each individual is firmly prior, for him, to that of any larger society: "The concern which we take in the fortune and happiness of individuals does not, in common cases, arise from that which we take in the fortune and happiness of society. . . . [O]ur regard for the individual [does not] arise from our regard for the multitude: but . . . our regard for the multitude is compounded and made up of the particular regards which we feel for the different individuals of which it is composed." (TMS II.ii.3.10). While Smith does, at times, take something like GDP as a measurement of the "opulence" of a society, it is important that for him this measures well-being only insofar as the goods so counted are available to every individual: "The high price of labour is to be . . . regarded as what constitutes the essence of public opulence. . . . That state is properly opulent in which opulence is easily come at, or in which a little labour, properly and judiciously employed, is capable of procuring any man a great abundance of all the necessaries and conveniences of life. Nothing else, it is evident, can render it general, or diffuse it universally through all the members of the society" (ED 12, LJ 567). GDP can at most be a symptom of wealth, not a criterion or definition of it ("what constitutes the essence" of it). Wealth consists ultimately in *each person*'s ability to gain "a great abundance of the necessaries and conveniences of life" by means of his or her own labor "judiciously employed," and that is not something that can be easily measured. An ability, a potential, diffused to each individual and enhancing the judicious efforts in each individual's life . . . if this is opulence, it will not fit into a calculus.

Smith's orientation toward the importance of each individual comes out similarly in his insistence that utilitarian considerations must not be allowed to trump matters of justice except in cases of extreme necessity,[2] and in a style that pervasively analyzes society by means of close examinations of its single members. The poor man in an urban context, we are told, can find a sort of moral protection in an extreme religious sect:

> A man of low condition . . . is far from being a distinguished member of any great society. While he remains in a country village his conduct may be attended to, and he may be obliged to attend to it himself. . . . But as soon as he comes into a great city, he is sunk in obscurity and darkness. His conduct is observed and attended to by nobody, and he is therefore very likely to neglect it himself, and to abandon himself to every sort of low profligacy and vice. He never emerges so effectually from this obscurity, his conduct never excites so much the attention of any respectable society, as by his becoming the member of a small religious sect. He from that moment acquires a degree of consideration which he never had before. All his brother sectaries are, for the credit of the sect, interested to observe his conduct, and if he gives occasion to any scandal, . . . to punish him by what is always a very severe punishment, even where no civil effects attend it, expulsion or excommunication from the sect. (WN V.i.g.12)

Like Smith's accounts of "the" landowner, merchant, laborer, soldier, student, or statesman, this description is convincing only if the reader imaginatively places herself in the situation of the individual described, imagines how she would think herself if she lived in such circumstances. Similarly, when Smith wants to show us how important the division of labor is in our own lives, he demonstrates how many different jobs go into an item of clothing that any one of us might wear; or, conversely, shows how a single random laborer might be said to "hold up" the lives and activities of thousands of other, less productive people. This approach to his subject, indeed, runs through the introductory section of every version of the lectures that eventually became WN:

> Of 10,000 families which are supported by each other, 100 perhaps labour not at all and do nothing to the common support. The others have them to maintain beside themselves, and . . . have a far less share of ease, convenience, and abundance than those who work not at all. The rich and opulent merchant who does nothing but give a few directions, lives in far greater state and luxury and ease . . . than his clerks, who do all the business. They, too, excepting their confinement, are in a state of ease and plenty far superior to that of the artizan by whose labour these commodities were furnished. The labour of this man too is pretty tollerable; he works under cover protected from the inclemency in the weather, and has his livelihood in no uncomfortable way if we compare him with the poor labourer. He has all the inconveniencies of the soil and the season to struggle with, is continually exposed to the inclemency of the

weather and the most severe labour at the same time. Thus he who as it were supports the whole frame of society and furnishes the means of the convenience and ease of all the rest is himself possessed of a very small share and is buried in obscurity. He bears on his shoulders the whole of mankind.[3]

What makes Smith unusual is that he combines this individualist orientation with such a thoroughgoing analysis of *social* structures. He is passionately interested in law, politics, history, and sociology, as well as economics. His moral treatise is devoted to showing how socially structured our selves are. He seems to want to resist the notion that the importance of the individual is necessarily threatened by the self's social relations. Mandeville saw the self as faced by an irresistible temptation to adopt social masks, as inevitably surrendering its own integrity to the need to fit into society. Hume dissolved the self entirely into the social transactions in which it participates;[4] for him, the apparent uniformity betokened by the use of the word "I" is in the end but a fiction, if a convenient one. Smith responds to these views by retaining the notion of a real, unified self while denying that that self is compromised by its social transactions: for him they are simply a "mirror" by which we can *see* ourselves.[5] We try to live up to the standards of our society, but that is not hypocrisy, nor a surrendering of integrity. It is, rather, the only way by which we can construct a true self, achieve integrity, at all. Not until Wittgenstein was anyone to surpass this insight into how autonomy and the social construction of the self might go together.

So how does this philosopher of social structures, this supremely acute observer of society's influence on the self, put his observations in a way that respects the ultimate moral importance of the individual? He simply looks at society from the bottom up rather than the top down, from the perspective of an individual who must move through social structures rather than the perspective, favored by political scientists and Pocockian historians of political thought, of one circling above the whole, to whom the interrelation of parts, the system into which individual agents fit, is much more interesting than the lifetimes of those agents themselves. Smith warns against such an approach to society, in a passage we have already noted:

> The man of system . . . seems to imagine that he can arrange the different members of a great society with as much ease as the hand arranges the different pieces upon a chess-board. He does not consider that the pieces upon the chess-board have no other principle of motion besides that which the hand impresses upon them; but that, in the great chess-board of human society, every single piece has a principle of motion of its own, altogether different from that which the legislature might chuse to impress upon it. (TMS VI.ii.2.17; compare also IV.1.11)

But if the concern of WN is with *each individual in* a society, as opposed to with "society as a whole" or some weighted sum of individuals, then we have to wonder whether it can really be all that devoted to the wealth of *nations*. And we have to suspect that Smith's criteria *for* the wealth of a nation, insofar as he has them, may be more Rawlsian than utilitarian,[6] more committed than those who read him for his sturdy common sense would suppose to the notion that a society is not well off if *any* of its members, or at least the typical individual in any rank of its members, has to suffer. It may turn out that for Smith a society is not wealthy, no matter how much it produces, if its poorest people are badly off.

II

Smith's concern for the worst-off pervades his work. Carl Menger claims, rightly as far as I know, that "there is not a single instance in A. Smith's work in which he represents the interest of the rich and powerful as opposed to the poor and weak."[7] Before Smith wrote, common wisdom held that the poor needed to be kept poor, else they would throw away their extra wages on drink—a line of reasoning that of course also fed neatly into the desire of employers to pay their workers as little as possible. Although Smith was not the first to oppose this position, he was by far the most influential,[8] arguing forcefully that high wages for the poor were not harmful at all, but a sign and a cause of economic health:

> The liberal reward of labour . . . as it is the necessary effect, so it is the natural symptom of increasing national wealth. The scanty maintenance of the labouring poor, on the other hand, is the natural symptom that things are at a stand, and their starving condition that they are going fast backwards. . . . Moreover, the liberal reward of labour . . . enabl[es the poor] to provide better for their children, and consequently to bring up a greater number. . . . To complain of it is to lament over the necessary effect and cause of the greatest publick prosperity. . . .
>
> . . . [And] as it encourages the propagation, so it increases the industry of the common people. . . . A plentiful subsistence increases the bodily strength of the labourer, and the comfortable hope of bettering his condition . . . , animates him to exert that strength to the utmost. Where wages are high, accordingly, we shall always find the workmen more active, diligent, and expeditious, than where they are low. (WN I.viii.27, 40, 42, 44)

In other respects, also, Smith champions the virtues of poor workers, and especially their ability to handle their own life decisions by themselves. To the complaint that workers are lazy, Smith maintains that in fact they will work too *hard* if they have incentive to do so, and defends the common practice of taking off "Saint Monday" as an appropriate reflection of the human need for leisure:

> Workmen, . . . when they are liberally paid by the piece, are very apt to over-work themselves, and to ruin their health and constitution in a few years. . . . Excessive application during four days of the week, is frequently the real cause of the idleness of the other three, so much and so loudly complained of. Great labour . . . continued for several days together, is in most men naturally fol-lowed by a great desire of relaxation, which . . . is almost irresistible. . . . If it is not complied with, the consequences are often dangerous, and sometimes fatal. . . . If masters would always listen to the dictates of reason and humanity, they have frequently occasion rather to moderate, than to animate the applica-tion of many of their workmen. (I.viii.44)

Elsewhere, he repeatedly upholds the superiority of independent work-people over those with supervisors or masters watching over them (e.g., I.viii.48); defends the ability of the poor to handle their own expendi-tures, rather than being restrained by sumptuary laws (II.iii.36, V.i.g.10);[9] recommends progressive tax measures (V.i.d.5, V.ii.e.6); attacks restric-tions placed on the movements of the poor and their choice of work (I.x.c.45–59, 12); and even tries to excuse, if not quite justify, mob violence:

> [The combinations of masters] . . . are frequently resisted by a contrary defen-sive combination of the workmen; who sometimes too, without any provoca-tion of this kind, combine of their own accord to raise the price of their la-bour. . . . [W]hether their combinations be offensive or defensive, they are always abundantly heard of. In order to bring the point to a speedy decision, they have always recourse to the loudest clamour, and sometimes to the most shocking violence and outrage. They are desperate, and act with the folly and extravagance of desperate men, who must either starve, or frighten their mas-ters into an immediate compliance with their demands. The masters upon these occasions are just as clamorous upon the other side, and never cease to call aloud for . . . the rigorous execution of those laws which have been enacted with so much severity against the combinations of servants, labourers, and jour-neymen. (I.viii.13)

Smith consistently adopts the strategy, in defending the rights or explain-ing the actions of the poor, of showing how they are just like "the rest of us" in virtue. Only the difference in their circumstances makes it occa-sionally appear otherwise. Thus masters, in the above passage, are just as ready to use illegitimate means against the rightful claims of their work-ers; that is indeed, Smith says a few lines earlier, "the usual . . . state of things." Thus, similarly, it is ridiculous to suppose that the profligacy of the poor is greater, or more dangerous, than that of their wildly irresponsible "kings and ministers" (II.iii.36). The famous passage in which Smith talks of the desire for self-improvement following us from womb to grave appears in this context:

> With regard to profusion, the principle, which prompts to expence, is the passion for present enjoyment; which, though sometimes violent and very difficult to be restrained, is in general only momentary and occasional. But the principle which prompts to save, is the desire of bettering our condition, a desire which, though generally calm and dispassionate, comes with us from the womb, and never leaves us till we go into the grave. In the whole interval which separates those two moments, there is scarce perhaps a single instant in which any man is so perfectly and completely satisfied with his situation, as to be without any wish of alteration or improvement, of any kind. (II.iii.28)

Smith is here conducting a polemic against people who consider "the passion for present enjoyment" to be so dangerous, so destructive to national capital, that governments should restrict its expression by law. He concedes that that passion is "sometimes violent and very difficult to be restrained." But he insists on his opponents recognizing that it is also "in general only momentary and occasional." By contrast, the desire underlying saving, "though generally calm and dispassionate," never leaves us twixt womb and grave. It is "uniform, constant, and uninterrupted," he says later (¶ 31), and overcomes the worst waste and destruction of capital—which are virtually always a product of government(¶ 31, 36). What Smith thus shows is that we need not worry about profligacy even if we accept the ugliest view of human beings: even then, the desire for social status will in the end defeat the passion for momentary pleasure. We must imagine him, as perhaps he imagined himself, in Parliament, fighting hypocritically pious aristocrats who profess their great concern for the wasteful indulgences of the poor. "Foolish, self-destructive passions overwhelm such weak people," they lament; "we must restrain their spending in their own long-term interest." To which, Smith: "Not so, Sirs, the foolish desire to become like yourselves will restrain them without any help from us."

Finally, as we shall note again below, Smith's criterion for the wealth of a nation is one linked inextricably to the well-being of the poor. The cheapness, hence ready availability, of grain, potatoes "or whatever else is the common vegetable food of the people" (I.xi.b.14) is what Smith takes to be the most important concern of public policy in economic matters.[10] As Istvan Hont and Michael Ignatieff have pointed out, it is to solve the problem of famines, above all, that Smith recommends a free market in corn.[11]

But if a sympathy and respect for the poor underpins the moral outlook of the entire work, it should seem strange that Smith rarely discusses policies that might alleviate poverty. There is one extended attack on the Elizabethan Poor Law, apparently arguing for its complete repeal without replacement, but no discussion of the major topics in most of his contemporaries' writings on poverty: (a) workhouses, (b) friendly societies and other voluntary relief efforts organized by the poor themselves,[12] (c) the question of whether the able-bodied poor should receive relief or not,[13] or (d) the role that churches might play in supporting those who could not support themselves.[14] There is also no mention of any literature on the poor aside from the one writer, a Richard Burn, on whom Smith relies to make his case against the Elizabethan Poor Law.[15] In a book that is otherwise remarkable for its vast erudition and range of economic topics, these are serious omissions, especially for a writer who so often professes concern for the poor. How can we account for them?

I suggest that Smith found most of the writings on poverty around him, and the policies based on such writings, nauseatingly patronizing. The accepted mode of proposing "solutions" to the problem of poverty in the eighteenth century seems to have been to show how one's plans would make the poor simultaneously more comfortable *and* more moral, with the emphasis, if anything, on the latter. Here is Daniel Defoe, rather a sympathizer with the needs of the poor than otherwise,[16] writing at the beginning of the century:

> [T]here is a general taint of Slothfulness upon our Poor, there's nothing more frequent, than for an Englishman to Work till he has got his Pocket full of Money, and then go and be idle, or perhaps drunk, till 'tis all gone, and perhaps himself in Debt; and ask him in his Cups what he intends, he'll tell you honestly, he'll drink as long as it lasts, and then go to work for more. . . . [I]f such Acts of Parliament may be made as may effectually cure the Sloth and Luxury of our Poor, that shall make Drunkards take care of Wife and Children, spendthrifts, lay up for a wet Day; Idle, Lazy Fellows Diligent; and Thoughtless Sottish Men, Careful and Provident . . . there will soon be less Poverty among us.[17]

Henry Fielding, in the middle of the century (1753), wrote a proposal "for making an effectual provision for the poor, [and] for amending their morals," in which not only vagrants but "persons of low degree found harbouring in an ale-house after ten o'clock at night" could be committed to a county workhouse, where they would be taught a trade.[18] Mandeville said that if a country is committed on principle to doing without slavery, "it is manifest that . . . the surest Wealth consists in a Multitude of labourious Poor," and that the best way to make sure the poor are labourious is to maintain their wages only just above subsistence level, and to keep them ignorant enough that they "submit to the Station they are in with Chearfulness"; Arthur Young echoed such views as late as 1771.[19] On the more humane side of the debate, we get Isaac Watts, who responded to Mandeville by calling for better schooling for the poor but couched his defense of this proposal in these terms: "[If the poor] have no manner of Learning bestowed upon them, . . . [h]ow little Sense will Servants have of the Honour and Obedience that is due to their own Masters?"[20] Watts had no doubt that the division between rich and poor was eternal, and ordained wisely by God. Hence the "Children of the Poor . . . should not be generally educated in such a Manner as may raise them above the Services of a lower Station."[21] The condescension of this approach to poverty, even at its most humane, continued into the next century (arguably, indeed, continues to the present day). Both when the original act for the protection of Friendly Societies was proposed, in 1793, and when it was amended, in 1819, the debate turned considerably on whether such laws would contribute to or detract from improvement of morals among the poor.[22] It is reasonable to suppose that most of the literature on poverty Smith could have known betrays a similarly paternalistic attitude,[23] by which the question is always, "What can we, who are both financially and morally better off than the poor, do to improve the material situation and moral health of those benighted creatures?"

Given Smith's respect for ordinary people's virtue, it would therefore not be surprising if he simply avoided most literature on "the poverty problem." Smith, on the subject that so troubled Defoe, rejects the notion that inherent vices cause alcoholism among workers:

> The education which low people's children receive . . . does them a great deal of service, and the want of it is certainly one of their greatest misfortunes. By it they learn to read, and this gives them the benefit of religion, which is a great advantage, not only considered in a pious sense, but as it affords them subject for thought and speculations. . . . [Putting a boy too soon to work entails that w]hen he is grown up he has no ideas with which he can amuse himself. When he is away from his work he must therefore betake himself to drunkenness and riot. Accordingly, we find that in the commercial parts of England, the tradesmen are for the most part in this despicable condition: their work thro' half the week is sufficient to maintain them, and *thro' want of education* they have no amusement for the other but riot and debauchery.[24]

Direct attempts to prevent drinking by the poor are merely inhumane: the only appropriate solution to the problem is to expand the educational opportunities offered to poor children. And while one advantage Smith offers for that expansion is that the children might then become religious, he does not recommend actually teaching them religion. Teach them to *read* and then they may become religious, says Smith, adding that the great advantage of religion is not piety but the fact that a person then has "ideas with which he can amuse himself." In several other ways, he is unsympathetic to policies by which governments try to press their notions of "virtue" on the poor. He is opposed to the establishment of religion, while defending, against standard Enlightenment objections, the sects that poor people tend to join (V.i.g.10–12). He also attacks sumptuary laws, as we have seen, which had traditionally been justified by a need to keep the poor properly humble or modest.[25] In general, he dismisses the notion that poor people need guidance, displaying instead a great respect for their decisions about how to run their own lives.

What the poor most need to rise out of poverty, of course, is adequate job opportunities, and it might seem that Smith is remiss in not requiring governments, when necessary, to provide them. But by freeing up labor markets, removing laws that provided incentives for poor people to stay in one place, and, as far as possible, cutting down on *masters'* combinations—unions to protect labor, insofar as Smith imagined them at all, are by all indications something he would have approved of[26]—Smith seems to have hoped that unemployment could be virtually eradicated. At the time he was writing, the period from 1740 to 1795 that constituted, for Britain, a prolonged boom in jobs and wages, this was not an unreasonable expectation. Had Smith foreseen a world in which government measures might be necessary to bring about full employment, it is not at all clear that he would have opposed such measures. Indeed, when Smith maintains that the sovereign has only three duties, there is nothing in that famous passage to preclude policies providing welfare to the poor: the "publick works and . . . publick institutions" that aid a great society could well include such programs, just as they include a public education system. But Smith had seen enough of government attempts to run the lives of poor people to have little reason for favoring programs that purport to alleviate poverty. Too often, their official purpose was merely a thin disguise for an attempt, hypocritically and paternalistically, to shove some upper-class person's notion of virtue down the throats of the poor. The fact that Smith valued independence so highly suggests that he recommended lifting the existing poor laws because he hoped to win, for those in poverty, an independence *from* "virtue."

III

It is Smith's concern for the worst-off that bars him from accepting the civic republicans' obsession with virtue. No society could consist entirely of landowners with the leisure to devote themselves to civic affairs, and for Smith, any society in which some achieved independence at the expense of making many others poorer and more dependent would be an exploitative society, not a realization of liberty at all. On the other hand, if governments are to encourage everyone in independence, as Smith seems to want, they must enable each of us to achieve the skills by which we can live as much as possible without having to depend on their patronage and protection, or on the goodwill of our neighbors. This independence is both a mental and a physical condition—we must both think and act independently—and while the material underpinnings of the physical condition are simply that we be subject as little as possible to coercion, the material underpinnings of the mental condition include the host of social institutions making it possible for us to develop (1) self-command, (2) a rich appreciation of empirical detail, and (3) the counterbalancing skill in taking a general view without which empirical detail is meaningless. I will argue that Smith praises market society in good part because he believes it can provide all of these conditions.

To begin with, as I suggested in the previous chapter, the famous passage about my appeal to the butcher and the baker can be read as, above all, about the *dignity* gained by speaking to someone else's needs rather than about one's own. We, unlike the puppy and the beggar, don't need to fawn on the butcher. But that allows us to achieve a distance from our own interests as well as an understanding of his—and such a distance is precisely self-command. Commerce thus takes the place, at least partially, of the military training that made for strength and fortitude in earlier, less economically developed ages.

The second condition is Smith's most obvious concern. The division of labor sorts us out such that we each become experts in something. Human beings begin more or less alike, says Smith, and become differentiated by what they do. Each of us acquires a knowledge of some specific subject matter, and a "talent or genius" in some area, that others lack. Economically, this means that we each acquire a comparative advantage over our fellows, which is what makes trade beneficial. Philosophically, what matters is that bodily immersion in a set of particulars gives us a kind of knowledge, a "knowing how," that no merely theoretical education could have supplied. Smith indeed exaggerates the ability of the division of labor to provide such mental goods, arguing, contrary to fact and even to claims he himself makes elsewhere, that improvements in machinery tend to come from those actually working with the machines: "A great part of the machines made use of in those manufactures in which labour is most subdivided, were originally the inventions of common workmen, who, being each of them employed in some very simple operation, naturally turned their thoughts towards finding out easier and readier methods of performing it. Whoever has been much accustomed to visit such manufactures, must frequently have been shewn very pretty machines, which were the inventions of such workmen" (I.i.8).[27] He goes on to say that the philosopher, from his general overview of the world, is also capable of imaginative inventions, but he never suggests that the philosopher, by means of theory alone, can adequately grasp the details of the working world, can exercise the delicate skill of the apothecary (I.x.b.35), or improve land as well as the merchant (III.iv.3). In a similar vein, as we have already noted, he argues that no one with a merely general view of the world, not the philosopher nor the social scientist nor the ever presumptuous politician, can acquire as precise a knowledge of each person's particular situation as the people themselves have who are immersed in those situations.

So the advantages of the division of labor in acquainting us with detail are clear. But if Smith thinks market society fosters what I have been calling *judgment*, and not mere perception, there must be another side to the picture. I think there is, but it is not obvious. In the *History of Astronomy*, Smith lays out an account of science that moves carefully between the need to take sharp note of particulars and the need to collect disparate particulars under general categories and principles. Now for Smith, science appeals to the imagination to judge its success,[28] and is thus measured by criteria that do not differ in kind from those by which we judge art. And Smith's view of those criteria, of what makes for beauty, is strikingly close to the view I have attributed to Kant: "A sort of uniformity mixd at the same time with a certain degree of variety gives [us] pleasure, as we see in the construction of a house or building which pleases when neither dully uniform nor its parts altogether angular" (LJ (A) vi.13, p. 335).

Put this together, now, with a remark about uniformity and variety in the characters of human beings: "[M]uch greater uniformity of character is to be observed among savages than among civilized nations. Among the former there is scarce any division of labour and consequently no remarkable difference of employments; whereas among the latter there is an almost infinite variety of occupations. . . . What a perfect uniformity of character do we find in all the heroes described by Ossian? And what a variety of manners, on the contrary, in those who are celebrated by Homer?" (ED 27). "Celebrated" by Homer: Smith's aesthetic preference between these two types of society is clear. Ossian's world is "dully uniform"; Homer's pleases by having "angular" parts. In the *Wealth of Nations*, Smith concludes his opening chapter on the division of labor with a virtual ode to the splendid differentiation it brings about:

Observe the accommodation of the most common artificer or day-labourer in a civilized and thriving country, and you will perceive that the number of people of whose industry a part, though but a small part, has been employed in procuring him this accommodation, exceeds all computation. The woollen coat, for example, which covers the day-labourer, as coarse and rough as it may appear, is the produce of the joint labour of a great multitude of workmen. The shepherd, the sorter of the wool, the wool-comber or carder, the dyer, the scribbler, the spinner, the weaver, the fuller, the dresser, with many others, must all join their different arts in order to complete even this homely production. How many merchants and carriers, besides, must have been employed in transporting the materials from some of those workmen to others who often live in a very distant part of the country! How much commerce and navigation, in particular, how many ship-builders, sailors, sail-makers, rope-makers, must have been employed in order to bring together the different drugs made use of by the dyer, which often come from the remotest corners of the world! What a variety of labour too is necessary in order to produce the tools of the meanest of those workmen! (I.i.9)

This calls up, not accidentally I think, the joyous survey of creation in Psalm 104, which climaxes with the words: "O LORD, how manifold are thy works!" In the eighteenth century, God's excellence was widely held to be manifested in, even to consist in, the *variety* of the world's contents. So it is hardly fanciful to suppose that part of Smith's point in this passage is to vindicate modern commercial society by way of the wondrous manifold into which it splits human nature. Contra Ferguson, Smith sees the effect of the division of labor on human personality as something to be embraced, not lamented. Commercial society is an intrinsic good because it is richly diverse, because it expresses, and enhances, the beauty of human differentiation. The African king at the end of WN I.i is not only poorer in material terms than the European common laborer, not only the agent of oppressive tyranny, but the master of a simpler, hence duller world. This rhetoric constitutes a polemic against primitivists like Rousseau and Ferguson. Commercial society is *admirable*, says Smith, a flowering of the human spirit, and not merely something ploddingly peaceful and opulent. The drawbacks of market society are present in WN and given serious attention, but they are drawbacks of an inherently admirable process, not of a neutral instrument.

But on Smith's own terms, the beauty of this kind of society, depends on its having a certain *uniformity* as well as variety, a certain organization or order as well as a multifold of particulars. And it is the loss of a *general* perspective, of the ability to take an overview, that most disturbs him about the lives of those who inhabit very specialized nooks of the division of labor:

In the progress of the division of labour, the employment of the far greater part of those who live by labour, that is, of the great body of the people, comes to be confined to a few very simple operations. . . . But the . . . man whose whole life is spent in performing a few simple operations, of which the effects too are, perhaps, always the same, or very nearly the same, has no occasion to exert his understanding, or to exercise his invention in finding out expedients for removing difficulties which never occur. He naturally loses, therefore, the habit of such exertion, and generally becomes as stupid and ignorant as it is possible for a human creature to become. The torpor of his mind renders him, not only incapable of relishing or bearing a part in any rational conversation, but of conceiving any generous, noble, or tender sentiment, and consequently of forming any just judgment concerning many even of the ordinary duties of private life. (V.i.f.50; cf. I.x.c.24)

Marx later came, famously, to worry about a similar problem in terms of "alienation," rooting the worker's disastrous differentiation from himself in the loss of connection between labor and its products. Control over the fruits of one's labor was therefore his key to restoring freedom and well-being. But this is not Smith's concern, nor was it that of the first generation of respondents to his, and other Scottish, accounts of civil society. What Hegel sought in the state, what Kant, Schiller, and Humboldt, like Smith, agreed was necessary but believed the state could *not* effect, was some element of society that might constitute a principle of "generality" to counter the excessive specialization brought about by the division of labor. The justification Hegel offers for moving to the state at all, in his *Philosophy of Right* (§§ 255–6), is that it counteracts the intense division of labour characteristic of towns by (1) joining them, in one political unit, to the less differentiated world of the country, and (2) establishing a civil service, separate from the market, that represents a principle of unity to the whole society. We may take this notion that a sphere of unity should balance the commercial sphere of differentiation as an expression of the principle of judgment, spread now across an entire social structure.[29]

The Hegelian solution is not open to Smith himself, however, given his individualist orientation. What does it matter if the state as a whole, by embracing agricultural and urban spheres, or by having a centralized civil service, somehow "expresses" the principle of universality as well as that of particularity? As long as each individual belongs either to the sphere of differentiation or to the sphere of unity, no one will have the two sides of judgment built into his or her own self. Smith must ensure that *those very individuals* stuck in specialized sectors of the economy can somehow build into themselves the general perspective they are in danger of losing. Insofar as he worries about this problem, even if he addresses it only with the disappointing recommendations of small public schools and militia training, he has more to say to modern liberals than anyone in the Hegelian tradition of statecraft.

Moreover, I am not sure that those two "homeopathic remedies" *are* all he has to offer on the subject. There are several "principles of unity" that go along with, and in part directly counter, the specialization so emphasized in WN. Some of these are very similar to the components of Hegel's state. Let us lay them out and consider whether they suffer from the problem I have attributed to Hegel.

First there are the philosophers, who do nothing in particular but observe everything, and therefore can connect things up that might otherwise remain separate: "Many improvements have been made [in machines] . . . by . . . those who are called philosophers or men of speculation, whose trade it is, not to do any thing, but to observe every thing; and who, upon that account, are often capable of combining together the powers of the most distant and dissimilar objects" (I.i.9).[30] It seems that such philosophers should be asked to use their capacity for bringing things together to help those in more limited occupational circumstances:

> In a civilized state, . . . though there is little variety in the occupations of the greater part of individuals, there is an almost infinite variety in those of the whole society. These varied occupations present an almost infinite variety of objects to the contemplation of those few, who, being attached to no particular occupation themselves, have leisure and inclination to examine the occupations of other people. . . . Unless those few, however, happen to be placed in some very particular circumstances, their great abilities, though honorable to themselves, may contribute very little to the good government or happiness of their society. (V.i.f.51)

Smith uses "philosopher" in a rough and loose way, and I think we can pretty well include all academics under his description. There is thus some suggestion here that academics, in their writings and their teachings, can help hold the fragmented parts of an advanced society together.[31] Exactly what this means is unclear, but it could be something as blunt as a suggestion that academics be required to share their research, in public forums, with ordinary workers. Smith's colleagues in Glasgow lectured on natural science to working men, and Smith himself helped try to set up a school for dancing, riding, and fencing.[32] So when he says that the state should "render almost universal" the study of science and philosophy among people of middling rank, he may not only be offering an antidote to "the poison of enthusiasm and superstition" (V.i.g.14), but hoping that the broad vision characteristic of the academy (in his time, at least) can filter throughout society and thereby correct for the limits on people's everyday perspectives.

Second, the state itself is supposed to have some ability to take a view of the whole. That is why Smith expects it to take care of "public goods," including his remedies for specialization, and that is why he, however reluctantly, puts in its hand the option of overruling "the system of natural liberty" in some limited cases.[33] In addition to these ways in which the state can compensate for *failures* of the market, moreover, it uses its central position in society to ensure that markets perform their healthy social functions at all. Most obviously, this means that it provides the general framework of external and internal security (defense and the administration of justice) without which no one would pursue long-term investments.[34] Slightly less obviously, it corrects for "blockages" in the free channels through which markets would otherwise enable goods to circulate. Smith explicitly urges governments to do what they can to prevent the combinations of masters:

> People of the same trade seldom meet together, even for merriment and diversion, but the conversation ends in a conspiracy against the publick, or in some contrivance to raise prices. It is impossible indeed to prevent such meetings. . . . But though the law cannot hinder people of the same trade from sometimes assembling together, it ought to do nothing to facilitate such assemblies; much less to render them necessary. A regulation which obliges all those of the same trade in a particular town to enter their names and places of abode in a publick register, facilitates such assemblies. . . . A regulation which enables those of the same trade to tax themselves . . . renders such assemblies necessary. An incorporation not only renders them necessary, but makes the act of the majority binding upon the whole. In a free trade an effectual combination cannot be established but by the unanimous consent of every single trader, and it cannot last longer than every single trader continues of the same mind. (I.x.c.27–30)[35]

Although "incorporation," in this passage, refers primarily to the guilds that regulated, and thereby restricted entry to, most professions carried out in a town (more or less as the Bar and medical associations do in contemporary America), Smith's savage criticisms, elsewhere, of joint-stock companies allow for an easy extension of the point here to "incorporations" in the modern sense. In particular, when criticizing the East India and South Sea companies (IV.vii.c.101–6, V.i.e.18, 26–30), Smith makes observations on the potential conflicts of interest among managers, employees, and shareholders, on the difficulty of governing any large and widely dispersed workforce, and on the tendency of merchants to employ political force, where possible, to further their economic ends, that apply to any large firm, whether or not it is publicly chartered. Throughout this critique, he describes merchants using political force "unjustly, . . . capriciously, . . . [and] cruelly" (V.i.e.29). A major theme of WN is that economic power should be kept as far as possible from political power: merchants should never govern people. But a large firm always requires a substantial disciplinary structure, if only to keep its various parts coordinated with one another. So while Smith says nothing directly about a free market consisting primarily of large, private firms—since no such thing was even on the horizon in his time—it is fairly easy to argue that this is not the free market he had in mind. If "a free trade" allows for combinations only "by the unanimous [and continuing] consent of every single trader," then the law, far from protecting and encouraging private incorporation, should refuse to put its weight behind any disciplinary structure shareholders or managers set up. At the very least, it should tolerate such structures with a sharply skeptical eye: eager to protect any subgroup of employees, or of rivals trying to enter the market, who claim that the firm stands in the way of their independence. For Smith, the state should use its centralized position to see, and its centralized power to combat, any combination in the private sphere that threatens to make nonsense of the "freedom" in free trade. This is supposed to help *every single trader*—in the modern context: every single employee—whose consent is then necessary to any combination and who can withdraw from it at the moment he ceases to be "of the same mind." In such a world, combinations will be relatively few and relatively weak. And if Smith is right, every trader, every consumer, and every laborer will be protected thereby.

Now of course the most famous of Smith's recommendations are those telling governments simply to get out of the business of regulating businesses altogether. But even this must be seen as in part a positive act, not a mere avoidance of action. The tendencies that lead governments to impose quality controls, maximum wages (Smith says nothing about *minimum* wages), and protective tariffs are deeply rooted in the beliefs of ordinary members of society. "Consumers need legal protection against bad quality," people think. Or: "The poor will waste money on drink unless their salaries are capped." Or: "We need to protect our industries against foreigners who undercut them." Sometimes these common superstitions are egged on by the disingenuous rantings of merchants who find such controls useful, but they are also based on old and widespread traditions about what fairness or honesty or divine will demands of the marketplace. Thus for governments to remove all such restrictions is not merely for them to go with the natural flow but to *make* that flow cut through hardened soilbeds of tradition and common belief. The Enlightenment ideal of replacing the prejudices of traditions with rational strategies, and thereby ending foolishness as well as oppression, is by no means absent from Smith's work, although it is tempered by a belief in gradual change.[36] He says that government can spread this enlightening wisdom, indirectly, through changes in laws governing markets:

The popular fear of engrossing and forestalling may be compared to the popular terrors and suspicions of witchcraft. The unfortunate wretches accused of this latter crime were not more innocent of the misfortunes imputed to them, than those who have been accused of the former. The law which put an end to all prosecutions against witchcraft . . . seems effectually to have put an end to those fears and suspicions, by taking away the great cause which encouraged and supported them. The law which should restore entire freedom to the inland trade of corn, would probably prove as effectual to put an end to the popular fears of engrossing and forestalling. (IV.v.b.26)

Not only should the law remove obstructions to the free trade of corn in order to promote agricultural production, but in so doing it will help to bring about *belief* in free trade among the people. Government can counteract prejudices based on tradition simply by removing its intellectual authority—the "great cause which encourage[s] and support[s]" popular ideas—from those prejudices. That alone virtually extinguished belief in witches; that alone, Smith argues, can eliminate analogous superstitions about economics. Note that the state compensates for the defects of specialization, again, not by simply *being* an institution that represents the universal, as it is for Hegel, but by diffusing the information it gains from its "universalist" position throughout society.

Third, arguing that agriculture encourages human unity more than other spheres do, Smith urges private people to invest in agriculture and the state to encourage commerce between town and country. He tells us that the division of labor cannot be taken as far in agriculture as in manufactures (I.i.4, IV.ix.35), and maintains that the conditions in which a farmer works, being highly variable, require and therefore cultivate "judgment and discretion" (I.x.c.24). He waxes rhapsodic about agrarian life:

The beauty of the country . . . , the pleasures of a country life, the tranquillity of mind which it promises, and, wherever the injustice of human laws does not disturb it, the independency which it really affords, have charms that more or less attract every body (III.i.3)

and describes new agrarian colonies in utopian terms:

Every colonist gets more land than he can possibly cultivate. . . . No landlord shares with him in its produce, and the share of the sovereign is commonly but a trifle. . . . [H]is land is commonly so extensive, that with all his own industry, and with all the industry of other people whom he can get to employ, he can seldom make it produce the tenth part of what it is capable of producing. He is eager, therefore, to collect labourers from all quarters, and to reward them with the most liberal wages. But those liberal wages, joined to the plenty and cheapness of land, soon make those labourers leave him in order to become landlords themselves, and to reward, with equal liberality, other labourers, who soon leave them for the same reason that they left their first master. (IV.vii.b.2)

So when Smith goes on to say, over and over, that there is no more important commerce than that between town and country (I.x.c.19, III.i.1, III.i.8, IV.ix.48), it is not unreasonable to see more than an exchange of "products" behind this insistence. *One* reason he urges trade between town and country is that he recognizes the importance of technological improvement to enlarging the agricultural sector—which in turn, as Hont and Ignatieff point out, would help stave off famines.[37] But another reason for emphasizing the intercourse of town and country may be that the latter can provide some balance between the differentiated and the universal perspectives that are jointly necessary for good human judgment.

Indeed, *all* commerce, within towns and between nations as well as between town and country, may serve for Smith as a way for people to share and "exchange" their virtuous qualities as well as their material goods. That commerce "brings people together" is a common eighteenth-century thesis, most famously expressed by Montesquieu. Smith echoes this thesis when he says that "Commerce . . . ought naturally to be, among nations, as among individuals, a bond of union and friendship" (IV.iii.c.9). He also makes "commerce" connote more than the exchange of goods by rooting it in conversation,[38] and using it to describe all ordinary social interaction (TMS III.3.7): a marketplace in ideas and virtues, as well as in material goods, is far from a foreign notion to Smith. He may very well, therefore, see the country as offering certain "generalist" virtues to counterbalance the town's "particularist" ones. If this is his hope, however, one wonders how well it can be realized on the individualist level we have been stressing. *That* there is a stretch of country outside one's town, or even that goods come in from there, will not help the poor workers in excessively specialized occupations to broaden their minds. Perhaps—in a Scotland where even the large city of Glasgow, in the 1770s, had a population of less than forty thousand[39]—Smith expected that workers, as well as merchants, would simply take frequent walks into the country and experience the "tranquillity of mind" he praises, or that buying one's goods from a farmer in the local marketplace would enable a worker, as consumer, to broaden his perspective to some degree. Certainly, the spread of philosophy, the protection of everyone's liberty by the state, and the establishment of public schooling and militia service are more likely to help the worker than commerce with the country, but when Smith rhapsodizes about the beauty of the country we get a hint that for him, as for Kant, natural beauty can go some way towards compensating for an excess of specialization: can literally "broaden our minds."

IV

Smith never quite tells us what the wealth of a nation is supposed to be. His title is odd in any case. Is he really interested in the wealth of *nations?* By far the largest section of the book is a polemic insisting that the notion of wealth as relative to "nations"—of international economics as a zero-sum game in which one country becomes wealthy only by beggaring others—is inimical to the economic health of every nation and every individual. Of course, the query that first leads us to read a book entitled *Inquiry into the Nature and Causes of the Wealth of Nations* may well take the form, "How can my nation become rich?" But the conclusion of that inquiry should show us that the wealth of *a* nation is inseparable from the wealth of nation*s*, taken together, such that the premise of the original question was faulty. We should conclude, that is, if we understand the reasoning along which we have been led, by recognizing that the economic health of all peoples is essential to our own; hence by rephrasing, if not withdrawing, our opening question. We might then read the title ironically, to suggest that there is no wealth "of" a nation in the sense we supposed when we picked up this book promising to show us its nature and causes. At least we must read the title against its most obvious grain: "the wealth of nations," we learn, is a sum possessed by all nations collectively, not by each nation distributively.

But if we should read "nations" ironically, or against the grain, then perhaps we should also read "wealth" that way. In any case, how exactly to define "wealth" is not a question Smith answers with his usual lucidity. There is the word, right in the title of the book, but when you try to locate a passage where Smith tells you what the title refers to, you will find him instead dancing around the question, suggesting here that it is "revenue and stock" (I.viii.21), there that it is the annual produce of land and labour (I.xi.m.21, IV.vii.c.35)—seeming not to notice that these are different things—and at yet another point describing it as the annual produce of labor alone (I.xi.e.33). The first chapter of part IV is devoted to how silly it is to suppose that gold and silver constitute the wealth of a country, but you will be hard pressed to discover what, as opposed to gold and silver, Smith thinks does constitute that wealth. The "annual production of . . . commodities" (¶ 33), "revenue or subsistence" (IV.intro.1), and whatever "creates the greatest employment to the people of the country" (¶ 10) are all candidates. A simple criterion appears in TMS:

one country is wealthier than another if its citizens "are better lodged, are better clothed, are better fed" (IV.i.11).

On the level of common sense, these casual remarks make good sense: a country is wealthy if its people can find the means to pursue their ends, if it has a good supply of food, houses, clothes, etc., and of jobs by which to earn those supplies. But how does this casual handwaving translate into a criterion for policy? When pressed, the formulations in the previous paragraph do not all cohere: measuring one is not the same thing as measuring another. How then can government officials, to whom above all WN is addressed, have any means of knowing whether their country is doing well or badly, whether Smith's recommendations work or whether they should look to someone else?

Well, how *do* you measure the opulence of a whole people? Do you add everybody's bit together, regardless of how the total is distributed? Do you take an average? Do you look at the well-being of one group, of each group, of the majority, of the average member of the majority? Finally, Smith suggests a test:

> [T]he low money price of some particular sorts of goods, such as cattle, poultry, game of all kinds, etc., in proportion to that of corn, is a most decisive [proof of a country's poverty and barbarism]. . . . [And] an easy proof of the prosperous condition of the country [is the] . . . increased fertility [of its land], or . . . its having been rendered fit for producing corn. . . . The circumstances of the poor through a great part of England cannot surely be so much distressed by any rise in the price of poultry, fish, wildfowl, or venison, as they must be relieved by the fall in that of [corn or] potatoes. (I.xi.n.2–3, 9–10)

Smith is perfectly serious about this, regarding the food of the poor as the most important of commodities, and in any case arguing that corn is the best approximation we have of labor value, to which all other value ultimately reduces. But it is hard to avoid the sense that he is mocking us when he makes the importance of rendering land fit for producing corn such a central achievement of his work: "it may be of some use, or, at least, it may give some satisfaction to the Publick, to have so decisive a proof of . . . its wealth" (I.xi.n.9). He refuses us any general, theoretically useful criterion for the wealth of a nation, but he assures us that in wealthy nations corn and potatoes are cheap relative to beef and chicken.

I suggest that part of what is going on here is that for Smith there *cannot* be a numerical expression for the wealth of nations. The goal Smith sets up for human life in TMS, as we have seen, is a balance of the passions—insofar as he answers the question of what our ends might be at all. That is not something that "adds up" across individuals. There is no "sum" of moderation or self-command in a society. But that means that the possessions and structure of a society can only be a rough guide to whether it is helping its individual members or not. And well-being, for Smith, is essentially an individual rather than a social phenomenon. He is far from an "atomic individualist" in his account of human nature, but he does firmly give *moral* priority to the good of human individuals over the good of human groups.

This makes him a sensitive and profound liberal, but it also deprives him of any easy, clear way to measure the economic health of a society. A society is economically healthy when it provides the means of independence to as many of its individuals as possible. But what are these means? It is clear that Smith wants a society to have as much as possible of the basic elements of material wealth—food, shelter, clothing—so that on any decent distribution the poorest will be as well off as possible, and it is also clear that, like Rawls, he objects to pure equality primarily because it will entail a lower standard of living for the poor. But it is not clear that Smith can say anything more than this about what material goods a society should have, because, beyond a certain minimum, the system of labor and exchange itself is as important to independence as what goods it produces. Recall LJ's encomium to commerce because of the independence it brings about:

> Nothing tends so much to corrupt and enervate and debase the mind as dependency, and nothing gives such noble and generous notions of probity as freedom and independency. Commerce is one great preventive of [having many servants and dependents]. The manufactures give the poorer sort better wages than any master can afford; besides, it give<s> the rich an opportunity of spending their fortunes with fewer servants which they never fail of embracing. Hence it is that the common people of England who are alltogether free and independent are the honestest of their rank any where to be met with.[40]

Here opulence and independence are interwoven so tightly that they are almost impossible to separate. Making the poor wealthier also makes them freer: people with greater means are not as desperately dependent on their bosses for employment. But another part of the reward of greater financial independence, it seems, is to have a mind less "corrupt[ed] and enervate[d] and debase[d]." People with greater means have more of the mental ease, and leisure, to develop judgment. Whether the material or the mental good counts for more here, it is hard to say.

Now if we bring Smith's concern for the worst-off together with his notion of independence, we arrive at some very interesting implications for political economy. As we said in the beginning of this chapter, Smith is concerned with what "renders [opulence] general," what "diffuse[s] it universally through all the members of society." But if opulence is independence, then independence must be "rendered general," "diffused universally." The goal of a Smithian political economy would seem to be to enable *each* person in a society, as far as this is possible, to attain independence. This does not require governments to equalize wealth—that, he believes, would merely make everyone equally poor—but it does suggest, insofar as necessary, that governments should ensure that people are equally provided with the conditions for independence. People start off essentially equal in talents or skills, for Smith, and become unequal as a result of specialization. That does not matter much, as long as the skills are merely instruments for acquiring material goods. But once the inequality in skills extends to qualities needed for the very achievement of independence, the possibility that each person can carve out his or her own path is seriously threatened. Smith famously says that courage and judgment, the "parts" necessary to being human at all, cannot just be allowed to atrophy, as they naturally will in the extremes of the division of labor (V.i.f.50, 60–1). Governments do not much need to redistribute goods, according to Smith. Once people have their basic material needs met, differences in wealth are mostly a matter of vanity. And governments should not enforce any virtuous actions except those required by justice. But they do need to make sure that everyone has the capacity to pursue virtues for themselves—the capacity to exercise and develop their "judgment," in the richest sense of that term.

Taken as the whole they are supposed to form, Smith's politics urge a widespread distribution of the conditions for judgment. With a free market imposing emotional discipline, spreading around greater means, and allowing more independent ways to work, with governments refraining as much as possible from regulating the daily choices people make, and with educational, military, and perhaps community-building institutions (V.i.g) in place to help counter the mind-deadening effects of the division of labor, a world of freely choosing, phronetic people might open up. I think this is Smith's utopia. Of course, the Industrial Revolution, and the power of large corporations, have blocked any such thing from actually coming to pass, but Smith opposes the development of large corporations,[41] and he seems not to have foreseen the spread of the factory system at all.[42] In Book III of WN, Smith describes how unanticipated events, together with the vices that characteristically beset the powerful, led feudal lords to lose their hold over their vassals. I think he both hoped and expected the same thing to happen to the hold that owners of stock have over their employees. People would wind up becoming more and more independent of one another, in their labor, as commerce progressed. Then the state might still have to protect people from becoming too *narrow-minded*, but not from becoming too *dependent*. That would explain why Smith never worries about the dependency of laborers under commerce: he did not see that dependency could again come to increase.

Once one supposes that he did not foresee the threat to independence that factories would introduce, his political views make complete sense. If the state just protects people from narrow-mindedness, he thought, and otherwise leaves them alone, they will all be independent in the full sense: free of coercion and capable of judging for themselves. Such a state, filled with independent citizens pursuing phronetic activities each in her own way, could rightly congratulate itself on its wealth. A wide distribution of independence, and of the ability to use one's independence judiciously: *that* is what constitutes the true "wealth of nations."

Chapter 9

KANT'S POLITICS, RAWLS'S POLITICS (I):

THE PUBLIC USE OF JUDGMENT

I WANT in this and the following chapter to show how Kant's political economy can be read as a version of Smith's. By this I mean that
Kant regards both modern commercial society and a presumption
against government interference in that society as ways to structure character—a character appropriate for freedom. If I am right, we will have
reason to make room for a Kantian politics that differs from the currently
dominant Rawlsian and Habermasian models in two important ways: (1)
in general, it will be more concerned with ensuring that ordinary citizens
can make their own daily decisions than with what principles guide the
society as a whole, and (2) specifically, it will favor market economies
over centrally organized ones for moral rather than merely pragmatic
reasons. Rawls and Habermas try to uncover a framework for just politics
from the structure of reason itself, and their projects fail, deeply and irremediably, because that structure cannot tell us anything, by itself, about
its own proper application to concrete matters of public policy. Kant's
own political writings are more closely engaged with specific, contingent
issues of his day. Surprisingly, perhaps, Kant has considerably greater respect for history, and for empirical fact, than do his modern-day followers. Unlike Rawls, especially, Kant does not conceive freedom as a
merely notional stance from which to construct general principles for the
distribution of material goods and social place; rather, freedom must be
worked out in and through the actual *practice* of social institutions, including the institution of the market. In seeing the market as something
that directly cultivates freedom, Kant and Smith are more intimately
linked, I believe, and stand further from the mainstreams of either left-
wing or right-wing politics than has generally been recognized.

I have argued elsewhere that Kant was one of the first figures in Germany to appreciate the importance and depth of the *Wealth of Nations*.[1]
Kant seems to have been inspired to take an interest in economic issues
by Smith, although, as we shall see, he seems also to have been critical of
Smith's overly empirical account of "value." In both these ways, Kant
gives WN much the same response he gave to TMS—borrowing empirical elements of the theory while insisting that its fundamental normative
principles have an a priori rather than a merely empirical grounding. By

means of this double response, Kant provides the theoretical basis for a liberalism that is more consistent and deeper than Smith's, while retaining the latter's rich respect for, and understanding of, the empirical world.

I present connections between Kant and Smith in parts I and II. Parts III to VI draw consequences from these connections for Kantian political theory in the present day.

I

The most obvious connection between Kant and Smith is their shared antipathy towards political leaders who treat citizens like children. Two of the passages in which Kant actually quotes Smith occur in the context of a critique of "tutelage" (*Unmündigkeit*). This is an obsessive concern for Kant. In *What is Enlightenment?*, in his *Reflexionen* of the same period, in *Theory and Practice*, and in his *Anthropology*, Kant condemns rulers who see themselves as the "father" of their people, and who thereby encourage in the people a childlike, passive disposition to avoid making use of their own reason:

> Kings as fathers treat their subjects like children, wanting to be the sole provider of their livelihood and well-being. Priests as shepherds [treat their congregants] as sheep and therefore indeed as the dear animal that can never become mature [*mündig*]. One makes the people first incapable of ruling themselves, and then excuses one's despotism on the grounds that they cannot rule themselves.[2]

> [T]here are naturally bound to be leaders who know how to use the docility of the great masses . . . and to represent as very great, even mortal, the danger of relying on one's own understanding, without someone else's direction. Chiefs of state call themselves *fathers of their country* because they understand better than their subjects how to make them happy, while the people, in their own best interests, are condemned to perpetual tutelage [*Unmündigkeit*]. And when Adam Smith says unjustly of these chiefs of state: "they are themselves, without exception, the greatest spendthrifts of all," he is effectively refuted by the (wise!) sumptuary edicts promulgated in many countries.[3]

> A government might be established on the principle of benevolence towards the people, like that of a father towards his children. Under such a *paternal government* . . . the subjects, as immature [*unmündige*] children who cannot distinguish what is truly useful or harmful to themselves, would be obliged to behave purely passively and to rely upon the judgement of the head of state as

to how they *ought* to be happy. . . . Such a government is the greatest conceivable *despotism*. (TP 290–91/74)

The main cure for *Unmündigkeit*, whether imposed by government officials or clergymen, academics or husbands,[4] is speech (the use of one's *Mund*)—as much speech, and as public speech, as possible: "But which sort of restriction prevents enlightenment, and which, instead of hindering it, can actually promote it? I reply: The *public* use of man's reason must always be free, and it alone can bring about enlightenment" (E 37/55). The single "transcendental formula" of public right is that "All actions affecting the rights of other human beings are wrong if their maxim is not compatible with their being made public."[5] Nor is this merely a transcendental guideline. The only empirical institution upon which Kant insists to safeguard the rights of citizens is the public use of reason.[6] He makes clear that by exercising your right to criticize your state—as well as your clergyman, your tax collector, and your military superior—you can develop the freedom that will allow you to emerge from tutelage. You can develop the freedom that will make tutelage, and the authority relationships it sustains, unnecessary.

Before we go any further we should note something very important, and curiously overlooked,[7] about this aspect of Kant's political philosophy. Freedom, it seems, is not always and necessarily there, nor does it come in a simple "on/off" state. Rather, it can be *developed empirically*, by engagement in certain kinds of activities. This is not necessarily what we would expect from Kant. Rawls says it is a Kantian but *not* Kant's own view that untoward empirical circumstances—above all, political oppression or great poverty—can serve as "limits on our reason," that "our freedom depends on the nature of the surrounding institutional and social context" (PL 222n).[8] Indeed Kant's moral philosophy seems not to allow for such empirical shaping of freedom. Claiming that will or reason can be empirically cultivated defies the sense in which that faculty is supposed to stand apart from all empirical influences on us. Repeatedly, Kant uses divine creation as the model for what truly free willing looks like, and suggests that transcendental freedom is beyond not only all empirical events but time itself.[9] If that same transcendental freedom is the ground of practical freedom and ultimately the only real freedom, one might suppose political structures to have no effect on freedom at all. Consistently with this interpretation, in the *Rechtslehre* Kant takes pains to make clear that his libertarian general principle for political order does not allow external structures of coercion to pay any attention to people's internal states: "It cannot be required that [the principle of right] be itself . . . my maxim, . . . for anyone can be free as long as I do not impair his freedom by my *external action*, even though I am quite indifferent to his freedom or would like in my heart to infringe upon it" (MM 231/56).

One would expect from this that institutions set up according to the principle of right could not either enhance or detract from anyone's ability to will freely.

But Kant's political writings run emphatically in the opposite direction: he has a rich empirical account of how social institutions and circumstances can shape freedom. An excellent example can be found in a passage from the *Idea for a Universal History*:

> Man has an inclination to *live in society*, since he feels in this state more like a man, that is, he feels able to develop his natural capacities. But he also has a great tendency to *live as an individual*, to isolate himself, since he also encounters in himself the unsocial characteristic of wanting to direct everything in accordance with his own ideas. He therefore expects resistance all around, just as he knows of himself that he is in turn inclined to offer resistance to others. It is this very resistance which awakens all man's powers and induces him to overcome his tendency to laziness. Through the desire for honour, power, or property, it drives him to seek status among his fellows, whom he cannot *bear* yet cannot *bear to leave*. Then the first true steps are taken from barbarism to culture, which in fact consists in the social worthiness of man. . . . [T]hus a *pathologically* enforced social union is transformed into a *moral* whole. . . . Nature should thus be thanked for fostering social incompatibility, enviously competitive vanity, and insatiable desires for possession or even power. (IUH 20–1/44–5)

Three features of this passage recall Smith's TMS: (1) the notion of social relations as a tension between two opposing impulses (for Smith, the feelings we have as "person principally concerned" in an event vs. the feelings we have as "impartial spectator" of that event), (2) the notion that one of those impulses is a desire for other people's admiration—here called "the desire for honour," but also, in more Rousseauian terms, "enviously competitive vanity," and (3) the notion that these at best *a*moral empirical impulses can yet bring about a "moral whole." It may seem inconsistent with everything Kant stands for that he allows a desire for admiration to motivate a moral development, but here, as elsewhere, his natural teleology comes into play. Just as, in the *Groundwork's* first example, the natural desire for self-preservation turns out to serve the rationally necessary function of preserving rational being itself, so here the desire for admiration imposes a discipline on us by which we can take the rationally necessary step of cultivating our natural talents rather than letting them play themselves out willy-nilly. Once we recognize the rational grounds for such discipline, we can and should of course be motivated by that recognition, rather than the mere "pathological" desire to be admired. But the pathological desire unavoidably occasions our coming to the recognition.

Empirically, then, Kant, like Smith, sees society as a world of simultaneous spectators and agents. Each of us constantly watches the others and constantly judges them morally and aesthetically. For moral purposes, we need to transform the causal structures that lead us to act well into *reasons* for good action, and once we work out the reasons behind what our neighbors admire and despise, we may in part turn our standards for judgment on that admiration and contempt itself. But the fact that ultimately we need to recognize a logical priority of reasons over causes, and that in practice we may then condemn some causal structures around us as *im*moral, does not imply that we could, in empirical fact, come to this free mental condition without being pointed there by our society.

Thus when Kant tells us that the public use of reason can bring people to a state of true freedom, he is not contradicting his moral philosophy. Rather, he is letting us know that he himself regards the freedom so important to his moral thinking to be something that allows of empirical conditioning, something that may increase over the course of human history, something that can be helped or hindered by the political institutions of each society. Perhaps he is introducing a somewhat new sense of "freedom." In one sense, freedom for Kant is of course a condition *for* the understanding of human decisions and history, but in this new sense it can also be conditioned *by* our individual and collective acts. He also, thereby, introduces a different role for political practice from the one he usually stresses—a role that makes freedom similarly a goal, as well as a presumption, of politics. Unsurprisingly, the public use of reason is something each individual must ultimately do for herself, but the powers that be in a society can also help this process along, by tolerating public expression and, ideally, creating forums for it to take place.

What relevance might all this have for political economy? Well, Kant's main cure for *Unmündigkeit* may be speech, but that does not seem to be his only cure. By repeatedly placing sumptuary laws in the class of institutions that encourage *Unmündigkeit*, Kant suggests that management of one's own income is also a way to develop one's freedom. Is it too much of a stretch to suggest that when Kant calls for the deregulation of commerce and, more generally, envisions a world where everyone earns their place by "talent, industry, and luck," he again has in mind the value of market activity for developing one's capacity for freedom? This would be a yet deeper recognition of the empirical conditions that make choice possible than his insistence on the public use of reason, for here it is the silent habits of working and saving, rather than conscious mental activities, that serve as a means to "enlightenment."

If this is right, a political policy of avoiding interference in the market will be not merely smart economics but a way for individual citizens to develop their own independence. This is not, however, nearly as close to libertarianism as it might look. Kant does not justify the market as a mere means to already chosen ends, an institution helping one to do what one likes, nor yet as a direct expression of freedom, but as a *training ground* for the full development of freedom. As such, it may indeed be a morally valuable institution, but one whose value will always depend on how much training in freedom it in fact provides. If, for certain individuals, other empirical conditions for the use of freedom are missing—and a high level of education, nutrition, health, and perhaps a good deal more might be included in this[10]—it will be in very bad faith to insist that the market gives them an opportunity to achieve enlightenment. We will discuss this further in the next chapter.

II

The connection between WN and Kant's *Critique of Judgment* is surprisingly straightforward.[11] Kant borrows Smith's phrase, "the division of labor," in a whole series of his works, from the *Groundwork* onwards.[12] In the latter, it justifies the distinction between philosophical and popular treatments of morality (G 388–9/4–5). Many years later, Kant uses the division of labor to explain how thinking should be organized:

> [I]t was not a bad idea to handle the entire content of learning . . . by *mass production*, so to speak—by a division of labor, so that for every branch of the sciences there would be a public teacher or *professor* appointed as its trustee, and all of these together would form a kind of learned community called a *university*. . . . The university would . . . be authorized to perform certain functions through its faculties (smaller societies, each comprising the university specialists in one main branch of thinking). . . . In addition to these incorporated scholars, there can also be scholars at large, who do not belong to the university but simply work on part of the great content of learning, either forming independent organizations, like various workshops . . . or . . . each working by himself. (CF 17–8/23–5)

In the light of this ongoing fascination with the division of labor, it is plausible to read Kant's introduction and first part of the CJ as governed by a picture of our mental powers by which each faculty performs its separate task and the results are brought together by the invisible hand of the "harmony of the faculties." Judgment would then be a product both of allowing the imagination to immerse itself as much as it likes in detail and of the cross-fertilization between such immersion and the unities, and tendency towards unification, fostered respectively by understanding and reason. The *Conflict of the Faculties* calls for a communal version of this cross-fertilization: in order to provide practical guidance to society at large, a learned community needs to foster interaction between specialized scholars in theology, medicine, law, etc., and a faculty that surveys and criticizes the whole.[13] This faculty, unsurprisingly, turns out to be philosophy. As it is for Smith, philosophy for Kant provides a counterbalancing force to specialization. And the product of combining specialization with the counterbalancing overview offered by philosophy is good judgment.

Returning now to CJ, we can illuminate the odd dip Kant makes into politics in § 40. We are told there that three maxims of the common human understanding also apply to common sense or judgment. The first two of these are "Think for yourself," and "Put yourself in thought in the place of everyone else." "Think for yourself" is very much the principle Kant described in *What is Enlightenment?* as crucial to coming out of tutelage (E 36/54–5). Here too it is described as that which brings "enlightenment" and overcomes "prejudice" (literally: prejudgment). Furthermore, the kind of thinking for oneself that Kant advocates in *What is Enlightenment?* concerns the search for public policies to which the entire society could agree, so the second maxim, which is described as the maxim of "enlarged thought" or of judgment proper, seems also a part of the conditions for bringing about enlightenment. Enlightenment consists in freedom from our "self-incurred tutelage" by thinking for ourselves rather than letting authorities do our thinking for us, but truly thinking for ourselves simultaneously frees us from the subjective conditions by which we constrain our thought to our individual experience rather than considering humanity as a whole. Kant here comes extremely close to Smith. Each individual is to think for herself, rather than having statesmen or clergymen think for her; to think from the enlarged or universal standpoint, which is very much like the viewpoint of the impartial spectator; and, if the *sensus communis* is truly a version of the harmony of the faculties, to hover reflectively around particulars in exactly the way that Smith says we do when we come up with moral rules. The last two of these connections have more to do with Kant's interest in TMS than in WN, of course, but they remain very much to the point. Kant's "purposiveness without purpose" in CJ seems clearly to be a descendant of Smith's aesthetic theory in Book IV of TMS—Smith proposes "appearance of usefulness without actual utility" as the criterion for beauty—and of his "invisible hand" teleology in both TMS and WN. If my account of "purposiveness without purpose" in chapter 4 is reasonable, however, then Kant shared something of Smith's teleological agnosticism in morality as well as aesthetics. Purposiveness without purpose gives us a placeholder for our ultimate moral ends, a general notion of a goal-directed life, without urging on us any specific shape for those goals. It enables Kant to avoid setting a specific end for our desires while still holding out the possibility that we might achieve a higher state of our "faculty of pleasure and pain," a state in greater harmony with our cognitive and moral goals. Analogously, we may take *What is Enlightenment* and CJ § 40 as giving us a model for how, in general, to think politically without urging us towards any specific political conclusions, and a model for how the political realm can encourage such individual thought while refraining from imposing any conclusions on the individual thinkers. Both politically and morally then, Kant, like Smith, points us toward an Aristotelian cultivation of our selves without committing himself to any specific telos at which such cultivation should aim.

III

As we noted in chapter 4, Kant himself strenuously avoids giving the freedom of judgment any immediate moral significance. In CJ, the freedom associated with judgments of beauty is a "symbol" of morality and can be a symptom of a good moral disposition, but Kant officially does not treat it as itself the kind of freedom on which moral thinking is based. Yet there are cryptic passages, like § 40, in which he almost recognizes a moral role for free judgment. Let us examine that section a little more closely.[14]

Kant begins by distinguishing between "common sense" and "common human understanding," insisting that judgment be identified with the former rather than the latter, but then tries to clarify "common sense" by way of maxims of the common human understanding. While he admits that these maxims "do not properly come in here," he still hopes that they will "serve to elucidate its fundamental propositions." In the Introduction to CJ he had suggested that the general principle of reflective judgment gets translated in scientific practice into such maxims as "Nature always takes the shortest way" (182/16). The maxims of § 40 seem to be a sort of aesthetic counterpart to these scientific rules of thumb—even if they "do not properly come in here." But, as we noted above, these maxims turn out to be very much what he had declared in *What is Enlightenment?* to be the heart of "the public use of reason," to be what releases us into true freedom. Part of why the maxims of § 40 are simultaneously introduced and withheld, part of what makes Kant so uncomfortable with them, may therefore be that he has elsewhere treated them as properly moral maxims, and he wants to keep morality and aesthetics apart.

One way to honor this separation without being enslaved to it is to introduce a distinction between morality and politics. Kant himself limits the political to a subset of the moral, but that is not what I mean. Besides the laws of justice, the laws providing a framework of protections by which I can exercise my freedom at all, which are what Kant primarily considered when he wrote a philosophical doctrine of "right," political theory is the study of the realm of *society*, of those projects that people pursue together and those institutions that must be run publicly, or at least by a group rather than by any single individual. Politics in this wide sense includes the structures that run churches and schools, museums and large businesses. In this sense, it provides the subject matter of sociability: not only what we *must* talk about with our neighbors, if we are to work with them in such institutions, but what in fact we *do* talk about most of the time. So when Kant imports into CJ maxims from *What is Enlightenment?*, perhaps it makes some difference, although he does not seem explicitly to realize this, that strictly speaking they are *political* maxims and not simply moral ones. For CJ is, among other things, one of Kant's most thorough studies of sociability. And politics, I have been suggesting, is a matter of sociability as much as morals.

Of course, Kant's understanding of sociability is odd, to say the least. As we have seen in section I of this chapter, Kant agrees with Smith that the social construction of the self consists in a tension between two opposing impulses, but Kant adds that it is our *dislike* for one another, as much as anything else, that incites us to moral development. Kant says in IUH that man is "unsocially sociable"; he "cannot bear" society, yet also "cannot bear to leave." "Unsocial sociability" is a phrase with much the same air of paradox as CJ's "disinterested satisfaction," "purposiveness without purpose," etc. It suggests that we come together in order to spark conflicts with one another, and that our continual pricking of one another is at the same time itself a form of "sociability." This is a wonderful empirical description of the arguments among best friends, the give and take of neighbors and colleagues who care about one another or participate in joint projects, the love of Beatrices and Benedicts. But I think it also represents a deeper insight. We saw in chapter 2 how the play of the faculties parallels and in part underwrites the play of conversation. According to CJ, moreover, reason requires this play of the faculties in order to get a grip on the empirical world. That suggests that it belongs to the very workings of our reason—and of reason embodied in any finite creature—that we simultaneously hold up our views as if they were the only correct ones and keep them open to correction by others. If we did not hold our own views correct, we would not, in any meaningful sense, be holding them at all; but if we did not also hold them open to correction, we would not have a proper notion of what "truth" or "correctness" *means*, at least for a being that does not invent the world in which it lives. So insisting on directing everything in accordance with our own ideas, while simultaneously seeking free agreement to or approval of those ideas from others, belongs to the essence of embodied reason. Conversation is necessary, rationally necessary, despite the fact that the first two *Critiques* and the *Groundwork* are written as if all rational achievement could take place within the mind of one thinker, alone in and with the world.

Now if CJ is Kant's deepest study of the nature of conversation, and if also, more famously, it is the work in which he gives "reflective judgment" some of the functions he had earlier attributed to reason,[15] then it would not be surprising to find that the political roles he attributed to "public reason" before CJ—in 1784, say, when *What is Enlightenment?* was published—might be taken over by "judgment" after CJ. That is just what we do find. In the essay on "Theory and Practice," published three years after CJ, Kant consistently uses "judgment" for the faculty by which citizens discuss political matters, reserving "reason," at most, for something that provides a regulative ideal *guiding* judgment:

[The "original contract"] . . . is in fact merely an *idea* of **reason** . . . [which] oblige[s] every legislator to frame his laws in such a way that they could have been produced by the united will of a whole nation. . . . But this restriction obviously applies only to the **judgement** of the legislator, not to that of a subject. Thus if a people, under some legislation, were asked to make a **judgement** which in all probability would prejudice its happiness, what should it do? (TP 297/79–80)

For the result usually affects our **judgement** of the rightfulness of an action, although the result is uncertain, whereas the principles of right are constant. . . . [It is a] fallacy [to] allow the principle of happiness to influence the **judgement**, wherever the principle of right is involved. (301/82–3)

[E]veryone has his inalienable rights, which he cannot give up even if he wishes to, and about which he is entitled to make his own **judgements**. (304/84)

[W]here the supreme legislation did . . . adopt measures [declaring religious doctrines or forms permanently valid, which would necessarily be unconstitutional], it would be permissible to pass general and public **judgements** upon them, but never to offer any verbal or active resistance. (305/85)

Nowhere does practice so readily bypass all pure principles of **reason** and treat theory so presumptuously as in the question of what is needed for a good political constitution. The reason for this is that a legal constitution of long standing gradually makes the people accustomed to **judging** both their happiness and their rights in terms of the peaceful *status quo*. (305/86)

The pattern of usage is too consistent to be written off as carelessness. Even where Kant wants to insist that our political opinions *should* be informed by "reason," he allows that they *are*, in fact, simply "judgements." Throughout this work, reason informs judgment but is not identical with it, and it is judgment, not reason, that comes to political conclusions.

We might now want to reconsider the famous principles of *What is Enlightenment?* in the light of their reappearance in CJ, rather than the other way around. Enlightenment consists in freeing ourselves from our "self-incurred tutelage" by thinking for ourselves rather than letting authorities think for us, and by freeing ourselves from the self-centeredness by which we constrain our thought to our personal experience alone. Political institutions can foster both sides of this intellectual independence by avoiding a paternalistic attitude towards the people, in the marketplace of material goods as well as the marketplace of ideas. Opposition to paternalism is the hallmark of Kant's politics, running through *What is Enlightenment?*, the *Idea for a Universal History, Theory and Practice*, and his unpublished political reflections. Kant characteristically translates this into policy by calling for freedom of the pen, which in *What is Enlightenment?* he terms "the freedom to make public use of one's reason."[16] We can now see that he might have entitled this freedom, had he written *What is Enlightenment?* after CJ rather than before, the "public use of one's *judgment*." The maxims of *What is Enlightenment?* certainly make better sense as principles of judgment than of reason proper. The kind of thinking for oneself that Kant advocates in *What is Enlightenment?* is concerned, after all, with specific political issues: the role and reform of the military, the tax code, the clergy. On Kant's account of reason—beyond time and all empirical phenomena, setting necessary conditions *for* the grasping of empirical phenomena—what can it possibly have to do with such specific political concerns? Specific conclusions are the province of judgment, surely, here applying a general concept or rule to particular instances, there interpreting a given particular case as falling under one concept rather than another. Reason cannot get a grip on such specifics except by means of judgment. How could reason alone pick out one policy rather than another as better suited to its purposes? Judgment would seem to be the faculty most appropriate for making both aesthetic and political assessments.

As it happens, aesthetics and politics are the only topics that inspire Kant to write sociably. The subject matter of aesthetics presumably makes it obvious, as the subject matters of science, theology, and morality do not, that one comes to reasonable conclusions by way of conversation with others, not by rational reflection alone in one's room. Kant therefore makes aesthetic interpretation a paradigm of what fills enjoyable and enriching talk. But what first breaks Kant of his methodological solipsism is the subject matter of politics. The occasional pieces of 1784–1786— *Idea for a Universal History, What is Enlightenment?*, the *Review of*

Herder, the *Conjectures on the Beginning of Human History*, and *What is Orientation in Thinking?*—are all written in an elegant and easily accessible style, addressed to issues of the day and devoted to explicit polemics with other authors (think also of the chapter headings of *Theory and Practice* : "Contra Garve"; "Contra Hobbes"; "Contra Mendelssohn"). When, therefore, in *Theory and Practice*, he explicitly comes to use "judgment" rather than "reason" to name the faculty best suited to coming up with political opinions, I think we can hear a more or less deliberate echo of CJ. Politics, like aesthetics, requires or even consists in dialogue.

Echoes of Plato should probably be heard here as well. Judgment is a descendant not only of *phronesis* but of *doxa*, the faculty that for Plato grasped the ever-changing flow of empirical particulars and hence, inter alia, the stuff of the political world. But for Kant, unlike Plato, particulars are not in the least unreal, do not dwell in some shadowy midregion between Being and Nonbeing, so the faculty that grasps particulars, the faculty of aesthetics and politics, can be a perfectly respectable source of truth. Of course it is not quite that easy. Kant is Platonic enough to make judgment a shifting business, and something regulated by the ideas of reason.[17] So unchanging rational norms are necessary to our conversations about politics. Still, they can never supply the actual subject matter about which we converse; they are necessary only as *background* to what we say. Reason cannot constitute any political (or aesthetic) view. Indeed, by handing them over to judgment reason acknowledges—nay demands—that aesthetic and political views be shifting, that we *not* attribute a fixed, general truth to them. As when we call something "beautiful," we lay claim to a universal voice in political judgment, but we can never prove that the instance we have picked out actually deserves that voice's approbation.[18] What we converse about, when we interpret politics or aesthetics, is *essentially* controversial, something on which multiple views are always rationally justifiable.

It follows that any theory of politics we could all agree to would be literally pointless: there would be no point to uttering it. If that is Rawls's project, he succeeds at the cost of emptiness. If the Difference Principle, for instance, means only that policies must aim to "help" the worst-off as much as possible, however "help" is defined and whatever factual claims are added in to interpret the aim of the policy, then it brings Plato's hierarchical utopia and Marx's egalitarian one, Milton Friedman's laissez-faire complacency and Harold Laski's stifling paternalism, too close together to have any bite. No polemic for or against current policies can easily be read off of Rawls's principles. And the most interesting aspect of his writings—of both *A Theory of Justice* and *Political Liberalism*—is their powerful running polemics: against, in the first case, the utilitarianism that was dominant when Rawls published it, and against, in the second case, those who take differences in religion and culture to be either the death knell for principled agreement in politics, or a clarion call for a "comprehensive" liberalism that would clear out such differences for good. Rawls is never more Kantian than when he is willing to engage in these polemics, and he would be yet more so if he included in his work essays directly responding to positions with which he disagrees ("Contra Nozick"; "Contra Marx"; "Contra Sandel"), or essays making clear how what he has to say might bear on the Vietnam war, on welfare policy, or on debates over free speech. For sociability, according to Kant, is nothing if not polemical, and the philosopher's role in society is to engage, and thereby help guide, those polemics.[19]

IV

As we have seen, Kant's society works empirically much like Smith's. It is a society of spectators as well as agents, a society in which we each constantly watch the others, and constantly judge them for moral or aesthetic worth and worthlessness. But this silent watching is not all we get from Kantian society. At best, we converse as well—and thereby share judgments, as well as impose them on one another. Both the conversation and the silent modeling are modes of education, modes by which we draw on one another's experience and judgment to refine our own. And in both the conversation and the silent modeling we are, ideally, as active as we are passive, refining the judgments of others as we refine our own, and indeed providing, in the actions we perform and things we say, the sparks of conflict by which all discipline, all refinement of our judgment, is made possible.

Now Kant reiterates the notion of an "invisible hand" making for freedom in another passage of IUH, which simultaneously introduces a remarkable metaphor:

Man, who is otherwise so enamoured with unrestrained freedom is forced to enter . . . [a just civil constitution] by sheer necessity. And this is indeed the most stringent of all forms of necessity, for it is imposed by men upon themselves, in that their inclinations make it impossible for them to exist side by side for long in a state of wild freedom. But once enclosed within a precinct like that of civil union, the same inclinations have the most beneficial effect. In the same way, trees in a forest, by seeking to deprive each other of air and sunlight, compel each other to find these by upward growth, so that they grow beautiful and straight—whereas those which put out branches at will, in freedom and in isolation from others, grow stunted, bent and twisted. All the culture and art which adorn mankind and the finest social order man creates are fruits of his unsociability. (22/46)

Our unsocial sociability leads us to "prune" each other, to compel each other away from easy, but self-destructive, paths of growth. It seems, moreover, that philosophy's specific role in the social order is to encourage this conflict, this mutual checking of impulses, this pruning of each person's growth by everyone else. Shortly after writing IUH, Kant objects to his former student Herder's speculative style in the following terms:

> But it is . . . essential that . . . our resourceful author should curb his lively genius somewhat, and that philosophy, which is more concerned with *pruning luxuriant growths* than with propagating them, should guide him towards the completion of his enterprise. It should do so not through hints but through precise concepts, not through laws based on conjecture but through laws derived from observation, and not by means of an imagination inspired by metaphysics or emotions, but by means of a reason which, while committed to broad objectives, exercises caution in pursuing them.[20]

Then, in the *Groundwork*,[21] Kant draws on Smith's "division of labor" to advise philosophers that they should practice a specific, disciplined craft:

> All trades, handiworks, and arts have gained by the division of labor, where . . . each [person] limits himself to a particular job which is distinguished from all the others by the treatment it requires, in order to do it with greater perfection and with more facility. . . . It might be worth considering whether pure philosophy in each of its parts does not require a man particularly devoted to it, and whether it would not be better for the learned profession as a whole to warn those who are in the habit of catering to the taste of the public by mixing up the empirical with the rational . . . that they should not at one and the same time carry on two employments which differ widely in the treatment they require. (G 388/4)

Kant seems to have maintained this conception of philosophy for the rest of his career, since it is crucial to the argument of *The Conflict of the Faculties*. Again drawing on Smith's division of labor for his central metaphor, Kant claims that philosophy's job is to stir up and preserve conflict with the other faculties at the university, because only by such agonistic questioning can the other faculties be forced to pursue truth, rather than merely purveying what people would like to hear.[22] This suggests that philosophers can be essential to a morally advantageous sociability. What we need from other human beings is above all that they *dis*agree with us. We are inclined to want to "direct everything in accordance with our own ideas" (IUH 21/44), and in consequence the reason of each of us comes into conflict with the reason of all the others. But it is precisely such conflict, and not any comfort we might take in "solidarity" with others, that provides the advantage of society of which reason can most approve: "Man wishes concord, but nature, knowing better what is good for the species, wishes discord" (21/45). Through discord, we correct our errors, discipline our minds, "prune" and simplify our profligate thoughts. The voice of philosophy maintains this discord, insists on such pruning, and thereby keeps our life in society invigorating and intellectually healthy.

So philosophy should prune the other disciplines, and more generally provide a cautious, limiting voice to counterbalance the wild—and in part wildly exciting and important—products of imagination. It is the voice of order over against variety, to use Leibnizian terms, of "taste," in Kant's own terms, over against "genius." It thereby expresses the natural tendency of social constraint itself: it *is* unsocial sociability, as an express, rational project rather than a mere unconscious tendency. Philosophy does explicitly what the "invisible hand" does implicitly.[23]

But doesn't the limitation of philosophy to the expression of pure reason, to a rational pruning of imagination's creative profusion, suggest that Rawls is right about Kant after all, that Kant himself would want to limit political philosophy to thought experiments and the laying out of abstract ideals, not to put it in an ever inconstant, ever tentative intercourse with facts of empirical history? Should we not just prune the ambitions of historians and political scientists, developing rational ideals for them to use as a guide?

I think there is a good deal to this objection, but I propose two lines of defense against it. First, Kant may well have less room for a sharp distinction between ideal and nonideal theory, or theory of any kind and empirical detail, than does Rawls. Kant is much more inclined than Rawls to make specific policy suggestions in his political writings, and is certainly much less abstract, less removed from the work of historians and the political controversies of his day. He calls, like Smith, for the abolition of entail and hereditary aristocracies, gives us not only a principle about but a detailed list of who should and should not have the right to vote, and offers a revisionary and somewhat unusual set of criminal penalties. In none of his political writings is he ever utopian. Even the *Rechtslehre*, far from presenting an ideal model of the state, simply follows the customary series of topics in courses on jurisprudence, offering analysis and commentary in line with Kant's overall rational system of morals along the way, but tending rather to toss off a criterion for just law or the like in the midst of detailed investigations of speech, voting rights, and the like, than to leaven an ideal theory here and there with a few details about how it might apply to actual political practice. Kant also directs Herder to "laws derived from observation" and emphasizes in IUH that the guidance he recommends is a guidance *of* empirical research: "It would be a misinterpretation of my intention to contend that I meant this idea of a universal history, which to some extent follows an *a priori* rule, to supersede the task of history proper, that of *empirical* composition" (30/53). Two paragraphs earlier, he proposes that we read European history in such a way as to "concentrate our attention on civil constitutions, their laws, and the mutual relations among states, . . . notice how these factors, by virtue of the good they contained, served for a time to elevate and glorify nations, . . . [and] observe how their inherent defects led to their overthrow, but in such a way that a germ of enlightenment always survived" (IUH 30/52). Kant has a research program, a philosophical ideal, to guide the kind of history we do, but that program or ideal is designed to explain actual empirical details, to fail if it cannot explain them well, and therefore to be open to revision if empirical facts show it to be unrealistic. By contrast, for all that Rawls talks about real psychological motivations, he gives no indication that any new psychological discoveries could vitiate the basic tenets of either the *Theory of Justice* or *Political Liberalism*.

Second, to the extent that Kant does conceive of philosophy's relationship to empirical work as one-way, as dictating ideals for historical investigation rather than itself being informed by history, we can see this as reflecting a central error in his theory of judgment. Kant too readily sees reflective judgment as merely preceding determining judgment, too readily sees concepts, once formed, as simply "containing" their instances. He does not fully follow out his own remarkable insight into the relationship between concepts and the process of judgment by which they are constructed. Reason need not give up its autonomy if it accepts the role of regulating a continuing *interaction* between the understanding and the imagination, rather than having the former impose a definite shape on the latter. In political philosophy, this means that working out the ideals of justice, or right liberal action, may consist as much in admonishing the abstract "[political] understanding" to pay heed to the concrete "[political] imagination" as vice versa. That is, the philosopher may want to advise political scientists—as Kant actually does advise Herder—to attend more to the actual psychological and sociological makeup of the people they want to regulate or explain, as much as, in other circumstances, the philosopher may want to admonish excessively empirical students of politics to pay more attention to human ideals. Sometimes institutions need to be designed or redesigned in accordance with new empirical facts, just as sometimes they need to be designed or redesigned to be more responsive to our ideals. It all depends on the particular balance in public discourse at a particular time. Philosophy *regulates* that balance; it should not add weight to one side alone.

For all the greatness of his achievement, I blame Rawls for adding too much weight to the side of an already excessively mathematical approach to economics in the current academy. Ever since Paul Samuelson's work of the 1940s, both left-wing and right-wing economists have been obsessed with the building of ideal models that they themselves admit have only a tenuous relationship to the prediction of actual economic behavior. Rawls began developing TJ after immersing himself in the writings of Samuelson, Hicks, Walras, and Von Neumann and Morgenstern,[24] and his work throughout has been characterized by an attempt to respond to the amoral abstractions of contemporary economists with an argument built from their own materials. The result is a Difference Principle that is all too easy to satisfy loosely and all too difficult to satisfy strictly, and a political liberalism that is too weak to have much bite when the conditions for reasonable discourse are taken loosely, and insufficiently open to disagreement when those conditions are interpreted strictly. If the Difference Principle requires of us merely that we *intend* our social arrangements to help the least advantaged as much as possible, it is compatible with defenses of everything from the most extreme versions of free-market capitalism to the most extreme forms of communism. Again, if it demands that our social arrangements *actually* help the worst-off more than any alternative arrangement, and help them in each generation rather than in some long-term future, then what system it justifies is severely underdetermined by theory. The free marketeer opposed to welfare policies can plausibly argue, after all, that precisely the removal of any safety net will in the long run raise the standard of living of those at the bottom more than policies that cut down on people's incentives to work. Even the Hindu caste system can be justified as aimed at the benefit of the untouchables, if we are allowed to include maximization over "success in future lives" as part of the benefit we are considering. Plato explicitly justifies his hierarchical utopia in terms of guiding the animalistic dross of society to a better life than they would have if left to their own devices. What differentiates the free marketeer from the socialist, and both from the believer in caste hierarchies, and what is supposed to differentiate the Rawlsian welfare state liberal from any of these other approaches, are controversial, highly specific factual matters of the kind that cannot enter into Rawls's original position. Without some supplementary account of how these factual matters are to be interpreted, we have no way of telling which of these applications of the Difference Principle is the right one.

The problem here is intrinsic to Rawls's project. If his conclusions are really supposed to follow as strictly from reason and the broadest of facts about human nature as he suggests, then they can hardly be such that reasonable people would disagree about them—or, conversely, that reasonable disagreements would be affected by them. This is the aspect of Rawls that makes his Difference Principle look acceptable to left- and right-wing academics alike—and, therefore, irrelevant to what divides them. When Rawls deploys the Difference Principle in a way that strays from the universal intuitions and principles that are supposed to underwrite it, on the other hand, one is hard-pressed to see how, on his own account, these conclusions could be the sole possible outcome of deliberations in the original position.

A similar problem arises for Rawls's more recent work. If political liberalism really endorses a rich pluralism of comprehensive views about how to live, the realm for a full-blooded, unhypocritical use of "public reason" will shrink to tiny proportions, while if it really requires that all reasonable comprehensive views come to a principled accord with the demands of public reason, the pluralism for which it allows will wither into uninteresting differences over such matters as what foods people eat and what holidays they observe. Again, the problem is endemic, not accidental, to Rawls's project. With a suitably jerry-rigged interpretation of "justification," "reason," and the like, practically any comprehensive doctrine can transform practically any of its demands into something merely justifi*able* in politically liberal terms. Where Rawls tries to move to a stronger condition, however—say, to the condition that constitutional proposals be actually justifi*ed* by his own account of public reason—he loses his grip on the uncontroversial intuitions that make his views appear to be entailed by reason alone. Imagine a fundamentalist Christian who insists that she regards all those cooperating in society as "free and equal" rather than "different and unequal," as required by Rawls (PL 110), and agrees that public decisions should be reached, among those free and equal cooperators, on the basis of "mutually recognizable reasons and evidence" (PL 115). She merely adds that the cooperators actually achieve the freedom that they each potentially have, receive what they potentially deserve as beings of equal worth, and grasp the reasons and evidence that are potentially available to them only once they have submitted in faith to Christ. She notes that the universal freedom and equality, and ability to recognize reasons, of which Rawls himself speaks is merely notional: he would not deny that in fact there are many who, for want of a fortunate upbringing or circumstances, or for reasons of mental ill-health or irrepressible perversity, will not be truly "reasonable." Reasons advanced by the latter, for Rawls, need not count as "mutually recognizable" ones even if the person advancing them sees them as such. Our fundamentalist Christian simply takes a lack of her faith to be similarly a condition barring people from achieving the freedom, equality, or capacity for reason notionally attributed to them: she believes that reasons, to be truly reasons at all, must be offered from a perspective of faith in Christ. But if this move is allowed, only political structures that advance the favored religious view will be liberally permissible structures. Of course Rawls would not allow this. To disallow it while preserving his neutrality about comprehensive conceptions, however, he would have to show that the fundamentalist Christian's notion of what is reasonable is incoherent. He would have to show that the fundamentalist is not properly using reason to come to her definition of "reason," and show this without appealing to any facts that might be in dispute between her and a person with a more secular view of the world. Any such attempt to settle what counts as reason without taking a view on disputed matters of fact is, I believe, hopeless. Its hopelessness is but a symptom of the way Rawls's philosophy radically disengages itself from the world it tries to address.

Not unrelated to this problem is the fact that Rawls's mode of doing political philosophy is strongly elitist, even though his conclusions oppose elitism. In principle, Rawls seeks a "reflective equilibrium" between ordinary moral intuitions and higher-level theory, but in practice he moves to the theory after but a quick glance at intuitions—themselves far from ordinary, as we shall see in the next chapter—and never really returns from his theoretical structures to show how they might solve real problems we face. What kind of redistributive policies Rawls himself favors, or even whether he prefers market socialism to market capitalism, has remained notoriously uncertain throughout the quarter century over which his work has dominated political philosophy.[25] We might say that Rawls in principle sees judgment—a balance among reason, understanding, and sensibility—as the touchstone of good political philosophy, but in practice takes the side of reason so much as to overwhelm the intuitions with which it should be negotiating. And the social version of this mental faculty talk is that Rawlsian theorizing overwhelms ordinary conversation. The philosopher tells the historian or political activist that he or she just "doesn't understand the argument" and that's the end of the discussion. Disengagement ensues between philosophy and the political world it might try to shape, rather than the rich "pruning" relationship that Kant describes. The abstract philosophical apparatus one needs to engage in debate with Rawls's theories descends more from Plato than from Kant, or from the less appealing side of Kant, the side that insists on "philosophy as a special task." Rawlsian philosophical experts stay remote from the humdrum confusions of real political debate, which means in practice that the "people," for all their supposed autonomy and need for self-enlightenment, must take direction on their ideals from philosophers.

Such an undialectical division of labor encourages *Unmündigkeit* rather than working to lift it.

V

Jürgen Habermas, I think, makes a similar complaint about Rawls:

> [M]y universalization principle differs from the one John Rawls proposes [in that] . . . Rawls views the substantive parts of his study . . . , not as the *contribution* of a participant in argumentation to a process of discursive will formation regarding the basic institutions of late capitalist society, but as the outcome of a "theory of justice," which he as an expert is qualified to construct. . . . Moral argumentation . . . serves to settle conflicts of action by consensual means. . . . If moral argumentation is to produce this kind of agreement, however, it is not enough for the individual to reflect on whether he can assent to a norm. . . . What is needed is a "real" process of argumentation in which the individuals concerned cooperate.[26]

Habermas himself is not known for the wide accessibility of his work, nor, as we shall see, do his ideal speech conditions really serve as "the contribution of a participant in argumentation" to real debates over institutions, but he rightly objects to the model of the philosopher as moral "expert," as an expert on justice, or liberty, or right action in general. Political philosophers who take their bearings from Kant's insight that all human beings are equally deserving of respect must enact that respect by *actually listening* to what all human beings have to say, even if they also hold out an ideal of rationality from which many, much of the time, will fall short.

In one way Habermas does get closer to this actual listening than Rawls does: he takes the risk of mentioning real political issues and taking some sort of stand on them. But there is too little of this, and he presents his stands as if they were consequences of his ideal theory, rather than "substantive contributions" to the debate among citizens. It is his considered view that moral theory should avoid taking particular positions, that this is immodest, a way of setting philosophy up too much as a kind of expertise: "What moral *theory* can do and should be trusted to do is to clarify the universal core of our moral intuitions and thereby to refute value skepticism. What it cannot do is make any kind of substantive contribution" (p. 211). Again, I share his aversion to the philosopher-as-expert model, but ironically his refusal to allow philosophy any substantive role itself helps *make* it a kind of expertise: his modesty bends over into immodesty. By seeming to be above the fray, the principles philosophy supposedly yields are made too unassailable by common experience, are lifted too far off from the discourse they are supposed to help shape. One consequence of this is that when Habermas proclaims that "human rights obviously embody generalizable interests" (p. 205), or that "disparities of social wealth" in the West are one of the great "moral-political liabilities of our time" (p. 211), these come off, not as Jürgen Habermas's personal opinions on controversial political issues, with which traditional Muslims and hard-line defenders of laissez-faire, respectively, might reasonably disagree, but as if they were Philosophy's conclusions on the subject, dicta from beyond the fray that silence opposing views because they follow from conditions that any morally acceptable discourse must meet. Habermas may well not intend this tone but the entire separation he wants to make between justification and application (pp. 86, 103–5, 206–7, 210), and the approach he endorses to this separation, by which one settles the first first and then moves on to the second, makes the philosopher's work too ideal a business, something surrounded too much by an aura of apriority, an aura protecting the philosophical expert from the layperson and silencing the layperson in the presence of philosophical conclusions. What we need instead in political philosophy is a constant *interplay* between justification and application, by which one moves back from the second to clarify the first and then, temporarily, forward again. To say anything of significance about the nature of moral discourse, one must also make a contribution to that discourse. Of course, *as* philosophers we are not experts on any substantive moral issue, as Habermas rightly points out, but perhaps this simply means we should become such experts, acquire some expertise in economic or social issues, as Adam Smith did, or in a cultural or religious tradition, as did Gandhi and Kierkegaard, and present our "theoretical" positions together with and through this mastery of certain particulars—if only in order to make the theoretical position itself properly clear. To the distinction quoted above from p. 211 of Habermas I would respond: if moral theory does not make a "substantive contribution" to actual moral debates, it cannot "clarify the universal core of our moral intuitions" either, since clarification requires examples, concrete material to work with. Otherwise we don't know what "a discourse among citizens," in *our* time and cultural setting, so much as looks like: *what* norms might appropriately be taken as disrupted, for instance.[27]

More specifically, the conditions for morally acceptable discourse Habermas offers us are, without examples, so vague as to be empty. Habermas draws from his "principle of universalization" that is supposed to guide argument such seemingly concrete rules of logic as:

(1.1) No speaker may contradict himself.

(1.2) Every speaker who applies predicate *F* to object *A* must be prepared to apply *F* to all other objects resembling *A* in all relevant aspects.

(1.3) Different speakers may not use the same expression with different meanings. (p. 87)

Each of these rules, however, is open to interpretations so widely different that they cease quickly to be concrete. This is most easily illustrated with the second rule. Just what is supposed to count as "relevant aspects"? Suppose speaker X applies the conjunction of predicates "blasphemous," "unacceptably offensive to others," and "legitimately restricted by law," to Andres Serrano's photograph *Piss Christ*. In response, speaker Y, while accepting the linkage of the three predicates for the purposes of argument, suggests that both Dante's *Divine Comedy*, in which Mohammed is placed in hell as a heretic, and the New Testament, which is filled with passages Jews consider both blasphemous and unacceptably offensive, would then have to count as "objects resembling *A* in all relevant aspects." It is more than a little likely that the success of the one or the other in winning the debate will turn on *whether* the resemblances between the first and the latter two objects count as relevant or not, that settling *this* question will be dispositive of the general one, "Should blasphemy and legal restriction be linked?" X and Y presumably agree, that is, that Dante and the New Testament are paradigms of particular works whose publication should *not* be restricted by law, and their agreement or disagreement on the general issue will hinge on whether one can persuade the other that the particular object, *Piss Christ*, is legitimately interpreted as like these paradigms in relevant aspects or not. Now the debate between X and Y, in this case, can be understood not merely as a debate, *within* morally acceptable discourse, on a specific issue, but as a debate *about* the limits of morally acceptable discourse itself. X and Y are arguing about limitations on free speech, after all, and each may well regard the other as stretching the limits of what morally acceptable discourse should consist in. Y may see X as a demagogue dishonestly appealing to widely held notions of "offensiveness" in order to further an agenda suppressing the speech and ways of life of people he dislikes, while X may see Y as a demagogue dishonestly using the freedom of religion as a cover under which to promote licentiousness. But if I am right about what needs to be done to demonstrate that X's proposed restriction on discourse is or is not justifiable, and that either X or Y is applying predicates in a sophistic rather than a reasonable way, then Habermas's universal rule of rational argumentation will do no work in this case, will come on the scene after all the work has been done. As it often does, judgment—the interpretation of cases, and of rules in the light of the cases to which they supposedly apply—here precedes reason.

The same goes, if less obviously, for rules 1.1 and 1.3. "No speaker may contradict himself" can be taken in a broad or a narrow sense. In the narrow sense, only the most blatant utterances of "P and not P" are ruled out, and even then only when they do not serve as part of some ironic, shocking, or other nonliteral performance (as they do, for instance, in Zen parables)—precisely the kind of role in which anyone is ever inclined to utter them in the first place. In the broad sense, the rule against self-contradiction might come to prohibit all Zen-type parables, along with any tension in one's position and perhaps even any change of mind over the course of time. Then, however, it ceases to be an obvious rule of logic and becomes an arbitrary restriction on content. Broad and narrow interpretations of "the same expression" and "different meanings" similarly make 1.3 either useless or arbitrary.

Now one might suppose that the emptiness we keep running into results from the rules in question here being purely *logical* ones, that Habermas's *ethical* rules for argument would fare better. I think not. Rather, the problems with the logical rules provide an excellent model for what is wrong with the ethical ones. Here are some of the latter:

> (2.1) Every speaker may assert only what he really believes.
>
> (2.2) A person who disputes a proposition or norm not under discussion must provide a reason for wanting to do so. (p. 88)

In particular cases, of course, we know exactly how these rules work, and why they are ethically appropriate. If Habermas means by 2.1, for instance, that no one should make "hypocritical" assertions (to use a morally loaded term) or that no one should imitate Newt Gingrich's mode of assertion on family values (to illustrate the loaded term with a yet more strongly loaded particular example) then I certainly agree, and I laud his ethical sensitivities—for reasons I could explain in detail by expatiating on the degrading effects on public discourse of Newt Gingrich's rhetoric to those who might suggest, for instance, that hypocrisy is acceptable, even justifiable, for democratic politicians. But my argument in that case would consist of a set of highly contestable *judgments*, heavily dependent on contingent details rather than philosophical principles. If Habermas means 2.1 to follow from philosophical principles alone, such that both positions in the dispute over democratic hypocrisy, for instance, would accept it—the defender of hypocrisy explaining, say, that what an elected representative "really believes" simply *is* the platform on which he was elected—then we face the same danger of emptiness as we did with the logical ones. For what people in general "really believe" can analogously be interpreted as just what they are "really willing to assert," as long as "believe" is construed widely enough to include positions upheld by virtue of a certain social role, or by virtue of sub- and unconscious desires, or by virtue of a philosophical antirealism by which one regards "warranted assertibility" rather than "truth" as the proper norm for conversational utterance. If "believe" is construed narrowly enough to rule out these possibilities, however, then it represents too tendentious a view about what political, psychological, and epistemological positions are legitimate to serve as a meta-norm for all discussion.[28]

Moving now to the ethical rules for conversation for which Habermas is best known—those making participation in any conversation as universally accessible as possible—we find a similar equivocation. Reason interpreted one way demands much too little, interpreted another way demands much too much. Rule 3.1 tells us that permission to participate in the discussion should be granted to everyone "with the competence to speak and act" (89), and "everyone" is glossed a little lower down as meaning "all subjects . . . who have the capacity to take part in argumentation." Rule 3.2 (c) tells us that every such person should be allowed "to express his attitudes, desires and needs." But what is the competence or capacity in question here? Bare linguistic ability, such as a psychotic, or a seriously retarded or autistic person might have? Then we are asking for considerably less than what we ordinarily consider "reason," and may be opening ourselves to carrying on permanently irresolvable disputes—to say nothing of having to take on a surface level the concerns of someone whose "attitudes, desires, and needs" may be best expressed in terms he himself cannot muster. If we read much thicker norms of rationality into Habermas's "competence" or "capacity," however, we will quickly find ourselves excluding everyone from the poorly educated to the dogmatically religious. We might put this point in another way by noting that competence for speech and argumentation is normally something relative to the particular criteria that structure a particular *kind* of argument. Entirely different skills and knowledge are needed to participate competently in a Talmudic dispute, a philosophical debate, or a debate over evidence among journalists. If only people "capable" of taking part in *this* sense are admitted to a particular discussion, the rule picks out a severely restricted group. If not, however, the rule evens out differences among types of argument, such that the criteria reasonably favored by Talmudists, philosophers, and journalists, respectively, must disappear in favor of some obscure ideal holding all arguments up to the same canons of general "rationality."

Similarly, when the three parts of Rule 3.2 tell us that "everyone is allowed" to question any assertion, to introduce any assertion, or to express any attitude or desire, we need at least to know *when* they are so allowed. At all points, even when the question has been repeatedly answered, the assertion or attitude repeatedly responded to, by all the other participants? Then filibustering and similarly coercive performances become part of fair discourse. Or only when the point introduced is relevant and new? But then "relevance" becomes an excuse which the powerful can use to censor anyone they like. A few pages after these rules,

Habermas himself acknowledges that real discourses "take place in particular social contexts and are subject to the limitations of time and space," that therefore "topics and contributions have to be organized," openings, adjournments, resumptions, etc., "must be arranged" (p. 92). The passive voice in these sentences betrays a deep failure: *who* does the organizing, the arranging, is something Habermas simply does not address, does not give us so much as a theoretical tool for addressing. And the language of "topics and contributions," "opening[s], adjournment[s], and resumption[s]" puts in mind two clear paradigms: academic conferences and parliament meetings, in both of which those who already have power ensure that the kind of discussion they want to see takes place. In these cases, it is ridiculous to suppose that "the idealized conditions always already presupposed by participants in argumentation can at least be adequately approximated" (p. 92). A far more powerful contribution to bringing about *that* result would have been an example of a specific way in which specific discussions might be restructured—even though the particularity of the example would make it unlikely if not impossible that any fully satisfactory, fully general rule could be derived from it.

It is not clear, furthermore, that a conversation that *anyone* could enter, and help set the agenda for, is really an ideal for human interaction. This is the counterpart, in Habermas, to Rawls's tendency to overload judgment with reason. In real conversations, some people always have more right to enter than others: when they are already engaged in the conversation and are reaching a point where they think they are clarifying something to one another, when the conversation bears on issues that matter more to their lives than to others', when, perhaps, they have shown in the past, and are currently showing, more respect for the rules of conversation or more knowledge of the subject matter than someone trying to enter, and in many other circumstances. So construing the ideal as something equally open to all merely finesses the question, in real, particular cases, of to whom a given conversation should be particularly open—a question, often, to which justice demands an urgent solution. If the main problem of discussions of poverty in the United States is, as I believe it is, that the poor have too little say in solutions proposed, then it is a red herring, and a dangerous red herring that obstructs justice, to complain simply that these discussions are not open enough to "all." The right of wealthy college students, for instance, to have their equal say is not the problem that the discussion actually faces. Nor, if I am right to say that *poor* people are the group most wrongly ignored here, will it necessarily be the case that the same goes for the groups picked out (simply) as "African Americans" or "women." Of course, the latter claim is highly controversial. But the real debate over who most needs to enter this particular conversation is one to which empirical evidence and interpretive sensitivity are most needed, not general principles of reason. The debate is indeed one in which philosophers can have a useful role—helping to define what counts as a "voice" or to defend a relevant notion of "having a right to speak"—but that role is not well filled by noting that everyone with rational capacity has, in principle, a right to speak.

Now, I do not think the problem here is that Habermas has failed to carry out his own program well enough. It is not that there might be some better, clearer, less equivocal general rules by which to lay out ideal speech situations. On the contrary, it seems to me, the ideal conditions for any "speech situation" must always be constructed in part out of the *content* of the debate at hand, and not by procedural rules alone. This entails that such conditions must always be constructed anew, interpreted and reinterpreted as times and issues change. But this consequence appropriately reflects what it is that conversation does. We might say—on the model of the claim that the general condition for the application of a concept to an object include the fact that other concepts have already been applied to that object[29]—that one condition for the possibility of conversation is that conversations are already afoot. Of course, this is going too far. We do not talk all the time, and we can perfectly well begin a conversation nevertheless. But when we start to talk to someone else, and particularly if our talk goes beyond perfunctory exchanges of ritual greetings or the like, we always bring to bear a background of other conversations in which we have taken part and a presumption that our conversational partner has a similar background. This is not as trivial as it may at first seem. I can spark up a conversation with a total stranger in the U.S. (anywhere in the world, probably) by making a remark about O.J. Simpson, but not about the philosophy of religion, and I know that because I know something about "what is being talked about" in my world and my time. Not coincidentally, my example is political. If in Kant's day it would have been much easier to chat about the philosophy of religion with a stranger, that is because the abstract question of how a perfect Being might reveal Itself in historically given texts was then (in the context of the *Pantheismusstreit*) a hot *political* topic. We talk to new conversational partners about things that we think they are talking about with others and that we have ourselves, usually, discussed with others. We do not talk to them about something that interests very few human beings (the chemical composition of oak leaves) or something on which give and take is impossible (obvious mathematical or perceptual truths) or something for which the rules of conversation normally require a history of intimacy (our sex life or digestive problems). It is because small children do not yet grasp these principles that they engage mostly in monologues and make awkward conversational partners when they do trot out one of their non sequiturs for a potential response.

I have moved away, here, from what might strictly be called the "logic" of conversation, what makes conversation possible at all, to something like "conversational implicature" or "pragmatics." But that is the arena in which Habermas takes his stand; that is the arena in which normative guides for how we talk to each other must do their work. In this arena, I would say that *one* rule for a fair conversation is that it be built out of the topics going into other conversations, that it take its ground from what, at a given historical time and place, happens to interest the people around.[30] That condition, however, will build an element of recursiveness into the conditions for the ideal speech situation, such that it cannot be defined purely a priori. What actually counts as a fair conversation will have to be judged case by case, in part on the basis of how it fits in with the history of conversations to which it is meant to belong.

VI

In general, I have been trying to show that both Rawls and Habermas use Kant to promote a notion of philosophy that attempts too much to settle the question of what counts as, respectively, a fair society and a fair conversation in advance of the actual histories in which actual societies and conversations find themselves situated. Kant himself, I believe, recognized that there is no way to avoid the particularity of real judgments, the particularity of what people actually talk about. As this applies to politics, it suggests that philosophers cannot afford to stay above the political fray if they want to say something significant. We cannot insulate our positions against political controversy and still say something that can improve people's lives. Perhaps we can peek above the fray, but we must always remain in the midst of it at the same time. Here we may take guidance from Smith, who, when admonished that his remarks on the American controversy at the end of WN made the book too "topical," too relevant to one time period rather than to all time, understood instead that the commentary on a specific, historical issue gave his principles clearer, more specific meaning.[31] Even if it is far from easy to extrapolate today from Smith's views on how to settle the American controversy, still the fact that we have a stance on a particular case, in a particular context, helps limit the acceptable interpretations of Smith's general principles. Kant, although to a lesser degree, similarly took stands: on capital punishment, on aristocratic privileges, on the separation of church and state.

But one respect in which I want to follow Rawls and Habermas, and in which they are truly Kantian, is their insistence that too *much* emphasis on the actual, too much of a notion that we need to immerse ourselves in the particular, overlooks the way in which reason can and must set conditions in advance *(a priori)* for the grasping of particulars, the way in which rational beings like us always do and should see particular situations in the light of more general principles. We do not respect ourselves and others enough if we see people only as particular beings, immersed in and at the mercy of historical and biological contexts; the reason by which we recognize the proper role for this particularism also helps free us from it. How then to negotiate between the legitimate demands of reason and the way in which a philosophy transfixed by those demands can lose contact with real human lives? How to keep philosophy a rational "pruning" device for politics but not a realm of experts urging people to ignore their own eyes and their own feelings? I propose a philosophy that uses judgment, the faculty of conversation and commensuration, to bridge also the gaps relevant to its own place in society: between the academic and the popular, between the philosophical and the political, and between authoritative and autonomous modes of coming to moral and political ideals.

To elaborate the first of these dichotomies, I want to recall, from chapter 2, the notion that concepts function properly at all only when they include some specific intuitions and exclude others, only when they draw borders between one kind of similarity and another. This is probably too weak a condition for conceptualization, but it is at least a minimal such condition. But a relationship of similarity that includes some and excludes other instances must itself be defined by similarity and contrast with other relationships of similarity—with other concepts—since "sameness" in itself has no content.[32] Any shift in one concept therefore implicitly affects all the others. For this reason, and since the attachment of concepts to specific intuitions is always made by way of judgments, which can always be reinterpreted by subsequent judgments, concepts are always in the process of construction, always being made and open to being remade.

Now if this is right, one can never so much as *identify* a concept properly without giving some example of its use. This goes for practical as well as theoretical terms, and for "lower-level" as well as "higher-level" abstractions. It goes, that is, for "justice" as much as for "biological explanation," and for "lifeplan," "primary good," and "interest" as much as for "justice." If one does *not* give an example of a concept one is using, that simply implies one is assuming a background usage by which the audience already knows what intuitions belong and what intuitions do not belong to the concept in question. Thus "gene," in a contemporary article on biology, does not normally need examples because its use currently picks out and excludes well-defined sets of intuitions. As genetics developed from Mendel's experiments to the discovery of DNA in the 1950s, however, as it moved, even earlier, from crude speculations about inheritance to something that fit into a well-defined experimental program, the term "gene" surely *did* need frequent exemplification, to distinguish the limited empirical objects scientists wanted to include under the term from the loose and wider set of objects included under the term in popular usage. And should genetic explanations change significantly in the future, scientists making the change will have to again give examples of specific chemicals or traits they think should and should not be tied to the word—both when they present their work to their immediate judging audience of research colleagues, and when they explain their work to the wider public.

But what happens only occasionally in the history of scientific language happens constantly in the history of moral, aesthetic, religious, and other evaluative language.[33] Concepts like "justice," "equality," "well-being," even "person," are continually up for grabs. To make clear just *what* case they are making, therefore, let alone to make it persuasive to a wider audience, philosophers must give real instances of what they want to include in and out of their conception of ideal distribution, ideal conversation, etc. Moral philosophy that wants to have an impact on real moral practice *must* draw on "popular" issues and examples, if only to make clear how its recommendations would endorse or reject common intuitions.

As to the second dichotomy, between the world of political philosophy and the world of politics: the question we, all of us, need to face is not so much "what is just?" but "which of the policy choices before us, or institutions within our imaginative and political reach, is *most* just?" We do need people refining answers to the first question alone, and perhaps some philosophers should devote their academic lives to it, but it should never embrace the whole of what political philosophy does. We need a Hannah Arendt, commenting on the Eichmann trial, on politicians' lies, on the history of civil disobedience, as much as we need a John Rawls, giving us theoretical accounts of fair distribution or political reasoning. Specific institutional proposals, which litter the pages of Smith and Mill, and occasional writings on political events, like those of Michael Walzer and Ronald Dworkin, provide content to philosophical sketches of justice or liberty or equality, and such content is not merely a heuristically helpful illustration of the principles involved but a theoretical necessity: without intuitions showing how they might apply, the principles will be indeterminate. Political philosophy must aid political judgment, not detract from it, and detract it will do if it tempts us to contemplate ideals of reason that have no interplay with empirical particulars.

This brings us to the third dichotomy, crucial to a political philosophy that sees itself as aiding political judgment. All of us, philosophers included, take certain moral intuitions and practices on authority. Often the relevant authority is our parents, or our childhood teachers, or the apparent consensus of those with whom we share a culture, but sometimes it is another philosopher, living or dead, or a scientist, or a consensus among academics in a discipline. Autonomy demands that we question such authorities, but such questioning cannot be comprehensive—certainly not directed to all parts of our worldview at the same time—else we will have no paradigms of true or good answers to use as criteria in settling, or even appropriately posing, the questions we ask. One virtue of an account of freedom or justice is that it fits in with the going authoritative theories in political science or philosophy, or corrects them in terms they themselves hold out as legitimate. Perhaps the greatest strength of Rawls's work is the way it fits in with and reinterprets the Kantian tradition, and the critique it offers of rival, utilitarian theories. The greatest weakness of his work, by the same token, has been its attempt to play down these historical and polemical aspects of the project, to present itself as a freestanding view whose merits can be evaluated independently of its placement in a series of ongoing arguments. Insofar as a philosophical view fails to address previously and currently respected positions, it fails to say anything interesting. Interpreting the past of our discipline is thus a part of proposing new ideas in it, as well as an exercise in humility. And recognizing that ideas always appear in a polemical context, are always in conversation with other writings of their time, reminds us that in the end the best each of us can do is *judge* the reasonableness or imaginativeness or usefulness of an idea against some background that remains unjudged (prejudicial), not deduce conclusively that it is correct or incorrect.[34]

A battle over Kant's mantle thus represents a deeper division over the extent to which the wisdom of his work and of the liberalism it represents—a wisdom we cannot, because it has shaped us so deeply, judge with full autonomy—licenses communitarianism or individualism, a centralized or a market economy, a respect for cultures or a universal ethics, in our own time. If judgment as I have characterized it defines discussion in general and political debate in particular, there will be no purely philosophical way of removing the differences between one who favors Rawls's or Habermas's approach to Kant's and one who favors mine. Of course, one can distance oneself from one's political views—I don't mean to suggest that philosophical stances are always tailored to justify a set of immediate political allegiances. I am proposing something less reductionist yet in a way more threatening to the self-sufficiency of political philosophy: what counts as a good political theory must, I think, be *settled*, even as a philosophical matter, in part by how well, in a reader's judgment, the theory handles current problems. The yielding of better normative insights into concrete problems is a criterion, not merely a motivation, for preferring one political philosophy over another. A scientific theory is judged, in part but significantly, by the predictions it yields; a political philosophy must be judged by an analogous return to the empirical world. In the next chapter, I attempt such a return.

Chapter 10

KANT'S POLITICS, RAWLS'S POLITICS (II): TALENT, INDUSTRY, AND LUCK

KANT is never farther from Rawls's interpretation of him than when he says, in *Theory and Practice*, that status and property ought to be distributed in accordance with each individual's "talent, industry and luck."[1] The context is an attack on hereditary prerogatives—serfdom, entail, primogeniture, and the like, which Kant takes to be arbitrary barriers in the way of everyone having the same chances in life—but it is clear that he does not consider the accidents of natural endowment and personal history to be similarly invidious. Rawls, famously, takes talent and industry to be products of luck, and luck, here and everywhere, to be at best irrelevant to what people deserve:

> It seems to be one of the fixed points of our considered judgments that no one deserves his place in the distribution of native endowments, any more than one deserves one's initial starting place in society. [The] assertion that a man deserves the superior character that enables him to make the effort to cultivate his abilities is equally problematic; for his character depends in large part upon fortunate family and social circumstances for which he can claim no credit. The notion of desert seems not to apply to these cases. (TJ 104)

The point is repeated several times, and some commentators have indeed suggested that it provides the core of Rawls's entire argument in the *Theory of Justice*.[2] Rawls seems to consider this intuition almost a direct consequence of the Kantian principle that each human being is equally an absolute end. I try in this chapter to show how Kant's views can just as easily justify the opposite position, the position that the ideal equality of human beings *requires* that the achievement of status and goods reflect, to some extent, the accidents of biological and historical fortune. Then, relying in part on Martha Nussbaum, I soften the laissez-faire Kantianism I have developed by way of some restrictions on what kinds of luck are morally tolerable.

I

The "fixed point in our considered judgments" by which, according to Rawls, differences in talents and willingness to make an effort are clearly undeserved, the intuition so fundamental to his work and supposedly so obvious, in fact makes nonsense of the whole notion of "desert." If one does not deserve the character that enables one to make efforts, then a fortiori one does not deserve what those efforts themselves achieve, but if one does not deserve so much as what one devotes efforts to achieving, then one does not deserve anything. Perhaps this is a reasonable interpretation of what Christians mean by saying that everyone is equally sinful. But then at least it is a controversial theological view, not an uncontroversial ethical one. As an ethical view, it is wildly counterintuitive.

Yet when we reflect on the chain of intuitions to which Rawls directs us, it does seem true that talents, and even the willingness to make an effort, can no more be considered "earned" by us than our race or our gender. Those with better childhoods, or a luckier endowment of genes, tend to develop greater talents and healthier personalities than those unfortunate enough to be born with shoddy parents and less useful genes. But luck is supposed to be irrelevant to moral desert. So families and genes, and what families and genes produce, including talents and the willingness to develop talents, must be irrelevant to moral desert.

If we revert, now, to the anti-Rawlsian intuition according to which we do deserve what we achieve by talent, we may feel tempted to treat Rawls's attempt to urge us otherwise as a perfect example of how Bertrand Russell once characterized philosophical thinking: begin with the obvious and proceed from there by careful logical steps to the absurd. Making this overall assessment, however, is easier than challenging any of the argument's parts. *Should* luck be considered unproblematically relevant to moral desert? That's a position quickly made counterintuitive, and one that certainly runs up against any morality founded in freedom. Is it, then, not a matter of luck what genes we have, and what family we are born into? How could it not be? Well then, perhaps talents, and the willingness to make an effort, are not a product of genes and upbringing. But all empirical evidence suggests that they are . . .

Rather than engage directly with the train of thought stringing these intuitions together, I suggest we see what happens if we simply pursue a different line of intuitions altogether. This one *begins* with our inclination to claim that we earn our talents, indeed earn everything about ourselves: our personality, our family upbringings, our entire history. "What you inherit from your parents, earn it daily in order to possess it," says Goethe,[3] and I think this is a sensible way to embark on exactly the opposite Kantian road from Rawls's. For the person with Goethe's perspective, nothing inherited is yet necessarily given, not talent, not the value of a strong personality, not the bare ability to cultivate abilities. Everything, even if inherited, needs yet to be earned, can be traced to the activity of our wills. We have talents, but they are mere capacities until we actively cultivate them. We are born with failings and we meet with misfortune, but we can take actions to compensate for such failings and misfortune.[4] By our actions we can increase our chances of meeting with good or bad luck, we can thrive on or thwart the consequences of luck, and we can more or less adapt our emotions and expectations to living with those consequences. Only with such a view, one might say, can the hypothesis of an active will, of moral desert, be given empirical meaning; otherwise we had better do without the notion altogether. I take responsibility for my entire array of accidental characteristics, which means that I work on them and work with them: trying to use some, develop others more fully, eliminate or mitigate still others. I thereby attribute a grip on the world to my will, and moral value to my empirical personality. *I*, this particular person, not some universal will, can take credit if I use intelligence or charm to achieve a good end, and I too must take responsibility for distasteful habits of jealousy or self-pity, rooted though all of these things may be in my genes or childhood.

Now before we examine this train of intuitions for its intrinsic merit, and possible advantages over the Rawlsian route, let us note that it follows just as readily as the Rawlsian alternative does from Kantian premises. Kant argued for the absolute, and hence equal, value of every rational agent, and located the source of that value in the agent's capacity for freedom. But this basic human equality can just as well play itself out by *means* of our talents and luck as it can require us to ignore such features of ourselves. Kant's view of transcendental freedom leaves undetermined how we should relate to our "initial endowments" and our history: we can either take responsibility for none of our accidental characteristics or take responsibility for all of them. At times, especially when he urges every individual to view her entire empirical life as "but a single phenomenon" under the control of her "intelligible consciousness" (CPrR 99/102–3), Kant himself leans towards the latter interpretation of how will relates to history. Of course this is to make our ability to take control of our lives a nonempirical presupposition, rather than the sort of thing that might itself be subject to the vagaries of upbringing. Rawls, realistically, urges us to take a more empirical attitude towards people's ability to shape their own characters, by which that ability depends on "fortunate family and social circumstances for which [one] can claim no credit" (TJ 104 ; cf. PL 7). But even Rawls must posit some basic moral capacities to flesh out the equal worth he attributes to people, and his presupposition that everyone has "a capacity for a sense of justice and a capacity for a conception of the good" (PL 19, and TJ § 77) is just as nonempirical as any presupposed universal capacity to make an effort. So Kantian theory will not settle the question of how to view desert. Indeed, it is possible to understand Kant's egalitarianism such that *both* views of desert are legitimate. We can see the two trains of intuitions as representing an antinomy of justice: the fundamental moral principle that all individuals have equal worth may license *both* treating their talents as inessential to that worth *and* treating their talents as essential to it. This is not as paradoxical as it may seem. Kant suggests in a number of places that moral principles are guides to the interpretation of the facts around us for the purposes of practical reason, as scientific principles are guides to such interpretation for the purposes of theoretical reason.[5] Both ways of treating talents and luck can serve as such guides, as long as we separate the purposes for which we use the one from the purposes for which we use the other.[6]

It follows that we need to look at the various advantages of adopting one or the other perspective for the purpose of enabling the freedom of each rational being to play itself out, rather than to insist that one or the other is the true consequence of moral egalitarianism. One obvious disadvantage of the Goethean line of intuitions is that it appears to justify whatever level of material comfort or social status everyone achieves, no matter how magnificent or how desperate. Nobody's place in any system of material and social distribution would seem to be unjust; justice would be unable to distinguish among systems of distribution. This is a cruel result, and even more wildly counterintuitive than Rawls's. Surely it is unjust for people to starve even when they have tried to work, even when, perhaps, their failure is purely a matter of luck or indeed of having been too honest or loyal in a corrupt world. Few would deny this. Even those, like Friedrich Hayek, who most strongly defend the vast inequalities of market capitalism tend to do so while lamenting them as a regrettable but necessary price to pay for the supreme social good of freedom. I do not want simply to replace Rawls's dismissal of our talents and luck as irrelevant to economic justice with a wholesale endorsement of them as, in fact, somehow willed. But I do think the approach that starts from that end, from the recognition that it is not *impossible* for us to "will" our talents or our luck and that sometimes we surely do so, yields interesting insights, and insights that go a great distance towards explaining Kant's express endorsement of distributing goods and political status in accordance with "talents, industry, and luck." Correlatively, I believe, and think Kant believes, that the inequalities of the market system are not wholly a bad thing. To some extent they may indeed be necessary to a morally healthy social order, and even Hayek, who accepts considerably *more* inequality than I consider either healthy or justifiable, has underplayed the reasons why *some* inequality can be a good. I think people commonly have an intuition that equality for its own sake is not necessarily good, may even be a little repulsive, although they rarely admit this intuition even to themselves, since they find themselves thrown back by the repugnance of the full-fledged "willed luck" view.

So, abstracting now from any reliance on Kantian principles, let me try to lay out some of the non-Rawlsian intuitions I think most of us have about talents, luck, and inequality. A view that it is *simply* good for "gifted" human beings to thrive is morally unacceptable, I believe, as is any view that allows some individuals to be sacrificed for the sake of others. In selecting non-Rawlsian intuitions, I have taken the fundamental egalitarianism of the Kantian tradition to set the boundaries of an acceptable moral view. Insofar as our intuitions belie such egalitarianism, we may simply want to reject them. I do not think inequality among human beings can be justified except by derivation *from* the equally valuable, free choices of each human being.[7] But if it turns out that human beings in fact *will* to live in a world of luck and social inequality, even where they themselves may have bad luck or live on the lower ranks of a social hierarchy, then we may be required to develop a Kantian politics that accommodates such choices. If the intuitions that some luck and some social inequality constitute an essential part of the goods that free beings will, then we may need to accommodate those intuitions even while guarding against their potential for justifying cruelty.

1. *Earned Talents.* It is an old story, at least as old as the fable about the ant and the grasshopper. Two children study piano: one practices, the other doesn't. Perhaps the second "could" have been a great pianist, but she isn't; the first one turns whatever talent she has "natively" into enough for a career. Has she not earned it? Has the other not earned her failure? Perhaps the first child's parents pushed her. So what? Some children react to their parents' pushing by going in the other direction, some work hard despite lack of encouragement from their parents. Surely the first is not wrong to insist that she *chose* to go with her parents' direction rather than against it. And if the second blames herself for not working harder, we will surely look on her as having a good sense of responsibility, not as having made some moral error.

Of course, the story can be changed, such that one child is forced to the piano by violence and psychological threats or the other, for equally horrific reasons, can preserve her sanity only by *not* practicing. We might well withdraw the "one earns, the other doesn't" conclusion under such circumstances. But these are not the usual stories and they are certainly not the only ones. The point at the moment is that if *any* version of this story leads us to insist on seeing *any* talent as earned, Rawls' intuitions on the subject will at best be incomplete, inadequate.

2. *Compensation.* Sometimes, although certainly not always, inequality in social status or material goods masks a deeper equality in well-being. Status and material goods are notoriously insufficient for happiness, and the search for them is notoriously capable of making one *un*happy. Adam

Smith treats the pursuit of such things as empty vanity beyond a certain minimal level, for which reason he worries little about distributive justice.

For two reasons, moreover, equality might be unappealing even if status and goods *were* sufficient for happiness. First, people succeed and fail in different spheres of life, such that a fairly poor and politically insignificant person may have a terrific marriage, a rich or famous person suffer from psychological or physical illness, a lonely person find satisfaction in art, etc. Now some of these arenas are susceptible to political control and some are not. If we even out status and wealth, therefore, we may simply remove something that now compensates for differences in health, attractiveness, psychological stability, and the like, rather than truly making everyone's quality of life equal. We can overrule or abolish academic scores for many positions, but we cannot compensate for the differences in social status due to varying levels of personal charm. Similarly, no political program yet devised, and no nonmanipulative such program on the horizon, can compensate for the differences in human lives due to genetic or early-childhood-induced proneness to depression or calm. Unless we can be sure that politically controllable goods, like income or some combination of Rawls's primary goods, really stand proxy for all things people need and want, political and economic equality may detract from rather than contribute to the achievement of full human equality.

Second, what we take pleasure in is very often *relative to* the talents, personality, and history we have as a matter of "luck." A lifetime membership at the opera is of no use to someone who hates classical music, nor is a senatorial position much of a reward for the pathologically shy, nor would a high-profile academic job be more than embarrassing for one whose skills are political rather than intellectual. As adults, we tend to regard our taste in music, our shyness or extrovertedness, our political or intellectual abilities, as matters of where we choose to spend our energies as much as what abilities we had to begin with. We seek arenas where we have a talent that makes for success, but also where we have the talents needed for enjoying the successes in question. We are thus in a very literal sense "responsible" for making ourselves happy.

And we can maintain our sense of responsibility for this entire realm of activity only as long as the rewards of different projects remain appropriate to those projects. Translating all job satisfaction into income, replacing all opera houses with more widely accessible sources of entertainment, making the status that accompanies educational and political positions a perk to distribute rather than an achievement to be earned are ways of defeating this specificity of the rewards we seek. If a government treats all our pleasures as fungible, it deprives us of the rewards that come of developing tastes and enjoying the results of achievements. It deprives us of what I called in chapter 5 "proper pleasures," encouraging us to satisfy animal needs instead.

3. *Comforts of Inequality.* In a way that is perhaps related to the specificity of human pleasures and abilities, there can be some comforts in occupying a low rung of a hierarchical ladder. Where some have substantially greater shares of material resources than others, they are inevitably expected to have rather greater social responsibilities. Adam Smith points out how wealth is automatically a marker for status—we "sympathize" with the wealthy, imagine ourselves in their shoes, hence pay more attention to them than to our average fellow citizens—and how that entails that the wealthy have their behavior more closely watched than other people. A wealthy person is more liable to being resented, and sometimes to certain kinds of ostracism, than others tend to be. In addition, the wealthy are a natural target for charitable causes and for the support of artistic and political causes, and in most societies they are expected to regard themselves as especially obliged to help such causes. All of these are of course ways in which rich people are *privileged*—it is gratifying to be so well attended to, and there is a thrill in having political power—but they are also, to some degree, burdens. And while wealth itself unquestionably gives many the power to shirk these burdens, the public contempt that an irresponsible rich person can face is a real concern for some. From here we can see why many people in an unequal society rather like *not* being rich, rather let someone else occupy such visible, time-consuming, and precarious social positions. At the same time, if the wealthy take their role seriously, having people around with a substantial edge in purchasing power can mean that eccentric artists get patronized, minority political views funded,[8] museums or parks built and maintained. Where this is so (and it is worth repeating that it is not always so), one may enjoy living in an inegalitarian society while precisely *not* occupying any of its top strata. There is a kind of division of labor in cultural and political leadership in such a society, and while that often entails paternalistic attitudes or cruel lack of attention to the poor, a certain low degree of it fits human nature better than any strict egalitarianism. I may well not want to lead while still wanting there *to be* leaders, and this need not be an irresponsible attitude. Some people simply, and with perfect legitimacy, prefer "cultivating their own garden" to the theatrics of the public realm.

4. *Living with Our Luck.* Making use of one's luck is itself an accomplishment, and we tend to regard people who turn whatever hand they have been dealt to its best possible use as admirable, as achieving much more than those merely lucky enough to have been dealt a good hand in the first place. We tend to consider noble a person who attempts to live with whatever condition he is thrown, and regard everyone as obliged to live with *some* of the conditions he is thrown. In this way we can consider ourselves, as we like to do, to be *using* or *appropriating* our luck rather

than enduring it passively. I put this at the moment simply on the level of what we "like" because, although there are philosophical justifications for the attitude, it is an important brute fact that we enjoy appropriating our luck, that this is a brute element of the human good. People deliberately take up risky hobbies and professions; people emigrate from socialist states to capitalist ones, and from kibbutzim to urban marketplaces; people read books about the ups and downs of other people's lives, and discuss such shifts of fortunes in their own lives with friends, rather than concentrating their attention on what remains the same across time, or on those changes completely under their control. People enjoy games that have an element of luck, although they often prefer games that require skill in addition to luck. Chess and Go are ancient, wonderful games, but so are bridge and poker, and social "games" in many cultures, from courting rituals to transferals of power, resemble the latter much more than the former: in part because people, quite simply, like to *play* that way. Perhaps we like these games for psychoanalytic reasons, because we get thus to stage consciously, and thereby gain control over, the frightening dependence we have on what the empirical world happens to do to us;[9] perhaps we have evolved, biologically, a tendency to enjoy the challenge of facing and trying to overcome luck since this is otherwise a useful skill for survival. Whatever the explanation, many people, probably most, do not really want to live in a world that does away with luck, including the luck of our initial "draw" in natural endowments and family upbringing. Hence the instability of socialist communities, even on a small scale, their tendency to develop their own inequalities of status and games for distributing those inequalities, and their tendency, as we saw in 1989, to be defeated by precisely the kind of overwhelming, spontaneous popular revolution by which Marx thought they would be installed. People want a chance to play somewhat risky games, including the games of the marketplace, and let the chips—some of the chips at any rate—fall where they may.

5. *The Need for Desert.* Finally, we have a moral need for some notion of desert by means of talent and effort. If we give up on the notion that we deserve any of our abilities, we abdicate responsibility for our own characters, and if we give up on the notion that the abilities take certain material ends as their fitting rewards, we undermine a primary means of moral education, a primary instrument of praise and blame in childhood: the appropriateness of achieving aims worked for, and failing when we work shoddily or not at all. Nor can we, as Rawls seems to want to do, hold on to any notion of desert, and correspondingly of freedom and responsibility, if we renounce desert for our amoral traits. If we give up on the notion that we deserve, that our choices have helped to bring

about, such fundamental character traits as our talents and willingness to make an effort, we can hardly hold on to a notion that we deserve our moral qualities. We must rather give up on desert altogether.

In this connection, we must deny Rawls his attempt to separate distributive from retributive justice:

[N]one of the precepts of justice aims at rewarding virtue. The premiums earned by scarce natural talents, for example . . . do not correlate with moral worth, since the initial endowment of natural assets and the contingencies of their growth and nurture in early life are arbitrary from a moral point of view. . . . The idea of rewarding desert is impracticable. . . .

No doubt some may still contend that distributive shares should match moral worth at least to the extent that this is feasible. . . . Now this opinion may arise from thinking of distributive justice as somehow the opposite of retributive justice. . . . [I]n a reasonably well-ordered society those who are punished for violating just laws have normally done something wrong. This is because the purpose of the criminal law is to uphold basic natural duties, . . . and punishments are to serve this end. They are not simply a scheme of taxes and burdens designed to put a price on certain forms of conduct and in this way to guide men's conduct for mutual advantage. It would be far better if the acts proscribed by penal statutes were never done. Thus a propensity to commit such acts is a mark of bad character.

. . . [It] is clear that the distribution of economic and social advantages is entirely different. These arrangements are not the converse, so to speak, of the criminal law, so that just as the one punishes certain offenses, the other rewards moral worth. The function of unequal distributive shares is to cover the costs of training and education, to attract individuals to places and associations where they are most needed from a social point of view, and so on. (TJ 310–5)

I quote at length because I think only the whole flow of the argument shows how consistently Rawls treats "virtue" and "moral worth" as interchangeable, and both as entirely separate from "talent." Since Rawls takes for granted that "virtue" means "*moral* virtue," it is obvious for him that the "premiums earned by scarce natural talents" do not reward virtue. A more Aristotelian conception of virtue, a conception by which virtue consists above all in the cultivation of natural human capacities for excellence, might make it seem equally obvious that *only* premiums "earned by" talents could possibly count as rewarding virtue. Next, it seems clear to Rawls that to offend against "natural duties" (the duties of not injuring others, depriving them of liberty, etc.) is a mark of bad character, while one's talents are wholly irrelevant to character: something society merely has an interest in training and educating, in attracting to places where they might be needed, etc. Perhaps Aristotelian notions of virtue as "excellences" are too amoral—too showy, too elitist—for any

Kantian egalitarianism, but what has happened, even then, to the Kant of the third example in the *Groundwork*, the Kant who gives us a *moral duty* to cultivate our talents? Are we supposed to cultivate them while treating the rewards that might be fitting to such cultivation as mere means of social manipulation, to be redistributed away from any requirement of fit whenever convenience so dictates? How would *that* be different, if cultivating our talents is indeed a mark of good character, from treating the appropriate punishments for bad character in purely utilitarian fashion? Conversely, if cultivating our talents is not a mark of good character, merely a reflection of an arbitrary natural endowment, why should we regard propensities to violate "natural duties" as a mark of *bad* character? Why not say then, with some penal reformers and many utilitarians, that a criminal's desire to commit antisocial acts is merely his or her misfortune, and should be treated with exactly the combination of incentives and restraints by which, in the economic sphere, we encourage people to develop some talents and squelch others?

On the empirical level, it is likely that a society urging citizens to distinguish their "true selves" from their talents and industry would be unable to keep those same citizens feeling responsible for their inclinations to dishonesty and fraud, to callousness and cruelty, to sexual faithlessness and violence. We do not tend much to separate, in our views of our own personalities, between natural excellences and moral virtues, at least insofar as we are asked to take responsibility for them.[10] If we have responsibility for any feature of our personality, despite its dependence on environmental accidents, then we have responsibility for the moral features among others. If we lack responsibility for any feature because of its dependence on our environment, then we lack responsibility for the moral ones as well.

At the very least, this is the common view, and experience suggests that societies accept or give up on one notion of responsibility only together with the other.[11] It is therefore hard to believe that a "public conception of justice" that endorsed holding one's talents at arm's length could in fact at the same time bring about the respect for persons, and for acting on principles, that Rawls takes as such an important goal of a theory of justice (see TJ 133, 177–81, 472–9, 496–501). It is hard to see, that is, how Rawls' conception of the human being could in fact "generate its own support," how, if it were instituted as the official basis for all distribution of material rewards, it could encourage any sense of responsibility for actions, let alone the "corresponding sense of justice" to Rawls's two principles (cf. TJ 177).

We feel intimately connected with our talents, our personality traits, our tastes and energies, even our history, especially as we grow older. I may well regard some of my talents as merely "external" to me, and perhaps I regard all of them that way until I train them, live with them for a while, or otherwise appropriate them, but surely I find it hard to figure out who, specifically, I am independently of some combination of the contingent facts that I live in this country, live with that person, run fast or slowly, am attractive or not, fix cars or trade bonds, and spend my leisure time at the basketball court or in front of a chessboard. And to be told that societal reward ultimately should not depend on how I succeed in these things is to be told that they do not matter, that they are irrelevant to my "real self." But most of us are not satisfied to endorse pure will or reason as our real selves, and there is a good reason why we should not be: if our wills do not come to include the empirical ways in which they get used, they are nothing but mere capacities, not something whose effectiveness in the world can be asserted at all. Effectiveness depends on our being able to say that the development of some talent or trait or taste is the product of our will. We therefore feel we more truly *have* a self when we can take responsibility for our own history. To reward people as if what they do with their luck does not matter is to reward precisely those who shirk any responsibility for their actual doings, to provide incentive for not regarding one's will as effective. This is perverse, discouraging people from identification, not only with their contingent features, but with the real self that is supposed to underlie such contingencies. We come to see it as something that does not exist empirically, that can be ignored for empirical purposes.

Now Rawls may think he has accommodated this problem because the people in his original position allow themselves to compete for higher positions and rewards once a just framework has ensured that the differences thus secured benefit the worst-off. But the intuition we need to hold on to is that we deserve some rewards intrinsically if we earn them by talent and effort, that certain rewards somehow *fit* what we have done.[12] Rawls says that his Difference Principle "represents, in effect, an agreement to regard the distribution of natural talents as a common asset and to share in the benefits of this distribution whatever it turns out to be" (TJ 101), remarking later that for people to regard talents in this way is for them "to express their respect for one another in the very constitution of their society" (TJ 179). Here one's talents are seen as something useful for society as a whole, and our respect for one another must sidestep, must ignore, the role of our talents in making up who we are; but we would like our talents, at least when we have developed them and plugged them into channels our society has held open to us, to be *admirable* as well as useful. Our proper pleasures, which are centrally even if not solely displayed in the marketplace, depend on our phronetic activities being rewarded for the virtues they display, and not merely for the material benefits they produce and distribute. To regard one's developed talents as merely useful for the production of social benefits may well be to take up a noble moral attitude, but at best it is surely a supererogatory one, not the readily expectable element of ordinary moral psychology on which Rawls says we should rely when constructing basic principles of justice (TJ 176–7). Rawls uses arguments drawn from moral psychology as a strong recommendation for his own principles vis-à-vis utilitarian ones. Utilitarian principles, he says, require either such a strong altruism or such a willingness to live with one's risks that individuals cannot rely on one another to adhere to them—"the strains of commitment" in living with them will be too great (TJ 176–7). Precisely this is what I think we can say about Rawls's own account. A society publicly proclaiming that talent earns rewards only because and when the least advantaged are thereby helped will not inspire the people living in that society to feel that it "affirms their own good", and thus will fail to meet Rawls's condition of "stability" (TJ 177). One could maintain the society instead by means of a *pretense* that the rewards are really being made available on the basis of their intrinsic suitedness to an exercise of talents, but this would violate Rawls's condition of "publicity" (TJ 133).[13] The kind of respect for each other's talents that I am recommending needs to belong to "the very constitution of . . . society," needs to comprise a basic part of respecting each other as persons, not come in, under constant suspicious scrutiny, as a provisional secondary principle after the basic outlines of justice have already been accommodated. If the thought that rewards should be earned and not merely distributed, that we are intimately tied up with our abilities, and that our material achievements should somehow reflect that fact—if these intuitions are indeed deeply rooted and rationally endorsable—then Rawls's own principles require us to accommodate them in the basic stucture of our society.

II

I have traced five linked intuitions, not presented an argument that refutes Rawls. What matters is that these intuitions make both common and Kantian sense, and that they fit the overall view I have been urging in this book: a view placing judgment, in political matters, over reason. The acceptance of luck that the intuitions all require is an intrinsic part of any politics focused on our capacity for judgment. A politics of judgment needs to allow for luck, for people to see themselves as making their own way amid contingencies, integrating their accidental qualities into their wills where they can, and learning to live with accidental limitations where they cannot. Kant's appeal to talent, industry, and luck in TP thus supports a reading of his own politics as a politics of judgment. It suggests, that is, that Kantian social and economic institutions should constitute a realm where judgment can play itself out, rather than one in which reason decides in advance what the end-state should look like. The "antinomy of justice" I described earlier lets us know that reason, if called upon to do so, *could* stipulate our ideal political ends, and this is perhaps what has transfixed Rawls. Because reason *can* set us an ideal here, because it can resolve the issue of what distribution of goods would be ideally just, perhaps he thinks it *must* find this resolution, must be called upon to give us an answer. But the answer reason gives a priori is not necessarily the answer we would give as rational *as well as historical* beings, so calling on reason here preempts the actual living out of human lives, the histories which philosophy should follow and, at most, "prune," not rewrite. We live out our own lives by acting on our own individual capacities for judgment, despite or even because this puts us in the hands of our talents and tastes and at the mercy of our luck, not by waiving our judgment in favor of our own, or anyone else's, principles of reason. Reason should guide our individual judgments, not overwhelm them.

It follows that one ground for relying on markets, rather than even the most decent and reasonable philosopher, to guide our distribution of material goods is that they enhance, play to, and train us in judgment. They enable us to develop specialized skills, force us to attend to the specific nature and needs of others, encourage us in the "self-command" that is a precondition for reflecting usefully upon our desires, and leave us alone enough that we can shape our own history. People who favor heavily planned political economies often suppose that this development of skills and character can take place entirely outside the economic realm. But where? We spend a huge proportion of our lives in labor and consumption, so if those realms of activity are tightly controlled, we will lack much opportunity to emerge from paternalistic tutelage. Moreover, a government that plans prices and production must inevitably stretch its tentacles into every arena of life, from amusement parks to printing presses to schools and churches. George Kateb describes our current political economy as already dangerously close to this:

> [T]he growth of state activism in a democracy is the growth, as well, of that . . . dependence which makes it easier for the government to think of itself as . . . an entity that is indispensable to all relations and transactions in society. . . . The government becomes all-observant, all-competent; it intervenes everywhere; and as new predicaments arise in society, it moves first to define and attempt a resolution of them. My proposed idea is that as this tendency grows—and it is already quite advanced—people will, to an increasing degree, come to accept the government as [indispensable]. . . . People's dependence

on it will gradually condition their attitudes and their sentiments. Looking to it, they must end by looking up to it.[14]

The idea that judgment and its correlated virtues might be trained as a luxury, outside the economic realm, is unlikely to be realized even in the affluent utopias that Marx and other socialists have imagined. Some of these socialists, influenced by the civic republican tradition, have looked to participation in communal debates as a better training ground for freedom than the market. But this misses the need for freedom, if it rests on judgment at least, to be developed ultimately *by* each individual *for* that individual. Political debates and voting procedures are blunt and occasional instruments, far from the ubiquitous, diffuse, subtle incentives and interactions by which markets provide each of us with constant, individuated guidance.

It follows that one good justification for an unequal distribution of rewards in a society is that that enables markets to work, and enables the virtues markets encourage to meet with proper recognition for success. Again, Kateb expresses this well:

> Of course, scarcely any idea lends itself more easily than does desert or merit to the rationalization of abuse, punishment, neglect, and cruelty. But the idea at its worst may still be better than a practiced rejection of it. As long as it remains out of the power of reason to decide the question of free will, then it is better for the sake of human dignity to continue to accept free will, and, along with it, the idea of desert or merit. That acceptance could mean, in turn, that justice does not require radical socioeconomic equality but that . . . justice is, even if reluctantly, on the side of inequality. . . . I do not mean to suggest that a market economy is a perfect indicator of the comparative moral worth of people. It does not bestow distributive justice. But it does often give greater rewards to greater energy, skill, or cleverness, not only to blind luck or the human vices.[15]

"It does not bestow *perfect* distributive justice," I would say, or, even better: it is generally just because it does not "bestow" or "distribute" at all. We *earn* our own lives in a market economy, if, and insofar as, we ever earn them. We earn them not despite luck but because of it: because there and there only can we take true responsibility for our luck.

III

None of this goes to show that anyone deserves to starve, simply because luck would have it that way, or deserves to have the colorless, mind-numbing lives of many middle-class workers. (Nor does it show, for that matter, that anyone deserves fabulous luxury.) Kateb continues the passage I have just quoted by saying, "To reject the project of ever greater socioeconomic equality is not . . . to ignore misery or even to ignore bare poverty." Accepting the luck that brings inequality and, through markets, gives individuals control over their work and goods does not mean accepting everything that falls out from luck and history, from the "accidental" features of our lives. Surely it is disingenuous to claim we are respecting people when we let them live in the streets or grow up without education. At that point, respect requires us to *override* luck, not to accept it.

One way to respond to this challenge is to return to Kant for, at last, something of a critique of Smith. The *Groundwork*, in addition to a paragraph that makes interesting use of the division of labor,[16] contains an odd passage that juxtaposes markets and prices with the absolute value of human being. The passage is odd because it is quite unnecessary to the argument. "In the realm of ends everything has either a *price* [Preis] or a *dignity* [Würde]," writes Kant at G 434/53, and for the next four paragraphs he compares the two. If one were to cut out these paragraphs, they would not be missed. The sentence that precedes them splices directly on to the one that succeeds them, there is no reference to price elsewhere in the *Groundwork*, and insofar as they describe the sublimity of the will, they merely duplicate other material to be found in the chapter (for instance, at 427–8/45–6). It is as though Kant tried to stick a theory of value in *Groundwork* II wherever it would look least out of place. For *as* a contribution to the philosophy of economics, these paragraphs do say something new and interesting.

Price, writes Kant, is the mark of what "can be replaced by something else as its equivalent." This seems to mean that price is essentially something relative, and that impression is supported by an equation Kant draws, a few lines later, between "price" and "relative worth": "[T]he condition under which alone something can be an end in itself does not have mere relative worth, i.e., a price." Kant's analysis of this relative worth is not entirely clear—he does not, for instance, explain exactly what prices are relative *to*—but he is ahead of his time in rejecting any attempt to ground value in precious metals, in land, or in labor. He does not allow any empirical thing or human activity, that is, to serve as an absolute standard for measuring prices. And if he had read WN by this time, as I believe he had, one can imagine that what he learned from it, and particularly liked in it, might be its criticism of the various empirical fetishes of the mercantilists and Physiocrats.

I say one can imagine he particularly liked this because I think what Kant admired about Smith may have been very similar to what he admired in Smith's friend Hume. Hume had unmasked various epistemological superstitions, above all that there was any empirical evidence for a unified "self" and that there was any empirical justification for belief in causality. Kant admired the incisiveness of these attacks and responded by accepting them as accurate depictions of the empirical phenomena regarding selves and causes, while arguing that a transcendental assumption of a unified self and law of causality was still necessary. Smith unmasks economic superstitions about the superiority of land over any other kind of investment (physiocracy) or the superiority of precious metals, or manufactured goods, over any other kind of comparative advantage in trade (mercantilism).[17] Both the skeptical stance that enabled him to perceive such errors, and the detail of his explanations as to why they are erroneous, would likely have held great appeal for Kant.

But there is a point at which Smith's healthy willingness to submit everything to empirical tests appears to break down, and it is here that we may begin to locate where Kant might have tried to use Smith against himself, to borrow his work, as he had Hume's, as a weapon *against* thoroughgoing empiricism in the explanation of human knowledge or action. Smith finds no absolute standard of value *within* the market, but he does seem to hold a labor theory of value as a kind of absolute standard *beyond* the market. At times his account of labor value can be quite confusing, and may indeed be confused.[18] Kant, by contrast, neatly dismisses labor as a standard for value. *All* empirical things have a relative value, for Kant (428/46), and the abilities and energy that go into labor are in the end just empirical things: "Skill and diligence in work . . . have a market [price]" (435/53).[19] Only *rational being,* that which makes and assesses all claims to relative value, can itself have absolute value: "A thing has no worth other than that determined for it by the law. The legislation which determines all worth must therefore have a dignity, i.e., unconditional and incomparable worth" (436/54).[20]

Now what, concretely, might follow from a claim that relative values or prices are grounded in the absolute value of the human being? That human beings should not be bought and sold is surely one implication, and Kant thus provides theoretical grounds for the antislavery position that Smith held but could justify only contingently. More deeply, some aspect of human thought—the capacity to value things itself—must be beyond price; whatever goes into deliberation should not, therefore, be something we can ever be justified in trading off for other goods. The policy consequences of this implication might include a demand that anything feeding into the human capacity for evaluation should lie beyond the market, that education and access to information, at least, should be guaranteed to everyone regardless of market distribution.

So much for a general principle for where market mechanisms might be morally inadequate. But a problem remains. We need somehow to distinguish between those features of our characters essential to our "capacity for evaluation" and those features we can allow luck to shape. Can we do this? Drawing a nonarbitrary line between the luck relevant and the luck irrelevant to character-formation seems next to impossible. Surely either *all* luck is relevant or *all* luck is irrelevant. If reason can embrace arbitrary happenings as its own products, can it also distinguish nonarbitrarily among these arbitrary happenings?

I turn to Martha Nussbaum for hints as to how we might do this, how we might respect people's capacities enough to let them embrace their luck while at the same time respecting their need for help in avoiding incapacitating misfortune. Nussbaum is a particularly appropriate thinker for my concerns since she shows beautifully how an ethical view that stresses judgment needs to accept the importance of luck in our lives rather than trying to overcome it.[21] Judgment is directed to particulars, and the realm of particulars is a realm where quirky things happen, where we cannot count on the certainty of abstract generalizations always to guide us aright. At the same time, Nussbaum displays, in all her writings, strong political commitments to what we today consider liberal causes, including the cause of alleviating—if possible, eradicating—poverty. So she will hardly be one to accept the complacent coldness, sometimes cruelty, of those who delight in luck enough to regard even welfare programs as detracting from our responsibility for what happens to us. Nussbaum points, I think, to how we might humanely accommodate luck in a liberal politics. If so, she enables us to satisfy the powerfully decent call of egalitarianism in the Kantian tradition without alienating us from our talents and personalities. What follows is a short commentary, directed to the concerns of political economy, on *The Fragility of Goodness*.

"But human excellence grows like a vine tree, fed by the green dew, raised up, among wise men and just, to the liquid sky." So Pindar displays a problem that lies at the heart of Greek thought about the good life for a human being. . . . [T]he excellence of a good person is something of that person's own, for whose possession and exercise that person can appropriately be held accountable. . . . [But it] is [also] like a young plant: something growing in the world, slender, fragile, in constant need of food from without. A vine tree must be of good stock if it is to grow well. And even if it has a good heritage, it needs fostering weather . . . , as well as the care of concerned and intelligent keepers. . . . So, the poet suggests, do we. We need to be born with adequate capacities, to live in fostering natural and social circumstances, to stay clear of abrupt catastrophe, to develop confirming associations with other human beings. . . . And all these needs for all these things that we do not humanly control are pertinent . . . not only to feelings of contentment or happiness. What the external nourishes, and even helps to constitute, is excellence or human worth itself. (p. 1)

Luck is necessary not merely to enjoy the fruits of excellence but to *be* excellent at all. We are lucky if we have the healthy childhood to develop good moral habits, and we are lucky if we have the leisure, later in life, to make use of those habits. We may even be lucky, sometimes, to have setbacks and failures forcing us to concentrate on why life is truly worth living—at least if these are the right kind of failures, the ones that allow for such reflection.

> [Pindar] displays the thorough intermingling of what is ours and what belongs to the world, of ambition and vulnerability, of making and being made, that are present in this and in any human life. . . . To what extent can we distinguish between what is up to the world and what is up to us, when assessing a human life? To what extent *must* we insist on finding these distinctions, if we are to go on praising as we praise? And how can we improve this situation, making progress by placing the most important things, things such as personal achievement, politics, and love, under our control? The problem is made more complex by a further implication of [Pindar's] poetic image. It suggests that part of the peculiar beauty of *human* excellence just *is* its vulnerability. (p. 2)

We identify ourselves with our luck, take responsibility for it, in part *because* we cannot draw a sharp line between the internal and the external. Not mere pragmatic considerations, moreover, but virtue requires this. It belongs to human excellence to reconcile oneself to the paradox that part of what it is to "create one's self" just is to *be created by* something "outside" of oneself. We will not be who we are and aim to be, we will not be true decision-makers who can be praised and blamed for our acts, if we do not keep ourselves vulnerable to luck, and to loss.

It may indeed be important, *pace* Nussbaum, that "making progress" *not* be identified with bringing such things as personal achievement, politics, and love, under our control—at least under more control than we need to appreciate, still, our vulnerability.

> In general, to eliminate luck from human life will be to put that life, or the most important things in it, under the control of the agent (or of those elements in him with which he identifies himself). (pp. 3–4)

"With which *he identifies himself*": Nussbaum rightly leaves both open, and significantly up to the agent himself, what counts as "properly" drawing the line between internal and external.

> That I am an agent, but also a plant; that much that I did not make goes towards making me whatever I shall be praised or blamed for being; . . . that an event that simply happens to me may, without my consent, alter my life;

. . . —all these I take to be not just the material of tragedy, but everyday facts of lived practical reason. (p. 5)

And if everyday facts of lived practical reason, then, a fortiori, of political economy. Which means that we must allow for luck, accept it, not only in what we, as individuals, expect praise or blame for, but in what we, as a society, praise and blame. When we set up the institutions that, directly or indirectly, distribute praise and blame, reward and punishment, we must not simply ignore or overrule luck. Rather, we must enable ourselves, as individuals, to continue to live with it.

> On the other hand, it seems equally impossible, or equally inhuman, to avoid feeling the force of the Platonic conception of a self-sufficient and purely rational being, . . . freed from contingent limitations on its power. . . . And if to feel this tension [between the need for luck and the desire to be free of luck] is not an idiosyncratic or rare experience, but a fact in the natural history of human beings, then good human practical reasoning about the self-sufficiency of the good life seems to require an inquiry that explores both pictures, feeling the power of each. (pp. 5–6)

This tension is the tension of judgment, I believe, as well as the tension to which judgment responds. That is how "good human practical reasoning" consists in good judgment. We need to treat our contingencies "responsibly" in both senses of that word: we must truly respond to them and we must try to control them. We must also recognize the tension between these attitudes for what it is: "not an idiosyncratic or rare experience, but a fact in the natural history of human beings," perhaps the defining fact, the fact that makes us human.

> [I]t is [the Greeks'] instinct that some projects for self-sufficient living are questionable because they ask us to go beyond the cognitive limits of the human being; and, on the other hand, that many attempts to venture, in metaphysical or scientific reasoning, beyond our human limits are inspired by questionable ethical motives, motives having to do with closedness, safety, and power. (p. 8)

It is remarkable how much of this can be transposed directly to issues in political economy, particularly the last remark. The Marxist project of a community that no longer faces scarcity, that protects all its members from financial failure, and that has done away with envy and vanity, has been often and rightly criticized for "go[ing] beyond the cognitive limits of the human being," and for being motivated by an obsession with "closedness, safety, and power." I have argued that even the more flexible and modest project of John Rawls tries too hard to insure human safety rather than accepting the fact of, the need for, and even on occasion the joy in human vulnerability.[22] In this, Rawls is really more Platonic than Kantian, more in search of a rational ideal that will overcome the limits on our knowledge and emotional capacities than willing to accept Kant's own concessions to the empirical responsibilities of judgment.

Now, how to draw the line between the luck that must be embraced, and the luck that should, as much as possible, be controlled? How draw a line between "external" and "internal"? Well, we might start by insisting that the luck necessary for us meaningfully to *have* an "internal" at all is strictly "external," that no line could be drawn unless and until we are lucky enough to have a realm we control, a perspective and personality we can regard as our own:

> Aristotle plainly does believe that our worldly circumstances affect, for better or for worse, . . . good character itself, not just its expression. It is obvious that the world, in his view, affects decisively the character-formation of children; the case for adult vulnerability is not as obvious, but it can still be convincingly made out. . . . [C]ircumstances of life can impede character itself, making even acquired virtues difficult to retain. . . . Love and friendship require trust in the loved person; generosity is incompatible with continual suspicion that the world is about to take one's necessary goods away; greatness of soul requires high hope and expectation; even courage requires confidence that some good can come of fine action. . . . [V]irtuous condition is not, itself, something hard and invulnerable. Its yielding and open posture towards the world gives it the fragility, as well as the beauty, of a plant. (pp. 336–40)

Luck makes possible "virtuous condition" itself. *This,* however, is the vulnerability that needs to be controlled, the luck we cannot, as a society, merely stand by and let happen. Where virtue is already possible, there luck can and should be allowed to play—virtue requires a negotiation with some luck—but the luck that brings virtue about must be limited. As a society, we are obligated to put every resource we can muster into preventing and overcoming the circumstances that make children unable to grow up with good characters, and to provide insurance to adults against events that "dislodge" them from so much as having control over their own characters, from retaining the virtues that enable them to handle and appreciate luck at all.

"Dislodge":

> The good person, Aristotle said, could not easily be dislodged from *eudaimonia*, but only by "big and numerous misfortunes." Once so dislodged, however, "he will not become *eudaimon* again in a short time, but, if ever, in a long and complete time.". . . . A purely external impediment to good action

could be set right immediately by the restoration of good fortune. A person who has been enslaved in wartime can be set free in a moment. A sick person can as quickly be cured. . . . What does take time and repeated good fortune to heal is the corruption of desire, expectation, and thought that can be inflicted by crushing and prolonged misfortune. . . . It takes a long time to restore to the slave a free person's sense of dignity and self-esteem, for the chronic invalid to learn again the desires and projects characteristic of the healthy person, for the bereaved person to form new and fruitful attachments. (p. 337)

We need enough external goods to be strong enough to handle loss: not more, but also not less. Above that threshold, handling one's own luck is appropriate. But it is not appropriate to let luck provide whatever it takes to insure that people not get entrenched in starvation, in slavery, in illness or despair sufficient to "corrupt . . . desire, expectation, and thought," in miseries sufficiently "crushing and prolonged" to break their self-command. The material security to prevent such disintegration of virtue is the "guaranteed minimum" of political economists. This minimum we as a society must supply, must distribute to each, not expect each to earn for himself. We must "distribute" it, despite our general preference for "earning" over distribution, because otherwise we cannot meaningfully expect each to be able to "earn" at all. Only those lucky enough already to have the wealth to avoid great misfortune would then be capable of such a responsible mode of taking possession. We can now put in better perspective Kateb's reminder that rejecting the project of "ever greater socio-economic equality" does not mean ignoring poverty. Kateb's concern for the poor is not merely a humanitarian oscillation from his concern with desert but the flip side of the very justification for inequality he has invoked. For the essence of the market economy as a virtue-enhancing system is that it trains us to make and to live with free choices, so insofar as it depends on actions that can not reasonably be interpreted as a matter of "free choice" at all, its justification falls away. To hold each responsible for his or her own acts, to expect people to work for their own ends, we must provide them with the means that allow for responsibility: the means of health, leisure, and education by which they can judge intelligently of their lives and their conditions.

When he comes to the issue of justice across generations, Rawls insists that a nation needs enough wealth to maintain institutions of justice from one generation to the next, but not more (TJ pp. 287–90). Why not apply a similarly judicious criterion to the amount of wealth, or primary goods, each individual needs? The minimal level of support an individual needs is that which enables her to maintain her ability to reason—the equivalent, on the individual level, of a society's institutions of justice—from one day to the next. Beyond that level, she is responsible for her own luck; and that level is not arbitrary, because only with an ability to reason intact is responsibility of any kind, including responsibility for one's luck, possible. Such a guaranteed minimum for the worst-off seems to me clearly preferable to Rawls's always rising maximal index of primary goods. Of course, what specific forms the minimal means of health, leisure, and education should take may well vary from place to place, culture to culture, and time to time.[23] But the problem of how to apply a distributive principle of justice besets Rawls's maximin principle as well. The issue at the moment is whether there are moral reasons for preferring maximin, as the appropriate principle, over a stable minimum. And Rawls's argument for that preference depends entirely, I believe, on the intuition that differences in talent and industry are morally irrelevant. With a rejection of that intuition, the way is open to replace his controversial maximin with the much less controversial guaranteed minimum.

IV

I have not argued that we require instances to grasp a concept only to myself offer a concept with no examples. I therefore want to sketch how the "protection against dislodgment" I recommend might apply to our present circumstances.

In the first place, the "guaranteed minimum" needs to be considered as much an essential requirement of justice, as much something a just Constitution should guarantee, as any civil right. A respect for market incentives does, I think, lead one to prefer that this be provided outside the market as much as possible, perhaps by a negative income tax, as Milton Friedman has suggested, rather than by a minimum wage (supplemented, for the unemployed, by free shelter space and perhaps free bulk food). But at all events it is one of the most important obligations any government has to fulfill, and generously so if it is to serve its purpose, so those who go Friedman's route should never agitate against welfare programs without proposing immediately to replace them with, say, a negative tax ranging from 100 to 200 percent of income for everyone below the poverty level. Moreover, Friedman's route, though preferable, is not required by the liberalism I am expounding. Just as judgment itself comes in degrees, so the freedom that enables it comes in degrees. A little interference with the market here and there, a little dampening of some people's incentives for judicious choices so as to enhance everyone's capacity for judicious choice, does not an unfree people make. Welfare grants and minimum wage laws can therefore be justified wherever a better policy is not politically feasible. The point is to use market systems *as much as morally justifiable,* understanding "morally justifiable" to require a nonmarket guarantee that everyone have the health, the intellectual ability, and the options to choose judiciously at all.

By "options," I mean that a choice reflecting judgment must be a choice of one who has alternative possibilities to what he is now choosing, and, ideally, a choice of one who has experienced some of those alternatives in the past. If judgment is developed by habit and depends on felt similarities among particulars as well as thought-out generalizations, then first experiencing what it is like to work on an assembly line, in a mine, or as a typist may be essential to choosing judiciously whether one wants to continue doing so, or at what price, having done something different, one would be willing to return to it. More obviously, perhaps, a free market in labor requires not merely that jobs be "out there," but that each individual have as much access as possible to *getting to* the jobs she might like and for which she might be qualified. Smith dismissed the notion that markets in labor are as free as all that in a famously ironic passage:

> [T]he wages of labour in a great town and its neighbourhood are frequently . . . twenty or five-and-twenty per cent higher than at a few miles distant. . . . Such a difference in prices, which it seems is not always sufficient to transport a man from one parish to another, would necessarily occasion so great a transportation of the most bulky commodities, not only from one parish to another, but . . . almost from one end of the world to the other, as would soon reduce them more nearly to a level. After all that has been said of the levity and inconstancy of human nature, it appears evidently from experience that a man is of all sorts of luggage the most difficult to be transported. (WN I.viii.31)

The mobility of labor might be increased if the costs of transportation were underwritten (directly by the government, or via incentives to private companies) for every individual who lacks the means to cover them herself. This is a condition for a true free market in labor—along with unemployment insurance, well-funded opportunities for retraining, and well-publicized information about job openings. Without all of these conditions in place, people may make some sort of choice about their employment but not a judicious choice. Only where they are capable of making judicious choices, however, can we truly speak of a free market.

By "intellectual ability," as a condition for judicious choice, I mean to pull together all the qualities we have seen judgment to entail. We saw in chapters 2 and 5, for instance, that the reflection going into judgment takes *time*: one needs to interpret oneself and one's situation in an unhurried way if one is to pick up its details sensitively and categorize them appropriately. Thus one who must choose a job, let alone make long-term plans about what kind of work to pursue, should not be desperately in need of the first opportunity that comes along, nor so pressured by work obligations that he cannot think straight about where his skills might truly lie and what he truly wants. A need for substantial leisure—say, six weeks a year, or a several-month sabbatical every few years—thereby becomes a condition for freedom. In this the liberalism I am proposing fits with the normative concerns of a long liberal tradition. A two-week "vacation" is just what it sounds like: long enough to "vacate" one's life—one's projects, thoughts, long-term commitments—in favor of the beach or the gambling table. If workers are to develop new habits and/or new interests, they need enough time to take classes, to try out new activities, to look for a job, or even, quite simply, to reflect on themselves. Those without an adequate minimum of leisure cannot be regarded as having properly "chosen" anything at all. A substantial amount of leisure is a condition for judicious choice, and the worker who makes do with two weeks of vacation in return for more consumer goods is no more rightfully considered free in making this choice than is the slave who has been in her condition so long that she "chooses" to remain in slavery rather than face the risks of independence.

In addition, the kind of market that cultivates intellectual and moral virtues, the kind of market where individuals are faced daily with the need to make judicious choices, is only one along the lines Smith originally praised: a system of small firms and consumers, in which no one has enough power to evade the discipline of competition. "Combinations" of merchants, as he stressed again and again, defeat this diffusion of power, and large firms are prime examples of unacceptable combinations—considerably more so than trade unions. Where a few companies dominate what kinds of car are produced in a country, and especially where one or two companies dominate a small town's labor market, there is no reason to interpret the choices made by the car consumers and the workers, respectively, as reflecting a judgment among real options. Moreover, where workers are each but tiny cogs in a huge bureaucratic apparatus, their daily decisions are likely to matter little to anyone but themselves. In order to foster the sense of daily responsibility so important to developing judgment, therefore, a liberalism that stresses judgment will campaign on principle for strong antitrust legislation, indeed ideally for the replacement of large firms by small, local ones. Economists have shown that this is not the most efficient way to run an economy, that economies of scale entail that better and cheaper goods will be produced by large firms, and that competition will lower prices adequately even where but two giant firms compete. But if we are concerned with more than the satisfaction of "expressed preferences," this is not the end of the story. If we want freedom and responsibility for all workers, and truly free, judicious choices going into the preferences consumers express, then we need to break up gluts of economic power despite the inefficiencies entailed.

What if the inefficiencies are simply unacceptable, if they would impoverish everyone? To the extent that they would, we can compromise, accepting a lower degree of freedom in our society in return for better and cheaper goods. But compromise must at least require insuring that the gluts of power in the hands of employers and shareholders are balanced by equally powerful gluts in the hands of workers (trade unions) and consumers (consumer advocacy groups). The power of the state, on the view I have been laying out, is legitimately used precisely to keep all loci of power small, to minimize the obstacles to each individual's ability to develop and use his or her own judgment.[24] It keeps its own power small by limiting its tasks to the minimal functions Smith lays out for it: defense, the administration of justice, and large public works, where the latter includes the provision, for all, of the conditions for judgment. And it keeps the power available to other groups small by favoring small businesses over large ones, workers over their employers, and, in general, the weak over the strong. It must guarantee rights of exit from all "private" loci of power, and should urge the provision of a voice within them and the proliferation of competing alternatives to them. Only where the control of both public and private groups over resources and opportunities is severely limited will each individual have the independence to carry out her own judgments.

Finally, the judgment that we need for truly free choices requires, in addition to good information about the options among which one is choosing, a thorough education in the skills of interpretation and the assessment of evidence. As regards the information alone, workers and consumers alike need easy access to rich, clear, and clearly organized facts about products and jobs. Where the market does not itself provide such information, centralized computer services open to everyone are thus a legitimate task for public funding. In addition to this, however, not only must the public underwrite an excellent system of education, but that system needs to help people acquire the skills of aesthetic interpretation, and learn the relevance of those skills to the decisions they need to make about running their own lives.

I would be much readier to believe the claims of hard-line "free marketeers"—that everyone is really living out the consequences of their own choices regardless of the hardships of their work, or lack of work—if conditions of this sort were in place. If people were all raised from childhood on with adequate nutrition, shelter, and health care, if they knew they would receive considerable aid in unemployment, if they could take any job in the country because funds were available to transport them

there, if they were well trained in evaluating evidence and had easy access
to a large amount of information about their opportunities, and if they
had sufficient leisure to reflect on their lives and alter them if necessary, it
is likely (a) that they would not put up with the exploitation and manipulation they now accept, (b) that they would become more flexible, better
adapted to a dynamic marketplace, and (c) that they would, where necessary, pursue the formation of unions, a right to representation in management, or political change, with more wisdom, and willingness to compromise, than they do now. It is likely, that is, that the *facts* of our political
economy would change. And insofar as they did not change, one would
have good empirical reason to believe that people were truly *choosing* not
to change them, that they had truly understood and were rejecting alternative options. Then one could say that the market was enabling people
to live out their own choices, not only better than any planner could do,
but *well*—full stop.

PART III

THE FREEDOM OF JUDGMENT

Chapter 11

A THIRD CONCEPT OF LIBERTY

FROM SMITH AND KANT we can draw a view of judgment that redeems, I believe, the promise I made in the introduction to enrich our understanding of liberty. It may sound unexciting to announce that one wants to make the world free for good judgment but this quiet doctrine turns out to be the most sensible, most decent, and at the same time richest concept of liberty we can possibly find. What is unexciting about it, indeed, reveals its overwhelming coherence with the intuitions we already have. A world where everyone can develop and use their own judgment as much as possible is closer to what we really most want out of freedom than any of the standard versions of negative and positive liberty: consumer sovereignty or "solidarity" with a community, a right to "private" choices or choice by our general will, expressive individualism or Marxist species-being.

This final chapter explores Berlin's two concepts of liberty, places the freedom of judgment in relationship to them, and lays out some advantages of a liberty based on judgment over the other two concepts. I follow Berlin's famous essay in three main ways: (1) in preferring an historical to a merely logical analysis of the concept of freedom, seeing concepts as interwoven with the historical traditions in which they have been used, (2) in sympathizing rather more with the negative than the positive tradition of liberty, and (3) in abstracting from metaphysical questions to focus on political ones. Political freedom may in fact be linked to freedom of the will, but I do not think arguments establishing such a link have yet been successful. And whether government should help us attain, or could possibly interfere with, the freedom of our wills is a question that I do not know even how to begin answering.

1. One way of taking Berlin's distinction is to make it a debate over the importance of political participation. Berlin himself allows for a number of other ways to put the distinction, but describes the central issue dividing the two concepts as follows:

> Liberty in [the negative] sense is principally concerned with the area of control, not with its source. Just as a democracy may, in fact, deprive the individual citizen of a great many liberties which he might have in some other form of society, so it is perfectly conceivable that a liberal-minded despot would allow his subjects a large measure of personal freedom. . . . Self-government may, on

the whole, provide a better guarantee of the preservation of civil liberties than other régimes, and has been defended as such by libertarians. But there is no necessary connexion between individual liberty and democratic rule. The answer to the question "Who governs me?" is logically distinct from the question "How far does government interfere with me?" It is in this difference that the great contrast between the two concepts of negative and positive liberty, in the end, consists.[1]

Many have read Berlin as an updated version of Benjamin Constant, who put matters similarly. Constant distinguished between the liberty of the ancients and the liberty of the moderns, saying that "an Englishman, a Frenchman, and a citizen of the United States" understands liberty to be the right of everyone "to express their opinion, choose a profession and practise it, to dispose of property, . . . to come and go without permission, . . . to associate with other individuals, . . . to profess the religion which they . . . prefer, or even simply to occupy their days or hours in a way which is most compatible with their inclinations or whims." For the ancients, by contrast, liberty consisted in jointly carrying out the affairs of state: "in exercising collectively, but directly, several parts of the complete sovereignty; in deliberating, in the public square, over war and peace, . . . in voting laws, in pronouncing judgments; in examining the accounts, the acts, the stewardship of the magistrates."[2] Constant's comparison is subtle and complex—representative, if not participatory, democracy turns out to be part even of the liberty of the moderns—but he puts into sharp contrast a liberty that makes individuals "sovereign in public affairs" but "slave[s] in . . . private relations" with one that makes them "independent in . . . private life" but publicly a cipher. From this contrast, debates over the importance of political participation to freedom take their cue. In these debates, negative liberty represents a "private" freedom, the freedom economists tend to assume, in which I can do what I want with a minimum of interference by others but may or may not have a voice in the governing structures around me, while positive liberty represents the notion that participation in government is necessary to my freedom, so that I can be free only in a democracy. A liberal state, on the first notion of liberty, need not be democratic, and the undemocratic structure of private corporations does not in any way diminish the freedom of the workers they employ. According to the second notion of liberty, both the state and the workplace should be democratic.

Note that there need be little difference over policy between upholders of the negative and upholders of the positive view. As Constant's concession to representative democracy reveals, and as Berlin explicitly points out, upholders of negative liberty can agree that democracy is an excellent, even a necessary, way to protect noninterference with individual activities. Democracy serves as a check to tyranny and corruption; it provides an incentive encouraging those in power to protect the liberties of the people over whom they rule. Of course it does not *always* do this. When a populace is religiously biased, strict rule by the majority may oppress minorities. When a populace does not understand or is indifferent to the condition of poverty, rule by the majority may obstruct options giving the poor a way out of their condition. The first kind of case explains why we in America declare an absolute individual right to religious expression, and put the power to enforce that right in the undemocratic Supreme Court. The second kind of case explains how progressive voices in the nineteenth century could give the interest of workers themselves as a reason to *oppose* extending the franchise. Whether democracy will enhance or detract from liberty in any given case is an empirical question. But it is probably safe to assume that in most cases, where elections are open, speech is free, and some medium of speech conveys the issues fairly well to the voters, democracy will protect liberty. Indeed, these instrumental reasons for democracy are sufficient to underwrite a strong case for democracy in the workplace: insofar as a workplace monitors and imposes discipline on a large section of its workers' lives, it can constitute as significant a threat to liberty as the government, and the best safeguard against that threat, in many cases, will be democratic accountability. But if one who holds the negative view of liberty can be a social democrat as easily as a libertarian, then policy commitments will not mark the distinction between holders of the negative and holders of the positive view.

2. What is at stake between negative and positive views of liberty is whether democracy forms an *intrinsic* part of freedom. Supporters of positive liberty believe, as Quentin Skinner puts it, that "we need to establish one particular form of political association—thereafter devoting ourselves to serving and sustaining it—if we wish to realise our own natures and hence our fullest liberty."[3] Our freedom depends on our pursuing our "most distinctively human purposes," and since human beings are most distinctively "social and political in character" (pp. 21–22), the pursuit of such purposes requires that we have a role in the political structures that govern us.

What can be said in defense of such a claim? One might advert to the Aristotelian and Thomistic philosophies that describe human nature as distinctively social and political, but this is not really much of a defense. The science that justified this description for Aristotle is no longer plausible today, while Thomas's premises, insofar as they are not drawn from Aristotelian biology, depend on a scriptural faith. It is characteristic of the modern condition, as Berlin stresses, to recognize an "inherent variety of human aspirations and goals" (p. 35), or at least the reasonableness of vast disagreement over such goals. Skinner himself elegantly describes contemporary calls to return to Aristotle and Thomas as an attempt "to seek by some unexplained means to slip back into the womb of the polis" (p. 37). So why else might we believe that democracy is an essential part of our liberty? Suppose our individual activities, under an absolute monarchy, are as free as they can possibly be from interference by others. Would we become more free simply by living under, or participating in, democratic structures?

According to the argument most favored by contemporary defenders of positive liberty, democracy enhances our freedom (a) by giving us more control over our options than we would otherwise have and (b) by fostering in us excellences proper to life in community with others, without which our individual capacities for action will be thin simulacra of what fully free, fully human action requires. These two points are of very different merits. The first is seriously confused, I think, while the second is quite true—but provides only a weak case for the importance of democratic citizenship. Let us take them in order.

The first part of the argument tends to get defended by an empirical falsehood disguised by metaphysical hocus-pocus. The empirical falsehood is that individuals in modern societies can have any regular imprint on the course of political affairs. Constant put the response to this claim nicely:

> The share which in antiquity everyone held in national sovereignty was by no means an abstract presumption as it is in our own day. The will of each individual had real influence . . . Consequently the ancients were ready to make many a sacrifice to preserve . . . their share in the administration of the state. Everybody, feeling with pride all that his suffrage was worth, found in this awareness of his personal importance a great compensation.
>
> This compensation no longer exists for us today. Lost in the multitude, the individual can almost never perceive the influence he exercises. Never does his will impress itself upon the whole; nothing confirms in his eyes his own cooperation. (p. 316)

At least insofar as we belong merely to the electorate, rather than to those elected, none of us today really gets to see our desires, beliefs, judgments, etc., reflected in what goes on politically. Whatever candidate you vote for, you will rarely hear him say something in terms you use yourself. If you hold a view on an issue that differs in the smallest nuance from the standard positions on that issue, moreover, you can be sure it will never show up on a ballot or in the mouth of a candidate you get a chance to vote for. Send a letter to your senator or congressman and you will get back a letter addressed to "the multitude": a form letter, registering your response as but one of a crowd. This is certainly true for national, state, and city politics, but it is also true in the politics of unions, the public school system, and many churches and activist groups. Modern economic structures and technology have made the groups we live in so large and so closely interwoven with one another that most problems cannot be solved by communities intimate enough to give their individual members a real influence or voice.

Here the defender of political liberty may come back by reminding us that, as we vote or otherwise participate in politics, we are part of a larger whole, that it is not our individual votes to which we should be looking: "my" will is realized in politics, I am "self-governing," insofar as a majority I vote with passes a law. This is the move that takes us from empirical error to bad metaphysics. One needs a good deal of fudging about who the "self" is to make it plausible that a majority's decision expresses my "self-"government. Skinner, who claims that political participation is a part of *negative* liberty, and whose defense of political participation is therefore one of the most reasonable going, draws the following comparison:

> To allow the political decisions of a body-politic to be determined by the will of anyone other than the entire membership of the body itself is, as in the case of a natural body, to run the gratuitous risk that the behaviour of the body in question will be directed to the attainment not of its own ends, but merely the ends of those who have managed to gain control of it. It follows that, in order to avoid such servitude, and hence *to ensure our own individual liberty*, we must all cultivate the political virtues and devote ourselves whole-heartedly to a life of public service. (p. 31, my emphasis)

I think Skinner wants primarily to make an empirical statement here, to the effect that "our own individual liberty," construed negatively and distributively, is best protected by a democracy of active citizens, but, as we have seen, this is not necessarily true, and perhaps on that account he tries to strengthen his position by slipping between "our own individual" wills and "the will of . . . the entire membership of the body[-politic]." This is metaphysical hocus-pocus. As long as we begin from individual wills, there is no such thing as a "will of the entire membership," at least aside from the extremely rare cases in which everyone in a society agrees exactly on what the society should do. There is no "it" to have "its own ends" in a society; there are merely coalitions of larger and smaller numbers of individuals who happen to agree, here and there, on things that further their various individual ends. Even when a particular such coalition gets its policy enforced, moreover, the mere fact that that coalition has won out over other coalitions does not mean that the policy counts as the action of any individual within the winning coalition. Sometimes the world does what I would like it to do and sometimes it doesn't: this needn't have anything to do with my actions. Just because I want the country to have a large potato harvest, and it does, does not mean that I brought about that harvest—even if I did a nice job of cultivating the potato plants in my kitchen garden. Similarly, just because I want a candidate to win and she wins does not mean I brought about that victory—even if I voted for her.[4] If the argument is still concerned with *my* freedom, with the ways in which an individual will may be reflected in the world, it does not matter in the slightest what groups that will may happen to be aligned with. It is an uninteresting coincidence, as far as *my* freedom is concerned, whether the majority happens to agree with me today or disagree with me tomorrow. If, on the contrary, the argument has switched its locus of concern to the freedom of a *communal or collective* will, then we need a reason for considering such an entity to have any relevance to what we do as individuals, or for regarding its actions, rather than our individual actions, either to require or to express "freedom." Unless we leap to a faith in the weakest elements of Hegel's ontology, moreover, there is no reason to believe so much as in the existence of such an entity. A faith in a traditional God is rather more plausible—it is certainly no less plausible—and no modern political theory would rest its case on that.

Democracy as an expression of "our" control over our environment is thus, it seems to me, a hopeless proposition. There is no "our" to have such control. This leaves out, however, the second half of the argument for democracy as essential to freedom. And democracy as a mode of training in the skills necessary for (individual) self-government can be given a rather better defense. By participating in voluntary associations, Alexis de Tocqueville claimed, "Feelings and ideas are renewed, the heart enlarged, and the understanding developed."[5] By participating in town government, one develops yet more important qualities: one takes an interest in one's community, comes to understand the need for procedural justice, "develops a taste for order, . . . and in the end accumulates clear, practical ideas about the nature of his duties and the extent of his rights."[6] Aside from safeguarding negative liberty (Tocqueville's main point here), these qualities may help us come to the kind of moderate balance of passions, the concern for others together with self-command, needed for true "independence." Still, in the end what matters is independence itself, not the mode of reaching it, and it is far from clear that participation in government is the only way to develop that quality. Nor is it clear that participation in government always in fact breeds virtues of any kind. Arrogant, self-deluded, and otherwise morally incompetent people abound who participate well in communal government. Political activists, kibbutz leaders, school and church board members—anyone who has spent a significant amount of time with such people knows plenty who are shallow, ambitious, and vain, whose service to their cause or community is a means of self-promotion or, at best, a distraction from personal failings.

We forget, in addition, how often we have an impact on our society's decisions quite independently of formal political processes: in writing letters to the newspaper; in asking questions at public lectures; in attending or avoiding a politically oriented house of worship; in providing financial support for public radio and television, for museums, for churches and private charities; in buying certain newspapers and avoiding others; in meeting with our children's teachers and principals, making clear how we would like our children to be taught; in protesting ways that our offices are run, our garbage is picked up, our streets and houses are preserved, our teachers, and lawyers, and doctors behave—or, on the contrary, in complimenting a teacher, a doctor, a police officer, a postal clerk, for a small courtesy or job well done; even, finally, in the way we speak to friends and neighbors, influencing their opinions and actions. . . . In a liberal democracy, where much public work is done by private associations, or on a very local, loosely supervised level, a great deal of what we do has a political dimension.

It is indeed quite possible that, in modern societies, we develop and exercise our communally oriented virtues *better* by "private" than by "public" activities. Every time I buy a company's products, I in effect vote for that company's public policy views, internal structure, mode of advertising, and relationship to the environment, even as I also satisfy my private desires or needs. My economic vote is indeed rather more effective than my vote in large elections, since it is part of a smaller pool, and it may be just as publicly motivated; hence the campaigns to "buy American," to boycott Nestle's, to support small stores over supermarkets, and the like. Furthermore, every time I so much as walk along the street, my clothing expresses to others a class identification, a view of modesty, a notion of the importance or unimportance of fashion, perhaps even an explicit religious or political point of view. Every time I speak up on a moral issue, I influence the views and practices of those around me (sometimes by driving them *away* from my own position), and every time I speak up even on a matter of fact, I express a view about where facts are appropriately to be sought: I endorse mainstream or eccentric newspapers, government officials or Marxist activists, New Age astrologers or respected scientists.

And recognizing this public, even political dimension to all human behavior diminishes the importance of political behavior strictly so-called. If I "vote" every time I enter a mosque or buy a box of cereal, then the vote I cast in the ballot box is not necessarily of greater value to the public world. Odd as this may sound, I think it is true. Elections are blunt instruments. Ultimately the choice is almost always between two or three candidates, each of whom represents a basket of views from which, in part, I almost always dissent. To get to the final stage of an election, moreover, each candidate must go through a process that at best (even, that is, in the absence of strong moneyed interests) selects for an ability to compromise among different views. Any positions that I think should not be compromised, and any eccentric views I hold, will not be well represented in this process. I can more clearly and effectively express my uncompromising pacifism, say, by conscientious objection and a refusal to buy from companies with military contracts, than I normally can in the electoral arena. I can express my eccentric opposition to all television more clearly and more effectively by not buying a television set, and telling my friends about the advantages this has, than by voting for a candidate who opposes one or another kind of TV programming. The pattern of my purchases, conversation, sexual choices, and behavior towards family and neighbors issues both in a sharper, subtler message and in a more regular effect on my social environment than will the occasional votes I drop into the electoral bucket. This is an extension of Constant's point about the modern world. The size of the societies we live in ensures both that no individual has much influence over political decisions, relative to the citizens of ancient republics, and that political decisions have less influence over every individual's activities. Our large-scale anonymous societies ensure that political organizations find it much more difficult to control our everyday activities than the ancient polis did. As individuals, therefore, we have rather greater influence over each other's lives.[7]

Furthermore, explicitly political actions in a mass democracy are not all that expressive of the individual will even for those who do have political influence. Suppose I actually occupy political office. Then I presumably have much more influence over public policy than I would have as a private citizen, but then the positions I maintain will also be more distant from what I actually believe than they would be if I did not occupy public office. If I am elected to office, I need to say things that will please, or at least not horrify, my constituents, which means suppressing my more eccentric positions; if I am appointed to office, I need to do the same thing with regard to the attitudes of those who appointed me. When I take part in public deliberations, I soften what I say, eliminate detailed considerations that I fear might be confusing, turn specific charges into vague, general noises of complaint, and stress considerations I think others are likely to agree with even when I personally consider those considerations fairly trivial. Of course, all this can be a means for me to learn tolerance, openness, compromise, etc., and that can be a form of moral growth. But on some issues, compromise is repulsive, and quite often getting ahead of what people think has advantages even for satisfying those people's wishes. (Hence leaders of undemocratic organizations—foundations, churches, colleges, and the like—can sometimes exhibit more wisdom and foresight in their policies than can leaders responsible to regular democratic checks.)

Recognizing this potential tension between integrity and popularity means that it is never unreasonable to shun public office. Participation in public office, in legislative debates and the execution of public policy, can be an intensely *alienating* experience, rather than, as Rousseau, Marx, Arendt, and others seem to have supposed, the highest fulfillment of our destiny as self-legislating creatures. We legislate most successfully for ourselves, we govern our own lives most fully, by controlling how we individually run our most important individual decisions, not by participating in group attempts to coordinate human actions—although, on some occasions, our individual self-legislation should and will take us to an endorsement of democratic politics. So while participating in one's polis *may* contribute to a person's development of self-rule, it is by no means identical with such self-rule.

3. By moving from "self-rule" as political participation to "self-rule" as the individual's rule over herself, we point the way to what I call the third concept of liberty. For rule over oneself is quintessentially the exercise of judgment or phronesis, the making of choices guided by judgment. But to see the exercise of this quality as constituting a concept of liberty at all, we need to recast Berlin's distinction so that it does not turn on political participation.

Berlin's own presentation very much allows for that. A philosophically deep way of taking his distinction, and one that enables us to situate Kantian judgment in the middle of it, is to see it as a division between two understandings of human nature. Suppose one begins the case for positive liberty from within the notion of negative liberty. Freedom *from* restrictions, one says, is impossible without some freedom *to* combat the internal as well as external obstacles to my action. The notion of an "internal" obstacle—an obstacle *to* me that is also *within* me—then requires some notion of the self as divided, as split between, standardly, a set of merely given desires and some controlling agency over those desires. The arguments for this view make more philosophical sense than the arguments that self-government requires political participation, although they can lead to rather more dangerous political conclusions. And the liberty of judgment I derive from Kant and Smith can be clearly seen as an alternative to the two traditional concepts of liberty if we put the issue in these terms.

Berlin defines negative liberty as a freedom from obstructions or interferences.[8] This leaves open the question: obstructions to what? The absence of interference with what *aspect* of myself constitutes freedom? To which most accounts of negative liberty, including Berlin's own, reply: "obstructions to my *desires*." I am free when I can act to satisfy my desires, unfree when such action is thwarted. "The negative conception of liberty in its classical form," says Berlin, is the notion that "all coercion is, in so far as it *frustrates human desires*, bad as such, although it may have to be applied to prevent other, greater evils."[9] Pleasure, the satisfaction of desire, is the central term in this conception, for which reason Hobbes and Bentham are its standard founders. Constant writes that the "aim of the moderns is the enjoyment of security in private *pleasures*, and they call liberty the guarantees afforded by institutions to those pleasures" (p. 317, my emphasis). This does indeed seem to be the dominant modern view. Among economists, the notion that liberty protects private pleasures is taken as almost tautologous. And the prominent political philosopher Joel Feinberg begins an introductory text to his subject with the claim:

> Because of the intimate tie between constraints and desires, it is natural to think of the abridgment of freedom as necessarily productive of frustration. When we are constrained in the most obvious cases, our wants are denied their satisfaction.[10]

Sometimes this linkage of liberty to desire is qualified to acknowledge that some of us, and all of us on some occasions, feel coerced by our desires. Negative liberty for a psychotic or drug addict may depend precisely on obstructing some desires, if only so that others can be more readily satisfied. When this account is extended to cover people other than the mad and the addicted, the relevant desires to be constrained are picked out by appeals to qualitative differences among desires (J. S. Mill) or to higher-order desires and their relationship to our lower-order desires (Harry Frankfurt). Even when so qualified, negative liberty remains essentially defined by means of the satisfaction of desires. Mill's higher pleasures still fulfill desires, while Frankfurt's case for heeding our second-order desires depends on a demand, within our first-order desires, for a fuller or more coherent satisfaction than the first-order desires themselves can achieve.

That negative liberty is a liberty to satisfy desire becomes yet clearer when it gets contrasted with positive liberty. Berlin describes positive liberty as a "freedom to" act, as opposed to a "freedom from" interference, but the point of this characterization comes out only when we recognize that the aspect of ourselves we are free to act *on* is our "true" or "deep" self, our will as opposed to our desires, etc. Kant draws a contrast between a self of desire and a self of reason,[11] and it is to that contrast that

Berlin again and again returns.[12] Positive liberty divides me into a "transcendent, dominant control[ing]" self and an "empirical bundle of desires and passions to be disciplined and brought to heel" (p. 134), into "reason" or a "latent rational will" and "irrational impulse" or an "empirical self in space and time" (pp. 132–3). Insofar as I follow the former rather than the latter, I am "autonomous," I "obey laws . . . [that] I have imposed . . . on, or found . . . in, my own uncoerced self," I am "lifted above the empirical world of causality" (p. 136). Berlin seems to find this Kantian language the strongest way of providing a case for the positive liberty that he mostly dislikes. He does bring in other languages for it, but tends to view them as grafted, to more or less unjustifiable degrees, onto the core of truth in the Kantian conception. Thus "Platonists or Hegelians" (p. 132), with their unKantian fondness for nonnatural entities and "higher natures," wander through the essay, and Berlin notes that the autonomous self can blur into "a social 'whole' of which the individual is an element or aspect: a tribe, a race, a church, a state," with a "collective, or 'organic,' single will" of its own. That is to say, the Kantian division of the self can be and has been made use of to justify nationalism, racism, and other collectivist doctrines.[13] At the hands of Romantic nationalists, positive liberty is often based on some sort of nonrational will rather than Kant's "will as practical reason," but this mystical monad is just as unempirical as Kant's, and it is the will's evasion of empirical criteria, rather than its rationality or irrationality, that best explains the tendency it has had to get translated into oppressive collectivism.

So Kant's philosophy, both because of its historical influence and because of its characteristic problems, serves as an excellent location for the split between the two concepts. But the history of Kantian politics is more complicated than Berlin's presentation of it suggests. The influence of Adam Smith on Kant, particularly in the third *Critique,* and the influence of that *Critique* on Humboldt and Schiller, and, through Humboldt, on J. S. Mill and Alfred Marshall, do not fit neatly into the traditions Berlin identifies with either the first or the second concept of liberty. To bring these figures together, we need to attend to their shared concern for judgment, the subject of Kant's third *Critique.* We then can distinguish the strand I am calling the third concept of liberty from the other two. By using the Kantian language of "desire" and "reason"/ "will" for the foci of the other two concepts, therefore, we may make clear the advantages of a freedom based on judgment over both positive and negative liberty.

In the first place, by emphasizing judgment we are able precisely to *finesse* the question of what constitutes "essential human nature." As we noted in chapter 4, judgment is a "mediating" faculty, by which I may identify myself either with my desires or with my will. A political view that treats people as if judgment were central to their nature, therefore, actually enables them as much as possible to decide what is central to their nature for themselves. In a world where the human essence is very much up for grabs—since the human telos is very much up for grabs—giving the question over to individuals is a tremendous advantage for any political view.

In the second place, while everyone equally has desires and everyone either equally has or equally lacks freedom of the will, it is widely accepted that some people have more judgment than others. Liberals generally try to argue that psychotics and children lack reason, and this may be true but is not so easy to prove, but psychotics and children certainly have deficiencies in judgment. More importantly, some sane adults have excellent judgment while others have barely any. This indicates both (a) that what it is to have judgment is an empirically discoverable fact, and (b) that judgment is a faculty that can be cultivated, that it is not merely there or not there. Recognizing whether another person has judgment, or is able to act on his judgments, may require a fairly complex set of empirical criteria but does not, like recognizing someone's will, evade such criteria altogether. At the same time, unlike both my will and my desires, my judgment is corrigible, open to development. My desires are either satisfied or they are not satisfied; my will expresses itself or it does not. But judgment uncontroversially comes in degrees, so basing political liberty on it allows us to talk, as we are normally inclined to do, about degrees of liberty, about being *more or less* free to do something rather than simply free or unfree.

This is to say that the freedom of judgment allows more room for growth than do freedom of desire or will. One of the things we mean when we say we are "free" is that we are free to change our desires in a reasonable way, and not merely to act on whatever desires we already happen to have. But if freedom *consists in* acting on my desires, it becomes quite unclear how I could ever enhance my freedom by changing my desires, why I should regard even preferences induced by indoctrination or manipulation as unfree. There are ways of getting around this by introducing second-order desires and the like, but they tend to be less than satisfying. It is simpler just to start with judgment instead of desires. Our judgments must always be responsive to our desires, but they are not identical with them. If judgment is a negotiation between desires and reflection, I could never appropriately judge something to be good for me that thwarts all my desires, but at the same time the reflection that interplays with desire allows me standards by which to shape my desires, to determine which of them are worth encouraging and which I should try to eliminate. Thus the freedom of judgment represents a more refined "me" than the freedom of desire, but, unlike the freedom of will, still a very recognizable version *of* me—not something indistinguishable from other rational creatures, or blended into a larger social whole. I can regard a me capable of exercising good judgment as truly a better, more actualized version of myself as I currently am—clearer about what I want, more in harmony with myself, more what I would like to be— without distorting what either "better" or "myself" means. Me with better judgment is beyond me with worse judgment, but not so radically beyond the latter as to defy any claim of continuity.

Third, a point that at first will seem in tension with the last one: we tend to presume that everyone is capable of a high degree of judgment. People do develop the faculty unevenly, but it seems that anyone who has a variety of experience, and attends to that experience with due seriousness, *can* develop judgment. Judgment is not an elitist mental faculty. People of all classes and levels of education display it, and people lack it across all classes and levels of education. Unlike mathematical reasoning, artistic genius, or the skills needed for historical or scientific research, judgment is a widely distributed mental skill, and it is not unreasonable to suppose that, with the right experience and training, everyone could have good judgment. Those who want to combine egalitarianism with a respect for skill and effort would therefore do well to structure society to reward good judgment above theoretical or technical skills.[14] We will return to this point below (§ 6).

Fourth, the freedom of judgment is rather more open to the influence of cultures or traditions than is either the freedom of desire or the freedom of reason. In one sense, this is obvious. Judgment and interpretation are crucially important skills in many non-Western societies, and an emphasis on developing and using them is central to the educational systems of practically all traditions that have a central text or set of stories. It is plausible, therefore, that urging a freedom to judge will not require nearly the overhaul of other cultures that the freedoms to fulfill desires, and to rely on reason rather than tradition, have tended to bring about.

More deeply, reason is supposed to transcend traditions, to be beyond anything as empirical as the beliefs of a given society at a given time, while desires tend to be understood as either bound by or opposed to traditions. Either I have been socialized into having the desires my group expects of me, or I have defied those expectations and come to "my own" desires as opposed to the ones any social group tried to foist on me. What counts as "my own" judgment, by contrast, is considerably harder to separate from the normal judgments and standards of judgment upheld by the society with which I converse. Socialization is a condition *for* competent judgment. Unlike both freedom of desire and freedom of the will, the freedom of judgment cannot be regarded as a part of our empirical or transcendental "natural condition," to be interfered with or preserved by society. Rather, it comes into existence only *with* society, and the opportunity for developing it can be greater or lesser, and distributed more or less widely, depending on what positive conditions for its development each society sets up. At the same time, unlike positive liberty, the freedom of judgment requires no empirical or metaphysical "solidarity" between me and any social group. It is just that the modes of classification, and canons of empirical and moral argument, upheld by the social group or groups around me form the indispensable starting point for my own interpretive reflections. In the judgments to which I then come, I am free to reject any of those modes of classification and argument, although I cannot reject them all, or indeed reject any substantial part of them at a single moment. Similarly, I can reject any one social group or set of groups in favor of another (convert, emigrate, change my friends), but I will not be able to judge at all if I lack relationships to any group. So to lead everyone to freedom of judgment, society does not need to force them to conform their behavior to its laws or customs, or induce them to have just the desires it holds they ought to have. When it informs or guides them, moreover, it helps constitute, rather than detract from, their individual freedom. As long as society's proper role is seen as merely to *guide* individuals, not to absorb them or to express their "true essence," we may be able to justify liberal communitarianism or nationalism,[15] but never the totalitarianism that Berlin rightly associates with most versions of positive liberty.

4. Two advantages of basing liberty on judgment for the relationship between theory and ordinary political discourse:

(a). I noted in the beginning of this chapter that I follow Berlin in separating questions about liberty from questions about freedom of the will. One reason for doing so is that liberty is something both governors and governed need to be able to recognize easily, while this is not true for metaphysical freedom. Concepts of liberty, of the kind of freedom relevant to politics, need to remain literally "superficial": close to the surface of the way we all already use the term. Especially in a democracy, liberty can be protected only if it is widely understood and its importance widely accepted. Hence one wants a theory of it not to depend on complicated metaphysical views, about God or *Geist* or the will, or controversial empirical ones that only social scientists can appreciate. By this criterion, some famous accounts of freedom are suspect. It is too hard to understand how Marx's species-being is a conception of freedom, too easy to misinterpret Rousseau's being "forced to be free." The freedom of judgment, by contrast, is an easy notion. We are all very familiar with what it means to say that one person "has judgment" or that another lacks it; this is something we do every day. And whether someone gets to act on his judgment or not is equally easy to grasp, certainly as much so as whether he gets to act on his desires. What it *takes* to have good judgment is a more complicated matter. But since we know what the results look like, we can at least have a good idea, in ordinary practice, of whether a given society nurtures judgment in its individuals or not.

(b). Emphasizing judgment helps theorists avoid arrogance in the tone with which they make political demands. Whether we have a certain desire or not, and whether a given object satisfies our desires or not, are normally incorrigible claims, made by individuals about themselves with no expectation of contradiction by others. What someone rationally wills is also supposed to be, at least in principle, susceptible of absolute determination: there is supposed to be one most rational answer to every question and one most rational decision in every situation. By contrast, as we have seen, it is of the nature of judgment to be indeterminate, to allow always of further debate. When we judge, we fit one claim in with a number of neighboring claims—"Winning this contract gives me my best shot at promotion" where I already hold a number of factual judgments about what makes for promotion, and normative judgments about what constrains my notion of a "best shot"—and the notion of "fit" allows more corrigibility than desire has, while the fact that we seek a mesh with other views we already hold allows us to be agnostic about whether there is some judgment in this situation that *any* human being would have to make, regardless of what else she already believes. Because he wanted a "view from nowhere," Descartes subordinated judgment to understanding, and the project of foundationalism ever since has been to try to discover an indisputable ground beneath all the disputable judgments we make every day.[16] In moral and political philosophy, the shape that foundationalism tends to take is an insistence on expressed preferences, or a theory of the right or the good, as the indisputable starting point for the assessment of policies or institutions. That insistence translates in practice into the unshakable complacency of a Milton Friedman as well as the totalitarian inclinations of a Herbert Marcuse or Catherine MacKinnon. People with a firm foundation for their views tend to believe that their vision must be correct, any policy not coherent with it straightforwardly wrong, and anyone advocating such a policy stupid, deluded, or ill-willed. Emphasizing judgment forces each of us, including the theorists who advocate the freedom of judgment, to *work out* our visions for the political and moral good bit by bit, in conversation with others, and without hope that we can ever conclude the process. Hence the appealingly open, tentative tone of Smith's and Kant's political writings. They are trying out ideas for policies and institutions, rather than recording what they consider the only right way to proceed, and one imagines, on reading them, that in person they would respond readily to discussion and correction.[17] They display a rather more flexible, undogmatic approach to public policy than one usually finds among either the theorists of positive liberty or the Hobbes-Bentham tradition of negative liberty. Emphasizing judgment is "freeing," in the most ordinary sense, for the multitude of citizens who dissent in some way from the negative libertarian insistence on the sovereignty of expressed preferences as well as the positive libertarian visions of true autonomy.

5. Some advantages of the freedom of judgment over other contemporary theories of freedom:

(a) Charles Taylor talks of "self-realization" and "authenticity" when cashing out what he wants from the positive liberty tradition, but he has no more success in defending or defanging these notions than have his many predecessors.[18] To begin with, "self-realization" suggests that a self other than the one I actually have already exists, at least *in potentia*, and simply needs to be brought out. Where is this "real" or "authentic" self supposed to be found? Taylor does not explain this much, except by indicating that it is the self that pursues our "basic purposes" (p. 216). But this brings up the second major problem with his argument. Taylor draws a distinction between those of our desires that are "import-attributing" and those that are merely "brute," notes that we regard the import-attributing ones as capable of being mistaken, and suggests that we regard ourselves as unfree, bound by our desires, precisely to the extent that our import-attributing desires are mistaken. All this seems right, especially as a phenomenological description of what we mean by "being bound by our desires," but it does not follow that we can expect to discover any broadly acceptable theory of just *what* import-attributing desires truly deserve to be endorsed. And Taylor needs such a theory. "[F]reedom is . . . the absence of external obstacle to significant action," he says, "to what is important to man" (p. 218). He does not explain what he means by "significant" and "important," although he uses such notions throughout the article: "[T]he meaningful sense of free, that for which we value it, [is] the sense of being able to act on one's important purposes" (p. 227; see also 228). What our important purposes might be, however, he never tells us, any more than he makes clear what self is supposed to be realized.

Taylor could avoid this whole nest of issues by turning to judgment instead of import-attributing desires. To identify freedom with judgment, we need not gesture towards a self independent of the me who is actually around right now. I may improve my current self by developing better judgment—and thereby see how to change some current desires I dislike—but my judgment is not separate from my current self, does not dictate to it from outside.[19] My judgment is a process that tracks my desires, experiences, and actions, not an entity or potential entity serving as their ultimate source or aim.

Finally, even if we grant Taylor everything he wants to say about authentic versus false selves, important versus trivial desires, he omits a step when he moves from my capacity for being *wrong* about my desires to anyone else's capacity for *correcting* me about them:

> [We may think we can] avoid any . . . second-guessing of the subject. . . . [W]e would [thereby] retain the basic concern of the negative theory, that the subject is . . . the final authority as to what his freedom consists in, and cannot be second-guessed by external authority. . . . I think that this hybrid or middle position is untenable, where we are willing to admit that we can speak of what we truly want . . . , and of some desires as obstacles to our freedom, while we still will not allow for second-guessing. For to rule this out in principle is to rule out in principle that the subject can ever be wrong about what he truly wants. And how can he never, in principle, be wrong, unless there is nothing to be right or wrong about in this matter? (pp. 222–3)

Four pages detailing how we can "admit the possibility of error" (p. 226) about our desires follow this passage. But to say that there is something to be right or wrong about in a matter is not yet to show that someone else can *tell* us what is right or wrong. Ruling out second-guessing, even in principle, need not presuppose ruling out that the subject can ever be wrong about what he truly wants.[20] One may presuppose instead that no one *else* is more likely to be right, or that even if someone else were correctly to second-guess the subject, it is bound up with attaining what we truly want that we come to such realizations, and choose to act or not act on them, by ourselves. The first line of argument is unappealing if taken to presume a pre-Wittgensteinian, "private access" view of the mind, but makes considerable sense if grounded in the Smithian point that in general no one knows the details of a subject's empirical situation better than the subject does herself. In Kant's *Critique of Judgment* we have a striking indication of how to understand the second line of argument, of why it may be appropriate for us each to determine what we truly want by ourselves, regardless of whether others could in principle second-guess our judgments. For Kant, the purposiveness that reflective judgment models helps us shape our actual purposes, but that model depends on our each feeling for ourselves the pleasurable harmony among the faculties to which such reflection can lead. Both lines of argument support the conclusion that governments should leave individuals alone as much as possible, which captures the core political intuition shared by Smith and Kant. I think that intuition is correct, but is best expressed by avoiding all talk of desires until we have defined liberty first on quite a different basis. The liberty to act on our own judgments is in fact likely to help us fulfill our most fundamental or important desires, and that may be a happy coincidence or an empirically establishable effect of judgment that confirms the aptness of defining freedom in its terms. But desires cannot substitute for judgments in the definition without implausible and dangerous implications.

(b) Harry Frankfurt might be said to offer a kind of negative liberty, insofar as his work bears on political questions. If so, I think certain problems with his work show us why we might want to supplement negative liberty with borrowings from the "positive" tradition.[21] Frankfurt argues, plausibly, that the mere absence of a possibility that I could have done otherwise does not of itself establish that I did not act freely. The example he gives is one in which I opt for A believing that I might just as well have chosen B instead, but in fact, unbeknownst to me, B was not available. A mad scientist, perhaps, was monitoring my movements, and would have stopped me had I opted for B. Since I opted in any case for A, he did nothing to block me. Given a story like this, or any analogous scenario in which the unavailability of alternatives does not actually affect my decision-making process, we can agree that I chose A freely, should be held legally and morally responsible for it, should be judged virtuous or unvirtuous on the basis of my choice, etc.

But this type of scenario does not generalize. Had I known what was going on in this case, we can expect my decision to have been very different, if only to spite the mad scientist at work. And if something like this is understood to have gone on throughout my lifetime, throughout the time over which I have developed whatever decision-making capacity I have, we can rightly complain that that capacity itself was not freely developed. Frankfurt's story only works, that is, if we presume that the agent in question already *has* a real capacity for making his own decisions, on the basis of which we can evaluate this choice as one he "would have made anyway." We lose grip on that notion, if the agent-candidate (we cannot say "agent" outright without begging the question) has never made a decision without a scientist doing his manipulative bit in the background. Of course in principle it remains still imaginable that the agent might have had desires, reflected on them, and acted, in *all* cases, without happening to go against what the scientist happened to want, so that the unavailability of options has always been a merely potential fact rather than an actual one. Then we might still say the agent is fully free and accept Frankfurt's notion that freedom consists in endorsing the motivations and actions open to one regardless of whether different possibilities were also open, but if the story is to be taken seriously, this would have to count as a remarkably unlikely coincidence. That is, if people remotely like real human beings were in the positions of scientist and victim, we would expect them to *differ* frequently in the outcome they would select. If that appeared never to happen, we would almost certainly read the evidence as a case in which either the victim in fact lacked any distinct power of agency at all or the scientist in fact lacked the powers attributed to him. So the effectiveness of this story in gauging our intuitions about freedom trades on its resemblance to cases, real and fictional, in which a person is bullied, hypnotized, brainwashed, etc., into doing what he would *not* otherwise have wanted to do. Given the notion of a free development of agency, we can make sense of extraordinary cases in which an agent might freely choose what he could not but have chosen, as in Frankfurt's story. But without a background notion of agency-development, I think the story says very little to us. And if we are given such a notion, but the person in the story is thwarted repeatedly from considering or adopting alternatives during the period when her agency should have developed, then it seems reasonable simply to deny that she has ever been capable of freedom.

More generally, any notion of human freedom must explain how we develop that freedom, not simply how we exercise it at one moment or another. A freedom that does not need development could be a freedom for God, or some other eternal agent, but not for human beings. This much Frankfurt would surely accept, but then perhaps he does not appreciate the role of alternate possibilities in learning to be free. For it is natural to say that I develop a sense of what I truly want by trying out here one possibility, there another, in similar situations, and that if I cannot, or even *do* not do this, I will lack the self-knowledge by which I could so much as recognize any option as one that meshes with my preferences.

This point cuts especially against a certain kind of economist's version of the Frankfurt argument. Libertarian economists often write as if a worker is "free" to take a job even if no other job is available—so long as the job is one he or she *would* have chosen if there were other jobs out there. Similarly, a consumer might be free to choose a given product even though there are no alternatives to it, as long as we can say that this is the product she would have chosen if there *were* alternatives. In economics, this is an extremely useful claim, because one can work out what workers or consumers "would" choose by assuming that they are all "rational choosers" in the economist's special sense of that phrase (materially self-interested, well-informed, instrumental reasoners) and arguing that the job or product in question is, respectively, the best paid or lowest priced to be expected in its particular category. But the argument I have offered should begin to show what is wrong with this approach, and with the whole notion of rational choice on which it is based. If the worker and the consumer learn what kind of job or product they want and what they are willing to pay for it, only by actually going through a history of choices in which alternative jobs and products are available, then only in exceptional cases can we call them "free" when they plunk for one option despite the fact that no others are available. You can intelligibly attribute "free choice" to me when I choose a job with IBM on January 2 1995, although that is the sole job available to me, only if I have a background of choosing jobs among many available options against which you can determine what my preferences actually are. I can intelligibly attribute free choice to *myself* only against a similar background. Thus a world in which each person always has only one job available to him or her is not a world in which workers freely choose their employment.[22]

One advantage of defining freedom by means of judgment, in this light, is that such a definition does not allow us to ignore the connection between freedom and alternate possibilities. To put my objection to Frankfurt simply, freedom as endorsement of one's given options takes for granted a fully formed capacity for choice antecedent to all actual choices, while most of us would insist that we can only say what actual choices we would freely make after we have actually made many choices.[23] To suppose, as rational choice theorists tend to do, that we can say in advance what every worker or consumer would choose is precisely to deny the reality of freedom, and I see no reason to say anything different about Frankfurt's metaphysical version of this view. Of course, one may want to deny the reality of freedom, but if one does not, then surely one must affirm that we can never quite be sure what any individual would choose in advance of whatever it is that he actually does choose. Now judgments are indeterminable prior to the actual particulars with which the world confronts us. As Kant says, "We cannot determine a priori whether an object will or will not accord with [judgment]; we have to try it out" (CJ 191, my translation). I do not know in general how I will judge; I have to find out.[24] It makes sense to presume that there is a most rational response to each situation that anyone could figure out, but much less so that there is a best judgment of it independently of each person's actually coming into the situation and judging. So the notion that freedom includes, at least to some degree, my right to stipulate what I will *count* as realizing my freedom, is built into the concept of freedom as judgment.

(c) Building the importance of actually living through a variety of options into freedom brings us close to the position advocated by Joseph Raz in his influential book *The Morality of Freedom*.[25] Raz assimilates his view to the tradition of "positive liberty" (pp. 408–12, 425), however, while I see mine as belonging neither to this tradition nor to its usual counterpart. I think this is more than a terminological disagreement between us.

Raz's position is generally very appealing. He recognizes that freedom consists, not only in the absence of coercion but also in having an adequate variety of options and favorable natural and social circumstances for choice (pp. 154–6); he recognizes that these circumstances and the absence of coercion are *jointly* necessary for freedom (p. 425); he is a gradualist who respects the rootedness of individuals in ongoing "concrete social forms" (pp. 307–13, 426–7); and he sums up his notion of freedom as autonomy in terms I want almost entirely to endorse:

> The conditions of autonomy are complex and consist of three distinct components: appropriate mental abilities, an adequate range of options, and independence. . . . If a person is to be maker or author of his own life then he must have the mental abilities to form intentions of a sufficiently complex kind, and plan their execution. These include minimum rationality, the ability to comprehend the means required to realize his goals, the mental faculties necessary to plan actions, etc. For a person to enjoy an autonomous life he must actually use these faculties to choose what life to have. There must in other words be adequate options available for him to choose from. Finally, his choice must be free from coercion and manipulation by others, he must be independent. All three conditions . . . admit of degree. (pp. 372–3)

I only "almost" endorse these lines because they retain a trace of the instrumentalist model of rationality that Raz wants to get away from. It looks here a bit too much as if we choose freely by *first* "planning" (forming intentions, comprehending means, etc.), *then* plugging the plans into outside options ("actually us[ing] these faculties"). Judgment builds more of an ongoing interplay between actions taken and intentions formed into the process of making choices, but this, I suspect, marks but a trivial difference between it and Raz's "autonomy." Raz can build the interplay into his own account without changing any important conclusions.

Another objection to Raz's account is, however, significant. Raz moves too close, I think, to allowing one vision of the good life to be imposed on all. Repeatedly, he ties the value of autonomy to particular kinds of goals, particular visions of the good life. "Autonomy is valuable only in pursuit of the good," he says (p. 381); the value of autonomy disappears when it is used for "immoral" or "worthless" ends (pp. 133, 379, 417). The state has a legitimate interest in discouraging "worthless", "bad" or "repugnant" conceptions of the good life (pp. 411, 417–23), and by Raz's own, appropriately broad understanding of "morality" (pp. 213–6), this does not mean only conceptions that lead one person to harm another. Such philosophically controversial goods as those of art or of pride in one's nation belong under the absolute ends autonomy must respect (pp. 215–6), and Raz makes clear that an illiberal culture, even one that does not harm others and enables its members "to have an adequate and satisfying life," may yet inadequately foster autonomy—in which case it deserves to be considered "inferior" to liberal cultures, and to be urged to disappear (pp. 423–4).

Raz develops a conception of well-being that is supposed to give content to this notion of "worthless" ends while allowing for a wide plurality of autonomous courses of life (pp. 288–320). This qualification is not terribly reassuring, however. The directedness of Raz's conception of liberty towards a thick notion of what makes life "worthwhile," "rewarding," etc., entails imposing on people precisely the kind of comprehensive view about human ends that Kant and Smith, like Rawls, rightly ban from a polity's role. Yes, freedom requires conditions, but no, those conditions do not include any thick view of what the freedom ought to be used for. The third concept's resistance to *that* tendency in the "positive liberty" tradition has important political implications. One is that the third concept view emphatically does not encourage any cultures to disappear, as long as they do not harm others and they allow their members "adequate and satisfying" lives. Another is that, for all the conditions it requires, the third concept still draws a sharp line between a permissible and an impermissible extent to which the state can shape our choices. While Raz is right to argue that coercion is unproblematically permissible for a liberal in many cases (pp. 410–19), he comes dangerously close at times to endorsing a picture in which there is only a vague continuum between what may and may not be coerced. The notion of conditions for judgment provides at least some line, rather than just a continuum, between the two: freedom will have conditions, but will not have them all the way along. As soon as judgment is recognizably in place—the person has her basic biological needs met, has the experience and mental training to reflect on ends as well as means, and is not being coerced by anyone else—what one does with one's judgment is none of any government's business.[26] The notion that we could decide in advance what count as "worthless" or "immoral" judgments and, correlatively, as properly "valuable" ends for autonomous choice, is no part of the third concept of liberty. In consequence it makes room for a wider range of cultures and modes of life than Raz does. At some point, a concept of liberty must break free *of* conditions for freedom if it is to track what "liberty" ordinarily means; there must be a significant role for the individual to determine what the ends of freedom ought to be.[27]

(d) There are interesting similarities as well as differences between what I am proposing and Michael Sandel's call for "self-government" in *Democracy's Discontent*.[28]

Here is a dilemma that liberal political views often face: On the one hand, if people vote for their leaders purely on the basis of their private interests, and their leaders use the positions so won purely to serve their constituents' private interests, then the public realm does nothing to discourage selfishness, and the needs of those whose interests are poorly represented will not be addressed, even if they, above all, require public attention. For these reasons, a regard solely for one's own interests corrupts democratic politics, hurts the needy, and threatens the virtue, and perhaps even the liberty, of us all. On the other hand, if people vote, and leaders act, with regard to a "public interest" alone, then a doctrine of public interests as opposed to private interests grows up by which it becomes all too tempting to regard individuals as "limbs" of a large social "organism," that can be amputated from it if necessary.

It is to address this dilemma that Sandel has urged a return to "republican liberty." He describes how American political discourse comes out of two traditions about the nature of liberty—a "liberal" and a "republican" one, which closely correspond to negative and positive liberty[29]—but has in the twentieth century moved increasingly towards the former at the expense of the latter. The liberal tradition, he says, in its concern for rights and procedure, has both presumed and promoted a self "unencumbered" of communal ties or higher moral commitments, thereby contributing to the increasing emergence of self-centered, atomistic, amoral individuals. The republican tradition, by contrast, understood that "political discourse [must] engage rather than avoid the moral and religious convictions people bring to the public realm," and that it is essential to building a healthy community that a society "cultivate in citizens the expansive self-understandings that civic engagement requires" (p. 7). Our negative liberties themselves may be seriously threatened if we cannot, to some extent at least, remove ourselves from our private interests when we select our governing officials. We therefore need an education for citizenship. Nor does education simply mean what our schools do. Sandel devotes particular attention—and particularly valuable attention—to the way that debates over political economy in the United States, from Thomas Jefferson's advocacy of agrarianism to the concerns of the Progressivists in the early twentieth century, have until recently focused as much on whether the conditions of labor promote civic virtue as on whether the rights of laborers are being protected or not. The well-being of our nation requires that our schools, our workplaces, and all other important institutions in our lives promote a sense of communal belonging[30] and the virtues necessary to carry out the duties of citizenship. Against Rawls, Sandel claims that the state must endorse a comprehensive picture of how to live, at least to the extent that it holds up "self-government" as an intrinsic part of that picture. He looks to a pluralist community, a society open to diverse ways of pursuing the good life (pp. 7, 320–1), but wants pluralism to be constrained by a set of political virtues, virtues that make all the communities in our society share at least a commitment to a common whole.

I like the details of Sandel's proposals, and share his complaints about what he calls the "liberal" tradition. That the negative liberty tradition is based on too thin, too narrow, too atomistic a conception of the self, that our pursuit of our different ends should be constrained by a set of virtues, that the state has some legitimate role in encouraging those virtues, and that our workplaces, as well as our schools, should be structured with these virtues in mind—on all of these points Sandel is surely right. But the goal of the virtues we need for freedom is not "self-government," as Sandel construes that term—active participation in our political structures—nor do we need self-government in that sense to preserve the health of our democracy. That political participation is unnecessary for true freedom, that "self-government" is not even an appropriate name for such participation, I discussed above. Nor does Sandel's version of this notion escape the confusions that beset other positive libertarians. Trying to fend off the objection that republican virtue can be coercive, that it tries to dissolve individual selves into a larger, collective whole, Sandel distinguishes between the republicanism of Rousseau and de Tocqueville (pp. 319–21, 347). Rousseau, he says, construed the common good as a "unitary and uncontestable" ideal, and was consequently "[u]nable to abide disharmony" (p. 320): all citizens had to be brought to agreement, by coercion if necessary. Tocqueville, by contrast, understood that the common good could be a matter for endless deliberation, and that a *variety* of public institutions—"townships, schools, religions, and virtue-sustaining occupations"—could cultivate the virtues necessary to participate well in such deliberation. Tocqueville's variety of virtue-promoting institutions, Sandel seems to think, will prevent the coerciveness of Rousseau's vision. But this is a mistake. Tocqueville may split the groups that claim us into smaller and more various units than Rousseau does, but nothing he says rules out the possibility that these smaller groups will in turn be oppressive vis-à-vis their individual members, coercing them into agreement. Labor unions, small townships, and churches have in many times and places been notorious for the coercive pressures they bring to bear on their members, for the stifling effect they have on the thought and behavior of individuals who dissent from the group. A politics that urges everyone to belong to some such group need not in the least be a politics cultivating what Sandel calls "the independence and judgment to deliberate well about the common good" (320). Far better to turn away from belonging altogether, at least as a direct goal, and focus on independence and judgment themselves. These are the virtues that really give individuals freedom, that grant them literal "self-government."

They are also the virtues we need for a healthy democracy. The neutrality that a state should have towards our comprehensive goals includes, I think, an abstention from insisting that anyone place "o'er all, Supreme, a passion for the commonweal."[31] Active citizenship, per se, need not be something most individuals prize highly. What liberalism does need, to preserve itself if nothing else, is that every citizen's comprehensive conception of the good include a healthy respect for the liberty of others—and for the common good insofar as the common good serves that liberty. Suppose that each citizen develops for herself a comprehensive picture of the good life that transcends her duty to her fellow citizens. Suppose, in addition, that each citizen recognizes that her individual search for that higher good is but an example of how individual human beings in general best come to the goals they pursue, and considers her free adoption of her goal essential to the way it ought to be pursued. One citizen might pursue salvation by Christ, one Buddhist self-renunciation, and one a secular appreciation of aesthetic pleasures, while all three see the ability of each individual to come to his or her own goals as sacrosanct—even if they believe that others should ideally come to the same goal they have come to themselves. All *such* citizens will be both motivated by something nobler than their own material interests and jealously protective of individual liberty. Herein lies the right middle way, I think, between a dangerously selfish and a dangerously self-sacrificing citizenry.

And this middle way can be achieved by structuring society so as to promote everyone's capacity for judgment. To emphasize judgment is to emphasize a skill valuable simultaneously for political participation and for the conduct of one's everyday life. The line between purely moral and purely political judgments is not sharp. Ideally a citizen will shape her moral judgements so as to include some political commitments while choosing leaders out of a worldview informed by her morality. This is one reason why a liberal polity needs to encourage judgment in its citizens and not merely political commitment. A second reason is that one's specifically political judgment will be both richer and freer—more sensitive to what goes into other people's conceptions of the good life and less bound to any particular such conception—if it starts from a commitment to a good beyond the well-being of the polis itself, if it makes room for the possibility of a nonpolitical conception of the good life. Finally, it is better that each individual citizen understand and promote everyone else's judgment than everyone else's well-being. By cultivating judgment in everyone, rather than mere fellow feeling, the society is likely to produce citizens who look out for one another's freedom, who tolerate dissent from the group, and who avoid the paternalism that an excess of compassion often produces.

6. The freedom of judgment helps alleviate the longstanding tension between the ideals of equality and liberty. Even people suspicious of egalitarianism tend to grant that we are all entitled to equal shares of liberty itself. Our equal liberty, or right to liberty, has historically been the clearest sense in which humans can be described as equal at all. But if freedom consists, as it does on positive libertarian views, in expressing an abstract reason or hidden will, then it probably cannot be distributed equally. Berlin begins the positive tradition with Plato, who suggests in the *Republic* that we are most fully ourselves when we are philosophers, as well as that philosophy requires skills much like those of mathematics. It follows, notoriously, that society has to be set up in an elitist way, with the few who can master the rigors of dialectic guiding the rest of us. Modern, egalitarian versions of Plato simply hope that we can all become philosophers, all achieve the skills of a logician. IQ tests probably tell us little about intelligence as a whole, but they have shown, if showing was needed, that we cannot all become logicians. There has never been a nation of philosophers and there never will be: the abstract abilities required by philosophical argumentation are simply not equally or indeed widely shared among human beings.

A different tradition of positive liberty, rooted in German Romanticism and to be found in figures ranging from Herder and Wordsworth to Marcuse and Foucault, asks that we all become artists. This tradition, known as "expressive individualism," has had a powerful impact on both nineteenth- and twentieth-century social movements in Europe and North America. Freedom, says this tradition, is what releases our individuality, what enables us to find and express the unique spirit ("genius") in each of us.[32] This leads to an appealing picture of everyone as an artistic creator, either literally painting, composing music, writing poetry, and so forth, or at least giving their lives a unique aesthetic flair—as recommended or demonstrated by the likes of Nietzsche, Paul Bowles, or Jack Kerouac. But the results in practice have been the thousands of terrible writers encouraged to think they "had a poem in there somewhere" (only to be bitterly disappointed by other people's reactions when they actually produce that poem), the violent religious and political cults (the Manson family and the Branch Davidians, but also the Red Brigades and the followers of Mishima) that have attracted people by their promise of something more unusual and interesting than everyday life, and the millions of young people in the past three decades or so who have played the same guitars, donned the same jeans, and grown their hair to the same considerable length in order to express their "individuality" in the manner expected of them by their peers and role models. The sad truth is, we can't all be artists any more than we can all be philosophers.

Negative libertarians might seem to come closer to respecting the abilities of ordinary people. Everyone has desires, after all, and normally knows what they are and how to satisfy them. Negative libertarians do in fact appeal to precisely such considerations to recommend the market over central planning, and individual choices about how to live over moralistic and paternalistic legislation. But it is easy to slip from strict negative libertarianism to utilitarian fantasies that are every bit as coercive as their positive libertarian counterparts. For if freedom consists in our ability to satisfy our desires, then the market has merely *instrumental* value, as does the government's abstention from regulating morality. If empirical evidence shows, as it has so far, that people satisfy their desires more readily when they do so on their own, then the case for the market and against paternalism is made. If we can satisfy more desires of more people by means of intelligent central planning and moral regulation, however, believers in negative liberty may well have to advocate that route instead. The quarrel between Friedrich Hayek and B. F. Skinner becomes merely a tactical one. On both of their views there is a theoretical possibility that social science experts can lead government to provide us with what we most want from our freedom. Hayek and his followers have indeed not objected very vigorously to the elitism by which social science experts dominate our current political system. Someday economists, psychologists, political scientists, and sociologists may really figure out how to satisfy everybody's desires much better than everybody can do by themselves. Should this still theoretical possibility become a reality, those libertarians who treat preference-satisfaction as sovereign should view a planned utopia as the best way to accomplish negative liberty's goals.

The freedom of judgment, by contrast, allows a principled opposition to other people running our lives for us, regardless of whether those other people are philosophers who want to impose their own comprehensive vision of the good, or social scientists who think they know, or even really *do* know, what we desire better than we do ourselves. Judgment is something we must each exercise for and by ourselves, and judgment, unlike philosophical or artistic skill, is something we can reasonably expect all people to be able to achieve. Judgment is enough of a skill that it requires training and practice, but it does not allow of expertise, or depend on rare talents, in the way that abstract reasoning and artistic creation do. At least, there are empirical reasons to think that a whole society of good judges is possible.

Treating judgment, for the moment, as more or less identical with aesthetic interpretation, let me give two examples of what I mean and then adduce some broader considerations. My first example is the Orthodox Jewish community, which I know intimately. The central sacred practice for most Orthodox Jews is close reading of the Talmud and the first five books of the Hebrew Bible. One is not only permitted but encouraged to ask challenging questions of the text,[33] and is then expected to come up with answers to one's own questions that fit well both with the details of the text and with general moral and religious conceptions in the Jewish tradition.[34] This is not an easy intellectual exercise, but I have heard it done well by people from all classes and educational backgrounds, and by people who otherwise did not strike me as particularly intelligent. When I spent six months at a yeshiva in 1982, I heard readings of the Torah from little known rabbis that for depth and interpretive virtuosity equaled or bettered the very best lectures by the most famous "close readers" I heard during nine years at Yale. I also received at least one memorable piece of personal advice from a nineteen-year-old student at the yeshiva couched in the form of a clever and wise analogy to episodes in the Book of Exodus. In a tiny, hole-in-the-wall Orthodox synagogue in New Jersey, I have seen a part-time rabbi who pretends to no great intellectual gifts, lecturing to a crowd of middle-class businesspeople, frequently come up with very subtle and original interpretations. I want to draw attention especially to the audience for these interpretations. Long out of school, and in some cases never schooled in the liberal arts, the people I have met intelligently studying Torah or Talmud probably could not follow a fairly elementary scientific or philosophical argument. Ordinary people give interpretations, or ask their children to give interpretations, at home over Sabbath meals, and many people of all ages and backgrounds attend a Talmud class every day. For the last half century or so, there has been a project by which people read the entire Talmud, one page a day, over seven years (in the United States, one can participate by dialing an 800-number which provides an interpretation, in Yiddish, of the page for each day). This emphasis on close reading, moreover, is a longstanding feature of Orthodox communities. "Rashi" is the acronym for an eleventh century grammarian and somewhat difficult commentator on the five books of Moses (*Chumash*), and *Chumash with Rashi* has been for several centuries the most widely read text in Orthodox Jewish homes and the basis of Jewish education. I cannot imagine any other intellectual activity becoming such a widespread feature of a community's daily life, any other intellectual activity in which people with such otherwise varying abilities and experience could participate equally.

My second example, from a very different culture, is the tradition of shadow puppet theater (*wayang kulit*) in Java. A puppeteer (*dhalang*) comes to town half a day or so before the scheduled performance in order to learn the local gossip. He then works allusions to current town affairs into the story from the Ramayana or whatever that he puts on that night.[35] He may also allude to the generosity or stinginess of his sponsors, or to any of a number of other subjects, in ways that only a deep understanding of the conventions of wayang kulit will enable one to grasp:

> Dhalang often laugh . . . at the way sponsors overinterpret remarks made in the course of a performance. Stories are told of the elaborate lengths to which some sponsors have gone . . . in search, say, of a particular kind of fish just because a character in a play in progress has expressed a desire for it. In their nervousness, sponsors think a dhalang is making demands when he is actually just following the plot. Dhalang do, however, voice dissatisfactions and demands in just this way, occasionally for themselves, more often on behalf of their troupe. If, for example, a performance is well under way but the musicians have not yet received tea and snacks, a dhalang may have a character . . . remark on how thirsty the soldiers are getting. No high-status wayang figure would normally allude to such a common need, and the break in tone makes the dhalang's meaning clear. . . . The audience roars at such times, and their laughter is very much at the sponsors' expense. (pp 175–6)

The sponsor may "overinterpret" but the audience "roars" at these references. So the references are hardly unambiguous, yet a mass audience laughs at them (and the audience for wayang kulit may include practically everyone, at least every male, in town).[36] That same audience expects idiosyncratic variations on the standard tales in every performance, and evaluates dhalang on how well they come up with such innovations and incorporate them into the traditional forms:

> Even dhalang who hold [school] degrees in awe . . . share the general view that a dhalang can and should introduce his own variations in performance. Otherwise he is scornfully labelled a student dhalang . . . , presumably not descended from dhalang and still dependent on book learning when he performs. The different lines of dhalang families in Java are expected to inherit variants in the tradition, and any member of such families retains at least a little of his father's style, as well as eventually adding his own variations. (p. 184)

The dhalang's role thus perfectly exemplifies the tension between revision and responsibility that I identified at the end of chapter 4 as the essence of judgment. Dhalang judge how they should perform, and are themselves judged by audiences, in accordance with the delicate line between varying a tradition and remaining faithful to it, keeping a tradition alive and making sure that there remains something *to* keep alive: "Both general expectations of a dhalang and certain more technical constraints set up conflicting demands . . . that a dhalang be both conservative and flexible, impervious to influence and sensitive to his audience's wishes, 'original' in performance and yet 'respectful' of the tradition" (p. 188; see also 195–6).

Finally, the Javanese not only regard wayang kulit as their central art form but use it in everyday life as a means of interpreting their social and political milieu:

> Imagery taken from wayang crops up frequently in Javanese speech, and the art form provides many a metaphor to Javanese comments on all sorts of events. Children are nicknamed after the servant-clowns, and the labels for kinds of characters are used to characterise kinds of humans as well. In a religious mode, people often remark that we are all really just puppets, moved by the ultimate dhalang, God. In political discourse, any important political official is liable to be labeled a puppet manipulated by an unseen dhalang. Much discussion about the current regime has centered on who at any given [moment] the real dhalang is. (p. 15)

Perhaps not coincidentally, the Javanese are a paradigm example of what Clifford Geertz means by a culture that consists in the constant interpretation of its own behavior.[37]

Let me now move from particular cases to general considerations. If my examples of cultures of interpretation are unsurprising, it is probably because in recent decades we have become familiar with the idea that grasping and extending concepts are processes that belong together and that the combination of these tasks is essential to the use of language. Wittgenstein is probably the source of this insight. He is certainly an important influence on Geertz, as well as on Stanley Cavell, who expresses the point extremely well:

> We learn words in certain contexts and after a while we are expected to know when they . . . can appropriately be projected into further contexts . . . If what can be said in a language is not everywhere determined by rules, nor its understanding anywhere secured through universals, and if there are always new contexts to be met, new needs, new relationships, new objects, new perceptions to be recorded and shared, then perhaps it is as true of a master of a language as of his apprentice that though "in a sense" we learn the meaning of words and what objects are, the learning is never over, and we keep finding new potencies in words and new ways in which objects are disclosed.[38]

That is, our very ability to speak suggests that we are able to judge. Linguistic communication has indeed been called "a paradigm case of correct and reliable judgment."[39]

For all its familiarity we should not take this idea for granted.[40] In the first place, it is a remarkable thing—much ignored in the current climate of emphasizing differences in intelligence—that we all seem to have a roughly equal capacity for grasping and revising the application of concepts to particular cases. In America we display such trust in ordinary people's interpretive abilities by means of the jury system: we presume that practically any twelve citizens are capable of sifting through evidence to determine whether and how the law applies to a given case. In the second place, and more importantly for my purposes, this capacity is *only* a capacity, and while the skill it allows us to develop may have the potential for spreading more or less equally across a population, it can also remain undeveloped or atrophy. This is the consequence of the division of labor that most worries Smith in the *Wealth of Nations*:

> In the progress of the division of labour, the employment of the far greater part of those who live by labour . . . comes to be confined to a few very simple operations . . . But the understandings of the greater part of men are necessarily formed by their ordinary employments. The man whose whole life is spent in performing a few simple operations, of which the effects too are, perhaps, always the same, or very nearly the same, has no occasion to exert his understanding, or to exercise his invention in finding out expedients for removing difficulties which never occur. He naturally loses, therefore, the habit of such exertion, and generally becomes as stupid and ignorant as it is possible for a human creature to become. The torpor of his mind renders him, not only incapable of relishing or bearing a part in any rational conversation, but of conceiving any generous, noble, or tender sentiment, and consequently of forming any just judgment concerning many even of the ordinary duties of private life. Of the great and extensive interests of his country, he is altogether incapable of judging. (V.i.f.50)

In contemporary American society—where the language on the primary medium of entertainment gets flatter and less innovative every year, where politicians get away with speeches that lack wit, that lack all but the most obvious irony, that rarely allude to any texts or history and even more rarely mint a memorable new image, where telephone salespeople are expected to recite a fixed message rather than indulging in the traditional sales patter and people in clerical positions are often unable to understand even literal instructions, where both the jury system and the electoral system yield increasingly silly and arbitrary results—we are seeing an especially serious version of the atrophy of judgment. This problem is not separate, I believe, from what is widely perceived as a "malaise," a society of people who increasingly pursue only their most immediate and selfish pleasures, who are increasingly reluctant or unable to help others or to develop richer, more reflective desires for themselves. When one loses the ability to judge, one can no longer change one's desires rationally, nor seek, in politics or daily life, anything but the blindest, most immediate satisfactions. The moral, for a liberal who emphasizes judgment, is that government efforts to repair such social ills are a part of, not an interference with, our "natural liberty." We need to become a society of attentive readers again, not because reading is a "higher pleasure" or a means to some objectively given human end, but because it is part and parcel of our freedom to do anything else.

7. Finally, the freedom of judgment can bring together what is most attractive in both the "libertarian" and the "welfare state" heirs to classical Enlightenment liberalism, can craft a richer ideological position than those represented by either left or right on the contemporary political scene. A liberalism that emphasizes individual judgment would stand strongly for liberty rights (freedom of expression, worship, assembly, etc.), for a market free of tariffs, quality controls, wage and price controls, and centralized investment policies, and against imposing any religious code or comprehensive conception of the good life. All of these negative conditions are necessary to give people room for acting on their own judgments rather than on how someone else judges they should act. But such a liberalism would at the same time stand for government policies ensuring for everyone the conditions without which they cannot judge at all. It goes almost without saying that these include a decent minimal level of food, shelter, clothing, and health care, but if we recall the multifold features of judgment—that it requires leisurely reflection, that it is a socially directed activity, that it requires discipline, that it develops by being used, that we become conscious of it paradigmatically in the presence of beauty, and that it is above all a process of interpretation—they also include: enough leisure to engage in phronetic activities, develop one's interpretive skills, and exercise those skills in all one's major choices; job training or work for everyone who wants it (as protection against the loss of phronetic activities and the apathy that that loss can bring about); regular access to some kind of community; the opportunity to experience a position of responsibility (by way of universal military or civil service, or by assigning some positions in government by lot);[41] access to the beauty of nature and of art; and above all, of course, excellent education, for the young and for the older, and with an emphasis on the humanities skills needed for good interpretation just as much as on the more scientific skills needed to perform well in the marketplace. A liberalism of judgment would also favor the widespread distribution of information relevant to our lives as workers, consumers, and citizens, and of tools for properly sifting through and understanding that information—if need be with the aid of government funds. To Milton Friedman's famous list of things the government should not do,[42] it would restore the maintenance of public parks, given the importance of access to natural beauty, as well as public housing and perhaps military service. As he does, however,

it would prefer a negative income tax to a minimum wage as a way of helping the working poor,[43] and a direct distribution of necessities to the unemployed poor in place of such interferences with market incentives as food stamps and rent control.

In addition, because it looks to a flexible society in which institutions are both open to easy change and responsive to the judgments of those they affect, a liberalism of judgment would have a principled preference for the small and local over the large and centralized: small, local government over large central government, but also, and just as strongly, small, local businesses over large national and transnational ones. Antitrust laws, for the liberty of judgment, are not simply about keeping costs low to the consumer: they need to be widely applied in order to prevent a few large sources of labor demand from gaining either excessive control over the labor market or undue influence on government. A liberalism of judgment would for similar reasons prefer workplace democracy in each firm to large trade unions, although it would regard unions as an essential counterbalance to the power of big business wherever that exists. And in every one of these controversial areas, a liberalism of judgment would favor gradualism over revolution, small reforms over utopia. As judgment in everyday affairs works piece by piece, always open to partial correction but rarely to a complete overhaul, so a politics of judgment must seek institutional changes that people in their everyday lives can understand and live with. Thus a liberalism of judgment would truly walk between the libertarian right and the egalitarian left—and avoid at the same time the accusations of hypocrisy, lack of ideals, or excessive compromise that have dogged, for instance, Bill Clinton's centrism in America and Tony Blair's in Britain.

Over the long term, a doctrine promoting judgment should also be more successful in achieving its ends than Clinton, at least, has been. For the exercise of judgment makes for a more sensible citizenry, which is in turn a great advantage for the liberty it promotes. We would feel more comfortable about extending each other's rights if we had reason to think they would be used responsibly, more comfortable about allowing wider freedom of expression, fewer requirements on educational curricula, and fewer licensing practices, if we could trust that most everyday citizens were capable of acting with intelligence, and on tempered, reflected-upon desires. It would be easier to point out to such a public how ridiculous the perks, say, of agribusiness are, easier, perhaps, to persuade even those gaining from the perks to give them up (since they could substitute one desire for another more easily than we now can, and since each could trust the society as a whole to see them through if they fell, temporarily, into unemployment). It would be easier to explain to these citizens why they should invest heavily in public education, why that needs to include the humanities skills that teach interpretation as well as the technical skills that prepare one for a career, and why they might want to support universal service and/or some degree of participatory democracy.[44] It would also be easier to explain why arts funding should not mean underwriting the lavish, philistine entertainments of the Metropolitan Opera House,[45] nor underwriting anyone's "right" to express themselves, but allowing as many people as possible to have access to some thought-provoking painting, music, and theater, and some education in how such challenging work can ultimately be more beautiful than art that immediately gratifies the senses. Thus a liberalism of judgment would be self-sustaining; indeed, it would grow on itself. To represent freedom as based in good judgment is in part to help bring about people with good judgment. But that makes it possible to find votes for more judicious policies, which would include increased opportunities for each to use her freedom in her own way. Which in turn would increase the degree to which people develop their judgment. . . . Which in turn would increase the opportunity for liberal policies. . . .

What would a government premised on judicious liberalism *not* do? It would not try, so much as by symbolic means, to make people feminist or multiculturalist in outlook any more than it would try to make them Christian; it would not try to combat the evils of "consumerism" or divorce by law; it would not underwrite missions into space or protect animal species.[46] A liberalism of judgment would not make government the direct vehicle of any moral, or intellectual, or technological change. It would insist on the need for government action to provide a rich set of conditions for freedom but simultaneously maintain a presumption that those conditions should be limited, that whatever government can avoid doing, consistent with preserving everyone's liberty, it should avoid doing. And it would maintain this presumption because it sees a general favoritism for negative liberty as itself a positive statement, because the very absence of government interference encourages us to make our lives by ourselves. On the subject of paternalism George Kateb writes, sounding here exactly like Kant:

> The smaller the amount of explicit regulation meant to bind all, the more room there is left for individuals and groups to regulate themselves, to achieve a lawful autonomy. . . . The less paternalism there is, the stronger grows the readiness to reject paternalism in all the relations of life. It seems to me that necessary to the completion of constitutional representative democracy as a morally distinctive polity is limited, nonpaternalist government . . . . One's life is not supposed to be arranged or designed by government or to have meaning or coherence given to it by government; nor is one supposed to be helped too

much, or saved from oneself, or looked at closely or continuously. One is supposed to be free, autonomous, self-reliant.[47]

The structures of government represent moral qualities, for Kateb, and
thereby spread them throughout a society—both action and inaction by
government can do this. If true, which I think it is, this is another point
in favor of the liberalism of judgment. A society structured to provide the
basics of health, education, and information to its members, and beyond
that opportunities for leisure, responsibility, and community, would teach
that freedom is not simply there for the taking, that it has conditions and
needs development, but also that, after the conditions have been provided, we must each do the actual developing on our own.

What kind of citizen, if Kateb is right, might institutions based on the
third concept of liberty inspire? What kind of person does one who cultivates judgment make? Well, she stops to appreciate natural beauty and
therefore needs a little less in life than those who treasure material goods
alone. She also makes earnest efforts to replace or redirect her desires
when she finds them unfulfillable, and, to aid such changes in herself, she
seeks out phronetic activities and a supportive, healthy community. She is
therefore less self-centered, less anxious about her own satisfactions, than
one who regards his freedom as consisting in the pursuit of objects of
desire. Insofar as she has truly moved from aesthetic to moral judgment,
translating her self-reflection into strong and responsible action, this willingness to defer gratification becomes a source of courage. If she is a near
enough bystander to affect acts that, in her judgment, threaten some
human being's basic dignity, she will take considerable risks to fight those
acts.

Her reflectiveness also leads her to compromise when she doesn't get
exactly what she wants, and to a constant awareness that she must always
work amid the happenstance of good and bad luck. She is therefore a
good person to have on committees, or to come between feuding neighbors or colleagues. By example as well as advice, she encourages everyone
around her to compromise, to avoid being overly attached to their own
views. Similarly, she resigns herself, and encourages others to be resigned,
to compromise in public life: to gradualism in politics, and to the election, at times, of foolish or weak leaders. This compromise extends up to
the point at which political actions threaten the minimal conditions for
decent human life. There, she draws a sharp line.

In addition to these directly moral characteristics, she has a tremendous respect for empirical evidence. She tries to learn widely about the
world, and distinguishes carefully between appropriate and inappropriate
reliance upon expertise. She is a skeptic, not easily led by dogmas and

intellectual fads, but she is also flexible, coming around willingly, if slowly, to new paradigms of empirical research when they seem to her overwhelmingly successful. Her decisions about her own health are therefore sensible, neither superstitious—she gives no business to homeopaths or faith healers—nor overly cautious, and she supports public health policies that seem likewise sensible, after a reasonable survey of the information available to her. She is not easily taken in by fraudulent or empty advertising, but she does not put implicit faith in every utterance of the anti-establishment either.

Finally, her skepticism, general moderation of passion and expectation, and respect for empirical fact means she is not so much as tempted by religious and political cults—the Unification Church, the Spartacist League, Pat Robertson or Pat Buchanan, Ayn Rand's followers, etc.—although she may well be a devout believer in a religious faith or a committed communitarian. She is just, in this as in all things, a reflective religious or political believer, dissenting here and there from her authorities, and gently integrating her tenets of faith with common sense and common morality as much as possible. In this respect, for all that she might participate in and learn from a community, for all that she might acknowledge a religion or culture as providing the starting point for her reflections, she is still very much what Kateb calls an "individualist." By relying ultimately on her own judgment, she lives out his admonition that "[i]ndividualist forms of self-love. . . help check the horrors of group self-love" (p. 120).

It is hard to imagine a person who more readily deserves, and can more readily be trusted with, every kind of liberty and responsibility, who can run her own affairs better and be a better contributor to public decision-making, regardless of what specific political and comprehensive views she might hold. And it is hard to imagine a notion of political freedom that can more readily be trusted to encourage such virtues of health, calm self-command and decency—without telling us, overall, how we should live.

NOTES

CHAPTER 1
INTRODUCTION

1. Maurice Cranston, *Freedom: A New Analysis* (London: Longmans, Green, & Co., 1953), p. 65.

2. Isaiah Berlin, "Two Concepts of Liberty," in *Four Essays on Liberty* (Oxford: Oxford University Press, 1969).

3. For the system of abbreviation and pagination I use for Kant's texts, see the "Abbreviations" pages at the beginning of the book.

4. Those who urge "laissez-faire" economics are generally interested in freedom from paternalism precisely for the activities of these corporations and their already quite independent leaders. How much opportunity the poor have to think for themselves is rarely a focus of their polemics.

5. Will Kymlicka characterizes this as the best understanding of liberalism: "According to [Charles] Taylor, liberals teach us that the freedom to form and revise our projects is inherently valuable, something to be pursued *for its own sake*, an instruction that Taylor rightly rejects as empty. Instead, he says, there has to be some project that is worth pursuing, some task that is worth fulfilling. But the concern for freedom within liberalism doesn't take the place of these projects and tasks. On the contrary, the liberal defence of freedom rests precisely on the importance of those tasks and projects. . . . Freedom of choice . . . isn't pursued for its own sake, but as a precondition for pursuing those projects and practices that *are* valued for their own sake" (*Liberalism, Community, and Culture* [Oxford: Clarendon Press, 1989], p. 48). See also pp. 49–50.

6. "[O]ld age, as distinguished from mere adulthood, was felt by the Romans to contain the very climax of human life; not so much because of accumulated wisdom and experience as because the old man had grown closer to the ancestors and the past. Contrary to our concept of growth, where one grows into the future, the Romans felt that growth was directed toward the past" (Hannah Arendt, "What is Authority?" in *Between Past and Future* [New York: Penguin, 1968], p. 123).

7. Simon Schama, *Citizens* (New York: Alfred A. Knopf, 1989), pp. 174–82, 225–6; Robert Darnton, *The Literary Underground of the Old Regime* (Cambridge: Harvard University Press, 1982), pp. 202–5; Gordon Wood, *The Radicalism of the American Revolution* (New York: Vintage Books, 1991), pp. 43–4, 80–7, 92, 95–101, and chapters 10, 11, and 13.

8. In *What is Enlightenment?* Kant talks about the "public use of reason" as crucial to emerging from tutelage, but R 1508–9 bring judgment into the process, and in later political writings, "the public use of reason" seems to get transformed into "the public use of judgment." See chapter 9 of this book for further discussion.

9. For Schiller, see *On the Aesthetic Education of Man*, ed. and trans. Elizabeth N. Wilkinson and L. A. Willoughby (Oxford: Clarendon Press, 1967), especially

letters 1, 12–16, 20, and 27. For Humboldt, see *The Limits of State Action*, ed. J. W. Burrow (Indianapolis: Liberty Classics, 1993), chapters 3 and 8. Mill dedicated *On Liberty* to Humboldt, drawing on him throughout and especially for the much derided notion of "individuality."

10. Many current writers on liberty seem to have no interest at all in history. Gerald McCallum's influential "Negative and Positive Freedom" (*Philosophical Review* 76 [1967]) argues that every "freedom from" claim can be construed as also making an implicit "freedom to" claim and vice versa (we are always free *from* one thing *to* do something else) without ever paying attention to the fact that emphasis on one aspect of this freedom as opposed to another has made a tremendous amount of historical difference. And while Joseph Raz and others have recently proposed thoughtful new versions of positive liberty, they seem unconcerned about the fact that their gentle, relatively uncoercive versions of the notion have little to do with the way that notion has actually gotten used in the past. They rarely so much as attempt to allay the concern, therefore, that their own visions might be turned to coercive purposes were their theories to be put into practice by as large a body of people as put Rousseau and Marx into practice in the past.

11. This embraces both what Kant calls "reflective judgment" and what he calls "determining judgment" (CJ 179/15). I shall sometimes use "determinant" instead of "determining," but I think the latter term is clearer. I shall argue in chapter two, *contra* Kant, that every determining judgment relies on a reflective one, at least implicitly, and vice versa.

12. Oxford English Dictionary, 2nd ed., pp. 617–8. The two remaining illustrations are from the nineteenth century—Mill's "When the mind assents to a proposition it judges" (1843) and J. Martineau's "Understanding never judges. . . . It is the Will that really judges and decides on what is presented to it by the Understanding" (1885)—and may well be infested by the philosophical prejudices of German Idealism. Twelve of the thirteen definitions for "judgment" similarly fit the courtroom model.

13. This and the following quotations all come from the *New York Times* account of *Board of Education v. Grumet*, under the heading "Excerpts From Opinions and Dissent on Religion" (*New York Times*, 28 June 1994, pp. D20–1).

14. At least if Souter's convincing quotations from that decision, and Scalia's silence in response to those quotations, adequately let us know what Walz was about.

15. At least if the detail Scalia provides is representative of *that* decision.

16. Consider, for instance, the "Religious Freedom Restoration Act," passed by Congress in response to some very narrow construals of the freedom of religion by the Supreme Court in the 1980s.

17. Edward Levi, *An Introduction to Legal Reasoning* (Chicago: University of Chicago Press, 1949). Levi applies his model to constitutional interpretation on pp. 57–102.

18. And of related categories: of "terror" and "guerrilla activity," but also of "innocent civilian," "necessary force," "political means," etc.

19. CJ 179, my translation. I translate this passage myself since I dislike Bernard's term "determinant" for *bestimmend* (and find the recent translator Werner

Pluhar's term "determinative" even worse). It is important, to understanding Kant and to my uses of him, that we keep clearly in mind that *bestimmende Urtheilskraft*, like its *reflectirende* counterpart, is an activity, a process, and not merely a "result."

20. A rich and deeply thoughtful book on this last issue is Ronald Beiner's *Political Judgment* (Chicago: University of Chicago Press, 1983), which also focuses on judgment in part as a way of directing attention towards a capacity shared by all human beings, as opposed to something on which academics can set themselves up as experts (pp. 1–3, 8).

CHAPTER 2
AESTHETIC JUDGMENT

1. Kant himself would probably have been leery of any close association between aesthetic and moral decision-making, but ultimately I hope to suggest both why such anxieties may be misguided and how Kant, for all his leeriness of the association, in part succumbed to it himself.

2. I reiterate this account from "Frustrated Contracts, Poetry, and Truth," *Raritan* (Spring 1994); reprinted in *Beyond Representation: Philosophy and Poesis*, ed. Richard Eldridge (Cambridge: Cambridge University Press, 1996).

3. Both Romantic artists and neo-Romantic literary critics (Harold Bloom et al.) view Kant as vindicating their endorsement of the imagination over against the understanding, and this reading of Kant is widely held by commentators on the third *Critique*. Donald Crawford, for instance, says that "In the case of the experience of the beautiful . . . no concept is forthcoming" (*Kant's Aesthetic Theory* [Madison: University of Wisconsin Press, 1974], p. 89). Paul Guyer, wrestling explicitly with this issue, concludes that the word "definite" or "determinate" does no work in Kant's theory (*Kant and the Claims of Taste* [Cambridge: Harvard University Press, 1979], pp. 88–9 and note 60 on 408–9). Guyer here is rebutting Mary Warnock's suggestion that what understanding provides is an "indeterminate concept"; he notes that Kant never uses any such phrase (ibid.). But while he is right to refuse Warnock's interpretation, he is not right to ignore Kant's own repeated emphasis on the words "definite" and "determinate." To think without a determinate concept is not, indeed, to think with an *in*determinate concept—the phrase is close to an oxymoron for Kant (in practically the only place it appears in CPR [B 307], it represents a limitation to thought, something that cannot itself be thought)—but it could well be to use concepts without allowing any single concept to determine one's thought.

4. The word "definite" or "determinate" appears again and again in similar passages of the *Critique*. "Flowers, free delineations, outlines intertwined with one another without design . . ., have no meaning, depend on no *definite* concept, and yet they please. The satisfaction in the beautiful must depend on the reflection upon an object, leading to any concept (however *indefinite*), and it is thus distinguished from the pleasant, which rests entirely upon sensation." (CJ 207/41). See also CJ 222/58, 241/80, and FI 220/408.

5. See also FI 220–1/408–9: "So if the form of an object given in empirical intuition is of such a character that the *apprehension*, in the imagination, of the

object's manifold agrees with the *exhibition* of a concept of the understanding (which concept this is being indeterminate), then imagination and understanding are—in mere reflection—in mutual harmony, a harmony that furthers the task of these powers."

6. Kant's language suggests a considerably more interactive relationship between the faculties than Guyer's account allows. Guyer himself admits this, although he takes it as a failing on Kant's part (see Guyer, *Kant*, p. 87). Section 7 of the first Introduction, for instance, suggests that when the understanding's "presentation" coincides with the imagination's "apprehension of its manifold," the two faculties "*mutually* harmonize" (my emphasis). Section 8 goes even further: what we consider in the relationship of the two faculties "is how one *helps or hinders* the other in a given representation." Guyer responds to all this, weakly I think, by arguing that the two are in harmony since the imagination's play, solitary as it might be, contributes to the chief "business" or goal of the understanding (86–8). My account, by contrast, straightforwardly puts the two faculties into a relationship of "mutual assistance," and gives the understanding an active role that is perfectly described as the "presentation" of concepts to the imagination.

7. I would not claim that every passage in CJ supports such a reading, but it fits well with many passages, and there are several that practically require it. For instance, at FI 220–1/408–9, Kant speaks of the imagination's work having to agree with the understanding's "presentation of a concept . . . (regardless of which concept)," which Guyer can do nothing with but call the phrasing "inept," and at CJ 207 Kant says (my translation): "The satisfaction in the beautiful must depend on reflection on an object, which leads to some concept (undetermined which [*unbestimmt welchem*])." Consider also the following remarkable excerpt from a transcript of lectures Kant gave on aesthetics in the winter of 1794/95: "[Understanding and imagination] are like two friends who dislike but can't relinquish each other, for they live in a continuous fight and yet can't do without each other" (quoted in Dieter Henrich, *Aesthetic Judgment and the Moral Image of the World* [Stanford: Stanford University Press, 1992], pp. 52–3).

Sometimes Kant does hint that there are indeterminate concepts, in particular the indeterminate concept of "beauty," but there are problems with making sense of this, at least if the indeterminate concept of beauty is supposed to affect our judgments independently of any subordinate, more determinate, empirical concepts. Anthony Savile, in *Kantian Aesthetics Pursued* (Edinburgh: Edinburgh University Press, 1993), argues that Kant must allow some intermediate concepts to come between the supersensible and its supposed application to an empirical particular, else "there would be no way in which argument, even dialectical argument, could be properly sensitive to [aesthetic properties]. Any match that there might be between judgment and reality would only be fortuitous, and certainly could not *appear* as a match at all" (p. 56).

8. Twentieth-century modernist works of art serve as surprisingly exact illustrations for Kant's aesthetic theory, but the tension between form and chaos, between potentially unorganizable "nature" and the "art" by which we try to place nature into ongoing forms of organization, captures our everyday notion of what is beautiful about many different styles of art. Dickens's language, Tolstoy's characterizations, Mozart's vocal ensembles, all seem both wildly unexpected, elusive,

spontaneously "natural," etc., and remarkably controlled, shaped, intelligibly directed to some end. When we don't see any such intelligence, any such control—as we don't in some rambling novels and symphonies or much contemporary "express what you feel" art—there is nothing relieving, nothing exciting, about the wild or elusive content. When all we see is the artist's intelligence, a carefully constructed plan or message, we find the work coy or clever rather than beautiful. What makes moralistic art, and most allegory, so lifeless is not simply the fact that they convey simple messages but the fact that they are so strictly *controlled* (hence Dali, although without a simple message, is often equally lifeless). Kant has the balance here exactly right: "[T]he purposiveness in the product of beautiful art, although it is designed, must not seem to be designed, i.e. beautiful art must *look* like nature, although we are conscious of it as art" (CJ 306/149).

9. Reflective judgment is clearly a process, for Kant, something extended over time, not a single act. Determining judgments are acts (indeed, "deciding judgment" is another reasonable translation of Kant's phrase *bestimmende Urteilskraft*), sometimes included in, sometimes concluding, the process of reflective judgment.

10. CJ 219, translation by Guyer, in *Kant*, p. 94.

11. CJ 243, 222/80, 58. Guyer makes of this extension over time (a) that since manifolds are temporally successive, "it may always be appropriate to think of their unification as a temporally extended activity, even when it is also natural to specify a moment at which unification can be said to have been achieved," and (b) that the achievement of a goal can produce a pleasure that lingers on in the memory after the moment of achievement have passed (*Kant*, pp. 95–6). But the temporal extension of perception in *(a)* takes place in cognition as much as in aesthetic response, while *(b)* gives us a pleasure that merely reflects back on aesthetic response rather than being identical with it. My retrospective pleasure in *having* achieved something could stem from pride in my abilities, or relief that I don't need to be ashamed of a lack of ability, or the simple comfort we often take, looking back over a day or two, in being able to find a recent stretch of our lives filled with pleasant rather than painful experiences. None of these can strictly be called pleasure in the achievement itself, especially where that pleasure is construed, as Kant explicitly does construe it, as the relief of a need, and the need disappears to the extent that the achievement has been completed. One virtue of my reading is that because the cognitive need for interpretation can never be fully met, because its completion is indefinitely deferrable, we can easily see how the satisfaction of that need might extend over time. There is nothing to be "grasped in a moment" about interpretation, so if the play of the faculties consists in interpretation, it is obviously an activity we can "linger" over.

12. Guyer's central account of the harmony of the faculties runs as follows:

Supposing . . . that the harmony of the faculties is a state in which the subjective condition of knowledge exists without the use of a concept . . . , we can think of this state as one in which a manifold of intuition, presented by the imagination, is unified . . . without the use of a concept. . . . The "sensible [or subjective] condition" of knowledge might thus be taken to be the contributions of both sensibility and imagination, as contrasted with understanding, to the production of cognition. If we turn to the *Critique of Pure Reason*'s model of the actual production of knowledge, namely, the first edition's theory of threefold synthesis, we will see that this includes all the aspects of synthesis except the actual application of a concept of the understanding to the manifold of intuitions. Specifically, the "sensible condition" of knowledge . . . must include the "synthesis of apprehension in intuition" and the "synthesis of reproduction in imagination." . . . Kant maintains that [these two syntheses are] "inseparably bound up" [with one another], and that the two together constitute the "transcendental ground of the possibility of all modes of knowledge whatsoever," prior to . . . the actual application of a concept to the apprehended manifold. . . . The harmony of the faculties is then a state in which, somehow, a manifold of intuition is run through and held together as a unity by the imagination without the use of a concept. (Guyer, *Kant*, pp. 85–6)

But Kant himself gives us no reason to suppose that anything in Transcendental Deduction A should be taken as a clue to what goes on in CJ. In the first place, this is the section that he most conspicuously withdrew in the revised version of CPR published three years before CJ. In the second place, the three syntheses of Transcendental Deduction A apply to the construction of *all* objects, to the way we must grasp *any* intuition, so it is hard to see how any two of them could be fitted to just some objects (the "beautiful" ones) among others. If one did want to draw on CPR to illuminate CJ, the discussions of judgment in the Metaphysical Deduction and the Schematism, the discussion of reflection in the Amphiboly, and the remarks on teleology in the Dialectic would all be more promising places to look (I am indebted to Béatrice Longuenesse for all textual suggestions about First *Critique*/Third *Critique* connections aside from the reference to the Schematism.)

In any case, Guyer's appeal to the three syntheses of Transcendental Deduction A fails. Kant *would* give us license to separate the first two syntheses off from the third as the "sensible condition" of knowledge, *if* he indeed said that the first two syntheses together constitute a transcendental ground for the possibility of any kind of knowledge and that they do so "prior to the application of a concept." But he does not say this. Kant calls the *first* synthesis *alone* "the transcendental ground for the possibility of all modes of knowledge," and uses that as a basis for the claim that the second synthesis, because "inseparably bound up with the first," should rightly be considered a transcendental "act" as well. The fact that Kant thus distinguishes conceptually between the two syntheses even while calling them inseparable, and calls them inseparable merely to buttress a claim about the second one, should warn us away from assuming that the third synthesis will be any more separable from the first two than they were from each other. And while Kant says nothing explicit one way or the other about this possibility in subsection 3 of the Subjective Deduction, he has earlier spoken repeatedly of a "*three*-fold synthesis which must necessarily be found in all knowledge" (A 97, my emphasis). He also gives us philosophical reasons to tie the third synthesis to the first two. "If we were not conscious that what we think is the same as what we thought a moment before," subsection 3 begins, "all reproduction in the series of representations would be useless." This is exactly the same type of argument that showed the necessity of the second synthesis: "But if I were always to drop out of thought the preceding representations . . . , and did not reproduce them while advancing to those that follow, a complete representation would never be obtained." We were told, regarding the synthesis of apprehension, that we need to grasp representations as a whole even in order to describe them as a manifold, that we need to introduce the one/many distinction into a manifold to make any sense of it at all. We were then told, regarding the synthesis of reproduction, that the ability to reproduce past intuitions in imagination is essential to the initial apprehending of representations in terms of the one and the many. Now, regarding the synthesis of recognition, we are told that the notion of "sameness," the conscious imparting of unity to different particulars that constitutes the concept of "concept" itself, is in turn necessary to the second synthesis—and therefore to the first as well. Without the synthesis of recognition in a concept, "[t]he manifold of representation would never . . . form a whole, since it would lack that unity which only consciousness can impart to it" (A 103). The application of concepts is thus essential to the finding of any unity *even subjectively, even in the imagination alone*: the imagination needs the understanding to complete its own work. (Longuenesse suggests an emendation of this reading: the imagination requires the understanding, the first synthesis requires the third, *if* what we apprehend is to count as an *object*.)

This is the crowning moment of Kant's exposition in the Subjective Deduction, the reason he talks of a "three-fold synthesis," the fullest elaboration of the initial insight of the whole *Critique*: that intuitions and concepts *differ in kind but need each other*, that "intuitions without concepts are blind" (A 51). Unity depends essentially on the action of concepts—imparting unity is indeed the essence of what concepts do—so there can be no obtaining of "the psychological concomitants of knowledge" (Guyer, *Kant*, p. 98) in the absence of concepts. Despite the distinction that Kant draws between imagination and understanding, he would find it unintelligible to talk, as Guyer does, of "the imagination's unification of a manifold without a concept" (p. 98). Guyer himself asks (p. 97) how Kant, given the theses he maintains in CPR, could "even consider the possibility of any apprehension of a manifold without a concept, let alone actually affirm the existence of such a state of mind?" Guyer responds to his own question by saying, "Obvious as this question might seem to his reader, Kant never raises it in the *Critique of Judgment*, and gives no hint at a solution." Reason enough, one might think, to look for an interpretation of CJ on which such a question does not arise. What seems not to have occurred to Guyer is that Kant might never worry about how to unify manifolds without concepts precisely because, in both the first and the third *Critiques*, he strictly rules such a possibility out of court.

13. Compare Wittgenstein, *Philosophical Investigations*, trans. 3d ed., trans. G. E. M. Anscombe (New York: Macmillan, 1958), § 72.

14. Importantly, the borders can be *vague*: Wittgenstein, and, following him, Crispin Wright, have offered excellent arguments to show that some of our linguistic concepts are *essentially* vague—"baldness," for example—and there is no reason to suppose that such concepts are either eradicable from our thinking or any less useful, in allowing us to draw distinctions, than concepts whose borders can be determined with exactitude. (See Wittgenstein, *Philosophical Investiga-*

tions, §§ 88, 98–101; and Crispin Wright, "Language-Mastery and the Sorites Paradox," in *Truth and Meaning: Essays in Semantics*, ed. Gareth Evans and John McDowell [Oxford: Oxford University Press, 1976]. "Baldness" is Wright's example.) That I cannot say precisely whether Danny de Vito should count as bald or not does not leave me in the slightest doubt about how to classify Telly Savalas. And when Kant rules out indeterminate concepts, there is no reason to think he means to rule out vagueness. Rather, there are some intuitions that clearly do belong, and some that clearly do not belong, to the domain even of a vague concept, and that suffices to constitute "determinacy." Without such minimal inclusiveness and exclusiveness there will be no concept at all. A more precise kind of border is unnecessary.

15. On the picture of objecthood I find in Kant, manifolds are ultimately unified only by the determinant application of a concept to them. They can be provisionally unified, however, whenever the understanding and imagination agree that some determinant application can be responsibly made. As long as they continue to consider other such applications as well, this is still reflective judgment. When these considerations are ended in favor of a single application, we have determinant judgment. There is, then, no unity without borders, even in reflective judgment. Unity without borders will not enable me to pick out a specific object among other objects. It is just that the borders do not always have to be determinate ones—sometimes they can remain "in play."

16. I am indebted to Ronald Beiner for pointing out the trouble this passage makes for the link I am drawing between aesthetic judgment and communication.

17. See §§ 6 and 7, especially; not coincidentally picked up by Stanley Cavell as the crucial premonition of ordinary language philosophy in Kant ("Aesthetic Problems in Modern Philosophy," in *Must We Mean What We Say?* [Cambridge: Cambridge University Press, 1969], pp. 88–96), as well as by Guyer, Cavell's student: "This excursion into ordinary usage [is] unparalleled in Kant's other *Critiques*" (Guyer, *Kant*, p. 137).

18. Guyer admits in several places that this view fits best with Kant's own text; see p. 155, which talks of the "incoherence" and the "absurdity" of saying that the universal communicability of beauty could be what leads to our pleasure in the beautiful object, and the "strangeness" of the claim "that the communicability of a representation is itself the mental state of free play." On my reading, the intersubjective validity of the pleasure, and what we might call the "interfaculty" validity of the pleasure are one and the same thing, which makes good sense, I think, of both of these central claims that Guyer must write off as "absurd."

19. Hannah Ginsborg takes this aspect of Kant seriously for much the same reason that I do; see "Reflective Judgment and Taste," *Noûs* 24 (1990), pp. 71–5. I disagree with her, however, on how to interpret the potentially endless pleasure of heautonomy. Ginsborg writes (p. 73) that "the purely formal and self-referential judgment that all perceivers of the [beautiful] object should share my present mental state" implies that "I demand of myself [as much as of others] that I remain in the same mental state as that in which I presently find myself." But this is to say that "my mental state at each moment . . . is a ground or reason

for its own continuation in me," and Kant characterizes pleasure, in general, as an awareness of "being impelled by one's representation of an object to continue in one's present mental state." So the mental state in which a beautiful object puts us is necessarily pleasurable.

The first objection to this account is that it does not explain how the pleasure in the beautiful is *different* from other pleasures. "We *linger* in our contemplation of the beautiful, because this contemplation reinforces and reproduces itself" (CJ 222/58). By implication, not all pleasures equally linger and reproduce themselves. Moreover, and here we get to the deeper problem in Ginsborg's account, we linger in our contemplation of the beautiful *because* this contemplation reinforces and reproduces itself: one cannot explain why the contemplation reinforces and reproduces itself by saying that it leads us to want to linger. Nor does it get us anywhere to say that the nature of lingering is to provide a ground for further lingering. So Ginsborg must be wrong to explain the harmony of the faculties as a state that licenses a purely self-referential claim. Rather, the nature of that harmony enables us to linger because of the *end* that that harmony achieves, because "our whole faculty of representative power gains" by it (CJ 231/67), and that is the ground for claiming that the pleasure of this state of contemplation is always "animating," "enlivening," or "quickening" rather than enervating. It is "animating," "quickening," etc., because it achieves cognitive ends that imagination alone, and understanding alone, cannot achieve. The self-referentiality that marks judgment's fundamental principle as "heautonomous" rather than just "autonomous" is thus indirect: the harmony of the faculties serves, in the first instance, a purpose beyond itself, but the acheivement of that purpose turns out to promote the flourishing of the faculties themselves. I think this indirect account is less mysterious than Ginsborg's translation of heautonomy into the directly self-referential claim that one wants to remain in the state of mind one already happens to be in.

20. This is in fact right, I think, at least on my account of what the harmony of the faculties consists in. Our faculties are in harmony if and only if concepts can get some grip on our intuitions—reflectively (in play) when they may also be released continually in favor of other concepts, or determinantly (in knowledge) when the grip is unbreakable for theoretical or practical reasons—and precisely if and only if that condition holds can we communicate. To say a subjective condition is "communicable" is just to say it is open to being determined by concepts, ready for knowledge. In order to communicate we need concepts, just as we need concepts in order to know. One thing this means is that if the pleasure of aesthetic response took place, as Guyer supposes, entirely "below" the reach of concepts, we could not communicate it, although we might be able to communicate the *fact that we were having* it, or something of the sort.

21. Kant regards the fact that communicability is pleasurable as too empirical to ground the claimed universal validity of the pleasure in beauty, but the fact that aesthetic response is communicable need not be (and is not, on Kant's account) something empirical.

22. See *Critique of Pure Reason*, B 139–40, 157–8, and A 123–4, B 151–2.

23. The connection of judgment to conversation is spelled out in a similar manner by Peter Steinberger in *The Concept of Political Judgment* (Chicago: University of Chicago Press, 1993), pp. 247–80.

24. See Wittgenstein, *Philosophical Investigations*, § 242: "If language is to be a means of communication there must be agreement not only in definitions but also (queer as this may sound) in judgments. This seems to abolish logic, but does not do so." This insight is elaborated in *On Certainty*—where it also becomes clear that Wittgenstein uses the term "judgment" in much the way I want to do. Wittgenstein's epistemology has indeed been an important source for me in thinking about the nature of judgment. See *On Certainty*, ed. G. E. M. Anscombe and G. H. von Wright, trans. Denis Paul and Anscombe (Oxford: Basil Blackwell, 1977), especially §§ 66, 124, 126, 128–32, 137, 140, 149–50, 232, 308, 490, 493–4, 517, 519, 603, 606, 615, as well as the passages cited in note 16, chapter 11 below.

CHAPTER 3
MORAL JUDGMENT

1. John McDowell, "Virtue and Reason," *The Monist* (July 1979), p. 332.

2. Nancy Sherman, *The Fabric of Character* (Oxford: Clarendon Press, 1989), pp. 38, 44, 48, and, generally, 29–48 passim.

3. Martha Nussbaum, *The Fragility of Goodness* (Cambridge: Cambridge University Press, 1986), p. 305.

4. This entire paragraph is influenced, overall and especially in the next few sentences, by a very helpful conversation with Yael Tamir.

5. Any other reaction, any other mode of perception, might indeed reveal a lack of appropriate moral emotions. In the circumstances of the Middle East struggle, a certain amount of clan loyalty may be justifiable for both Jews and Arabs. So the question is not simply whether a moral agent will perceive *correctly* in these circumstances but whether correct perception is adequate to do the moral job.

6. He writes ("Virtue and Reason," p. 347): "[T]hough Plato's Forms are a myth, they are not a consolation . . . ; vision of them is portrayed as too difficult an attainment for that to be so. The remoteness of the Form of the Good is a metaphorical version of the thesis that value is not in the world. . . . The point of the metaphor is the colossal difficulty of attaining a capacity to cope clear-sightedly with the ethical reality which *is* part of our world. [T]his . . . may actually work towards moral improvement; . . . by inducing humility."

7. "Moral philosophy is properly, and in the past has sometimes been, the discussion of [the] ego and of the techniques (if any) for its defeat. . . . To say this is of course also to deny that moral philosophy should aim at being neutral" (Iris Murdoch, *The Sovereignty of Good* [London: Routledge, 1970], p. 52).

8. "Humility is a rare virtue and an unfashionable one and one which is often hard to discern. . . . In fact any other name for Good must be a partial name; but names of virtues suggest directions of thought, and this direction seems to me a better one than that suggested by more popular concepts such as freedom and courage. . . . [A]lthough [the humble man] is not by definition the good man, perhaps he is the kind of man who is most likely of all to become good" (ibid., p. 103).

9. I bring in Sellars here because McDowell's account of teaching or reshaping perception in his recent *Mind and World* (Cambridge: Harvard University Press, 1994) relies heavily on Sellars's essay, "Empiricism and the Philosophy of Mind," (in Herbert Feigl and Michael Scriven, eds., *Minnesota Studies in the Philosophy of Science*, vol. 1 [Minneapolis: University of Minnesota Press, 1956]). The tie example in the Sellars article is on pp. 270–5.

10. It is also unclear whether such presentations should generally be considered "appeals to reason" at all. To get others to see things as we want them to, notes Ronald de Sousa, we need to "seduce" them. Arguments between people whose perceptions are charged with differently configured emotions will be "virtually impossible to resolve" (De Sousa, "The Rationality of Emotions," in *Explaining Emotions*, ed. Amelie Rorty [Berkeley: University of California Press, 1980], p. 147; hence to persuade someone who differs from us in this way we need to make use of "what Plato both practised as 'dialectic' and condemned as 'rhetoric'" (De Sousa, *The Rationality of Emotion* [Cambridge: MIT Press, 1987], p. 257). The "real seducer, the successful emotional persuader. . . . will point to features [of a situation] that have already captured the imagination of the 'mark.' The vulgar lovers' argument says, 'Come into my play: let me audition you for this part.' But the real seducer says, 'I come to you from your own play. Look: here is your part'" (ibid., p. 258).   This sounds exactly right. But there is something dishonest, something manipulative about the "lovers' argument": De Sousa's description nicely conveys an appropriate moral ambiguity. Seducing is *not* an "appeal to reason"—at least not normally, and at least not if "reason" is to play anything like the role, morally and epistemically, that it usually does. McDowell makes the gap between seducing and arguing an unintuitively small one, urging us to collapse the sharing of perception too straightforwardly into a form of reasoning.

11. Ross's translation of this word is misleading. Nancy Sherman proposes "consideration" instead, although she also notes the relevance of this quality, for Aristotle, to what makes for a good (courtroom) judge (*Fabric*, p. 37 and note). Beiner identifies *gnome* with "judgment," in roughly the sense I am using the term, but its relationship to *suggnome* (sympathy) suggests that it is better understood as something like psychological "insight" (see Beiner, *Political Judgment*, p. 76). The English word "judgment," I think, both in its legal connotations and in the philosophical history of its usage since the eighteenth century, fits *phronesis* better than *gnome*. Cardinal Newman translates phronesis as "judgment" in *An Essay in Aid of a Grammar of Assent* (Oxford: Clarendon Press, 1985), pp. 228–30.

12. "For [Aristotle] the mark of practical thinking is that it is concerned with particulars, and that some of the premises in practical reasoning are premises about particulars. Premises about particulars have no role in theoretical reasoning on his account. It is as animals endowed with needs, desires, and the power of voluntary locomotion that we are alive to particular facts through sense perception. By nature animals perceive or otherwise apprehend pretty much what they need to in order to act so as to live and propagate. Thus, to be one who takes in the particulars of one's circumstances is already to be an agent or an incipient agent" (Sarah Broadie, "The Problem of Practical Intellect in Aristotle's Ethics,"

in *Proceedings of the Boston Area Colloquium in Classical Philosophy*, vol. 3 [1987]). See also Terence Irwin, *Aristotle's First Principles* (Oxford: Clarendon Press, 1988), pp. 118–20, 261–3.

13. Ross translation, p. 1032, with the last word altered: Ross translates it as "judges," but it is a form of *krisis*, which Nussbaum and Sherman take pains to render elsewhere as "discrimination" or "discernment" (Sherman, *Fabric*, pp. 13, 35 and Nussbaum, *Fragility*, p. 300).

14. *Pace* Ronald Beiner: "In short: phronesis minus praxis equals judgment. Phronesis is the union of good judgment and the action which is the fitting embodiment of that judgment" (*Political Judgment*, p. 75).

15. As translated in Nussbaum, *Fragility*, p. 300; cf. also 1126b1–5.

16. "[Aristotle] says that the standard of excellence is determined with reference to the decisions of the person of practical wisdom: what is appropriate in each case is what such a judge would select. And he says that the 'judgment' or 'discrimination' in ethical matters rests with, or is 'in', something which he calls perception (*aisthesis*)" (Nussbaum, *Fragility*, p. 300). Sherman, who follows Nussbaum in objecting to the standard translation of *krisis*, does distinguish between the "discrimination" discussed in this passage and the actual moment of taking a decision, but does not make entirely clear to what extent the fact that phronesis must make decisions differentiates it from discrimination (Sherman, *Fabric*, pp. 34ff, especially p. 36).

17. One motivation for the current rejection of principle-based accounts of morality is that there seems something both phenomenologically and logically wrong about supposing good moral decisions to be always, or indeed generally, deduced from a set of rules. Phenomenologically, good moral decisions tend to have a certain ineffable quality about them; more often than not, they reflect good character and produce good results without the agent's being able to say exactly how (s)he reached them. Logically, it is simply false that what we intuitively consider to be the right decision in many circumstances can be justified deductively from any antecedently given premises. And if one says, "so much the worse for our intuitions about 'right' decisions!", one gives up on the evidentiary base from which one's theory can be shown to be about morality. (These last two sentences are inspired by a slightly altered version of an argument presented by Gopal Sreenivasan in a Princeton seminar.) Hence something other than, or in addition to, rules must go into the way we make moral decisions.

It may seem to follow from this that perception, which simultaneously tracks particulars and eludes full conceptual grasp, is the appropriate supplement to rules. But while there is something ineffable, something "below" the reach of concepts, about perceptions, there is something equally nonconceptual, equally resistant to being captured by rules, about the process of rule-following itself. If interpretation is a negotiation between universals and particular details, and one, moreover, that may result in either a modification of the universal or a different way of perceiving the particular, then it cannot be determined in advance by any set of moral rules, categorically imperative or otherwise. No rule, as Wittgenstein showed us, can possibly tell us how to follow other rules. Nor can there be a general account, or concept, of rule-following. If there were, that account (call it "G") would be translatable into a rule ("Do G!") that we could then use when-

ever we wanted to follow a particular rule—and that is what we have just pre-
cluded.

18. This is part of what Kant means, I think, by calling its principle "heautonomous." Compare also Wittgenstein: "My judgments themselves characterize
the way I judge, characterize the nature of judgment" (*On Certainty*, § 149).

19. I discuss the historical influence of TMS and WN on Kant in, respectively,
"Philosophy and Moral Practice: Kant and Adam Smith," *Kant-Studien* (1991),
and "Values Behind the Market: Kant's Response to the *Wealth of Nations*," *History of Political Thought* (Autumn 1996).

20. Both of the last two quotations are from TMS VII.iv.33.

21. This contrasts also with the views of Smith's teacher Hutcheson, who declared that the "moral sense," or benevolence, "from its very nature appears to be
designed for regulating and controlling all our powers" (Hutcheson, *A System of
Moral Philosophy* [London: A. Millar, 1755], 1:61). Smith ridicules this view, saying that "the soft power of humanity," the "feeble spark of benevolence," is
incapable of controlling our self-love: only "reason, principle, conscience" can
suppress our other passions. Small wonder that Smith was Kant's favorite of the
British moral sentiment theorists!

22. For instance, III.6.13 or VI.ii.1.22. On the importance of theater to
Smith's moral theory, see Charles Griswold, *Adam Smith and the Virtues of Enlightenment* (Cambridge: Cambridge University Press, 1998), chapters 1 and 2.

23. "I speak of pity, a virtue . . . so natural that even beasts sometimes give
perceptible signs of it. . . . [O]ne observes daily the repugnance of horses to
trample a living body underfoot. An animal does not pass near a dead animal of
its species without uneasiness" (Rousseau, *The First and Second Discourses*, trans.
Roger and Judith Masters [New York: St. Martin's Press], p. 130).

24. Aristotle, NE 1147b21–4: "[T]hose who have just begun to learn a science can string together its phrases, but do not yet know it; for it has to become
part of themselves. . . . [T]he use of language by [such people] means no more
than its utterance by actors on the stage."

25. Barbara Herman, *The Practice of Moral Judgment* (Cambridge: Harvard
University Press, 1993), p. 77, my emphasis.

26. We should remember here that Kant tells us that he intends the *Groundwork* to aid people in the day-to-day struggle of moral practice (G 404–5/21–2)
and that the second *Critique* condemns alternative moral positions because they
fail to "humble my pride," to "morally educate the soul," to "strike down all
arrogance [and] vain self-love" (CPrR 77/80, 85/88, 86/88). Kant writes to
instill humility, and he praises duty primarily because, as Smith had pointed out, it
is a supremely humbling principle.

27. His analysis of reverence for the Categorical Imperative as the feeling that
defeats all other feelings exactly parallels Smith's talk of reverence for law as that
which best restrains selfish passions (TMS III.5.2, III.6.10). See G 400–1/68–9
and note thereto, and CPrR part 1, chapter 3.

28. CPR A 107. See also B 133 and A 381.

29. Smith here distinguishes himself both from Mandeville's identification of
virtue with hypocrisy (as Nicholas Phillipson incisively explains in "Politeness,
Sociability, and the Science of Man: Adam Smith in Context" [unpublished

manuscript]), and from the blind emotional determinism of Hume. The pleasure in praiseworthiness and displeasure in blameworthiness arise from the presence or absence of a rationally appropriate object—from whether, in truth, we *deserve* praise or not—rather than from a conditioned response to external stimuli.

30. Tolstoy, *Anna Karenina*, ed. George Gibian, trans. Louise and Aylmer Maude (New York: Norton, 1970), p. 11.

31. Benedict Anderson shows wonderfully how novels came to define unified communities in the early history of nationalism in *Imagined Communities* (London: Verso, 1983).

32. Herman, *Practice*, pp. 76-7, 83, 87-8.

33. The intuitions that provide the starting point for moral thinking are always culturally charged, in a way that purely empirical concepts need not be. The paradigm beginning point for empirical knowledge is a tree or a house or a dog, perceived simply as such, while the paradigm beginning point for moral knowledge is a situation that is already loaded with an evaluative interpretation. Our communities encourage us to understand the perceptions of our daily, common-sense world in a way that endorses our individual senses, that cuts beneath communally passed-down ways of ordering the world, and may be held relatively firmly against our neighbors' attempts to persuade us otherwise. Only thus can individuals find their own way to basic nutrition, hygiene, avoidance of accidents, etc., without being led everywhere by others. The biological imperatives here mean that practically every culture allows for some significant degree of individualism in sense-perception. For moral purposes, by contrast, communities characteristically present their young with paradigms packaged in a way that is aimed at *molding* their individual perceptions. If there is any point to ethical codes, they must be able to shape our desires; what we would be inclined to do without them must in some way not be good. If ethical codes mandated just what everyone would do regardless of upbringing, there would just be no ethics, no set of norms we could distinctively pick out from prudence. So an ethical particular, a bit of ethical given, is a situation that comes already loaded with a normative interpretation: "Grandma's so nice to give us a present; say 'thank you' like a polite child."

34. What we get if we take the CI together with empirical facts about ourselves, as animals with certain features and needs, will still at best radically underdetermine anything like the bulk of the choices that ought to follow from an adequate moral theory. Ignoring this underdetermination is just the great Enlightenment error: the error of supposing that morality, like science, might be read off straightforwardly from culturally, traditionally, and religiously unmediated experience. We can refuse this error and still be recognizably Kantian.

The model I have offered, in which interpretation rather than perception constitutes the proper moral way to grasp a particular in any case, is similar to Herman's talk of rules of moral salience (RMS) as informing "a characteristic way of seeing" (*Practice*, p. 83). But I would take Herman's own emphasis on the Fact of Reason more seriously than she herself does, to rule out any possibility of some cultures having members who simply "happen" not to see themselves as agents at all. The attempt she makes on p. 92 to condemn Nazism while remaining silent on Ilongot headhunting is wrongheaded. The Ilongot can't possibly be regarded as not conceiving of themselves as agents—on the empirical evidence of the book she cites, to say nothing of the Kantian requirement that we read awareness of agency into the reflections of any rational being. No human community, no community of beings that talk, can be regarded as innocent of morality.

At the same time, I want to build reference to *some* human ends, although not to any particular human ends, into the basic conditions Herman gives for RMS to count as such (pp. 86–7). This opens up precisely the arena in which cultural difference most strongly tends to arise. We (Western Enlightenment folk) differ with the Ilongot, as with fundamentalist Jews, Christians, and Muslims, over what truly goes into human nature and human ends, not over how each individual should and should not relate to the moral rules that may follow from the true answer to those questions. Kantian moral principles neither resolve nor ought to resolve these differences (although empirical data gathered under a Kantian conception of *science* may contribute to this resolution): they mandate only that, whatever view of human nature/human ends a culture maintains, it allows its members to come to that view, and either criticize/dissent from it or exit from the culture upon maturity, in a way that recognizably allows for autonomous choice.

35. Herman, *Practice*, pp. 86 and 90.

36. As do Winterbourne in Henry James's *Daisy Miller*, Tom Fowler in Graham Greene's *A Quiet American*, and E. M. Forster's Philip, in *Where Angels Fear to Tread*, who is berated for precisely this character trait: "Oh, what's the use of your fairmindedness if you never decide for yourself? . . . It's not enough to see clearly; I'm muddle-headed and stupid, and not worth a quarter of you, but I have tried to do what seemed right at the time. And you—your brain and your insight are splendid. But when you see what's right you're too idle to do it. You told me once that we shall be judged by our intentions, not by our accomplishments. I thought it a grand remark. But we must intend to accomplish—not sit intending on a chair." To which Philip responds: "Some people are born not to do things. I'm one of them. . . . I seem fated to pass through the world without colliding with it or moving it. . . . I don't die—I don't fall in love. . . . You are quite right; life to me is just a spectacle" (*Where Angels Fear to Tread* [London: Edward Arnold, 1947], pp. 167–8).

37. Lawrence Blum, *Moral Perception and Particularity* (Cambridge: Cambridge University Press, 1994), pp. 36, 42, 58–9.

38. For instance, NE 1140b15–20, 1172a20–25, 1175a29–37, 1179b20–1180a24.

CHAPTER 4
JUDGMENT AND FREEDOM

1. Neiman explains and defends this throughout her *The Unity of Reason* (New York: Oxford University Press, 1994). See also Richard Velkley's *Freedom and the End of Reason* (Chicago: University of Chicago Press, 1989); and, for the relevance of teleology to Kant's moral concerns especially, Patrick Riley, *Kant's Political Philosophy* (Totowa, N.J.: Rowman and Littlefield, 1983).

2. I am indebted to Béatrice Longuenesse for an explanation of how judgment increasingly comes to take over some of the functions attributed to reason in the

first *Critique*. See also Hans Saner, *Kant's Political Philosophy*, trans. E. B. Ashton (Chicago: University of Chicago Press, 1973), pp. 92f.

3. The connection between judgment and purposiveness in CJ is so strong that one might think judgment is supposed to teach us what it is for anything to be a purpose at all. In fact, however, Kant calls the principle with which judgment is identified "the purposiveness *of nature* in its variety" (CJ 180/17), and generally takes care to bind the purposiveness of judgment strictly to empirical objects, rather than to suggest that we learn from judgment what "purpose" means in general. I made this mistake until corrected by Hilary Bok: to whom many thanks for the relevant clarification, which informs this whole section.

4. One of the things entailed by the priority of systematicity over actual system is that any given piece of empirical system we construct, any given set of general concepts and hierarchy among them, is always open to the possibility that a piece beyond that one, a better view of or approximation to the infinite system that might absolutely be there, will show that our piece is radically incorrect, that we need to redo the hierarchy or reinterpret the general terms. Placing systematicity before system promotes scientific *criticism*.

This offers a clue to how we may put Kant's view of science together with more modern views. Kant undoubtedly has Linnaeus in mind when he describes empirical science as a matter of fitting species under genera. This makes science too classificatory rather than explanatory an enterprise, and suggests that in principle we could bring all phenomena under one large hierarchical tree, branching out neatly from a single concept at its top. Few scientists or philosophers of science would accept such a view today. Rather, they see science as primarily explanatory, and measure their higher-order laws and concepts not by yet higher-order "genera" but by canons of scientific theory-building like simplicity, consistency, explanatory power, and fertility, which are criteria for but not themselves part of the general terms and modes of explanation under which particulars are brought. But Kant is not so distant from all this. In the first place, he does not separate classification from explanation: for our understanding to find a "comprehensible order" in nature is for it "to divide its products into genera and species, so as to use the principles which explain and make intelligible one [thing] *for the explanation and comprehension* of another" (185/22, my emphasis). In the same passage, and elsewhere, Kant moves easily between talk about bringing species under genera and talk about unifying empirical *laws* (e.g., 180, 185/16, 24). Nothing he says denies that a theory, even in biology or chemistry (which Kant regarded as incapable of being pure sciences like physics), is a comprehensive set of laws explaining particular phenomena rather than a mere taxonomy of those phenomena under general headings. His point is merely that classification is preparatory to, perhaps even coeval with, explanation, and this is surely right. We cannot explain anything except by reference to general groupings of particulars and principles by which the particulars can be recognized as similar. Furthermore, the notion of general canons of science, outside of and helping us to evaluate the particular systems or hierarchies we construct, has an explicit place in Kant's account: he cites simplicity and continuity as "maxims of the judgment" which "present themselves in the course of . . . science often enough" (182/18). Most deeply and importantly, the fact that Kant denies us knowledge of what the final cause of nature or any natural object actually is, that what he wants from the distinction between genera and species is only the ability "to use the principles which explain and make intelligible one [thing] for the explanation and comprehension of another," that he sees judgment as discovering only "that two or more empirical heterogeneous laws of nature may be combined under one principle comprehending them both" (187–8/24), means that in practice he demands only the *possibility* of ordering phenomena, and not any specific order of them.

We might want to push these ideas in Kant against his Linnaean tendencies by moving from the notion that the sciences might one day be reducible to a single theory—history and economics to psychology, psychology to biology, biology to chemistry, chemistry to physics—towards a view of many different fields of explanation, each with its own canons, general concepts, and ways of looking at the particular data, sometimes intersecting, sometimes unifiable in this or that respect, but at least at the moment and perhaps permanently incommensurable. No full account of biology can be given from the physicist's perspective, just as no full history of physics will explain physical laws. The canons of explanation for solving a murder mystery are different from those accounting for an economic trend, although simplicity will be a virtue of both and the canons for the first in the realm of fiction will be related to those by which murders in the real world are detected. No overall picture of explanation emerges from all this, and no overall picture of explanation is necessary to understand that explanation, in every field, requires systematicity and canons of evidence. What Kant allows us is precisely the possibility of partial explanation: good theories must maneuver between particulars and generalities according to certain criteria, but they do not need to meet any single criterion, and we have access to no single, absolute account against which they might be measured.

5. Wittgenstein, *On Certainty*, §§ 140, 149.

6. Another way to put this problem is to note the oddity of supposing that aesthetic (as opposed to teleological) judgment could teach us anything about *objective* purposiveness, rather than only about our own purposes. Yet Kant says: "In a critique of judgment the part containing the aesthetical judgment is essential, because this alone contains a principle which the judgment places quite *a priori* at the basis of its reflection upon nature, viz. the principle of a formal purposiveness of nature, . . . without which the understanding could not find itself in nature" (CJ 193/30). The way objects universally or necessarily satisfy our feeling of pleasure and pain in beauty is a model for purposiveness, for how anything can be said to have a purpose in general.

7. Anthony Savile, *Kantian Aesthetics Pursued* (Edinburgh: Edinburgh University Press, 1993), pp. 57, 60. He notes, before saying this, that "although the text does indeed speak of the supersensible substrate of phenomena (at §§ 57.4 and 57.7), . . . it is notable that, as Kant goes on, his predominant way of speaking of the supersensible is as that *in us*, or as the supersensible substrate of *humanity*" (§§ 57.5 and 57.8). See also the whole of chapters 3 and 5.

8. The details of this view are rarely examined closely enough. Kant says that "Nature is beautiful *because it looks like art*; and art can only be called beautiful if we are conscious of it as art while yet it looks like nature" (my emphasis). And the natural beauties he finds especially important are those in which nature "speaks to

us" (301/143; cf. 302/144, on lilies and colors), those which an artist might well be tempted to imitate but which are beautiful only so long as "the thought . . . that nature has produced it" can legitimately accompany our reflections. At the same time, art is beautiful only when produced by a kind of natural force: "genius," the means by which "nature gives the rule" to the artist (307/150). I suggest that the priority of our interest in the beauty of nature signifies nothing more than that we must recognize beauty as out of our control, beyond us, given, rather than something we merely decree or construct. We need to find the possibility of order "out there," and to be responsive and responsible to it, not to withdraw into the solipsism of assuming that all order is merely projected by us. Solipsism of that kind breeds irrationality in epistemology and nihilism or utter selfishness in morals. Once we recognize beauty as representing something "out there" to which we respond, we may indeed attribute a special importance to the beauty that we find in nature. At the same time, we need not diminish—as Kant himself does not diminish—the importance of the beauty in art. We must simply view works of art *as if they themselves were products of nature*: as products of "genius."

9. The pleasure in natural beauty does not after all encourage any other activity just as well: it doesn't particularly encourage me to play a boom-box, read the day's newspaper, eat a piece of chocolate cake. Such activities seem irrelevant to natural beauty, even offensive to it, while thinking about the order of the world, about how to make sense of certain data, or how to conclude a moral argument, seems an appropriate *continuation* of the pleasure in the beauty itself.

10. The importance of literature to the moral imagination is a central theme in much of both Iris Murdoch's and Martha Nussbaum's work. See especially the latter's *Love's Knowledge: Essays on Philosophy and Literature* (New York: Oxford University Press, 1990). A wonderfully imaginative account of the importance of the imagination—imagination in storytelling in particular—is to be found in Salman Rushdie's *Haroun and the Sea of Stories* (New York: Penguin, 1990).

11. The example comes from Clifford Geertz's nuanced account of incommensurability and related problems in chapter 8 of *Local Knowledge* (New York: Basic Books, 1983). See especially pp. 195–207.

12. Bjørn Ramberg explains incommensurability as a way of describing the relationship between *speakers* at a certain time, rather than a relationship of "meanings" themselves: "Incommensurability is a disruption in the conventional *production* of meaning, not a disintegration of meaning. . . . [It] is a diachronic relation, not a synchronic one; it is not a relation between [linguistic] structures, but a symptom of structural change" (*Donald Davidson's Philosophy of Language*, [Oxford: Basil Blackwell, 1989], pp. 130–1). Ramberg uses this account to explain both scientific paradigm change and encounters between radically different cultures, noting—helpfully, for my purposes—that "phronesis" is the faculty essential to getting through such structural changes (128–9). A diachronic, and provisional, notion of incommensurability along these lines has been proposed by a number of people today, and is, to my mind, the only understanding of that notion that makes good sense of it. See Alasdair MacIntyre, "Tradition and Translation," chapter 19 of *Whose Justice? Which Rationality* (Notre Dame: University of Notre Dame Press, 1988); Elijah Millgram, "Incommensurability and

Practical Reasoning" in *Incommensurability, Incomparability, and Practical Reasoning*, ed. Ruth Chang (Cambridge: Harvard University Press, 1997); and chapter 6 of my *The Ethics of Culture* (Ithaca: Cornell University Press, 1994).

13. Hegel is practically the only philosopher to have fully recognized this and stated it frankly, but to his methodology contradictions were all too welcome, and he overcame them all too easily. I do not say that judgment *solves* the antinomy between empirical and transcendental freedom, resolves them into some new, single entity, only that it reduces the difference between the two.

14. This example, and many of the other reflections in this paragraph, are inspired by Juliet Floyd, "Heautonomy: Kant on Reflective Judgment and Systematicity," in Herman Parret, ed., *Kants Ästhetik/Kant's Aesthetics/L'Esthétique de Kant* (Berlin and New York: Walter de Gruyter & Co., forthcoming).

15. This allows for what Charles Taylor calls "strong evaluation" ("What is Human Agency," in *Human Agency and Language* [Cambridge: Cambridge University Press, 1985]; and "What's Wrong with Negative Liberty," in *Philosophy and the Human Sciences* [Cambridge: Cambridge University Press, 1985]). Taylor objects to Harry Frankfurt's model of how we evaluate ourselves because he thinks it is too dependent on internal coherence, does not say enough about how we might decide that one of our ends, even if it coheres with the others, is simply *wrong*. But Taylor has to introduce notions about what is essential to human nature in order to make room for such strong claims. With the notion of purposiveness without purpose in hand, we can open our self-evaluation to the rejection of any end or set of ends without buying any such metaphysical views. We can judge one sphere of ends simply against another such sphere, while abstracting from the question of what our "ultimate" ends might be. I might judge my career ends to be bad from a medical or a political point of view, or judge my political activities or health obsessions to be bad for my career. The networking of judgments allows me to deliberate over ends without assuming the existence of either an "authentic" self or some ultimate ideal to which all human beings should attain.

16. Wittgenstein, *Philosophical Investigations*, p. 227:

Is there such a thing as 'expert judgment' . . . ? —Even here, there are those whose judgment is 'better' and those whose judgment is 'worse.' . . .

Can one learn this knowledge? Yes, some can. Not, however, by taking a course in it, but through '*experience*.'—Can someone else be a man's teacher in this? Certainly. From time to time he gives him the right *tip*.

CHAPTER 5
PROPER PLEASURES

1. Much of what I am about to say is an extension of Aristotle, NE Book 10, chapters 1–6; and Alasdair MacIntyre's use of those ideas to characterize "internal" and "external" goods, in *After Virtue* (Notre Dame: University of Notre Dame Press, 1984), pp. 188–93. The best account I have ever seen of the cognitive aspects of pleasure and pain—again an Aristotelian one but developed, entirely without textual commentary, in the most rigorous analytic terms—is Elijah

Millgram's "How to Keep Pleasure in Mind," in *Practical Induction* (Cambridge: Harvard University Press, 1997).

2. The entire doctrine of the mean, and repeated concern to give a nuanced account of pleasure (in NE, Books I, III, VII, and X) can be seen as serving the overall end of preserving our phronesis—our ability to judge being the essence of our ability to choose, hence the hinge on which all other virtue turns. If this is indeed the organizing principle of Aristotle's ethics, his affinities with Kant are strong. For rich discussions of the relationships between Kant and Aristotle, see Christine Korsgaard, "From Duty and for the Sake of the Noble: Kant and Aristotle on Morally Good Action," and Barbara Herman, "Making Room for Character," in *Aristotle, Kant, and the Stoics*, ed. S. Engstrom and J. Whiting (Cambridge: Cambridge University Press, 1996).

3. The need for temporally limited goals arises not merely because of the approach of death but because of our aging (I am indebted to Jacob Meskin for bringing out the importance of aging to me). The Heideggerian view of human temporality is simplistic, I now believe. Were we, like most animals, to remain roughly the same in characteristics and abilities from the age of two or three until we died, we might well feel no more immediate pressure from time than a sheep or a cow seems to do. The fact that we need in our early years to acquire a large number of physical and mental skills, bear and raise children during a fairly limited period after that, and start losing health and strength long before we are finished with the child-rearing, imposes severe constraints on how much time we have for what we see as our ethical tasks. Practically all cultures—but few ethical philosophies—implicitly recognize these limitations in the way they structure the duties and expectations they impose upon their members.

4. In any case most fantasies have an urge to realization built into them that makes them less than what they purport to be so long as they remain *mere* fantasies.

5. *This* is the ultimate failure of stoicism. I cannot even keep willing if the world thwarts me at every turn. In a peculiar way, the stoic sees my will as too powerful. *Pace* the stoic, I lack the power to will that I might be satisfied with willing alone.

6. See Arendt, *Lectures on Kant's Political Philosophy*, ed. Ronald Beiner (Chicago: University of Chicago Press, 1982); and "The Crisis in Culture," in her collection, *Between Past and Future*, 2d ed. (Harmondsworth, U.K.: Penguin, 1968). Arendt's account of judgment is said to have influenced Jürgen Habermas's theory of communication and politics, and in recent years it has been very important to the work of Ronald Beiner, Seyla Ben Habib, and Richard Bernstein, among others.

7. Who would, I submit, have been an important source for Arendt herself had she known the *Theory of Moral Sentiments*. While Arendt comments thoughtfully on Smith's notion of labor in *The Human Condition*, and occasionally mentions other aspects of the *Wealth of Nations*, she never refers to TMS.

8. "Politeness, Sociability, and the Science of Man": see chapter 3 above, note 29.

9. The subtleties are thickly massed here. Although independent of the actual opinion of other members of our society on each occasion of its use, the standard for virtue remains something constituted by the *general standards* of excellence

abroad in our society. "The love and admiration which we naturally conceive for those whose character and conduct we approve of, necessarily dispose us to desire to become ourselves the objects of the like agreeable sentiments, and to be as amiable and as admirable as those whom we love and admire the most. Emulation, the anxious desire that we ourselves should excel, is originally founded in our admiration of the excellence of others" (TMS III.2.2). So the standard for virtue is essentially relative to a society—to that society, for each of us, in which we first come to see behavior to emulate, characters to admire. But at that initial point we desire "being merely admired for what other people are admired. We must at least believe ourselves to be admirable for what they are admirable." A counterfactual—*if* others saw us in the proper light, they *would* admire us—later takes the place of a straightforward factual condition—others admire us—as the proper test for determining the presence or absence of the object at which our desire for virtue aims. With that counterfactual we move inward, to the "impartial spectator" within our breasts as the prime judge of our conduct instead of our actual neighbors. So on particular occasions of use we treat virtue exactly as we treat factual matters, as something whose presence or absence is not constituted by what people say or think, but behind each of those particular occasions lies a standard that is, in general, dependent on how our society evaluates conduct.

10. Compare Jon Elster, on the irrationality of direct attempts to raise one's self-respect: *Sour Grapes: Studies in the Subversion of Rationality* (Paris: Maison de Science de l'Hommes, and Cambridge: Cambridge University Press, 1983), pp. 44, 99–100.

11. See J. G. A. Pocock, *The Machiavellian Moment* (Princeton: Princeton University Press, 1975).

12. Pocock suggests the influence of Machiavelli on Marxism (ibid., pp. 461, 505, 551), but does not develop this suggestion. Jeff Weintraub, in his independent study of the same civic republican tradition, develops Marx's use of that tradition in *Freedom and Community* (Berkeley: University of California Press, forthcoming).

13. When the *Politics* is taken together with the *Ethics*, as it should be.

14. I discuss WN V.i.g, and the need for liberalism to foster such small-scale communities, in "Insignificant Communities," in *Freedom of Association*, ed. Amy Gutmann (Princeton: Princeton University Press, 1998).

15. Marx, *Capital*, volume 1, chapter 14, section 5.

16. On the idea and its disappearance from political agendas, over the past quarter century, see Juliet Schor, *The Overworked American* (New York: Basic Books, 1991).

17. J. S. Mill, *Utilitarianism*, chapter 2; and *Principles of Political Economy*, ed. W. J. Ashley (New York: Longmans, Green, & Co., 1909), Book 5, ch. 11, §§ 8, 15.

18. Mill, *Principles*, Book 5, chapter 11, § 8.

19. Alfred Marshall, *Principles of Economics* (London: Macmillan, 1936), VI.xiii.1–3, 15. See also III.ii.4, III.iii.2; and Mill, *Principles*, § 12.

20. The early writings of Paul Samuelson, Kenneth Arrow, and Milton Friedman agree entirely on this—a fact for which their education in a positivist philosophical milieu is surely responsible.

21. Steven Gerrard works out this reconstruction in nice detail in "Desire and Desirability: Bradley, Russell and Moore versus Mill," in *Early Analytic Philosophy: Frege, Russell, Wittgenstein*, ed. William W. Tait (Chicago: Open Court, 1997). See also Mill, *Principles*, Book 5, chapter 11, §§ 6, 8–10.

22. Mill, *Utilitarianism*, ch. 2, ¶ 12, 13; *On Liberty*, ch. 4, ¶ 1–5; *Principles of Political Economy*, Book 5, chapter 11, §§ 6, 8. Compare also Marshall, III.ii.4: "[A]lthough it is man's wants in the earliest stages of his development that give rise to his activities, yet afterwards each new step upwards is to be regarded as the development of new activities giving rise to new wants, rather than of new wants giving rise to new activities" (p. 89).

22. "Tradeoff" is standard economists' language, especially when talking about the supposed choice, by American workers at least, to reduce their own leisure time; see Schor, *The Overworked American*, for a critical approach that tracks the standard discussions very well.

CHAPTER 6
THE *WEALTH OF NATIONS* (I): JUDGMENT

1. On Kant's admiration for Smith, see my "Values Behind the Market," cited above in chapter 3, note 19. On Smith's importance to Condorcet and Tom Paine, see Emma Rothschild, "Adam Smith and Conservative Economics," *The Economic History Review*, vol. 45, no. 1 (Feb. 1992). On Sieyès, see Ian Simpson Ross, *The Life of Adam Smith* (Oxford: Clarendon, 1995), p. 390. And on the Americans' admiration for WN, see Jefferson's letters to Thomas Mann Randolph and John Garland Jefferson, of late May and early June, 1790, Madison's 1783 list of books for the proposed Library of Congress, and, especially, his speech to Congress on April 9, 1789. Smith's influence on Pitt and Dundas is well known.

2. Hume also believed that self-interest was a less dangerous passion than many others (unselfish religious or political fanaticism, for instance, or the passion for revenge), as Stephen Holmes demonstrates in his "Secret History of Self-Interest," in *Passions and Constraint* (Chicago: University of Chicago Press, 1995). But this nuance will not affect my overall argument.

3. Hutcheson, *System*, 1:296.

4. For example, in *System*, 1:29, 121.

5. Ibid., pp. 31–2, 59–61, 121–2, 133.

6. Hutcheson, *A Short Introduction to Moral Philosophy* (Glasgow: R. Foulis, 1747), pp. 62–8; *System*, 1:160–8, 2:317–8.

7. Hume, *Enquiry Concerning Human Understanding*, chapter 1.

8. James Tully, introduction to *On the Duty of Man and Citizen*, by Samuel Pufendorf, trans. Michael Silverthorne (Cambridge: Cambridge University Press, 1991), p. xvii; see also p. xix. Perhaps the most obvious way this comes out in Pufendorf's thinking is the fact that he gives a Hobbesian derivation of the human tendency to live in organized societies from the need to avoid war rather than taking that tendency, as Aristotle had, to be an essential feature of human nature (see, for instance, Pufendorf, Book 2, chapter 5, § 2). Pufendorf matters here because he is an extremely important influence on Hutcheson, and, through him, on Smith.

9. Vico might be an exception to this generalization.

10. There is a wonderful discussion of this in Garry Wills, *Inventing America* (New York: Vintage Books, 1978), chapter 10.

11. William Wollaston, *Religion of Nature Delineated*, in vol. 1 of *British Moralists, 1650–1800*, ed. D. D. Raphael (Indianapolis: Hackett, 1991), § 297. See also §§ 295–8.

12. Knud Haakonssen, *The Science of a Legislator* (Cambridge: Cambridge University. Press, 1981), pp. 79–82.

13. The argument of the work is indeed largely *built* out of these historical investigations: "He appears to be engaged in composing not a theory, but a history of national wealth. He dwells indeed on principles, but nearly always . . . for the purpose of explaining the facts which he narrates" (E. G. Wakefield, quoted in Frances Hirst, *Adam Smith* [New York: MacMillan, 1904], pp. 166–7). I would say not so much that the *purpose* of the principles is to explain the facts, as that the ability of the principles to explain the facts is meant to be their proof.

14. Arguments for this claim about the social sciences go back as far as Dilthey. Prominent advocates of it today, almost all of whom are seen as Aristotelians of some kind, include Hans-Georg Gadamer, Charles Taylor, Alasdair MacIntyre, Michael Walzer, and Clifford Geertz. For a lucid exposition of the issues, see Taylor, "Interpretation and the Sciences of Man," in *Philosophy and the Human Sciences*.

15. Wills, *Inventing America*, p. 278.

16. John Locke, *Essay Concerning Human Understanding*, ed. A. C. Fraser (Oxford: Clarendon, 1894), IV.xiv.3.

17. Locke, *Second Treatise of Government*, ed. Peter Laslett (Cambridge: Cambridge University Press, 1988), §§ 240–1. Compare also §§ 21, 242.

18. Hume, *Treatise of Human Nature*, 2d ed., ed. L. A. Selby-Bigge and P. H. Nidditch (Oxford: Clarendon Press, 1978). I.iii.7, p. 96n.

19. See, respectively, *Treatise* pp. 108 and 112 (in I.iii.8), 456 (but cf. 470), and 459–61. All the latter citations are from III.i.1.

20. Ibid., p. 470.

21. Thomas Reid, "Essays on the Active Powers of Man," in *British Moralists 1650–1800*, ed. D. D. Raphael (Indianapolis: Hackett, 1991), § 858. Further references to Reid will be incorporated into the text, with section numbers referring to this volume.

22. Ibid., § 878.

23. *System*, 1:294, my emphasis.

24. I take the connection of commerce to speech in Hutcheson to be implied by the placement of the chapter on commerce in the *System*: between two chapters on the duties of speech and contract (see *System*, Book 2, chapters 10–13). The connection is explicit in Smith: see *Lectures on Jurisprudence* (LJ), pp. 352–3 ("If we should enquire into the principle in the human mind on which this disposition of trucking is founded, it is clearly the naturall inclination every one has to persuade" [LJ (A) vi.56]), 493–4, and WN I.ii.2.

25. Hutcheson, *Inquiry Concerning Moral Good and Evil* (London: J. Darby, 1726), § 3, ¶ 8. Hutcheson is said to have invented this phrase. See Wills, *Inventing America*, p. 150; and Raphael, *British Moralists*, p. 284, note 1.

26. And it is a somewhat different moral sense: "sympathy" rather than "benevolence."

27. See Griswold, *Adam Smith*, chapters 5.e, 6.b, and especially 7.a, on the importance of such "irregularities" in Smith's moral theory.

28. On judgment as what the "impartial spectator" does, see, e.g., I.iii (chapter title), III (chapter title), III.2.31, and III.iv. On the impartial spectator *as* a judge, see II.ii.2.4, III.1.2, III.1.6 and the whole long passage cut from edition 6 that Raphael and Macfie place in a footnote on pp. 128–30.

29. A more or less complete list: intro.3, I.i.3, I.v.40, I.v.42, I.vii.11, I.viii.19, I.ix.3, I.x.c.12, I.x.c.24, I.xi.n.10 (twice), I.xi.p.9, I.xi.p.10, II.ii.62, II.iii.32, III.iv.10, IV.i.10, IV.ii.10, IV.ii.39, IV.iii.a.9, IV.iii.c.11, IV.v.b.3, IV.v.b.4, IV.v.b.16, IV.v.b.25 (twice), IV.vi.32, IV.vii.a.19, IV.vii.b.44, IV.vii.c.70 (three times), IV.vii.c.71, V.i.e.30, V.i.f.9, V.i.f.26, V.i.f.47, V.i.f.50 (twice), V.i.f.51, V.i.f.61, V.ii.c.18, V.ii.e.5 (twice).

30. Thus the increased "dexterity" that the division of labor brings to workers is made to look, in its initial appearance, almost machinelike, and on each of the two subsequent occasions on which he explicitly compares industrial workers to machines, the word "dexterity" is again used to designate the machinelike quality about them (see I.i.6 and I.x.b.6.). Similarly, "toil and trouble" are given an almost technical sense distinguishing them from such more positive aspects of labor as "skill," "dexterity," or "industry" (see I.v.2).

31. Any reader who has waded through the tiresome repetitions of the phrase, "the ____, or what comes to the same thing, the price of the ____ ," will know exactly what I mean.

32. 1. "ascertain": I.iv.8, I.viii.34, and I.ix.3.
    2. "rate," "value," and "consider": I.v.29, 34, 37, I.x.b.8, 27–8, I.xi.n.1.

33. WN I.viii.23, I.viii.34, I.x.b.28, I.xi.g.10, IV.v.b.30. It is worth noting that Smith rarely mentions mathematics in WN without adding some at least mildly acidic comment about doubting the value of calculations for political economy. Smith is clearly more a founder of a historical or narrative conception of social science than of those paradigms, especially in economics, that treat the human sciences as if they were like physics.

34. By Smith or someone else: I.viii.34, 50, I.xi.n.7; I.viii.34 makes clear that this sort of evidence is also what Smith means by "proof," as does I.xi.n.1.

35. 1. "appears evidently": I.v.17 and I.viii.31.
    2. "is found by experience": I.v.41, I.xi.b.26.
    3. "suppose" and "apprehend": I.v.12, I.viii.4, I.ix.9, I.xi.b.26, II.iv.10.

36. Smith practically always uses these terms to describe people who believe something that is in fact wrong: "The over-weening conceit which the greater part of man have of their own abilities, is an antient evil remarked by the philosophers and moralists of all ages. Their absurd *presumption* in their own good fortune, has been less taken notice of" (I.x.b.26). Or: "Oatmeal indeed supplies the common people in Scotland with the greatest and best part of their food, which is in general much inferior to that of their neighbours of the same rank in England. This difference, however, in the mode of their subsistence is not the cause, but

the effect of the difference in their wages; though, by a strange misapprehension, I have frequently heard it *represented* as the cause" (I.viii.33. See also I.v.11, I.x.b.30, II.iv.9, III.ii.16, IV.ii.10, and IV.ix.28.).

37. The lone exceptions are I.vii.11 and V.ii.g.7.

38. Stated at IV.iii.a.4, implied at IV.iii.c.10 and IV.v.b.23–6.

39. One might object, recalling Smith's *Theory of Moral Sentiments*, that an impartial spectator can always judge a situation better than the (necessarily partial) agents immersed in that situation. But, in the first place, Smith makes clear in TMS that the impartial spectator judges better than the "person principally concerned" when and only when he or she observes precisely that situation in which the person principally concerned acts (or is acted upon), and there will normally not be such a spectacularly well-located spectator for each of the situations in which we act: certainly, no "expert" or government official, generalizing from far away, can count as such a spectator. And in the second place, the impartial spectator is ultimately something Smith expects us each to build into ourselves; so it remains true, of a person who has been socialized sufficiently to "watch" herself even as she acts, that she will be better able to judge her own acts than anyone else will.

40. See *Republic* 369e–370c: Each person is naturally fitted for one task, says Socrates, and this principle ultimately governs his entire account of justice (cf. 433a–434c, 441e, and 443c–d).

41. I am grateful to Jeff Weintraub for pointing out the second of these features to me.

42. This turns out to be one of the most problematic spots in Smith's entire analysis, but the mere fact that he tries to make such a claim suggests that he is trying to read the two-sided structure of judgment into the prime engine of his economic theory.

43. For the craft analogy see *NE* III.3, but contrast VI.4–5. Sarah Broadie and John McDowell discuss the role of this analogy interestingly in Broadie, *Ethics With Aristotle*, chapter 4, pp. 181–98, and McDowell, "Deliberation and Moral Development in Aristotle's Ethics," *Aristotle, Kant, and the Stoics*, ed. Stephen Engstrom and Jennifer Whiting (Cambridge: Cambridge University Press, 1996). On *deinotes* see NE 1144a25–35.

44. See Alasdair MacIntyre, *Whose Justice? Which Rationality?*; and Douglas J. Den Uyl, *The Virtue of Prudence* (New York: Peter Lang, 1991).

45. Compare WN IV.ii.39: "To judge whether such retaliations are likely to produce such an effect does not, perhaps, belong so much to the science of a legislator, whose deliberations ought to be governed by general principles which are always the same, as to the skill of that insidious and crafty animal, vulgarly called a statesman or politician, whose councils are directed by the momentary fluctuations of affairs."

46. See, for example, WN II.v.7; III.ii.21; IV.iii.a.1, 4; IV.iii.c.2; IV.v.a.20, 25; IV.v.b.23, 40, 53; IV.vi.32, IV.vii.a.19, IV.vii.b.59.

47. Joseph Schumpeter, *History of Economic Analysis*, ed. E. B. Schumpeter (New York: Oxford University Press, 1954), p. 184.

48. Quoted in Frances Hirst, *Adam Smith*, p. 165. Here is a sample of other

reactions to *WN* by Smith's contemporaries, all of which emphasize Smith's skills in explication and narrative above the novelty of his ideas:

> I Cannot forbear writing to you to Congratulate you upon your Book. . . . One writer after another on these Subjects did nothing but puzzle me. I despaired of ever arriving at clear Ideas. You have given me full and Compleat Satisfaction. . . . Nothing was ever better suited than your Style is to the Subject; clear and distinct to the last degree, full without being too much so, and as tercly as the Subject could admit. Dry as some of the Subjects are, It carried me along. I read the whole with avidity; and have pleasure in thinking that I shall within some short time give it a Second and more deliberate perusal. (Hugh Blair, letter to Smith, 3 April 1776 [Corr 187–8])

> [T]he world has seen no more important book than that of Adam Smith. . . . [C]ertainly since the times of the New Testament no writing has had more beneficial results than this will have. . . . [Smith's doctrines form] the only true, great, beautiful, just and beneficial system. (Christian Jacob Kraus, professor of political economy in Königsberg, quoted in Carl William Hasek, *The Introduction of Adam Smith's Doctrines into Germany* [New York: Columbia University Press, 1925], pp. 86–7)

> I owe to a journey I made with Mr. Smith from Edinburgh to London the difference between light and darkness through the best part of my life. The novelty of his principles, added to my youth and prejudices, made me unable to comprehend them at the time, but he urged them with so much benevolence, as well as eloquence, that they took a certain hold, . . . though it did not develop itself so as to arrive at full conviction for some few years after. (Lord Shelburne, quoted in Kirk Willis, "Ideas of Smith in Parliament," *History of Political Economy* 11 [1979], p. 529)

> [T]he author of the "Nature and Causes of the Wealth of Nations" has so clearly refuted all the gross and vulgar ideas upon [the supposed advantage of hoarding gold and silver, that] it cannot be necessary to say much upon it. . . . Dr. Smith, . . . it was well said, would persuade the present generation, and govern the next. (Sir William Johnstone-Pulteney, in Parliamentary debates of 1797, quoted in Willis, *Ideas*, p. 511)

49. Which mostly means laws getting rid of other laws that restrict trade—but the laws that ended the fears of witchcraft were also laws that undid other laws.

50. See, for instance, I.x.a.1, II.iii.19, V.i.a.14. In each case the argument depends on whose knowledge is likely to lead to the best economic decision (about the division of labor, about saving, about consumption, or whatever). That all candidates for making the decision—rich and poor, aristocrats, merchants and day laborers, private people and agents of the state—are motivated by their own interests is taken for granted, not stated. The controversial point, the one Smith argues for, is that the private person, even the private poor person, *knows what to do* to serve his or her interests, and thereby society at large, better than anybody else. Note that in the last passage cited, Smith argues that the state must provide

the economic basis for the military but takes pains to emphasize that this is primarily because the state is the only body with the capacity for the "wisdom" to make the relevant decisions, not because those decisions are in the state's *interest*. Interest alone is insufficient here.

51. Bernard Bailyn, *The Origins of American Politics* (New York: Vintage, 1968), p. 41.

52. Quoted in Hirst, *Adam Smith*, p. 143.

CHAPTER 7

THE *WEALTH OF NATIONS* II: VIRTUE AND INDEPENDENCE

1. Hutcheson, *System*, 1:25–7, 131–5, together with 53–5.

2. Ibid., p. 26, emphasis added.

3. "Every man, as the Stoics used to say, is first and principally recommended to his own care" (VI.ii.1.1). Smith attributes the notion that we need to care for ourselves to the Stoics and endorses both their claim that this is natural and their understanding of virtue as a fitting-in with nature. He criticizes the Stoics themselves, on the other hand, for not living up to this understanding in their endorsement of suicide and their rejection of all particularist passions and sympathies (VII.ii.1.47).

4. Smith calls Rousseau's *Second Discourse* an extension of Mandeville (Letter, pp. 250–1).

5. Hutcheson, *System*, 1:93–4.

6. Ibid., 2:105.

7. Ibid., 2:105–16.

8. "The moral primacy of individuals for which Smith argues here is a basic feature of his moral philosophy, which is often reflected in his language," Knud Haakonssen, *The Science of a Legislator* (Cambridge: Cambridge University Press, 1981), pp. 88–9.

9. Smith gives an elaborate and sympathetic account of classical doctrines in favor of suicide at TMS VII.ii.1.25–33, although he ultimately rejects those doctrines. "Nature in her sound and healthful state," he says, "seems never to prompt us to suicide" (VII.ii.1.34). Nor does the impartial spectator approve of suicide. At the same time, Smith regards attempts to punish suicide as "absurd" and "unjust," and says that suicides are the proper object of "commiseration" rather than "censure" (ibid.). All this is very far from regarding suicide as a violation of duty, a betrayal of the rights of humanity.

10. Charles Griswold and Douglas Den Uyl, "Smith on Friendship and Love," *Review of Metaphysics* 49 (March 1996), p. 616.

11. Smith seems increasingly to be a deist rather than a theist (certainly to be less and less a *Christian*), and his deism increasingly becomes a foreshadowing of Kant's: a matter of a morally necessary posit, rather than a metaphysical system or a guide to empirical reality. That, at least, is one way of explaining why in the last edition of TMS he suppressed the passage on atonement at the end of II.ii, and added III.2.12 and III.2.33. See, on this subject, Raphael and Macfie's Appendix 2 to their edition of TMS.

12. Hume, *Treatise*, II.iii.3, p. 415.

13. In, for instance, the two pages that follow the above quotation, which include the famous line, " 'Tis not contrary to reason to prefer the destruction of the whole world to the scratching of my finger" (ibid., p. 463), or in III.i (pp. 507–21, but especially 509–10), which contains the argument against deriving *ought* from *is*. Smith criticizes the "scratching of my finger" passage at TMS III.3.4 and III.3.26–7.

14. "It is reason . . . who, whenever we are about to act so as to affect the happiness of other, calls to us, with a voice capable of astonishing the most presumptuous of our passions, that we are but one of the multitude, . . . [who] upon many occasions prompts us to the practice of [generosity and justice]" TMS III.3.4.

15. Here Hume's repeated attempts to show us that animal psychology belongs on a continuum with our own—e.g., *Treatise*, I.xvi, II.xii, or *Human Understanding*, chapter 9—should be contrasted with the central place that Smith gives in WN I.ii to the differences between animals and human beings. Both Hume and Smith may be Aristotelians of a sort, but only one shares Aristotle's belief that human beings have a dignity to which animals can never attain.

16. If anything, Smith's own example in the passage supports such a heartless reading: he describes how the Count de Lauzun was able to amuse himself in the Bastille by feeding a spider, remarking that if the Count had been less "frivolous" in his everyday pursuits he would have recovered his tranquillity sooner. The Count was imprisoned, according to Raphael and Macfie's footnote, for insolence to Louis XIV. Presumably Smith does not commend that imprisonment—but that only goes to show that he does not think the king should have guided his actions by their probable effect on the Count's happiness.

17. Hutcheson, *System*, vol. 1, chapters 7 and 8, pp. 116–68.

18. Nicholas Phillipson seems to believe this. For all that I disagree with that claim, my account of propriety in Smith is considerably influenced by Phillipson's in "Politeness, Sociability and the Science of Man."

19. Note that I am *not* saying that Smith was an agnostic about the existence of *God*—he seems clearly to have been at least a deist instead—only that he was agnostic about what precise ends God, or anything else, has laid out for us. There are devout believers in God, even in a theistic God, who are agnostic about teleology in this sense: the Jewish tradition, especially, is marked by this combination (that is, for many Jews, what a "pre-Messianic" attitude consists in). Herder strikes me as the best example of a Christian contemporary of Smith's who expressed such an attitude: "History may not manifestly be revealed as the theatre of a divine purpose on earth . . . , for we may not be able to espy its final end. But it may conceivably offer us glimpses of a divine theatre through the openings and ruins of individual scenes" (*J. G. Herder on Social and Political Culture*, trans. & ed. F. M. Barnard [Cambridge: Cambridge University Press, 1961], p. 187). Isaiah Berlin comments: "[Herder] speaks as if history were . . . a drama, but one without a *dénouement*: as if it were like a cosmic symphony of which each movement is significant in itself, and of which, in any case, we cannot hear the whole, for God alone does so" (*Vico and Herder* [New York: Viking Press, 1976], p. 192).

20. Rawls consistently misinterprets Smith as a utilitarian: see *Theory of Justice*,

(Cambridge: Harvard University Press, 1971), p. 22n; and *Political Liberalism* (New York: Columbia University Press, 1993), p. xiv. (Further references to these works will be incorporated into the text by, respectively, "TJ" and "PL," followed by a page number.) At TJ 184 he claims that for Smith, as for Hume, a just society is "one meeting the approval of . . . an ideal observer." But while it is true that Smith considers things to be right and good only when an impartial observer approves of them, it is not true that he thinks that such an observer appropriately evaluates a society by taking it as a whole. Rather, he insists quite explicitly—and contra Hume—that justice is a virtue directly concerned with the rights of *individuals*, and only indirectly so with the good of society: "[O]ur regard for the multitude is compounded and made up of the particular regards which we feel for the different individuals of which it is composed" (TMS II.ii.3.10; see also the whole chapter). There are also good reasons to doubt that Smith understood "happiness" to be the *summum bonum* of either individuals or society, at least in anything like the same sense that Hume and Bentham did: see discussion in this chapter, above.

21. This and the next paragraph respond to criticisms made to me by Charles Griswold and a very helpful reader for Princeton University Press.

22. See Broadie, *Ethics With Aristotle*, chapter 4; and McDowell, "Deliberation and Moral Development."

23. See, for instance, Richard Kraut, "In Defence of the Grand End," *Ethics* (January 1993).

24. Stephen Macedo defends a view like this in *Liberal Virtues* (Oxford: Clarendon Press, 1990).

25. "By the time of the Union, Scottish political discourse was more concerned with 'independence' than with 'liberty,' and Scotsmen feared 'dependence' on the English more than 'despotism.'" (Nicholas Phillipson, "Adam Smith as Civic Moralist," in *Wealth and Virtue*, ed. I. Hont and M. Ignatieff [Cambridge: Cambridge University Press, 1983], p. 200).

26. The first passage seems quite literally to be talking about "commerce," but it does not take that to be the best or most effective school for the passions. The second passage acknowledges that the life of war or politics may best instill self-command, but notes that "the bustle and business of the world" may do so as well.

27. "When a Man acts in behalf of Nephews or Neices, and says they are my Brother's Children, I do it out of Charity; he deceives you: for if he is capable, it is expected from him, and he does it partly for his own Sake: If he values the Esteem of the world, and is nice as to Honour and Reputation, he is obliged to have a greater Regard to them than for Strangers" (Mandeville, "An Essay on Charity, and Charity Schools," in *The Fable of the Bees*, ed. F. B. Kaye [Oxford: Clarendon Press, 1924], p. 253). (See also the whole of this chapter.)

28. Compare LJ (A) vi.56–7, a predecessor of the passage we have been considering: "If we should enquire into the principle in the human mind on which this disposition of trucking is founded, it is clearly the naturall inclination every one has to persuade. The offering of a shilling, which to us appears to have so plain and simple a meaning, is in reality offering an argument to persuade one to do so and so as it is for his interest. Men always endeavour to persuade others to

be of their opinion even when the matter is of no consequence to them." That passage concludes by noting that certain monkeys, while just as capable as human beings of a jointly pursued activity insofar as they rob an orchard together, will then fight one another to the death over the apples because they don't *understand* that sharing is in all of their individual interests. Such understanding, not the individual self-interest, is what distinguishes us from them. And a paragraph remarkably similar to our passage was added to TMS for the 1790 edition: "The desire of being believed, the desire of persuading, of leading and directing other people, seems to be one of the strongest of all our natural desires. It is, perhaps, the instinct upon which is founded the faculty of speech, the characteristical faculty of human nature. No other animal possess this faculty, and we cannot discover in any other animal any desire to lead and direct the judgment and conduct of its fellows" (VII.iv.25). I am indebted for these references to Phillipson, "Adam Smith as Civic Moralist," p. 191 n. 52. See also Phillipson's remarks on conversation and commerce on p. 188, and on the importance of conversational clubs to Smith's model of society on pp. 198–202. In general, I agree strongly with Phillipson's characterization of Smith's moral and political writings as "a discourse on the social and ethical significance of face-to-face relationships between independently-minded individuals" (p. 198).

29. Smith increasingly realized this in later editions of TMS. Book 6, which was added in the last edition, divides virtue into three parts—self-regarding (prudence), other-regarding (justice and benevolence), and self-command—and it is fairly clear that self-command is meant to be at least the psychological foundation of the other two. Unlike Patricia Werhane (*Adam Smith and His Legacy for Modern Capitalism* [New York: Chicago University Press, 1991], pp. 41, 45), I do not think this is a radical change from Smith's views in earlier editions (compare, for instance, I.v.1 and III.5.12), merely a clearer way of presenting those views.

30. Although Allan Silver has shown, ingeniously reading this same passage, just how Smith's "society of strangers" does provide the condition of possibility for the peculiarly intimate modern form of friendship: see "'Two Different Sorts of Commerce': Friendship and Strangership in Civil Society," in *Public and Private in Thought and Practice*, ed. Jeff Weintraub and Krishan Kumar (Chicago: University of Chicago Press, 1997).

31. Surprisingly, Michael Ignatieff gets Smith wrong here. In "The Market and the Republic" (chapter 4 of *The Needs of Strangers* [New York: Viking, 1984]), Ignatieff argues that, while Rousseau understands that the virtue of self-command requires a particular set of social and material conditions, self-command is just a matter of "will" for Smith (pp. 120–2, 124–5), something that everyone can, and therefore should, just summon up the internal resources to achieve. Smith makes quite clear in TMS III.3 that self-command is made possible by material and social conditions. It is just that he sees a much wider range of conditions than Rousseau's as capable of doing the job: among the most important of which, in the modern world, is the market itself.

32. J. G. A. Pocock, *The Machiavellian Moment* (Princeton: Princeton University Press, 1975). This marvelous work has taught me everything I know about Harrington and his influence on republican thinking. Pocock has written more directly on Smith in his collection *Virtue, Commerce and History* (Cambridge:

Cambridge University Press, 1985) and in Hont and Ignatieff's collection *Wealth and Virtue*, and he seems greatly to have influenced Donald Winch's excellent *Adam Smith's Politics* (Cambridge: Cambridge University Press, 1978).

33. Pocock, *Machiavellian Moment* 499–501; and Ferguson, *An Essay on Civil Society*, ed. Fania Oz-Salzberger (Cambridge: Cambridge University Press, 1995), pp. 194–220. Quotation on p. 218.

34. Ferguson, *Essay*, p. 183.

35. Ignatieff, *Needs*, pp. 113–9.

36. Rousseau, *Discourse on the Sciences and Arts*, part 2; quoted in Ignatieff, *Needs*, p. 109.

37. Ignatieff also fails to comment on the fact that Smith *praises* Rousseau so highly in the letter, that Rousseau seems so important to him. This alone suggests that "morals and virtue" were as central a concern for Smith as for Rousseau. For if Smith found Rousseau so inspiring and profound on topics like property and growth at the time he was writing the economically relevant sections of TMS, then we have reason to suppose that his thoughts on economic matters were, from the beginning, permeated with moral concerns, even if he avoided mentioning such concerns explicitly. Perhaps he had moral reasons *for* such avoidance; perhaps virtue *should* not be the direct concern of political economy, for virtue's own sake. In any case, it is startling to see such a sensitive reader of Smith as Ignatieff suggest that Smith regarded freedom as "the leisure of emancipated desire" (p. 118), or that he validated capitalist society by its encouraging "passive freedom to enjoy one's property" (p. 124). This consumerist talk is something Smith explicitly and vehemently set his face against all through his career, more and more so as he got older. For an excellent account of Smith's opposition to the consumerist mentality, particularly in the last edition of TMS, see John Dwyer, *Virtuous Discourse: Sensibility and Community in Late Eighteenth-Century Scotland* (Edinburgh: John Donald Publishers, 1987), chapter 7.

38. See also WN I.i and LJ (A) vi.6–7, iv.7–8, (B) 20–1, and contrast Ferguson, pp. 182–4, 186: "If the savage has not received our instructions, he is likewise unacquainted with our vices. He knows no superior, and cannot be servile."

39. Smith does, after all, propose solutions to the problems worrying the Harringtonians, just not as drastic ones, nor any single vision of how they should hang together. While he rejects the notion of an "agrarian law"—a proposal of Harrington's by which agrarian holdings would be limited so that they could be spread around widely—he condemns entail and primogeniture over and over for tying up lands unjustifiably in a few hands (compare Winch, *Smith's Politics*, pp. 66–7). He also repeatedly urges the government to spend as little as possible on defense, showing here how idle and unproductive soldiers are, there what ruin warfare wreaks on a nation's stock, and allowing that "defense is of more importance than opulence" only in the context of a paragraph designed above all to show, against received wisdom, that the Navigation Laws were of no *economic* value whatsoever. This is not a case against a standing army, but it does offer grounds for keeping such armies small. Finally, Smith's fondness for America, and his proposal that if it remains British, it should essentially swallow up the rest of the kingdom (IV.vii.c.79), are surely not unconnected to the vision of independence—indeed, agrarian independence—he saw there.

40. Revolutionary change, as the French were shortly to find out, cannot possibly be long-lasting in any case: a sudden radical change, whether for better or for worse, disrupts ordinary people's course of life so much as to undermine their confidence that they can use their own judgment at all. If given a choice, the people will therefore eagerly revert to a world much like the one they had before, even if the new one is better in many ways. Hence only force can keep the change going.

CHAPTER 8
THE *WEALTH OF NATIONS* (III): HELPING THE POOR

1. What many of the *Wealth of Nation's* first readers seem to have taken away from it is a profound commitment to human equality. Thomas Paine was an enthusiastic admirer of Smith. John Millar, Smith's most devoted student, is best known for his *Origin of the Distinction of Ranks*, which fleshes out an account Smith himself offered in TMS, and made use of in WN, to explain all hierarchical distinctions in society as rooted in historical accident rather than natural human differences. Millar was personally active in the strongly egalitarian, Jacobinic movements in Scotland of the 1790s, influencing radical worker advocates like Thomas Muir. Across the water, it was Madison and Jefferson, Thomas Cooper in his antislavery youth, the abolitionist Benjamin Rush, and the fervently anti-aristocratic John Taylor of Caroline who were most favorably impressed by Smith. Jefferson and Taylor, especially, are usually associated with a primarily agrarian political economy, Jefferson and Madison were suspicious of banks and paper money, and all the Americans I have mentioned supported protectionist measures at times. What they learned from Smith was thus not necessarily free trade, nor the importance of manufacturing and banking. The one thing they all share with one another and with Smith is a tremendous avowed respect for "the common man," a belief that all people are equally deserving of, and more or less equally capable of, participating in the highest human life. How sincere this respect was is hard to say in many cases, but it certainly marks an ideal they set for themselves, and an ideal that differentiated them from the Federalists and from most of the intellectual and political elite in Europe.

As mentioned in note 1, chapter 6 above, the Americans' admiration for WN comes out in, for instance, Jefferson's letters to Thomas Mann Randolph and John Garland Jefferson of late May and early June 1790, Madison's 1783 list of books for the proposed Library of Congress and, especially, his speech to Congress on 9 April 1789. Seventeen eighty-three, and even 1790, are extraordinarily early years in which to take an interest in Smith. Smith's economic ideas were not widely discussed in France and Germany until after the French Revolution. Even in Britain, they came to prominence only when Lord Shelburne became prime minister in July 1782, and even then, only slowly; see Kirk Willis, "The Role in Parliament of the Economic Ideas of Adam Smith, 1776–1800," *History of Political Economy* (1979): 505–44; and Salim Rashid, "Adam Smith's Rise to Fame: A Re-examination of the Evidence," in *The Eighteenth Century; Theory and Interpretation* 23, no. 1 (1982): 64–85. The influence of Smith on Madison is discussed by Roy Branson in "James Madison and the Scottish Enlightenment," *Journal of the History of Ideas* (1979), and the influence of Smith on Taylor is nicely laid out by Paul Conkin in *Prophets of Prosperity: America's First Political Economists* (Bloomington: Indiana University Press, 1980), chapter 3.

2. "To hinder . . . the farmer from sending his goods at all times to the best market, is evidently to sacrifice the ordinary laws of justice to an idea of publick utility, to a sort of reasons of state; an act of legislative authority which ought to be exercised only, which can be pardoned only in cases of the most urgent necessity" (WN IV.v.b.39).

3. LJ A vi.27–8. Cf. LJ B 211–3, ED 4–6, and WN I.i.11.

4. Phillipson, "Politeness," p. 8:

Mandeville had been interested in the moral conventions which made men sociable. Hume, famously, went further, showing that conventions shaped every area of our cognitive life. To be sure, they all had their roots in the self. But Hume was able to show that the self itself, was the product of conventions and the socially interactive world in which conventions were created. In his brilliant and still neglected analysis of the passions in Book II of the *Treatise*, he showed how those sentiments of pride and humility, love and hatred, . . . which Mandeville had regarded as the primary motors of human conduct, could all be deconstructed into a network of conventions which shaped our cognitive world to the point that it was impossible for us to form a wish "which has not reference to society." (T.363)

5. See TMS III.1, III.2.1–9, 31–2, III.1–3.

6. On Rawls's misinterpretation of Smith as a utilitarian, see above, note 20, chapter 7.

7. Quoted in Emma Rothschild, "Adam Smith and Conservative Economics," *The Economic History Review*, 55, no. 1, February 1992: 89. Rothschild's article is an excellent survey of how Smith's quite radical ideas, especially as regards government concern for the poor, were distorted by their uses in later, more conservative politics.

8. See Daniel A. Baugh, "Poverty, Protestantism and Political Economy: English Attitudes Toward The Poor, 1660–1800," in *England's Rise to Greatness*, ed. Stephen Baxter (Berkeley: University of California Press, 1983).

9. "Moral disapproval of the luxurious spending of the poor" pervades the writing of Smith's contemporaries, according to Neil McKendrick ("Home Demand and Economic Growth," in *Historical Perspectives: Studies in English Thought and Society*, ed. N. McKendrick [London: Europa Publications, 1974], p. 167). Even Elizabeth Gaskell felt compelled "to offer some explanation of the extravagance of . . . working class wives," who indulged in ham, eggs, butter, and cream, while Sir Frederick Eden's famous report "constantly complained of the mis-spending of the poor on unnecessary luxuries and inessential fripperies." Henry Fielding complained that "the very Dregs of the People . . . aspire . . . to a degree beyond that which belongs to them," while J. Hanway said it was 'the curse of this nation that the labourer and the mechanic will ape the lord" (ibid., pp. 167–8, 191–2).

10. Indeed, the only price control he ever allows is one "[w]here there is an exclusive corporation" in bread, to regulate the availability of this "first necessary of life" (I.x.c.62).

11. Hont and Ignatieff, "Needs and Justice in the *Wealth of Nations*," in their *Wealth and Virtue*.

12. These had been around since at least the late seventeenth century, and were gaining strength rapidly in the eighteenth century. See Gordon Jackson, "Glasgow in Transition, c.1660 to c.1740," in *Glasgow*, ed. T. M. Devine and G. Jackson (Manchester: Manchester University Press, 1995), 1:93; Stana S. Nenadic, "The Middle Ranks and Modernisation," ibid.: 292–3 and Christopher A. Whatley, "Labour in the Industrialising City," ibid.: 373.

13. The crucial difference between the English and Scottish poor law; see Rosalind Mitchison, "The Making of the Old Scottish Poor Law," *Past & Present* 63 (1974).

14. He does, briefly, discuss the role that churches had in the *past* played in performing this function—V.i.g.22, along with a mention at I.x.c.46—making clear that church-based poor relief always came at the cost of increasing the dependency of poor people on the clergy.

15. Smith seems also to have owned no other books on poverty policy; neither the works cited below by Defoe, Fielding, and Watts, nor the writings on poverty of Richard Baxter (1673), Isaac Barrow (1671), Richard Steele (1684), Lawrence Braddon (1721), Richard Price (1771, 1789), or Baron Maseres (1773) appear in his library (at least according to the Bonar catalogue: James Bonar, *A Catalogue of the Library of Adam Smith* [New York: Augustus M. Kelley, 1966]; Nor are any tracts on poverty included under the headings "Pamphlets" and "Political Pamphlets"). Mandeville's works, and Arthur Young's, do of course appear, but he had other reasons for reading them and he never cites either one on the subject of the poor.

16. Baugh, "Poverty," p. 101 n. 49.

17. Defoe, "Giving Alms No Charity," in *The Shortest Way with the Dissenters and Other Pamphlets* (Oxford, 1927), pp. 186–8.

18. J. L. Hammond and Barbara Hammond, *The Village Labourer* (Phoenix Mill: Alan Sutton Publishing, Ltd. 1987), p. 151.

19. Quotations from Mandeville in Baugh, "Poverty," pp. 77–8, and from Young in Baugh, p. 103 n. 74. Baugh's essay is the best short account I know of Smith's relationship to the—overwhelmingly repulsive—other views of the poor in his day. Baugh does not, however, comment on why this great champion of the poor, and erudite reader, should omit even to cite any of the other literature on the subject.

20. Quotation (with inserts by author) in Baugh, "Poverty," p. 80.

21. Ibid.

22. From the Board of Agriculture report against benefit clubs, 1793:

benefit clubs, holden at public houses, increase the number of those houses, and naturally lead to idleness and intemperance;

From the preamble to the 1819 act for further protection of Friendly Societies:

whereas the habitual reliance of poor persons upon parochial relief, rather than upon their own industry, tends to the moral deterioration of the people . . . ; and it is desirable, with a view as well to the reduction of the assessments made for the relief of the poor, as to the improvement of the habits of the people, that encouragement should be afforded to persons desirous of making provision for themselves or their families out of the fruits of their own industry.

"Thus the aim of the act of 1793 remained unchanged: the poor rate was to be reduced and, if possible, the morals of the poor were to be improved; but the method of achieving this aim was to be more closely supervised than under the previous act for the magistrates were not merely to be asked to approve the rules of a society but also its tables" (P.H.J.H. Gosden, *The Friendly Societies in England 1815–1875* [Manchester, U.K.: University Press, 1961], pp. 3, 175).

23. "The Scottish Poor Law," says TM Devine, "was underpinned by a set of values and attitudes which assumed that . . . [t]he poor were poor because of defects of character, idleness and intemperance. In this view, only the combination of a rigorous poor law, expansion of schooling and the spread of evangelical Christianity could save urban society from moral catastrophe" (Devine, "The Urban Crisis," in Devine and Jackson, *Glasgow*, pp. 412–3).

The policies put in place by such views tended to tie material relief firmly to moral improvement. From church-sponsored poor relief, through the Poor Laws that Smith rightly attacked for restricting movement, to the workhouses where healthy and sick were thrown together (making them deathtraps in which a fever could wipe out half the inmates in one building: see Hammonds, *Village Labourer*, p. 147 and notes 2 and 3), public and private institutions alike attached moral strings to whatever aid they dispensed. See also Jackson, "Glasgow in Transition," pp. 93–4, and Nenadic, "Middle Ranks," pp. 296–7.

24. LJ (B) 330, my emphasis. Compare WN IV.iii.c.8, V.i.f.53.

25. Smith's contemporaries "complained that those becoming marks of distinction between the classes were being obliterated by the extravagance of the lower ranks; that working girls wore inappropriate finery, even silk dresses. By some curious alchemy . . . , the ability of working girls to afford fashionable clothes was transmuted into a further reason to attack the employment of women. It encouraged independence, it loosened their morals, it made them extravagant" (McKendrick, "Home Demand," p. 168).

26. I.x.c.25–29 bitterly attacks the "combinations" of masters, while I.viii.13 goes to some length, as we have seen above, to *defend* combinations of workers— at least in comparison with the masters they are combining against. And I.x.c.61, which contains the famous line, "When [a] regulation . . . is in favour of the workmen, it is always just and equitable; but it is sometimes otherwise when it is in favour of the masters," is on the whole an attack on attempts to cap wages— which it argues, summing up the entire chapter that preceded it, is something that masters naturally and constantly combine to do. Anything that might raise wages, against this unremitting attempt of masters to keep them down, would seem to be something of which Smith would approve. Finally, the last three sentences of I.x.c.61 suggest strongly that as long as masters *are* allowed to combine by law, workers should be able to combine as well. See also note 35, below.

27. Parallel passages appear in every draft of WN: compare LJ (A) vi.41–2, 53–4, LJ (B) 217–8, and ED 17–9.

28. See HA II.12 and III.3, and Charles Griswold, "Nature and Philosophy: Adam Smith on Stoicism, Aesthetic Reconciliation, and Imagination," *Man and World* 29, no. 2 (1996).

29. Hegel, *Philosophy of Right*, trans. T. M. Knox (Oxford: Clarendon Press, 1958), §§ 202–5, 229, 238, 247, 250, 256.

30. See also HA II.12: "Philosophy is the science of the connecting principles in nature. . . . Philosophy, by representing the invisible chains which bind together all these disjointed objects, endeavors to introduce order . . . and to restore [the imagination] . . . to that tone of tranquillity and composure, which is both most agreeable in itself and most suitable to its nature," and IV.19, on the way machines and "systems" resemble one another. Since Smith embraces both philosophical and social systems in his general use of that term, the passage in WN carries a clear implication that philosophers might help "introduce order" into societies as well as into machines and ideas.

31. As elsewhere, the pessimistic warning about what happens if the "few . . . are not placed in some very particular circumstances" is probably a rhetorical device to signal that the state should take care *to* so place them. On rhetoric in Smith, and a parallel to this rhetorical device in particular, see Jerry Z. Muller, *Adam Smith in His Time and Ours* (Princeton: Princeton University Press, 1993), pp. 65–8, 92–4, 150.

32. Hirst, *Adam Smith,* p. 98.

33. By restricting certain kinds of money circulation (II.ii.91–4), by controlling some businesses for defense purposes (IV.ii.24–30), and in rare cases, by imposing retaliatory tariffs to open other countries' markets (IV.ii.38–39).

34. Werhane and Muller stress this aspect of Smith's statecraft in their books.

35. When taken together with the well-known passage in which Smith says that laws that favor masters are often unjust, while laws that favor workers are always just, this gives us good reason to think that Smith would have opposed the laws Britain passed to prevent trade unionism (the Combination Acts of 1799 and 1800), and indeed have regarded unions as at least a necessary evil, so long as the combinations of masters could not be wholly prevented. It is interesting, in this connection, that the parliamentarians most active in repealing the Combination Acts in 1824—Francis Place and Joseph Hume—were devout Smithians, whose commitment to keeping the government out of the economy had earlier led them to positions that bitterly upset workers' advocates: See E. P. Thompson, *The Making of the English Working Class* (Harmondsworth, U.K.: Penguin, 1980), p. 565.

36. A wonderful discussion of WN as an Enlightenment text appears in Peter Gay, *The Enlightenment: An Interpretation* (New York: Alfred A. Knopf, 1969), 2:359–68.

37. See note 11, above.

38. See note 28, chapter 7 above.

39. T. C. Smout, *A History of the Scottish People, 1560–1830* (London: Fontana, 1969), p. 356.

40. LJ A vi.6–7; cf. B 20–1, 204–5.

41. V.i.e.15–40 makes this clear, and paragraphs 18 and 29 suggest strongly that his objections to them are not primarily ones of inefficiency.

42. C. K. Kindleberger suggests this in "The Historical Background: Adam Smith and the Industrial Revolution," in *The Market and the State*, ed. T. Wilson and A. S. Skinner (Oxford: Oxford University Press, 1976). But Kindleberger takes this to be a sign of Smith's poor observational skills, while I think there is no reason Smith *should* have foreseen the factory system. Most historians date the

Industrial Revolution in Scotland from the 1780s (see Smout, *History of the Scottish People*, p. 223—he suggests 1783 as a starting year), and the factory system does not seem to have gotten off the ground until the 1790s (Thompson, *English Working Class*, pp. 207-9; Peter Mathias, *The First Industrial Nation* [London: Methuen, 1969], pp. 114-20). As late as the 1830s and 40s, observers "were still exclaiming at the novelty of the 'factory system.'" (Thompson, *English Working Class*, p. 208).

Smith says very little about factory work throughout WN, although, of course, he opens the book with an example drawn from a pin factory. The significance of the example has been widely overrated, however. Smith himself makes clear, both before and after giving the example, that he regards it as a poor, an *untypical* example of the division of labor. He insists that it is a "very trifling" case (I.i.2,3,4), but says that it is one "that has very often been taken notice of" (I.i.3), and he justifies his own use of it only by the fact that it is a case where the division of labor is particularly easy to see (I.i.2). The example seems distasteful to him, he holds it at a distance, and the fact that his tone changes altogether in the joyful outpouring that ends chapter 1—describing the many independent crafts going into a day-laborer's coat—makes clear where he really welcomes the effect of the division of labor and thinks its effects are most importantly to be found.

In addition, the passages praising the increase in "independency" brought by commerce would be hard to understand unless he saw the ownership of stock as conferring to the owner considerably less power over others than the ownership of land had conferred in ages past. It would also be hard to understand why the street porter, a person with a hard and miserably *dull* but certainly not a *dependent* life, should regularly serve as Smith's example of the lowest of the low rather than a pin-maker. That employers would soon exercise practically tyrannical forms of discipline over workers seems simply beyond Smith's horizon. Here Ferguson was the more prescient writer.

CHAPTER 9
KANT'S POLITICS: RAWLS'S POLITICS (I): THE PUBLIC USE OF JUDGMENT

1. Samuel Fleischacker, "Values Behind the Market: Kant's Response to the *Wealth of Nations*," *History of Political Thought* (Autumn, 1996).
2. R 532 (from the 1780s), my translation. See also R 528-31, 1508-9.
3. A 209/80. It is important not to miss the heavy irony throughout this passage: Kant is of course in complete agreement with Smith here!
4. Both Kant's most misogynist and most feminist leanings can be found in this context. At R 528 and A 209, his official doctrine is that women are naturally not *mündig*. But in both places he seems at the same time quite uncomfortable with this position, and tries to justify it by saying that women do, after all, have more than adequate abilities to make use of their *Münder* (a backhanded compliment indeed!) and thereby can in fact attain a certain independence in the domestic context. And R 1508 lists the *Unmündigkeit* of gender in a series along with the *Unmündigkeit* established by academia and politics, and we know, from other contexts, that he disapproves of the latter two. At the end of R 528, he suggests that a period of *Unmündigkeit*, and even slavery, may be good for peo-

ple in some contexts, "but all these evils must still have an end sometime, and philosophy, if it is to have a role here, must give the principles." The overall current of Kant's thought, especially in R 528 itself, would include gender based *Unmündigkeit* among "all these evils," even if Kant never quite had the courage or foresight to do so himself.

5. PP 381/126. See also 386/130.

6. "Thus *freedom of the pen* is the only safeguard of the rights of the people" (TP 304/85).

7. Even Onora O'Neill's excellent "The Public Use of Reason" (*Political Theory*, vol. 14 [1986]), seems insufficiently impressed by the tension between Kant's account of transcendental freedom and the empirical processes by which he claims we actually achieve freedom. There are not many other scholarly studies of *What is Enlightenment?*, and those I have found focus only on the political role and structure of Kant's call for free expression, not its philosophical basis or implications: see, for instance, Dick Howard, *The Politics of Critique* (Minneapolis: University of Minnesota Press, 1988), pp. 11–2, and Allen Rosen, *Kant's Theory of Justice* (Ithaca: Cornell University Press, 1993), pp. 18–9, 137–8.

8. For references to Rawls's PL and TJ, see note 20, chapter 7 above.

9. On freedom and creation, see the Third Antinomy of CPR, and the Analytic of CPrR, especially the Typic, where we see ourselves as if we were to create an entire natural order by our wills. On freedom and time, see CPrR 86, where he suggests that our personality "has under it the entire world of sense, including the empirically determinable existence of man in time" (translation, p. 89), as well as pp. 94–9.

10. Herman has a wonderful sketch of why education is so important to Kantian agency, and mentions the possible extension of her argument to health care, in *Practice*, pp. 204–6.

11. Howard Caygill discusses the connection interestingly in *Art of Judgment* (Cambridge: Blackwell, 1989).

12. It is also implicit in IUH 20–1/44–5:

> *The means which nature employs to bring about the development of innate capacities is that of antagonism within society.* . . . By antagonism, I mean in this context the *unsocial sociability* of men, that is, their tendency to come together in society, coupled, however, with a continual resistance which constantly threatens to break this society up. . . . All man's talents are now gradually developed, his taste cultivated, and by a continued process of enlightenment, a beginning is made towards . . . transform[ing] the primitive natural capacity for moral discrimination into definite . . . principles.

I am grateful to Jeff Weintraub for pointing out to me the relevance of the division of labor to this passage.

13. Philosophy, he says, must be "free to evaluate *everything*" (CF 19/27, my emphasis).

14. Hannah Arendt discusses § 40 in interesting detail: see her *Lectures on Kant's Political Philosophy*, ed. Ronald Beiner (Chicago: University of Chicago Press, 1982), pp. 43–4, 70–2. But she simply identifies the *sensus communis* with the *gemeinen Menschenverstand*, ignoring Kant's explicit warning against doing this. (On p. 70, she simply moves from one to the other as if they were the same;

on p. 71, she calls the maxims Kant attributes to the latter "maxims of this *sensus communis*.") That the two are closer than Kant suggests can be argued, but to ignore the distinction Kant himself draws is unfair to his attempt to keep CJ away from political purposes.

15. Teleological ones, especially: compare the second half of CJ with CPR A 642 = B 670—A 668 = B 696.

16. E 37/55. See also PP 369, 382, 386/115, 126–7, 130; CF 19–20/27–9, 27–9/43–7, 32–6/53–61; and TP 304–6/84–7.

17. Which he explicitly brings together with Plato's Ideas (CPR A 312 = B 369—A 320 = B 377). But reason, far from transcending and triumphing over the conversational play in which judgment is at home, must itself require that play in order to arrive at some of its own conclusions, at least about things that are themselves a matter of sociability. It follows that Kantian political theory should not be as ideal, as removed from history and controversy, as that of either Rawls or Habermas.

18. CJ 214/49: "the taste of reflection . . . imputes [the universal validity of its judgments] to everyone . . . , without the persons that judge disputing as to the possibility of such a claim, although in particular cases they cannot agree as to [its] correct application."

19. For a profound and thorough examination of the polemical aspects of Kant's thought, see Hans Saner, *Kant's Political Thought*, especially pp. 73–213. Saner nicely delineates the importance of the *Critique of Judgment* to Kant's conception of philosophical debate (pp. 89–96), although he shares what I consider to be the misunderstanding that aesthetic response does without concepts (see pp. 90, 105). He also comes to the conclusion that *all* of Kant's philosophy is polemical, and that Kant's work in the end amounts "not [to] a certain field of thoughts but [to] the act of thinking" (p. 213), which is itself a matter of continuous, and endless, debate. I'm not sure I would go quite this far, but something of the sort does seem to me appropriate as regards Kant's thinking about *politics*.

20. Rev 55/211, my emphasis.

21. The *Groundwork* was published a few months after the review of Herder, and its third example parallels a section of that review; compare Rev 64–5/219–20 with G 423/40–1.

22. Which is, according to Kant (from clergymen, lawyers, and doctors respectively): "[I]f I've been a *scoundrel* all my life, how can I get an eleventh-hour ticket to heaven? If I've *broken* the law, how can I still win my case? And even if I've used and *abused* my physical powers as I've pleased, how can I stay healthy and live a long time?" (CF 40/49). What people want from the learned professions, Kant says, is a sort of magic or miracle-working, and philosophy must publicly combat scholars who yield to such demands, "not in order to overthrow their teachings but only to deny the magic power that the public superstitiously attributes to . . . them" (31/51).

23. This may explain why Kant, for all his admiration of Smith, is sometimes more willing than the Scot to countenance economic planning; see TP 299n/80n.

24. See the interview with Rawls in *The Harvard Review of Philosophy* (Spring 1991):39.

25. Compare Benjamin Barber:

Rawls . . . wishes to leave the choice between capitalism and socialism "open." [cf. TJ, p. 258] This, to me, is like developing a geometry in which the question of whether parallel lines meet is left open, or generating an aesthetic that refuses to take sides on questions of taste. Given the intimate interdependence of political and economic institutions in the West, and given the undeniable culpability of capitalism in the history of Western injustice, a theory of justice that sees nothing to choose between capitalism and socialism is either extravagantly formalistic to the point of utter irrelevance, or is a badly disguised rationalization for one particular socio-economic system, namely "property-owning democracy." ("Justifying Justice," in *Reading Rawls*, ed. Norman Daniels [New York: Basic Books, 1975], pp. 312–3)

Barber criticizes Rawls extensively for being "insufficiently political" and "egregiously ahistorical" (p. 309). I am very sympathetic to the criticism, while taking almost exactly the opposite side from Barber on the relative justice of "property-owning democracy" vis-à-vis socialism. History, it seems to me, has also decided against Barber on this question, although exactly what shape "property-owning democracy" should take remains open.

26. Jürgen Habermas, *Moral Consciousness and Communicative Actions*, trans. C. Lenhardt and S. W. Nicholson (Cambridge: MIT Press, 1993), pp. 66–7. See also pp. 68, 94, 106–8, 198, 204.

27. On the disruption of norms, see ibid., pp. 106–7.

28. In 2.2, "disputes," "under discussion" and "a reason" are similarly equivocal. Suppose I insist that I am not "disputing" a norm, merely reinterpreting it. Or I say: this norm *is* "under discussion," if not explicitly, and you are in bad faith to take its acceptance for granted. Or I offer a "reason" for rejecting some norm that you do not regard as a reason but as a prejudice, or irrelevancy, or position so uninformed as to be irrational.

29. See above, chapter 2, pp. 26–7.

30. The conditions for a fair conversation might also include such things, determinable only by reference to the actual conversation going on and perhaps even to the history of other conversations in the context of which it takes place, as the *relevance* of the points raised to the issue that the participants are trying to solve, and the importance of that issue itself.

31. See Winch, *Adam Smith's Politics*, pp. 146–7.

32. Compare Wittgenstein, *Philosophical Investigations*, §§ 214–6.

33. At least it happens constantly in a world of rapid change and widespread belief in the importance of individual creativity and autonomy, like our own.

34. The ineliminable importance of "prejudice" to interpretation, and the notion that the Enlightenment had an unjustifiable prejudice *against* prejudice, is a central theme of Hans-Georg Gadamer, *Truth and Method*, trans. Sheed & Ward Ltd., ed. G. Barden and J. Cumming (New York: Seabury Press, 1975).

CHAPTER 10
KANT'S POLITICS, RAWLS'S POLITICS (II): TALENT, INDUSTRY, AND LUCK

1. "*ihr Talent, ihr Fleiß, und ihr Glück*": the phrase appears twice on TP 292–3, and once, with a slight modification ("Vermögen" for "Talent") on 296.

Nisbet translates *Glück* as "good fortune," which is not as accurate as "luck" and obscures the connection, which I want to exploit, with Bernard Williams's and Martha Nussbaum's concerns.

2. See Brian Barry, *Theories of Justice* (Berkeley: University of California Press, 1989), pp. 213–25. Barry, it should be noted, prefers these intuitions to Rawls's official mode of argument: he says that "we would do better to go straight to Rawls's underlying moral intuitions and scrap their formulation in terms of choice in an original position" (p. 224).

3. Goethe, *Faust*, part 1, "Night," lines 682–3.

4. For this point, and for much else in this chapter, I am indebted to a very helpful conversation with Russ Muirhead.

5. Consider, for instance, how he treats the two sides of his third and fourth antinomies: the left-hand side becomes a guide to interpreting facts for the purposes of morality and religion, while the right-hand side guides our interpretation of facts for the purposes of science.

6. Not, in that case, unlike the approach P. F. Strawson famously recommends to the free will/determinist debate in "Freedom and Resentment" (*Freedom and Resentment* [London: Methuen, 1974]).

7. *Pace* Robert Nozick: "the foundations underlying desert" must indeed "themselves [be] deserved, *all the way down.*" See his *Anarchy, State, and Utopia* (New York: Basic Books, 1974), p. 225. I am indebted to Russ Muirhead for this reference.

8. The most convincing point, I believe, in the famous argument for capitalism of Milton Friedman: see *Capitalism and Freedom* (Chicago: University of Chicago Press, 1982), pp. 16ff.

9. Compare Sigmund Freud, *Beyond the Pleasure Principle*, trans. and ed. James Strachey (New York: W. W. Norton, 1961), pp. 8–11.

10. Nor *should* we so distinguish: charm is usually an amoral and honesty usually a moral talent, but charm can be needed to resolve many a moral problem and honesty can be a useful business trait. The latter is something Kant notes explicitly, at G 397/13–4, urging us to take on honesty *as* moral. Presumably we can do the same with charm—and intelligence, athletic ability, artistic creativity, and anything else.

11. Thus attempts in recent years to distribute economic and political positions on the basis of perceived social justice rather than talent have not coincidentally, I think, gone along with an increase in the number of "syndromes" invented to explain away, and sometimes to exculpate, criminal behavior. Of course, the converse—the combination, often associated with Puritan society, of forgiving no criminal trespass and regarding all material inequality as earned—should give us pause about the humanity of an unqualified enthusiasm for responsibility.

12. On the subject of whether fitness remains an appropriate subject for theories of justice, and in particular whether the work people do ought in some way to "fit" their interests and capacities, see J. Russell Muirhead, *Just Work* (Cambridge: Harvard University Press, forthcoming).

13. I am grateful to Peter de Marneffe for a conversation that helped me clarify this argument.

14. George Kateb, *The Inner Ocean* (Ithaca: Cornell University Press, 1992), p. 122.

15. Ibid., pp. 18–9.

16. And to economic metaphors and economic examples scattered all throughout the book; see, for instance, G 394/10, 397/13–4, 402/18–9, 419/37, and 422/40. I am increasingly convinced that Kant wrote the *Groundwork* soon after reading WN, and in part was concerned to provide a moral argument that would grant Smith all his empirical explanations of human behavior while making room for moral foundations that could not possibly be reduced to self-love. Of course, I believe that Smith himself did not want to reduce all human motivations to self-love; Kant may have seen Smith's empiricism as threatening to make such a reduction inevitable, whatever Smith himself intended.

17. On occasion, he explicitly takes his task to be the uncovering of prejudices. He explains that the activities of corn merchants in fact help rather than hinder the population's ability to avoid famines, and remarks about the contrary belief that "The popular fear of engrossing and forestalling may be compared to the popular terrors and suspicions of witchcraft" (IV.v.b.26). He also tries to exorcise the common prejudice against pharmacists (I.x.b.35) and, of course, the "fallacy" of equating wealth with money (IV.i.1).

18. He insists, for instance, that "Labour alone, . . . never varying in its own value, is alone the ultimate and real standard by which the value of all commodities can at all times and places be estimated and compared. It is their real price; money is their nominal price only" (I.v.7). On the other hand, this passage is embedded in a series of acknowledgments that labor's value is itself "commonly estimated . . . by the higgling and bargaining of the market," that "[i]t is more natural . . . to estimate [a commodity's] exchangeable value by the quantity of some other commodity than by that of the labour which it can purchase," and that "labour, like commodities, may be said to have a real and a nominal price" (I.v.4–5, 9). In a later chapter, "natural price" will be introduced as a counterpart to "market price." As opposed to "real price," "natural price" will not be strictly or entirely reducible to labor alone, but will function similarly as something outside the market that yet somehow grounds the market. Later economists did away altogether with these "real" and "natural" prices that have no direct empirical measure: see Schumpeter, *History*, pp. 309–11.

19. Beck puts "market value" here for some reason, but the German is *Marktpreis*.

20. If this is right, what Kant rejected in Smith may have been very much like what he rejected in Hume. Compare Smith's appeal to labor value and natural price with Hume's appeal to custom. Hume and Smith both discover the extreme relativism that pervades a realm of empirical analysis. Causes can only be understood as such relative to other causes, inductions relative to yet further inductions, prices relative to other prices. If we can be satisfied with an ungrounded system of interconnections, we can carry out here a causal analysis of a historical event relative to a psychological uniformity or vice versa, there an economic analysis of the price of silver relative to the price of corn, or vice versa; if we ask for some fundamental "stuff" or principle grounding all causes and prices, we will despair. Suddenly, into this hard relativistic teaching, along come "custom" and "labor" to ground what we've just been told are necessarily ground*less* empirical phenomena. Kant takes *these* grounds away and replaces them with transcendental assumptions—the transcendental unity of apperception, instead of custom, and

the absolute worth of the human being, instead of labor value. He sees himself as a more radical empiricist than the empiricists he follows, following their skepticism or relativism to the bitter end, and because of that seeing what they do not see—that an empirical system cannot underwrite its own rules. Rules are by their nature transcendental. They are not just another kind of empirical fact, but *norms*, both for justification and for prescription.

21. The importance of luck to a satisfying human life was first brought out, in recent philosophical literature, by Bernard Williams in his famous essay "Moral Luck" (in *Moral Luck* [Cambridge: Cambridge University Press, 1981]). But Williams does not particularly tie luck to judgment, nor, as far as I can see, does he have any special sympathy for the egalitarian intuitions that I find so valuable in the Kantian tradition.

22. This is one way of reading Bernard Williams's objection that Rawls builds "morality" too deeply into his starting position; see "Rawls and Pascal's Wager," in *Moral Luck*, pp. 97, 100.

23. This fits with Adam Smith's insistence on the historical relativity of the necessity/luxury distinction at WN V.ii.k.3.

24. This is, as it happens, an old liberal notion of what states should do. From Locke's argument that the state comes into existence as a substitute for the unreliable and arbitrary exercises of judgment that powerful individuals carry out in prepolitical societies, through Kant's claim that the essence of political morality is to ensure that "the freedom of choice of each can coexist with everyone's freedom" (MM 230/56), liberal thinkers have standardly held that the state maximizes the liberty of each individual by restricting the power of some individuals. Libertarians make three mistakes in interpreting these claims. First, they assume that the liberty of each individual is essentially an absolute, a fixed sphere around the individual that must be preserved whole. Second, they see only the state, not groups of individuals, as capable of constraining any one individual's private sphere. And, finally, they take "property," rather than any mental or physical ability, to be the central term for defining that sphere. These mistakes are interlinked: by construing only violence—the characteristic tool of the state—as a constraint on freedom (2), the libertarian can allow any concentration of property, no matter how large, to belong to the sphere of privacy (3), and thereby preserve the inviolability of that sphere against the demands of larger social purposes (1). The liberty I am proposing, by contrast, defines the sphere around the individual in terms of his or her ability to make judgments and act on them—an ability that is connected as much to the individual's *access* to resources she needs as to her actual *ownership* of any particular resources—and therefore allows the "right to property" to be treated as but one rough estimation of the freedom the state must protect, rather than so closely identified with that freedom that restrictions on the use of property will always be illegitimate.

CHAPTER 11
A THIRD CONCEPT OF LIBERTY

1. Berlin, "Two Concepts of Liberty" (cited above in chapter 1, n. 2), p. 130.
2. Benjamin Constant, "The Liberty of the Ancients Compared with That of

the Moderns," in *Benjamin Constant: Political Writings*, ed. Biancamaria Fontana (Cambridge: Cambridge University Press, 1988), pp. 310–1.

3. Quentin Skinner, "The Paradoxes of Political Liberty," in *Equal Freedom*, ed. Stephen Darwall (Ann Arbor: University of Michigan Press, 1995), p. 22.

4. In a very small community, of course, my speech in her favor (or, indeed, *against* her) might be crucial to the vote that puts her into office, but my vote alone, even here, and both my vote and my utterances, in a larger community, has such little effect on the outcome that that outcome cannot in any way be considered "my" action.

5. Alexis de Tocqueville, *Democracy in America*, ed. J. P. Mayer, trans. George Lawrence (Garden City: Anchor Books, 1969), p. 515.

6. Ibid., p. 70.

7. As Adam Smith, an important influence on Constant, emphasized in his TMS.

8. Berlin, "Two Concepts of Liberty," pp. 122–3, 127.

9. Ibid., p. 128, my emphasis. See also pp. 121, 127, where he talks about living "as I like" or as I "wish." Berlin brings out a problem with the conception on pp. 139–40, but that has to do with the possibility that defining freedom by my ability to satisfy my desires leaves room for me to attain freedom by getting rid of my desires, not with what I am concerned with here.

10. Joel Feinberg, "The Concept of Freedom," in *Social Philosophy* (Englewood Cliffs: Prentice-Hall, 1973), p. 5.

11. See MM 438n/234n, 335/144. Compare also G 451–3/69–71.

12. Berlin refers explicitly to Kant in "Two Concepts of Liberty" on pp. 136–8, 145, 147, 148, 152–3, 156, 157, and 170; to the heteronomy/autonomy distinction on 134, 136, 138, 142, 144, 149, 153, and 160; and to the empirical/noumenal distinction on 133–6 and 148.

13. For the connection of Kantian doctrines to nationalism, see also Elie Kedourie, *Nationalism*, 3d ed. (London: Hutchinson, 1985), chapters 2 and 3.

14. Which Murray and Herrnstein have taken, so misleadingly, to be crucial to intelligence. Stephen Jay Gould has long argued, against views like theirs, that "intelligence" must be understood as a composite of multiple skills. Selecting mathematical skills and the like then just reflects a particular choice someone or some society has made about which aspects of intelligence to emphasize—not a scientifically discoverable fact. I am proposing that our society make a different selection.

15. For excellent accounts of liberal communitarianism and nationalism, respectively, see Daniel A. Bell, *Communitarianism and its Critics* (Oxford: Oxford University Press, 1993); and Yael Tamir, *Liberal Nationalism* (Princeton: Princeton University Press, 1993).

16. Hence Wittgenstein, in his antifoundationalism, winds up explicitly endorsing judgment, indeed specifically the kind of judgment that takes place in the courtroom, over all philosophers' touchstones for truth. See *On Certainty*, especially §§ 8, 128–9, 149, 150, 220, 254, 325, 334, 335, 416, 453, 500, 557, 604–7.

17. A very misleading impression! Two more ornery critters than Smith and Kant would be hard to find. But I am talking about writing style and not person-

ality. In my experience, there is only a tenuous connection between how someone writes and how (s)he behaves in person. I think there is a rather stronger connection between *reading* tastes and personality, however, and that is all I need to make my point. Smith and Kant represent a truly open writing style, one that invites both admiration and criticism, and their readers tend to be people who themselves like that sort of thing. It seems to me that people who enjoy reading Smith, Kant, and Mill do tend towards a less dogmatic, more flexible approach to politics than those who prefer Friedman or MacKinnon.

18. Taylor ties freedom to "self-realization" or "what I truly or authentically want" on pp. 212, 213, 215, and 222 of "What's Wrong with Negative Liberty."

19. Alan Ryan writes of "the Kantian emphasis on the *dictatorship* of the rational will" (introduction to Ryan, ed., *The Idea of Freedom* [Oxford: Oxford University Press, 1979], p. 8, my emphasis) in contrast with Schiller's emphasis on "an aesthetically satisfying harmony of mind and heart." But Schiller's themes can be found in Kant's own aesthetics.

20. The closest Taylor gets to making an additional argument for this step is the following:

> But once we admit that our feelings are import-attributing, then we admit the possibility of error, or false appreciation. And indeed, we have to admit a kind of false appreciation which the agent himself detects in order to make sense of the cases where we experience our own desires as fetters. How can we exclude in principle that there may be other false appreciations which the agent does not detect? That he may be profoundly in error, that is, has a very distorted sense of his fundamental purposes? . . . All cases are, of course, controversial; but I should nominate Charles Manson and Andreas Baader for this category, among others. I pick them out as people with a strong sense of some purposes and goals as incomparably more fundamental than others, . . . but whose sense of fundamental purpose was shot through with confusion and error. ("What's Wrong with Negative Liberty," pp. 226–7)

Strictly, however, this still provides a reason to think only that I may be in error about my desires without being able to detect my error, not that anyone else is either more likely to detect such errors or justified in influencing my behavior if she does detect them. The examples of Manson and Baader take Taylor's case a little further, because most of us indeed have an intuition that we could do a rather better job at figuring out how Manson and Baader could have achieved satisfaction than they did for themselves. Yet a knockdown case this intuition is not, in part because Manson, at least, is too extreme an example, too close to psychotic for the most nonjudgmental of libertarians to have trouble writing him off as incapable of running his own life. In ordinary cases, unacceptably dangerous doors open up once we allow actions based on our "second-guessing" of other people's desires.

21. I shall restrict what I say here mostly to Harry Frankfurt's argument in "Alternate Possibilities and Moral Responsibility," but "Freedom of the Will and the Concept of a Person" and "Identification and Wholeheartedness" are also relevant. All are to be found in his *The Importance of What We Care About* (New York: Cambridge University Press, 1988).

22. What appears to insulate Frankfurt from this objection is that he is talking on a metaphysical rather than an empirical level, about counterfactual rather than real possibilities. To make the point that freedom of the will cannot be *defined* by a selection among alternate possibilities, he needs only one case in which the two can be distinguished. About the economic scenarios I have described, he could simply accept the empirical claims—agree that we need to explore different possibilities in similar situations in order to have a rich sense of the alternatives amongst which we cast our will—but then point out that "similar" is not the same as "identical," and that all the facts can be as I have described while a deterministic picture of the world remains true by which, in each situation, the agent has in fact only one real possibility for action. She then would still develop a rich notion of empirical alternatives, shape her desires accordingly, and come to her decisions with a background of informed reflection. But metaphysically one would have to say that she had achieved such freedom without ever having been able to do otherwise.

I have already suggested that this metaphysical story draws its plausibility from a related set of empirical stories in which the absence of alternatives cannot be thoroughgoing. I now want to make a stronger claim, which cuts against the story even as a piece of metaphysics. The story trades, I believe, on a distinction between *actual* wills and *possible* situations. The agent's will is presented as if we already know it exists, we can separate it from the situations that confront it, and we now need merely to ask when, in its embrace of possible actions, it accepts alternatives freely and when it is coerced or manipulated. But it is far from clear, at least if we rule out Cartesian introspection, that a will can be *identified* independently of a set of scenarios across which a pattern of rationally responsive decisions can be discerned. To identify a will at all, we need grounds to interpret a battery of evidence about some unified object's behavior such that it is more reasonable to attribute that behavior to a series of choices among alternatives than to any other cause. So if we have good reason, for any battery of such evidence, to think a controlling scientist is disposed to close off all but one alternative behavior in each case, then we also have good reason to regard the presence of a will here as at best indeterminable. All evidence that the object in question is "choosing" its behaviors, in such circumstances, can also be construed as evidence that the scientist in question is steering the object towards the alternatives it adopts. Even metaphysically, then, we cannot begin to identify something as a will, let alone a will exercising freedom, without assuming a real possibility of doing otherwise. The notion of will stands or falls together with the notion of there being alternate possibilities, even if, once in place, any single exercise of will might be free although one could not have done otherwise.

23. We are, in our capacity as agents, always already in the midst of actual choices, just as, in our capacity as thinkers, we are always already in the midst of concepts; compare chapter 2, 26–7.

24. Compare Stanley Cavell, writing on how we follow a rule, a topic he identifies, as I do, very closely with judgment: "*What* I take as a matter of course is not itself a matter of course. It is a matter of history, a matter of what arrives at and departs from a present human interest. I cannot *decide* what I take as a matter

of course, any more than I can decide what interests me; I have to find out" (*The Claim of Reason* [Oxford: Oxford University Press, 1979], pp. 122–3). Cavell has been much influenced by CJ; his early essay, "Aesthetic Problems in Modern Philosophy" (in *Must We Mean What We Say?* [Cambridge: Cambridge University Press, 1969]), is perhaps the first attempt to make use of it in contemporary analytic philosophy.

25. Joseph Raz, *The Morality of Freedom* (Oxford: Clarendon Press, 1986).

26. It should be clear that the condition "not being coerced by anyone else" rules out any use of judgment to coerce others. So it is the government's business, of course, to stop killing, theft, rape, assault, and the like: the whole libertarian program for government action is brought in by that condition. The point of my list of conditions is to go *beyond* the libertarian program. There is somewhat more for a government to do on my view than on a libertarian view—but less, firmly less, than Raz would allow.

27. In addition to the problems mentioned in the text, much of what Raz says suffers from the problem I attributed to Rawls and Habermas in chapter 9: vagueness about what, concretely, it entails. His talk about freedom requiring "the mental faculties necessary to plan actions" is wonderful—but just what *are* these faculties? Do they include the skills of interpretation and the appreciation of beauty that belong to reflective judgment? Do they include scientific knowledge of the world and of human nature, and if so, to what extent? More serious is a vagueness about what, outside of harming others, should be included in "immorality," and what, outside of some formal conditions, belongs to the important notion of "well-being." If the "immoral" is just whatever detracts from autonomy, and "well-being" is just whatever results from autonomy, then Raz's view is not far at all from the freedom of judgment—but then it does not really warrant the "perfectionist" label, or the assimilation to "positive freedom," that Raz claims for it. But if there is more to "morality" and "well-being," something thicker and more controversial, then we need to know why we should accept this something as necessarily belonging to human ends. The freedom that focuses on judgment abstains from determining what freedom is for; each of us must judge that for ourselves.

28. Michael Sandel, *Democracy's Discontent* (Cambridge: Harvard University Press, 1996).

29. Sandel cites one of Berlin's descriptions of the "first concept," along with passages in Hobbes, to characterize the liberal tradition, and contrasts the latter with the liberty of "the ancients," the liberty of citizens in Athens and Rome. See ibid., pp. 26–7.

30. Sandel points out nicely how even urban design can be understood in terms of civic virtue: "Following the example of nineteenth-century landscape architect Frederick Law Olmsted, Progressive advocates of municipal parks made their case in moral terms. They argued that parks would not only enhance the beauty of the city but also promote a spirit of neighborliness among city dwellers and combat the tendency to moral degradation" (ibid., p. 209).

31. Quotation from Thomson's *Liberty*, an anti-Walpole poem laying out the civic republican virtues associated with the Tory opposition in early-eighteenth-century Britain, discussed in Bailyn, *Origins of American Politics*, p. 50.

32. Charles Taylor describes this tradition best: see *Sources of the Self* (Cambridge: Harvard University Press, 1989), chapters 21 and 24. He rightly sees Schiller, Humboldt, and Mill as important to this tradition, but I think they can also be helpfully separated from it: by understanding their notions of individuality as dependent more on the skills needed to *interpret* art than to create it. See the discussion of Orthodox Jewish Torah study and Javanese *wayang kulit*, below.

33. For example: Why are there two stories of creation? How can God be described as "repenting," as he is before the Flood? Why does Abraham not protest God's command to sacrifice Isaac, as he had protested God's plan to destroy Sodom and Gomorrah?

34. A famous answer to the first question in the previous note—not the only answer, none of these questions are supposed to have only one answer—is that the two creation stories reflect two radically different sides of human nature. On the one hand, we are powerful, free creatures, made "in the image of God"; on the other hand, we are but dust, brought forth from our natural environment and destined to return to it. This matches the language of the two chapters in Genesis very well, and fits into specifically Jewish, as well as general philosophical, understandings of who we are. For an example of this reading, see Joseph Soloveitchik, "The Lonely Man of Faith," *Tradition* 7, no. 2 (Summer 1965). Ronald Beiner notes a similar notion of human nature in Kant's *Conflict of the Faculties*; see "Kant, the Sublime and Nature," in *Kant and Political Philosophy*, ed. R. Beiner and W. Booth (New Haven: Yale University Press, 1993), p. 286 n. 11.

35. I learned this detail from a lecture Tom Whitman, of the Swarthmore music department, gave at Haverford on the development of gamelan music. All other information here comes from Ward Keeler, *Javanese Shadow Plays, Javanese Selves* (Princeton: Princeton University Press, 1987).

36. See ibid., pp. 9, 12-3, 173-4.

37. See Geertz, *The Interpretation of Cultures* (New York: Basic Books, 1973), especially chapter 1. I say "perhaps not accidentally" because Geertz's first and most important fieldwork was in Java.

38. Stanley Cavell, *The Claim of Reason* (Oxford: Oxford University Press, 1979), pp. 169, 180. See also pp. 171-2, 181-3.

39. Steinberger, *Concept*, p. 157.

40. "The aspects of things that are most important for us are hidden because of their simplicity and familiarity" (Wittgenstein, *Philosophical Investigations*, § 129).

41. An Athenian idea worth renewing. It is highly unlikely, if designed to complement rather than replace representative democracy, to produce less competent, or less accountable, leaders than the career politicians, beholden to moneyed interests, we now have.

42. Friedman, *Capitalism and Freedom*, pp. 35-6.

43. Ibid., 191-2.

44. It would also be less dangerous to have members of this public selected randomly for public office.

45. This is not meant as a swipe at opera: I find opera, at its best, the most rewarding of all art forms. But (a) the Met, specifically, is a house that specializes in dull renditions of the most famous items in the repertoire, and (b) the idea that

an art form with such a small grip on the general public is worth supporting publicly just because the arts are generally worth supporting represents a misunderstanding of what the object of such support should be.

46. This leaves room for protecting the environment insofar as that is needed for *human* health and/or for the natural beauty that I have argued is important to human liberty.

47. Kateb, *Inner Ocean*, pp. 43, 123. See also p. 122, quoted above on pp. 227–8.

INDEX